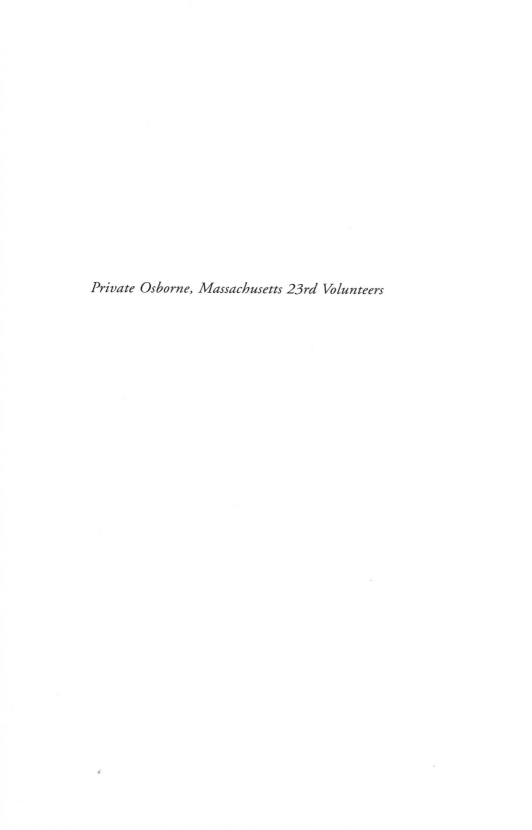

*Private Osborne, Massachusetts 23rd Volunteers*

# Private Osborne, Massachusetts 23rd Volunteers

*Burnside Expedition, Roanoke Island,
Second Front Against Richmond*

FREDERICK M. OSBORNE

*Edited by* Frank B. Marcotte

McFarland & Company, Inc., Publishers
*Jefferson, North Carolina, and London*

British Library Cataloguing-in-Publication data are available

Library of Congress Cataloguing-in-Publication Data

Osborne, Frederick M., 1845–1923
    Private Osborne, Massachusetts 23rd volunteers : Burnside
expedition, Roanoke Island, second front against Richmond / by
Frederick M. Osborne ; edited by Frank B. Marcotte.
      p.   cm.
    Includes bibliographical references (p.   ) and index.
    ISBN 0-7864-0554-6 (library binding : 50# alkaline paper) ∞
    1. Osborne, Frederick M., 19th cent. — Correspondence.  2. United
States. Army. Massachusetts Infantry Regiment, 23rd (1861–1865)
3. Massachusetts — History — Civil War, 1861–1865 — Personal
narratives.  4. United States — History — Civil War, 1861–1865 —
Personal narratives.  5. Soldiers — Massachusetts — Salem —
Correspondence.  6. Salem (Mass.) — Biography.  I. Marcotte, Frank
B., 1923–   .  II. Title.
E513.5 23rd.068   1998
973.7'44 — dc21                                  98-45428
                                                               CIP

Manufactured in the United States of America

*McFarland & Company, Inc., Publishers*
  *Box 611, Jefferson, North Carolina 28640*

For my Lady
and for
Juna M. Grass

# Acknowledgments

I want to thank my wife for encouragement and support during the years of research and for editorial help in manuscript preparation; the book exists in large part because of her participation.

Research assistance by Jean Carmosino was invaluable: her energy and enthusiasm served to unearth many long-buried historical gems which would otherwise have been lost to our story. Assistance by the reference librarians at the public libraries in Summit, Madison, Morristown, and Morris County, New Jersey, and Salem, Massachusetts, was critical and is much appreciated.

Jane Walsh and Susan Szpak of the Salem Public Library reference department were particularly helpful. Joan Vespe, bookseller, was an early fan of the book; her support lifted my spirits when hope sometimes waned. Special thanks are due to Thom Rogers for his help in computerizing the manuscript.

—FRANK B. MARCOTTE

# Table of Contents

# Preface

In the summer of 1990, a sheaf of letters was discovered in a safe in a house in Sugar Hill, New Hampshire, the home of Mrs. William H. Grass.

The well-preserved letters were dated almost one hundred and thirty years earlier. They had been written, it became clear, by a boy named Fred Osborne, who had served in the Union army during the Civil War.

There were fifty-two letters, along with most of the envelopes. The envelopes were addressed to Mrs. Stephen Osborne, 17 Oliver Street, Salem, Massachusetts. The letters were headed either "Dear Mother" or "Dear Jennie" and were signed "Fred" or "FMO." They were neatly written in a fine Spencerian hand with no crossed-out or written-over words.

Fred Osborne was in the Massachusetts Twenty-third Volunteer Regiment; he wrote about campaigns and battles, life in camp and on the march. His regiment was in the Burnside Expedition, the first amphibious operation in U.S. military history. It also figured in the battle of Roanoke Island, the first major Union victory of the war, and in many subsequent battles: New Bern, Kinston, Goldsboro, Charleston, Cold Harbor, and Petersburg.

Not written for publication, Fred's letters are lively, humorous, poignant, and unselfconscious. Something of a news hound, he kept up with events in the war, commenting on actions by President Lincoln and by generals that were in his world: McClellan, Grant, Sherman, Burnside, Foster, Hunter, and Butler.

The steady purpose of this soldier, his determination to fight the rebellion of the Southern states, and the cheerful account of his hard life impressed me as I read the letters, following the boy's adventures for three years. This adolescent, sixteen years old, had to deal with war all by himself, with no family near to guide and comfort him and never a furlough home; he had to carry on month after month, year after year. A remarkable young man.

*Camp Foster Roanoke Isld.*
*Feby 20th 1862*

*Dear Mother*

*We left the Schoner the 7th. in the evening, with three days rations, in our Haversacks and forty rounds, in our cartridge boxes. The gun boats had been up the Sound all day, having gone ahead of the Fleet in the morning. We were in sight of them all day. About noon they engaged with the Rebel batteries. The firing lasted until night. When we landed it was perfectly still. We had seen the fight to be sure, but we did not know whether they had been beat in off or not. And did know what we should meet when we did land. The Steamer "Pilot Boy" had a deck*

**A sample of Fred Osborne's handwriting, from a letter of February 20, 1862.**

It became something of a mission for me to dig into Fred Osborne's background, his education and early life, his family and its values and standards, and the milieu of his city, Salem, Massachusetts. All of this has helped me to understand this soldier and his willingness to risk his life for the Union cause.

A note on editorial method: Paper being precious, Fred wrote in the margins, filling in open spaces. Perhaps to save space there is little paragraph structure. To make his letters more accessible to the reader, I have added paragraphing as well as some punctuation; otherwise the letters appear exactly as written.

—FRANK B. MARCOTTE

## CHAPTER ONE

# Childhood and Home Life

We left the Schooner the 7th in the evening with three days rations in our haversacks and forty rounds in our cartridge boxes. The gun boats had been up the Sound all day, having gone ahead of the Fleet in the morning. We were in sight of them all day. About noon they engaged with the Rebel batteries. The firing lasted until night.

When we landed it was perfectly still. We had seen the fight to be sure but we did not know whether they had been beaten off or not. And did [not] know what we should meet when we did land.

The Steamer Pilot Boy had a deck of our reg't and was towing a string of boats besides. We were landed in a place all hummocks, salt grass, mud holes, etc. We could see the fires of the boys on the other side of the mud which was before us. Falling and stumbling round for about an hour, we got on terra firma, most of [us] wet with mud and water to our knees. We spent the night shivering round the fires. It rained all night, and we were miserable enough.

In the morning we marched up the road towards the woods where the Rebels were supposed to be. After getting through another mud hole, we heard firing ahead and orders came to hurry up the 23rd to support the 25th which had engaged the enemy.

At a turn of road where there was a place clear of trees, they had established the Hospital. The litters and the attendants standing round made a fellow feel kind of uncomfortable.

We pushed ahead and found the 25th had engaged the rebels who were in the woods on the edge of a clearing. At first it appeared they had no artillery as we could hear nothing but musket and rifle balls whistled past us. The rebels kept retreating through the woods and our colonel rec'd orders to deploy his Reg't to the right of the 25th to outflank the Secesh. We went right into a swamp where the water was about knee deep. When we had got pretty well in, we turned and marched by the right flank. The bullets, shell, grape shot, and cannister now began to fly about our ears in good shape.

Only one fellow was scared, he told the Captain he thought he had better go to the rear. He did not feel well. But it was no go.

We now turned and advanced by the left, which would carry us out of the swamp, but we encountered a close network of vines and brambles. We tried in vain to break through it and at last the officers had to cut through it with swords.

We pressed ahead then advanced by the right, the firing continuing brisk as ever. And the shells now began to fly pretty lively. We rushed ahead and just as we were getting out of the swamp and were in a puddle up to [our] waists, we heard a cheering and when we got out, found the rebels had a masked battery of four cannon and the 9th [N.Y.] Reg't "Hawkins Zouaves" charged on it and drove them out....

After staying at the battery about two hours, we marched down the road. It was strewed with knapsacks, blankets, and equipment. The arms we saw were either broken or thrown into ditches....

By this battle we got 10,000 [word unclear] of arms, 3,000 Prisoners and stores [of] flour, rice, pork, lard, sugar, molasses, etc. And as the whole Island is given up, we get 51 cannon.

The Secesh [secessionist soldiers] are miserable looking chaps, they average larger than we do, but do not look half so rugged, and are great braggers. ... When they saw us coming through, their Col. told them to run and they did. ... The woods were full of them when they were attacked. Some of the boys saw 40 in a ditch. I saw 4 new made graves myself....

This letter was written in my bunk, in the Rebel Barracks. Our Regiment was four hours in the swamp on the day of battle. I never got cold though I was wet to [the] waist till next morning....

I write in a great hurry as the mail goes by six o'clock in the morning. Direct your letters same as before. Excuse bad writing. Write soon and often.

Love to all.

F.M.O.

So wrote young Fred Osborne after his first battle, the battle of Roanoke Island, the first amphibious landing in United States military history. The battle was under the command of one of the most controversial generals of the Civil War; General Ambrose Burnside won this battle, the first major Union victory in the war, and he became a confidant of President Lincoln.

Fred Osborne, who was barely sixteen years old when he left his home and family to fight for his cause, was from Salem, Massachusetts, one of the great cities of the country, which undoubtedly helped shape this youngster's character and commitment.

In the 1850s, just before the Civil War, Salem was a lively, exciting, sophisticated city of 20,000. Fifteen miles north of Boston on the Atlantic coast, this maritime city was built on a slender finger of land jutting out into the ocean.

No house in the city was more than a few blocks from the water. Living in Salem made one conscious of water, of the sea and the tides, of boats and shipping and ocean commerce.

Fred's family had a maritime tradition. One of his older brothers, James Brace Osborne, was a sailor.[1] His mother was the daughter of Captain James Brace, an English shipmaster.[2] Mrs. Osborne probably passed on stories about her father's sea adventures. Fred's father also came from sailing people; his grandfather had been a captain as well as a shipowner. Captain Stephen Osborne had owned the sailing vessel *Sally* and had served as master of several other ships, including the schooner *Swallow*.[3] He captained the *Swallow* on a number of cargo trips from Salem to Maryland and Virginia in the late 1760s, according to sailing records.[4]

Captain Stephen Osborne, historical records indicate, was descended from the Duke of Leeds. The Osborne family is listed in *Burke's Peerage*, which reports that the first prominent Osborne family member was Sir Edward Osborne, who "filled the office of Lord Mayor of London in 1583 and was Knighted 2 Feb 1583-4."[5] Sir Edward's grandson Thomas Osborne was made the 1st duke of Leeds by Charles II.

Thomas Osborne, the 1st duke of Leeds, was an important figure in the government of Charles II in the late 1600s, the Restoration period of English history when England was recovering from Cromwell's excesses. "Charles's chief minister ... was Thomas Osborne. ... He was a shrewd politician ... adept at ... party machine tactics. ... His appointment was a ... milestone toward England's constitutional development. ... He was the real founder of the Tory party."[6] As a historical figure, Thomas Osborne may be more readily recognized by his other title, the earl of Danby.[7] The Osborne family continued down through the years to Captain Stephen Osborne and to his great-grandson, the Civil War soldier Frederick Osborne.

The maritime traditions handed down from his great-grandfather, Captain Stephen Osborne, undoubtedly influenced young Frederick Osborne, and Fred's home was only a few minutes walk from Salem Harbor and the ships tied up at the wharves. An alert, interested sort of boy, he could hardly have resisted wandering about the wharves, making friends of sailing men, and learning about the sea and ships. In his letters, he expressed no surprise about nautical matters when he was aboard various ships; they were quite familiar to him.

Fred's family lived in a big house at 17 Oliver Street. The house was on one side of the peninsula, a block from the water; across the peninsula, a half mile away, were the wharves along the shore of Salem Harbor. The house at 17 Oliver Street, which had been bought by his father, Stephen Osborne, about 1840, was large by standards of the time. It had been built in the early 1800s during the Federal architectural period. Today it is in the historic district of Salem, substantially unchanged from Fred's time and is included in a report on Salem historic houses.[8]

A visitor enters the spacious grounds along a walk leading from the street to a canopied side entrance. The front door opens into an entrance hall from which a curved stairway rises to the second floor. A left turn from the entrance hall takes the visitor into a sunny living room with a fireplace at one end. The long living room, enjoying the full width of the house, is cheered by windows along both sides. Beyond the living room is the commodious kitchen. On the second floor are many bedrooms, and there are more on the attic level.

The historical records tell us something of the social climate of Fred's Salem and give us a feeling for the milieu in which he lived. There was a tremendous interest in the printed word, in newspapers, in books, in pamphlets. It seemed almost an obsession. We will see numerous references to newspapers in Fred's letters; he reports that on one occasion, a truce was especially arranged to exchange newspapers with rebel soldiers across the fortified lines at Petersburg.

There were five newspapers in Salem in Fred's time. The printing business, the production of all kinds of printed materials, was growing rapidly and worried some people. Joseph B. Felt, a commentator on the Salem scene, was concerned about the growing power of the local printers: "Plain is the fact ... that from the introduction of printing among our population to the present the increase of its expedition in throwing off its impressions has been vast. As the power of this invention abounds, may it come under the control of right principle, be a purifier of the people from error, and an instructor to them in truth."[9]

Joseph Felt's concern about the effect printing might have on "error," "right principle," and "truth," reflected the strong public interest in morals. Morals held society together — that was the public's conviction. Morals were a public matter, and a number of social organizations concerned themselves with morals. These organizations included the Salem Society for the Moral and Religious Instruction of the Poor, the Female Auxiliary Moral Society, the Bible Society of Salem and Vicinity, the Washington Total Abstinence Society, the Female Washington Total Abstinence Society, and the Sons of Temperance.[10] Prominent individuals served as officers of these organizations, providing their stamp of approval and giving time and energy to the groups' objectives. Fred's future father-in-law was an officer in the Bible Society.

Salem people had an abiding concern for the poor, and helping them was the objective of a number of Salem societies.[11] The Salem Employment Society endeavored "to give sewing to poor women, at a fair compensation, who cannot obtain employment elsewhere." The Salem Dispensary contributed to "the relief of the poor by furnishing Medicines and Medical Advice, gratuitously." The Association for the Relief of Aged and Destitute Women supported "the Old Ladies Home." The Salem Female Charitable Society had as its goal to "support ... female children, and to assist that unfortunate class ... aged [and] infirm widows." The Samaritan Society had been established "for the purpose of relieving the sufferings of those persons who should be found destitute, and should be worthy objects of charity." The Salem Seamen's Orphan and Children's Friend

**The Osborne family home at 17 Oliver Street, Salem, Massachusetts, as it appears in an architectural rendering of the existing building modified to show its probable appearance at the time of the Civil War. Drawing by Roderick Carmosino, architect.**

Society had been founded "for the purpose of rescuing from evil ... children in indigent and suffering circumstances."[12]

A further measure of Salem's social character was the listing of "People of Color" which appeared each year in the Salem Directory. The name of each adult, his or her address and his or her occupation were given as for white people, except in a separate listing. Colored people were recognized as individuals, but of a different class. There were fifty-nine colored individuals listed in the 1842 Salem Directory out of a total population of about 20,000.[13] Salem also provided a school for colored children in a separate building with its own teacher.

Looking back into that time in Salem, trying to get a feeling for what life was like, it is illuminating to scan the kinds of daily work that individuals did for a living. This selection of occupations was taken from the records:

| | | |
|---|---|---|
| dressmaker | lawyer | gilder (applied goldleaf) |
| merchant | stocking factory worker | stonecutter |
| fisherman | chaisemaker (carriage | stagedriver |
| custom house agent | maker) | ropemaker |
| engineer | teacher | tobacconist |
| boarding house operator | wagoner | tailoress |
| mariner | chairmaker | blacksmith |
| notary | pilot | distiller |
| laborer | milliner | machinist |
| carpenter | cordwainer (shoemaker) | hatter |
| jeweller | sempstress (seamstress) | ship carpenter |

| currier (leather worker) | brewer | farmer |
| pattern maker | boat builder | clerk |
| last maker | bookbinder | newspaper agent |
| teamster | caterer | cooper (barrel maker) |
| nurse | clergyman | tinsmith |
| ship's captain | baker | music teacher |
| painter | printer | trader |
| innholder | peddler | grocer |

This was the Salem that Fred knew, that shaped his young character and his understanding of the world.

Despite their varied occupations, the people of Salem felt a special vigor, an intellectual stimulation generated by contact with the world, with people and goods and ideas from beyond the horizon, with ships coming in from Europe, from the Far East, from Africa, from everywhere.

American history was palpable in that city, whose citizens had fought the British in the Revolution and in the War of 1812; cannon and forts on Salem Neck protected the harbor. Salem privateering ships had scourged British shipping in the Atlantic and fortunes made from privateering had contributed to Salem's wealth.

Salem was a busy, bustling, active commercial city. On the wharves lining Salem Harbor, goods were unloaded from incoming ships and goods were dispatched into vessels going out into the Atlantic Ocean, heading for ports in all parts of the world. Shipowners and merchants made fortunes and erected fine houses on Essex Street, the prestigious main thoroughfare of the city.

Salem was a cultural city. A great wave of popular interest in literature and philosophy was building in Massachusetts, particularly in Salem and Boston. Nathaniel Hawthorne, James Russell Lowell, Oliver Wendell Holmes, John Greenleaf Whittier, and Henry David Thoreau were local heroes. People were tired of the Puritan repression and gloom which had carried over from colonial Massachusetts; the writings, the novels and poems, and particularly the lectures of these literate men gave them a new, cheerful, and hopeful view of the world.

The Salem of Fred Osborne's time was a city of civilized behavior. It was a time of entertainment in the home, of tea parties, a time of chaperones and of chivalrous treatment of women.[14] Everyone had a title of Mr. or Mrs. or Miss. Letters were carefully and graciously written. Officers in the army signed their letters, "Your Obedient Servant," even when writing to their enemies. Respect for women was a must.

Conversation, whether dinner-table talk or public speaking, was considered an art. Students took lessons in elocution and rhetoric. People paid to hear accomplished lecturers such as Dr. Oliver Wendell Holmes, an eloquent and powerful speaker. Elegant handwriting was admired as identifying a cultured person.

Fred Osborne grew up in a Salem which had an enthusiasm for knowledge and for culture. His father was an officer of the Salem Lyceum, one of the earliest in the remarkable lyceum period in our history.

## The Salem Lyceum

A craving for knowledge drove the lyceum movement of the nineteenth century; it thrived on the great desire for educational lectures. The name derived from the school in ancient Greece where Aristotle lectured to his students as they walked about the grounds of the Apollo Lyceus temple.

The lyceum movement blossomed in Fred's childhood, in the 1840s and 1850s. The Salem Lyceum was one of the earliest and most active and must have colored Fred's life as a youngster.

**Portrait of Daniel Webster by Harding. In the possession of Dr. Guy Hinsdale.**

Fred, with his family, sat in the audience to hear some of the great lecturers and orators of the time. Daniel Webster, America's greatest orator, fixed his audience with his piercing black eyes, convincing them with cool but passionate argument of his views on the Constitution and the Union. Other lecturers included Ralph Waldo Emerson, Henry David Thoreau, Horace Mann, Oliver Wendell Holmes, and other eminent literary and cultural figures of the pre–Civil War period. They appeared on the lyceum lecture circuit which went from Salem and Boston to New York and Washington and on to Cincinnati, Kansas, New Orleans, and Charleston. The lyceum was a national phenomenon.

Religion and politics were excluded in the early days of the lyceum. Knowledge of other fields was what people demanded. They wanted lectures on subjects that would give them intellectual growth and professional advancement. Clerks and farmers, apprentices and merchants paid their twenty-five cents to hear about botany or chemistry, electricity or geography, history or anatomy.

Middle-class people sought to learn about the world and to improve themselves. The lyceum movement was quite remarkable; it met a need that appeared and blossomed rather suddenly about 1830. Most people in the United States must have attended at least some lyceum lectures during its active period, from 1830 to 1860. The lyceum movement was interrupted by the Civil War; after the war, probably because improved schools slaked the thirst for knowledge, the movement did not regain its popularity.

The Salem Lyceum was a special case. Along with Boston and Concord (a few miles west of Boston), Salem formed the intellectual center of the United States. Salem was such an intellectually active community that it could support two lyceum lectures a week instead of the customary one. The Salem Lyceum had one of the most distinguished corresponding secretaries in the country: Nathaniel Hawthorne.[15] Nathaniel Hawthorne was an acquaintance of Fred's father since Hawthorne and Stephen Osborne were both officers of the lyceum and active in organizing the lectures.[16]

More successful in the North than in the South, the lyceum revealed economic and social differences between those two parts of the country that helped produce the Civil War. The North was egalitarian, with a large middle class which was eager for knowledge. The lyceum thrived on the middle class. The South had almost no middle class; slavery was central to its economy and to its culture. The plantation owner represented the Southern upper class, while slaves and poor whites made up the lower class, with few middle-class citizens in between. The plantation owner, with notable exceptions, was an outdoors man who was not a reader and not inclined to attend lectures. The Southern merchant or professional who aspired to be successful chose to join the upper class not by attending lectures but by acquiring some land and some slaves and becoming a plantation owner. The lyceum held little attraction in most of the South.[17]

The state of Virginia was different from the deep South. The lyceum did well in some of its cities such as Norfolk and Alexandria, but outside the cities Virginia was not a comfortable place for the ambitious. The slave economy discouraged struggling artisans who might attend lyceum lectures to get ahead; they would give up or move north. As cotton-raising moved toward the Southwest, Virginia turned to raising slaves for export to the cotton-producing states.[18]

The lyceum also measured intellectual interests in the West. The West of the 1850s was settled mainly by Southerners migrating north and by New Englanders migrating west. Southern Illinois was settled by Southerners moving up from the South, and it retained Southern culture, while northern Illinois was settled by New Englanders who came west via the Erie Canal. Lyceums appeared in the New England enclaves in northern Illinois but not in the southern part of the state.[19] Springfield was on the dividing line between the Southern and Northern cultures.[20] A lyceum was organized in Springfield at the time that Abraham Lincoln was practicing law in that city.

On January 27, 1838, twenty-nine-year-old Abraham Lincoln gave a lecture to the Young Men's Lyceum of Springfield; it has become famous for the insight it offers into his political philosophy.[21] Lincoln was beginning to stake out his positions on government and on slavery. That lyceum speech has been studied and argued about over the years. Edmund Wilson took it as a major subject in his 1962 book called *Patriotic Gore*, an analysis of Civil War literature. More recently historian Garry Wills cited the speech in his Lincoln study, the Pulitzer Prize–winning best-seller, *Lincoln at Gettysburg*.

The lyceum also became involved in the process of creating literature. A literary man had the opportunity to present his thoughts and essays in the form of a lecture as a first step; he would give the lecture on the lyceum circuit, perhaps changing and refining it, adjusting to the audience reaction. The lecture was then cast in final form and published. Some of the great literature of the time comes to us via the lyceum. Henry David Thoreau wrote of his method of composition: "From all points of the compass, from the earth beneath and the heavens above, have come these inspirations and been entered duly in the order of their arrival in the journal. Thereafter, when the time arrived, they were winnowed into lectures, and again, in due time from lectures into essays."

Emerson remarked in his journal for 1834: "When a village lyceum committee asks me to give a lecture, and I tell them I will read one I am just writing, they are pleased. Poor men, they little know how different that lecture will be when it is given in New York, or is printed. I 'try it on' them; 'the barber learns his trade on the orphan's chin.'"[22]

Thoreau's audiences were not enthusiastic about his lectures, but "through their very indifference they helped him to sharpen his words and to give added point to his ideas."[23]

Emerson on the other hand received only veneration from his audiences; his polished presentations probably did not need improvement. "Fully three-quarters of his published writing began as lectures."[24]

The lecture-based books on living a God-fearing life were most in demand. The "finger-shaking, cautionary lecture course for young men" was very popular. The lecture series by the prominent minister Henry Ward Beecher was an example; reader demand kept it in print in book form until 1925.[25]

The biology book *Methods of Study of Natural History* came from a series of lyceum lectures by Louis Agassiz, perhaps the most prominent botanist of the time. Sales were so good that it "had nineteen editions in one generation!"[26] Louis Agassiz was a world-renowned Swiss scientist who was lured to the United States to give lyceum lectures; he was offered a professorship at Harvard and never went back to Switzerland.[27]

The tales of travelers had a strong appeal for lyceum audiences. The Arctic explorer Dr. Elisha Kent published his suspense-filled lyceum lectures in a book called *Adrift in the Icepack*.[28]

The public library of each and every town and city, as we know it today, did not exist when the lyceum movement began in about 1830. The ground work for the public library was laid in part by the lyceum. The lyceum library, which had been accumulated for the use of members, often became the public library when the lyceum movement ended.[29]

## *Literary Salem*

Fred Osborne's early years were conditioned by a literary environment; his city was part of the writing establishment of the time.

**Nathaniel Hawthorne**

Nathaniel Hawthorne was a Salem native. His novel *The House of Seven Gables*, was published when Fred was a six-year-old scholar at the Phillips Grammar School. Near Fred's home was a large, many-gabled house on the headland overlooking the Atlantic Ocean that had belonged to one of Hawthorne's cousins. The windows of that house had watched many a sailing ship stand out to sea. It was the model for Hawthorne's novel.

Hawthorne went to live in nearby Concord when he was first married; it was perhaps the happiest time of his life. Hawthorne and his bride rented the "Old Manse," the family home of Ralph Waldo Emerson, for $100 a year, furnished.[30] Concord was also the home of Henry David Thoreau, who made a vegetable garden at the Old Manse for the newlyweds.[31]

At the end of this three-year stay in Concord, Hawthorne published *Mosses from an Old Manse*, a collection of tales which became popular with the reading public.

Nathaniel Hawthorne returned to Salem about 1850 and started writing *The Scarlet Letter*. It was during this period that Stephen Osborne and Nathaniel Hawthorne worked together as officers of the Salem Lyceum.[32]

## *At School in Salem*

School was a great influence in Fred Osborne's life. The Salem school system was one of the strongest in the country. As Fred Osborne studied his Latin and Greek and history and science and mathematics, he found a persistent theme in his school work: Preparation to lead a proper life. Students were taught rigorous moral principles; right and wrong were clearly defined. Discipline and behavior were serious issues and civil conduct was expected of an educated person. The Salem School Committee insisted on these matters.

Educated young gentlemen and ladies. That was what the Salem School Committee wanted. The School Committee, a select group of private citizens, had a long tradition of overseeing education. When Fred was in school the Committee had been overseeing Salem schools for one hundred and fifty years.

An educated young gentleman or young lady, the Committee believed, must be able to write well and to speak well. Much school time was spent on penmanship, spelling, syntax, and composition, to develop writing skills. And rhetoric and elocution were standard requirements to develop speaking ability.

The School Committee would have been proud of the writing skill that

**The House of Seven Gables in Salem, Massachusetts.**

Fred Osborne demonstrated in the fifty-two letters from Civil War camps and battlefields that he wrote to his mother and sister. His letters are clear and straightforward, with no crossed-out words or written-over sentences. And although he was writing on his knees, dipping his steel pen into a bottle of ink, there is only one ink blot in all the letters. Written for his family and not for expected publication, his letters are informal, but they show a nice expression of his thoughts and exhibit an excellent narrative style.

The schools reflected and contributed to the excitement of the times. Everything was possible; a person could do anything if he just got an education. Horace Mann, the secretary of education of Massachusetts, became an international celebrity for his work on public schools, but he met resistance to his ideas for improving schools.[33] Historian B. A. Hinsdale has noted: "There was ... a great amount of scepticism. ... Some thought it futile, and some undesirable to elevate the masses. ... [Social] classes were essential...; some [people] should be cultivated and refined, but others would meet their ends in toil and suffering, in living and dying in vulgarity."[34] Horace Mann rejected those views and had a passion for democratic education. He toured the state town by town, urging money and support for the public schools. When he found indifference, as when he had to sweep out the hall in Pittsfield before he could give his talk, he overcame it with his enthusiasm for developing the potential of all children, rich or poor, elite or workaday.[35] Massachusetts towns and cities caught the fire and set an example for the rest of the country and for the countries of Europe where Horace Mann had become famous. A semi-educated poor boy himself, he became an energetic and innovative leader who made a difference in public education in many countries. He was known to Fred and his family because he was a regular lyceum speaker.

In Salem, education was a democratic matter, not just for the elite. Preparation of a student might have been for college or for a life at sea or for life as a farmer or merchant. Females attended the same schools as males (the boys' and girls' high schools were merged in 1856, just before Fred entered high school).[36]

The Salem schools were in session throughout the year, except for the month of August. Christmas, Thanksgiving, July 4, and three other days were holidays; on Wednesdays and Saturdays, school was in session only in the morning. Hours were from 8 A.M. to 5 P.M. in the summer and from 9 A.M. to 4:30 P.M. in the winter, with a break for lunch.[37]

Although it was a challenge to students, one gathers from old reports that school was also exciting. In an 1897 speech, Miss Margaret Dalrymple, an eighty-seven-year-old Salem resident, spoke of young William Bentley, "an erudite scholar ... enlightened patriot, and broad-minded philanthropist [who] came to Salem a young man, endowed with uncommon powers," just after a schoolmaster had died and his school was to be closed because the School Committee could not find a teacher:

> He said, "Gentlemen have the school open in the morning. I will teach it till you can provide ... a teacher." The report spread with almost electric rapidity ... [and] brought every boy ... promptly at the hour for opening. After saluting them ... he walked into [school] at the head of quite an orderly procession. His style of dress ... the long academic gown ... the broad-brimmed hat ... his elegance and affability ... captured their admiration. His cheerfulness ... changed the atmosphere of that schoolroom. ... Work was no longer weariness. ... He spoke to the boys of the dignity of their human nature, the grand powers of the mind. The boys stood straighter and looked taller. ... Their work commenced. ... He spoke to them of the writer [of the piece to be studied], of the time he lived, of the subject and its purport ... and then, with all the magic of his rhetorical power, he read [the piece] to them. ... They had never heard anything like it. ... There was no more pouting ... obstinacy or truancy. His government was by reason, not by force.... Those boys became able, energetic and useful men, and [the] success of their lives ... they were proud to ascribe to their beloved friend and teacher.[38]

William Bentley later became a Salem minister and was active in the campaign to save the USS *Constitution*,[39] the ship that Oliver Wendell Holmes immortalized in his poem "Old Ironsides."

## CHAPTER TWO

# Talk of War

As a boy Fred Osborne was exposed to two sides of slavery: Salem's historical involvement in the slave trade, and the antislavery movement then intensifying in Salem and in the rest of Massachusetts.

## *Salem and Slavery*

In prior decades the slave trade had been a seafaring activity of great commercial importance. Before the Civil War, New England seaports sent ships to Africa to gather up slaves and deliver them to slave traders in the West Indies; the slave traders then sold the slaves to Southern plantations. For New England shipowners, the slave trade usually involved rum and molasses. Rum was carried in New England ships to Africa; there it was traded for slaves who were then exchanged for molasses in the West Indies. The molasses came back to New England to make more rum. At one time (1750), there were sixty-three distilleries in Massachusetts alone making rum out of molasses, and they could not keep up with the demand.[1]

Boston and Salem were the leading New England slaving ports, along with Portsmouth, New Hampshire; New London, Connecticut; and three seaports in Rhode Island.[2]

Although "most Americans were ashamed of the slave trade and eager to end it"[3] and President Thomas Jefferson had signed a law in 1807 which made the trade illegal, the slave trade was too profitable to be curbed. Fast ships were required to outrun government ships which tried to enforce the law, and "sleek, fast vessels with hollow-ground bows and capable of carrying an enormous press of sail came sliding down the ways of Baltimore and New England shipyards."[4] The illegal trade flourished for some years, not succumbing to efforts to curb it

until just before the
Civil War broke out.[5]

Tales of the slave
trade must have found
their way to young Fred
Osborne's ears as he
grew up in the seaport
of Salem. He would
have heard about the
slave ships out of Salem,
about shackling colored
men and women and
children together to
prevent uprisings, and

The *Nightingale*, slave ship out of Salem.

packing them side by side into lower decks to get the maximum number aboard.[6]

During the "middle passage," the months-long ocean voyage from the African coast during which the slaves were held below decks day after day, the desperate beings often tried to commit suicide to escape their misery. With little food and water and living conditions that were unsanitary in the extreme, many died en route and their emaciated bodies were pitched overboard.

There were stories too of captains who, when the slave trade became illegal, tried to remove proof that their ships were slavers when capture was imminent. When Captain Homans of the *Brilliante* saw four government cruisers bearing down on him, he tied his six hundred slaves to the anchor chain. When it appeared that he would be overtaken, Captain Homans dropped the anchor, which pulled the six hundred slaves overboard and under the sea so that he had no slaves aboard as evidence when he was finally caught.[7]

As a boy, Fred would also have heard tales about Zanzibar, the exotic Arabian city on the east coast of Africa that had been a slave market going back to the time of the Greeks.[8] Zanzibar filled a new need in the 1840s; the slave trade, though illegal since 1807, had picked up in intensity about the time that Fred was born. The Southern states needed more slaves to grow more cotton, which

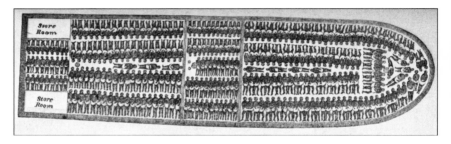

Method of stowing slaves in a ship.

had come into tremendous demand as an international commodity. Salem slave ships, looking for more slaves, discovered Zanzibar. "So many of the ships hailed from Salem that the Zanzibarians thought all white men came from this one New England town. English officers discovered to their indignation that Great Britain was considered to be a suburb of Salem."[9]

Little social residue from the slave trade remained in New England, but the Southern states were left to sort out the awkwardness of a society and an economy based on slaves. In a speech to the U.S. Congress, a North Carolina congressman, Robert Vance, said:

> Massachusetts is a state more responsible under heaven than any other community in this land for the introduction of slavery into this continent, with all the curses that followed. ... It is the nursing mother of the horrors of the middle passage, and ... after slavery in Massachusetts was found not to pay, her slaves were sold down South ... and then their former owners thanked God and sang the long-meter Doxology through their noses, that they were responsible no longer for the sin of human slavery.[10]

## Salem and Abolition

In the mid-nineteenth century, Salem tried to forget the awful years of the slave trade because the idea of human bondage was no longer tolerable. Although there had been antislavery sentiment in New England since colonial days, it did not engage the general public until just before the Civil War, when a wave of condemnation swept over the scene.

Antislavery organizations sprang up to support the cause. The Female Anti-Slavery Society was organized in Salem, and young Mrs. William Ives, wife of the publisher of the *Salem Observer* newspaper, was president in 1850.[11] Cornelia Ives, a niece of Mrs. Ives, was five years old in 1850 and would grow up to marry Fred Osborne.

Abolition became an issue with the literary men of Salem and Boston and Concord. John Greenleaf Whittier and James Russell Lowell gave lectures and wrote essays and poetry decrying the inhumanity of slavery. Henry David Thoreau was put in jail when he would not pay his poll tax to a government that allowed slavery; "Civil Disobedience," his famous essay, came from this jail experience. Thoreau wrote that slavery is a wound to the conscience of men: "Is there not a sort of blood shed when the conscience is wounded? Through this wound a man's real manhood and immortality flow out, and he bleeds to an everlasting death. I see this blood flowing now."[12]

William Lloyd Garrison, the well-known abolitionist, brought out his antislavery periodical the *Liberator* about 1840. "I will be as harsh as truth, and uncompromising as justice," he said in his first issue. "On this subject I do not wish to think, or speak, or write with moderation. NO! NO! Tell a man whose house is on fire to give a moderate alarm … but urge me not to use moderation in a cause like the present. … I am in earnest — I will not equivocate — I will not excuse — I will not retreat a single inch — AND I WILL BE HEARD."[13] Published in Boston, the *Liberator* was slow to catch on, but it soon became an engine of slavery reform.

**William Lloyd Garrison**

Harriet Beecher Stowe also aroused the public. Her novel *Uncle Tom's Cabin* was published in 1852 and caused a surge of emotion about slavery. Published first as a newspaper serial and then as a book, the book sold out the first printing of 5000 copies in one day. Fred was in grammar school when it was published. Like most Americans, he must have been gripped by the account of Mr. Shelby telling his wife that he has been forced to sell Tom: "What! Our Tom? — that good, faithful creature! — been your faithful servant from a boy! Oh, Mr. Shelby! — and promised him his freedom, too — you and I have spoken to him a hundred times of it." And the account of Tom on the river boat, going to his new owner, "chains on his wrists, chains on his feet." And the scene from Simon Legree's plantation: "'Now', said he, doubling his great, heavy fist into something resembling a blacksmith's hammer, 'do you see this fist? Well, I tell ye this here fist has got as hard as iron knocking down niggers.'"

President Lincoln is said to have remarked when he met Harriet Beecher Stowe: "So this is the little lady who started this big war!"[14]

## *Salem and the Politics of Slavery*

Slavery was the hot political topic when Fred was in high school, and his letters indicate that he was interested in politics.

The political winds in New England were beginning to blow with gale force. Factions lined up on both sides of the question of slavery. There were people in New England who wanted to leave slavery in the Southern states alone, to live and let live and, especially, to avoid rocking the boat and causing the southern states to secede. Business in New England had become entangled with slave labor in the South. The textile mills were a big industry which needed cotton, and the

South had to have slave labor to grow cotton. Bankers, manufacturers and retail people did not want to stop the flow of cotton to the New England mills. Slavery was viewed as evil, but doing something about it was not popular if it interfered with business.

Business people considered the abolitionists to be radicals and feared their passion to free the slaves. When mobs attacked abolitionist meetings in Boston, businessmen and newspapers supported this violence and the police looked the other way.[15] Fred's father, Stephen Osborne, was a merchant and must have worried about what might affect business, but since he was an officer in the Salem Lyceum, which sponsored many abolitionist speakers, his sentiments were probably not proslavery.

Daniel Webster had strong views on saving the Union which made him cautious about interfering with Southern slavery. He thought ill of abolitionists and said on one occasion:

> There are Abolition societies ... in regard to which I have very clear notions and opinions. I do not think them useful. I think their operations ... have produced nothing good. ... They have excited feelings. ... Public opinion, which in Virginia had begun to be exhibited against slavery ... drew back and shut itself up in its castle. ... Everything that these agitating people have done has been ... to bind faster the slave population of the South.[16]

Webster was in deadly fear of secession of the Southern states and the end of the Union: "I hear with distress and anguish the word 'secession.' ... I see as plainly as I see the sun what that disruption must produce; I see that it must produce war."[17] On another occasion, he said: "When mine eyes shall be turned to behold for the last time the sun in heaven, may I not see him shining on the broken and dishonored fragments of a once glorious Union; on States dissevered, discordant, belligerent; on a land rent with civil feuds, or drenched, it may be, with fraternal blood."[18]

There were many in Daniel Webster's camp, afraid of secession and loss of the Union; they would tolerate slavery to save the Union.

But the abolitionists, with their moral indignation, would not tolerate slavery even to save the Union. William Lloyd Garrison and his *Liberator* were putting out strong propaganda for ending human bondage, and a wave of mass repugnance for the practice of owning, trading, and abusing slaves was created by Harriet Beecher Stowe's *Uncle Tom's Cabin*. In the U.S. Congress, abolitionists were gaining strength. Fred Osborne's congressman Charles Francis Adams became a household name as a vocal antislavery advocate. Charles Sumner, another Massachusetts senator and a very popular lyceum orator, "could thrill and sway great audiences" with "his voice ... a great power ... [which he used] with great skill."[19] On the Senate floor, Charles Sumner attacked proslavery senators "who have raised themselves to eminence ... by the championship of human wrongs." He called Senator Douglas of Illinois "the squire of Slavery ... ready to do its humiliating offices," and he denounced Senator Mason of Virginia for supporting that side of Virginia "from which Washington and Jefferson [would have] avert[ed] their faces, where human beings are bred as cattle for the [slave trade]."[20]

Sitting at his Senate desk after one particularly strong speech, Charles Sumner "heard his name called. Looking up, he saw a tall stranger who said, 'I have read your speech...; it is a libel on South Carolina'...—and down upon the head of the defenseless man crashed a blow from a heavy walking stick. Pinioned to his desk, Sumner could not rise. ... Blow followed blow, till he fell bleeding and unconscious on the floor." The attacker was Preston Brooks, a congressman from South Car-

**John Brown**

olina; he was widely condemned in the North. Charles Sumner's wounds would take years to heal.[21]

Fanatical John Brown crystallized antislavery sentiment for many people in Massachusetts, perhaps for Fred Osborne. A few years earlier, in 1855, when Fred was in grammar school, the newspapers had reported bloody fighting in the new state of Kansas between the proslavery and antislavery settlers. The force of passion over slavery had built to the killing stage. The newspapers said that John Brown was a leader of guerrilla antislavery forces in Kansas. Prominent citizens formed a sympathetic "Massachusetts State Kansas Committee" to give John Brown moral support as well as arms and money.[22]

Four years later, in 1859, when Fred was in high school, John Brown attacked the arsenal at Harpers Ferry, Virginia, to obtain guns and ammunition for a slave uprising.[23] Harpers Ferry was a small town forty miles up the Potomac River from Washington, D.C. With a band of twenty-one men, five of them black and two of them his own sons, John Brown held the armory overnight waiting for slaves from the surrounding countryside to join him. His plan was that his army would then march across Virginia and the other Southern states, freeing slaves as it went. "Before I leave [Virginia] it will be a free state, and so will every other one in the South," one of John Brown's men had written home just before the attack.[24]

The newly invented telegraph brought immediate word of the attack on Harpers Ferry to newspapers in New York and Boston, in Alabama and South Carolina, in Virginia and Texas. The front-page headline in the *New York Times* read: "NEGRO INSURRECTION,"[25] but the slaves from the Harpers Ferry countryside did not come that day to join John Brown while he waited in the armory. Brown was captured by federal soldiers and held for trial. He was hanged a few days later, but the slavery question was never again the same.

Southerners were in a panic. An uprising of slaves was a fear in every Southern mind. Mary Chestnut, a Charleston lady, showed this fear as she watched her servants during the bombardment of Fort Sumter the next year: "[We cannot] detect any change in the demeanor of these Negro servants ... Lawrence [is] profoundly indifferent. So they all are but they carry it too far. You could not tell that they even heard the awful roar going on in the bay. ... They make no sign. Are they stolidly stupid? ... or wiser than we are: silent and strong, biding their time?"[26]

Suddenly rebellion was a reality. Southerners believed that John Brown was being used by the Northern abolitionists in a campaign to free the slaves. They feared Northern abolitionists would now come into Southern states and induce slaves to rebel, and slaves would react with violence, arson, killings, and rape. Slave rebellions had happened before. Southerners remembered the island of Haiti, where plantation slaves had rebelled. One of the slaves, Jean Jacque Dessaline, had been made governor, and in 1804 he had "inaugurated his rule with a bloodthirsty massacre of all the whites."[27]

The "Vesey Conspiracy" in Charleston in 1822 also haunted Southern memories. Some nine thousand slaves were, unknown to white owners, organized into a rebellion by Denmark Vesey, a freed slave. The conspiracy was discovered in time, and Vesey was hanged along with 36 others.[28] One Charleston white man, emphasizing that it could happen again, said: "Our negroes ... are the anarchists and the domestic enemy; the common enemy of civilized society, and ... would, if they could, become the destroyer of our race."[29]

The heavy slave population was frightening. Over half the population of South Carolina was slaves, with over eighty percent in some areas. In all of the Southern states, there were over two million slaves.[30]

The most vivid memory, perhaps, was that of the Nat Turner rebellion only thirty years before, in 1831. It was an uprising that was well publicized in the North and would have been in Fred Osborne's thoughts as he pondered the political scene. A brooding, religious black mystic, Nat Turner led a band of disgruntled slaves on a rampage, killing all the whites they could find on the farms in Southhampton county in southern Virginia. Hacking men and women and children to death with axes, beheading some, Nat Turner's band killed forty white people before they were stopped.[31]

Now, in 1859, when Fred was fourteen years old, John Brown had brought real fear to the Southern states. Southern towns formed "vigilance committees" to investigate strangers who might be abolitionists.[32] A slave owner worried in a letter to a South Carolina newspaper, "How easily Northerners travel across the South; any one of these men could be abolitionists from Ohio, bearing arms for the slaves."[33] Uneasiness about slave uprisings caused the governor of South Carolina to propose a law to "compel everyone that owns a farm with ... negroes ... to ... keep a white man constantly on the place."[34]

The Harpers Ferry raid was welcomed in the North. "At the very hour Brown was hanging ... church bells were tolling ... from New England to Kansas."[35] The usually reticent Henry David Thoreau "delivered an address in honor of the crucified hero."[36] Herman Melville, William Dean Howells, and Walt Whitman immortalized him in poems.

Reviewing the reaction to the hanging of John Brown, the Lawrence, Kansas, newspaper the *Republican* said: "The death of no man in America has ever produced so profound a sensation. A feeling of deep and sorrowful indignation seems to possess the masses."[37]

John Brown had opened Pandora's Box.

## CHAPTER THREE

# War

Fred Osborne began his third year at Salem High School in the fall of 1860. Abraham Lincoln was elected president in November. And then on December 20, just five days before Christmas, the newspapers blazoned the news that South Carolina had seceded from the Union.

Fred knew that South Carolina had seceded once before, back in 1832, and President Andrew Jackson had threatened to use force against the state. South Carolina couldn't get the other Southern states to go along on that occasion and secession was abandoned.

Now, at Christmas time in 1860, it was different; the disagreement over slavery had intensified. Abolitionists in the North loudly demanded that the slaves be freed, and Southerners hardened their position that slavery was their tradition, their internal affair.

Abraham Lincoln's election was the turning point for the South. Although Lincoln said Union first, that he would not press to end slavery, Southerners did not trust him and believed that with an antislavery president, the government in Washington would overrule the Southern states and free the slaves. They thought they had to secede.[1]

## Salem Watches Fort Sumter

The newspapers in Boston and Salem reported that the federal forts in South Carolina's Charleston Harbor were being seized by Southern forces. Major Robert Anderson and his sixty Union soldiers were in Fort Moultrie, on the edge of the harbor, when South Carolina seceded. He did not surrender but moved his troops over to Fort Sumter in the center of the harbor, a more defensible position.

The Southerners took this movement to be an aggressive act, and in late

December 1860 they laid siege to Fort Sumter. Major Anderson held out against the siege as December advanced into January, and he became a hero in the North. Philadelphia fired "three salutes of thirty-three guns each ... in honor of Major Anderson" and in Trenton "twenty-one guns were fired in honor of Major Anderson for the noble stand taken by him," according to the front-page story in the *New York Times* on January 2, 1861.

President Buchanan, who would be in office until March, when Lincoln was to be inaugurated, outlined the issue in a speech to Congress on January 5, 1861: "The seizure of this property [by Southern forces] ... has been purely aggressive ... [and] not in resistance to any attempt to coerce a state ... to remain in the Union."[2] After President Lincoln was inaugurated on March 4, Major Anderson continued holding Fort Sumter. He and his handful of soldiers were constantly in the newspapers: Would there be war? Would the South attack Fort Sumter? Would the North bring in a naval force to rescue Major Anderson from his perch in Charleston Harbor? High drama for a boy just turned sixteen who was watching and waiting.

The South amassed guns and troops in Charleston, and General Beauregard was put in charge of the Southern forces threatening Fort Sumter in the harbor. Neither President Buchanan nor President Lincoln wanted to use force to rescue Major Anderson because the North did not want the responsibility for starting a war. The stalemate continued.

Tension was in the Salem air. Fred came home from high school each day not knowing what news he would hear. His father Stephen Osborne brought home conversations with customers and merchants who had come into the fur store that day and had discussed secession or Union soldiers trapped on Fort Sumter or what the president should do. And Mary Osborne was quietly anxious about Fred and her three other sons, Steve, Orville, and Nate, all older than Fred, who worked in the family fur store. And Jennie, Fred's beloved sister who was close to his own age must have wondered what the future held for her brother.

Fort Sumter. What would happen?

Trying to avoid a war, President Lincoln sent a peaceable relief ship to Major Anderson, who was starving on Fort Sumter. It left New York Harbor on April 9, 1861. On April 10, Major Anderson rejected General Beauregard's ultimatum to surrender. The relief ship was still on its way when General Beauregard gave the order to fire on Fort Sumter on April 12, 1861.[3]

## War Erupts

Suddenly Northern minds converged, as the factions in New England came together. The Union must be saved. War was here and they had an enemy. Fred Osborne's mind must now have been made up. Secession must be defeated.

In Boston an observer reported: "I never before knew what a popular excitement could be ... never anything like this ... [not even in] 1775. ... The whole population seem to be in the streets with Union flags. ... Public meetings are held everywhere ... nobody holds back. ... Civil war is accepted everywhere."[4] A New Yorker noted: "The city is gay and brilliant with excited crowds ... thousands of flags, big and little."[5] In Ohio a man reported on the attitude of the West by saying "The West? The West is all one great eagle scream!"[6]

In the South, tension was also relieved. A Southern writer described the scene in Richmond, the capital of Virginia: "On April 12 ... news came of the bombardment of Fort Sumter, in Charleston Harbor, by Confederate troops, and its surrender by its Federal commandant. Alas, America! Civil War was a fact! Drunk with enthusiasm kindled by this first victory of Southern arms, Richmond people poured cheering into the streets."[7] Another Richmond observer recorded in his diary: "The crowded streets and wild shouts of the people, together with the lurid glare of an hundred tar-barrels, torches steeped in rosin, and rockets whirling high above the houses, presented a spectacle rarely witnessed by ... [the] people of Richmond."[8]

The Civil war had started, and for four long years the country would be drenched in fraternal blood, as Daniel Webster, now dead, had feared.

The bombardment of Fort Sumter by Southern artillery put the war in motion, but there was no formal declaration of war. The South had simply attacked the North, and the North had picked up the gauntlet.

The South, fueled by fear for some time, had soldiers mobilized and ready to fight. Since the Harpers Ferry attack more than a year earlier, Southerners had been recruiting and training soldiers. Richmond, soon to be capital of the Confederacy, "began busily preparing for war. ... Military companies were organized. The students of Richmond College formed themselves into [a military company]. Sometimes all other sights and sounds were blotted out by interest ... in a parade of one of the new military companies. ... The old Armory was aroused from its slumber and equipped with improved machinery for the manufacture of muskets and other arms."[9]

The Union army, on the other hand, was in a shambles. Most of the 16,000 men in the U.S. regular army at the start of the war were "scattered over the wide expanse of the western frontier."[10] U.S. regular army officers with Southern sympathies had walked away to join the Confederacy. Colonel Robert E. Lee was one such officer, and his aide Lieutenant J.E.B. Stuart was another; both men had been recently involved in capturing John Brown at Harpers Ferry. More than 300 of the U.S. Army's 1,100 officers resigned and went over to the Confederacy.[11] General Winfield Scott, the grand old hero of the Mexican War who was now old and feeble, had to put together a new fighting force that was larger than any in our history. Almost no Union army recruiting was underway when the war started, but in Massachusetts things were different. John Andrew, the new young governor, had been making military preparations because he believed war was coming. He had talked with Southern congressmen in Washington in

**A soldier in the Massachusetts Sixth Regiment.**

December, and he knew "the South [means] to fight [and that he] as Governor must have his state militia ready to move as soon as the first blow was struck."[12] By the first of April, Governor Andrew had companies throughout the state ready for active service.[13]

On Monday, April 15, 1861, two days after the attack on Fort Sumter, the newspapers carried President Lincoln's proclamation calling for 75,000 militia from the states. Troops were needed at once in Washington to protect the capital. Surrounded by two slave states, Maryland and Virginia, the city was in danger of immediate capture.

Governor Andrew started moving to fill the Massachusetts quota of troops. As Andrew's biographer, Henry Greenleaf Pearson, has noted, "In Boston ... men applied for commissions to raise companies. ... [In the State House] the [usual] quiet ... was destroyed by a swiftly growing crowd," all wanting to help answer the president's call for troops.[14] Soldiers arrived in Boston on trains from surrounding towns. Within two days, on the Wednesday after Lincoln's Monday call for troops, the Massachusetts Sixth Regiment, "the first armed troops to move anywhere in the war," was ready.[15] "By noon, the Sixth Regiment ... drew up before the long and broad flight of the State House steps, and Governor Andrew came down to give the regiment its colors and to bid it Godspeed. Throngs of people ... surged to meet them. Standing thus, the Governor for five minutes poured forth the feeling pent up within him ... surrendering himself ... to the fullness of eloquence. ... The regiment marched off, little dreaming what the future had in store for it."[16] Over six hundred thousand soldiers would die. This out of one million Confederate soldiers and two million Union soldiers.[17] Each dead soldier would leave behind a grief-stricken family, but these future sorrows were unforeseen as this regiment marched away from the Massachusetts State House in Boston on April 17, 1861.

The Sixth Regiment was on its way to Washington to save that endangered city, when it was attacked by a mob as it was changing trains in Baltimore, a city divided in loyalties, with strong elements of Southern sympathy. Four soldiers were killed,[18] and a sorrowful Governor Andrew telegraphed the mayor of Baltimore: "I pray you to cause the bodies of our Massachusetts soldiers, dead in Baltimore, to be immediately laid out, preserved with ice, and tenderly sent forward by express to me. All expenses will be paid by this Common-wealth."[19]

The attack brought a strong reaction in Massachusetts: "One thing was certain; the first blood had been shed; men of Massachusetts were lying dead in Baltimore; war was a necessity. From that moment everything was done with a difference."[20]

The Massachusetts Sixth moved on to Washington. Along with a handful of unarmed Pennsylvania men, they were the only troops that had arrived. Unprepared for war, the city quartered the regiment in the House of Representatives and in the Senate Chamber.[21]

According to historian Henry Greenleaf Pearson, days passed "and still there was no further sign of the 75,000 men Lincoln had called for. 'Why don't they come? Why don't they come?' he said, pacing his office, peering out the window."[22] On Wednesday, April 23, "when officers and men who had been wounded ... [by] the Baltimore [mob] called at the White House, he thanked them for their presence in the capitol, then added: 'I don't believe there is any North. ... You are the only northern realities.'"[23]

Washington had become isolated, cut off from the outside world. Maryland citizens, outraged at Northern troops coming through their state, destroyed railroad tracks and railroad bridges which led to Washington. Telegraph lines were cut, and mails were stopped. Lincoln was isolated from the North, waiting in the White House for troops that did not arrive.

Southern forces were gathering across the Potomac River from the capitol. On the Virginia shore, 15,000 Confederate soldiers had arrived; Washington could see their camp fires at night. The *Richmond Examiner* asked for "One wild shout of fierce resolve to capture Washington City, at all and every hazard. That filthy cage of unclean birds must and will be purified by fire."[24]

Meanwhile, Governor Andrew was furiously getting more regiments ready to send to Washington. John Andrew was making his reputation as the most active wartime governor. From boyhood he had been an abolitionist; as "a short, fat, chubby, curly headed little fellow" of fifteen he was exposed to Garrison's *Liberator* and the call for immediate emancipation. Then and for the rest of his life he "made the Negro's cause his own."[25] John Andrew had helped to give the Republican nomination to Lincoln. Now he was getting his chance to be an activist in the antislavery cause. John Andrew came from a Salem family, and his progress as the new governor was closely followed by Fred and his family.

Fred Osborne, who was still in high school, was swept forward by the excitement. On April 20, eight days after the South fired on Fort Sumter, he joined the Union Drill Club, which would soon become Company F of the Massachusetts 23rd Regiment.[26]

Washington was still isolated when Fred joined the Drill Club. He had read in the newspapers of the attack in Baltimore on the Massachusetts regiment and identified with the four dead soldiers coming home packed in ice. But immediately after that incident, the railroads and bridges to Washington were destroyed and news to the North was interrupted.

With no communications from Washington, Governor John Andrew became frustrated and concerned. He had troops ready to go to save that city, but he couldn't send them without an okay from the War Department. Washington was silent. To make contact with the War Department, John Andrew assigned former governor George Boutwell to get to Washington somehow, giving him "a hundred dollars in gold, an improvised cipher-code ... and a small revolver loaded."[27] When Boutwell did not get to Washington, Governor Andrew sent another messenger, Attorney General Dwight Foster. Boutwell and Foster tried to get to Washington by a water route via Chesapeake Bay and the Potomac River, but they were still trying when the emergency ended.

The isolation of Washington was ended by General Ben Butler, a brash, pushy, inventive former politician from Massachusetts who would compete for headlines with Lincoln and McClellan in the coming months of the war. In charge of a Massachusetts regiment on its way to Washington, General Butler was stopped by the torn-up railroads. He found a locomotive near Baltimore which had been put out of action by Southern partisans and called for volunteer mechanics to repair it. It happened that one of the volunteers knew the engine because he had helped build it a few years earlier. That volunteer mechanic, who came from Beverly, a town next to Salem, "passed ... [his] hands over the locomotive a few times" and "presently it was ready to whistle and ... gallop as if no traitor had ever tried to steal the go and music out of it."[28]

As the locomotive started toward Washington, it was preceded by repair crews who hunted down missing rails which had been hidden in bushes and ditches by Southern sympathizers. The repair crews put the missing rails back in the railroad track as the locomotive followed along behind them.[29] After six days of isolation, relief came to Washington on April 25, 1861, when "the piercing shriek of a locomotive broke the noonday stillness of the city ... a route had been opened to the North."[30]

## A Slow Beginning

Fred Osborne was learning to drill with his friends in the Union Drill Club when he read in the newspapers about General Ben Butler's rescue of isolated Washington. Now that the railroads were operating again, a number of regiments from Massachusetts arrived in Washington. But the War Department had made almost no preparation to deal with arriving troops. No plan for a Union army had been made. "Not one of the departments in Washington was in condition to run smoothly. ... The War Department was the worst case of all."[31] It was a "time of uncertainty as to the basis on which soldiers would be accepted by the national government."[32]

The Union government was not ready to provide for the troops, so it fell to the home states to help out. As Pearson, Governor Andrew's biographer, points out, "Massachusetts, having sent off … [several] thousand men, now found that she had on her hands the task of maintaining them in the field — a quasi-hostile country some four hundred and fifty miles away."[33] A month's supply of rations for the troops had to be got ready: "For a week [there] ensued … a bustle of preparation. … In kitchens and bakeries all about Boston … a cargo of beef, pork, and pilot bread, cheese and preserved meats by the ton, tea, coffee,

John Andrew

sugar, and pickles by the barrel, with candles, beans, dried apples, beets, onions, potatoes, and tobacco thrown in." The cargo was to be delivered by two hired, armed steamships; the state (with a bank loan) paid half and "the other half [was] raised by subscription."[34]

Governor Andrew was advised by one of his agents of the condition of the soldiers in the Capitol: "[the soldiers] need a health officer … Soap! Soap! Soap! I cry but : [no one] heeds … washer-women are needed more than nurses." Another agent criticized the colonel of one Massachusetts regiment: "An old gentleman of courage, patriotism and zeal, is understood to have brought with him in the hurry of leaving only about brains enough to command a single company." The agent further complained of "delay, waste, loss, and confusion."[35]

But plan for a Union army or no plan, preparations for war were moving forward in Massachusetts, where militia companies and regiments went into camp, waiting for a call from Washington. "Ambitious young men, with their eyes on captaincies and lieutenancies, were raising [troops] in every town and village throughout the state. … The whole state was enlisted for the war."[36]

Now Governor Andrew tried to hold back the companies and regiments. He had been attracting men to the Union's colors, but he "could not accept them; could not muster them; could not encourage them, further than with kind words, until answers were received from Washington. … Days passed on; no requisitions came. The companies held to their organizations; paraded the streets, partly for drill, but chiefly to pass the time. … They pressed daily to the State House; the Governor wrote and telegraphed again and again to Washington, beseeching the Secretary [of War] to accept the services of men anxious to serve their country."[37]

Simon Cameron, President Lincoln's secretary of war, was not eager to have more soldiers. John Andrew's biographer wrote: "The attitude of the ... War Department was persistently lukewarm. This was to be a little war, a gentle war,— in fact, almost no war at all. The fewer the troops ... the better."[38] Governor Andrew had two hundred companies ready, and Cameron would accept only thirty. After "weeks of hard work ... the ranks were full, and the disappointed ... went back to work or migrated to some other State."[39]

Secretary of War Cameron

**Simon Cameron**

was the bottleneck. Governor Andrew's agent in Washington reported that: no more regiments could "be received at present, and [that Cameron] could give no promise or encouragement for the future."[40]

Simon Cameron was not the man to get the Union army ready for war. He was a political payoff who had helped Lincoln get support from Pennsylvania for the Republican nomination. Lincoln replaced him as secretary of war a year later. As Pearson has commented: "Cameron would have been a millstone around the neck of any president."[41]

The slow and confused buildup of the Union army continued while the Confederacy established troops and war supplies on the Virginia shore of the Potomac River opposite Washington.

## The Union Army Is Tested: First Battle

In the spring of 1861, Fred Osborne and the Union Drill Club practiced in the armory on Central Street or in fine weather on the spacious green acres of Salem Common, half a dozen houses from Fred's home on Oliver Street.

Fred's brothers, Nathan, Stephen and Orville, were working for their father in the fur store on Essex Street. On May 14 Nathan, who was eleven years older than Fred, applied for a commission as a captain in the regular U.S. Army. While waiting to hear from that application, Nathan requested authority from Governor John Andrew to recruit a company of volunteers.[42]

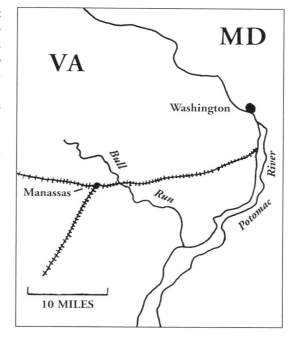

In the warming days of May and June, regiments arrived in Washington from New Hampshire and Rhode Island, from New York and Ohio, from Pennsylvania and Vermont, and from Maine and Massachusetts. A Union army was forming in and around Washington.

Colonel Ambrose E. Burnside, who was to be Fred's general in a few months, was among the officers in Washington who were drilling and marching the men into a fighting force. Colonel Burnside was in command of a brigade of four regiments, the 1st and 2d Rhode Island, the 2d New Hampshire, and the 71st New York. Still untrained, his men would face Confederate rifles and cannon in a few days.

July came and the battle of Bull Run. Stung by Fort Sumter, the North wanted to get a lick in against the Confederacy. Northern newspapers urged: Now that we have war, let's have a battle.

Manassas, a Confederate railroad junction in the Virginia countryside, across the Potomac River and twenty miles from Washington, seemed to be everybody's choice for a battle. To get to Manassas, the Union army would have to cross a stream called Bull Run; General Beauregard, in charge of Southern forces in the area, was busy fortifying the hills that overlooked Bull Run.

The Union army was inexperienced and only a few weeks old, but the newspapers and the politicians and President Lincoln wanted a battle. When General McDowell, who was in charge of the army in the Washington area, asked for more time to train his troops, Lincoln replied: "You are green, it is true; but they are green also. You are all green alike."[43] The three-month soldiers, the first men that Lincoln had asked for, were about ready to go home, their term nearly up. They had to be used soon, and they were most of the army.

The battle of Bull Run was fought on a hot, sunny Sunday, July 21, 1861. By 2 o'clock in the afternoon, it appeared that the Union had won a victory. The

**View of Washington, D.C., looking down Pennsylvania Avenue. From a sketch made in 1861.**

city of Washington was jubilant at the news it was hearing. "So soon as a dispatch was received at the War Department or by some ... newspaper man, it was ... read to the assembled hundreds, who joyfully greeted each and every word with rousing ... cheers and ... the word of glad tidings was read and re-read until the reader became hoarse."[44]

President Lincoln received a telegram from a Union general at the scene of battle saying that a "great battle had been fought, and victory won."[45] Lincoln went for a carriage ride in the country on that Sunday afternoon, believing that the Union had won.

But in midafternoon the tide turned. The Union troops gave way as they were pressed by the Confederates and gave way again. Then they panicked, and a rout was underway. "They turned and fled past officers on horseback flailing the smoke with sabers while screaming for them to stand. They ran and they kept on running."[46]

The battle of Bull Run was a surprise to the North. This was to be "a little war, a gentle war, ... almost no war at all." The Southerners had been expected to cave in at once. Secession was something done in a pique. Southerners would soon see that it was a mistake and rejoin the Union. Three-month soldiers would be more than enough to bring the South to terms.

The North was to learn better. The South would fight for four years — short of men, short of food, its soldiers barefoot in the snow — until it was completely spent.

The battle of Bull Run was a newspaper story for many days, and we can be sure that Fred read all the newspaper accounts he could lay his hands on.

The North was discouraged. The Union would not achieve a victory until General Ambrose Burnside led the ships of the Burnside Expedition to attack the Confederacy below Richmond. Fred Osborne was in the expedition, on the ship *Highlander*, on his way to the battle of Roanoke Island.

## Company F

In the summer of 1861, the city of Salem, like the rest of the North, was recovering from the stunning defeat at the battle of Bull Run. It was clear that the South would fight and that the North had a real war on its hands.

Nathan Osborne, Fred's 26-year-old brother, went off to war that summer. He had applied for a commission in the regular army back in May, and while waiting for an answer, he had been clerking in his father's fur store and raising a volunteer company. Nathan's handwritten synopsis of his military career, found in his military records, explains his activities: "On July 1, 1861 under authority from the Gov. of Massachusett, I commenced the recruitment and organization of a Volunteer Company. Before its completion I was notified of my appointment as a Captain in the 13th Infantry, U.S. Army to date from the 14th of May 1861. Having turned over my Volunteer Company to the Commanding Officer of the 17th Massachusetts Infantry, I reported at Washington for instructions and immediately after at Jefferson Barracks, Mo."[47]

Jefferson Barracks was an infantry camp just outside of St. Louis which had been set up in earlier years to train soldiers for the wars with the Indians.[48] Nathan Osborne and William Tecumseh Sherman formed a connection at this time: they were both assigned to the 13th Infantry of the U.S. Army, at Jefferson Barracks, Nathan as a captain and Sherman as a lieutenant colonel in command of Nathan's regiment.[49]

But Nathan and Lieutenant Colonel Sherman did not get together

**General William Tecumseh Sherman**

**General Philip Henry Sheridan**

for a while. Before he had a chance to move to Jefferson Barracks, Sherman, who had been president of a horse-car tram company in St. Louis, a job he held briefly after leaving a regular army career, was put in charge of a brigade which fought in the battle of Bull Run.[50] His men ran from the enemy, an embarrassment to this soldier who would later become Grant's main man and a hero in the North.[51] William Tecumseh Sherman would make Civil War history at the battles of Vicksburg, Chickamauga, and Missionary Ridge, and Nathan Osborne would be an active participant in these battles. Fred often mentioned the adventures of General Sherman and Nathan in his letters.

Philip Henry Sheridan also joined the 13th Infantry Regiment with Nathan Osborne.[52] Phil Sheridan had been fighting Indians in the Far West as a lieutenant in the regular army when the Civil War broke out; he was promoted to captain in the 13th Infantry. He would fight with Sherman and Nathan Osborne in the battles of Chickamauga and Missionary Ridge. Later promoted to general, Phil Sheridan became famous for his cavalry campaigns in the Shenandoah Valley of Virginia, which were critical to the final defeat of Robert E. Lee's Confederate army.

The Union Drill Club was a special project for the city of Salem during the summer of 1861. The military club had the support of the religious segment of Salem society; the Reverend Wilder, rector of Grace Church, was president of the Club. Also participating in the effort were Reverend Spaulding, pastor of the Universalist Church, Dr. Briggs, pastor of the First Unitarian Church, and Reverend Thayer, pastor of the Crosbie Street Congregational Church.[53] Reverend Thayer, "whose professional duties forbade his ardent desire to enlist," gave $100 of his own money to aid the club.[54]

Other important city people were involved: "As an indication of the standing of the Club in the community ... many prominent names ... freely [gave] both time and money. ... Hon. Stephen P. Webb, Mayor of Salem; Hon. W. D. Northend, Senator for Essex; Willard P. Phillips, Collector of Port; Allen W. Dodge, Esq., County Treasurer; Judge Otis P. Lord."[55]

Oliver Wendell Holmes's sister, Mrs. C.W. Upham, who lived in Salem and had a son in the Union Drill Club, wrote a poem for the club. A distinctly fiery message, the poem was presented at one of the club's "war meetings."[56]

PATRIOTIC ODE

Dedicated to the Union Drill Club of Salem.
Tune — "Scots wha hae."

Rally boys! Come forth to fight,
For the Union, Law and Right;
For the Nation's honor, bright,
Let us draw the sword!
By the wrongs vile traitors wrought,
By the ruin they have brought,
Tyranny of deed and thought,
Forward is the word!

See the Northern pride and flower
Gathering in this fateful hour;
Union is our strength and power, —
Let us join the van!
Lay the traitors in the dust;
Die they shall, and die they must:
They have broken every trust, —
Forward every man!

Massachusetts calls to-day,
Beckoning all her sons away;
She no longer brooks delay —
Not a man must lag!
Gird the sword, and join the throng;
Right must triumph over wrong;
In our cause we shall be strong, —
Raise the starry flag!

With these somewhat bloodthirsty urgings from his mother, Oliver Wendell Holmes Upham, an eighteen-year-old student, and the rest of the Union Drill Club were thus dedicated to the war against secession.

Oliver Wendell Holmes Upham would, in the fall of 1861, enlist in Company F, Massachusetts 23rd Regiment, and go to war with Fred Osborne. But in two months, before his first battle, he would be "discharged for disability" and return home to Salem.[57] The record does not disclose the nature of the disability.

His cousin, Oliver Wendell Holmes, Jr., son of the literary giant, joined the Massachusetts 20th Regiment and made a creditable record as an officer during the war; he later became chief justice of the U.S. Supreme Court.

The Union Drill Club voted for a uniform: "For the officers, a blue, straight-vizored kepi trimmed with gold, a gray, single-breasted frock, collar and cuffs of blue with gold braid, and dark blue trousers. The men wore a gray kepi and Zouave jacket, the latter of gray flannel widely faced with blue, but cap, jacket and dark-blue trousers all trimmed with red."[58] The Zouave uniform, an oriental style with flashy colors and loose pantaloons adapted from the French Foreign Legion, was

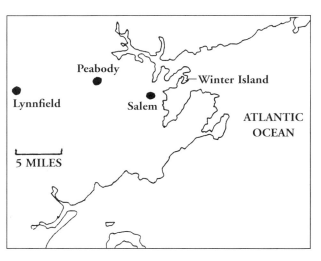

**Location of Lynnfield and Peabody**

a popular choice among volunteer companies in the Union army. Company F wanted at least the colorful jacket.

The Union Drill Club became Company F in September of 1861. A thirty-one-year-old Salem bookseller, George Whipple, received authority from Governor Andrew to recruit Company F. Captain Whipple would be Fred Osborne's commanding officer for the next two years.

On October 14, 1861, Company F marched off to camp on Winter Island, a peninsula of the city of Salem extending out into the Atlantic Ocean where the city had spent $400 to build barracks.[59] On the evening of October 14, "the

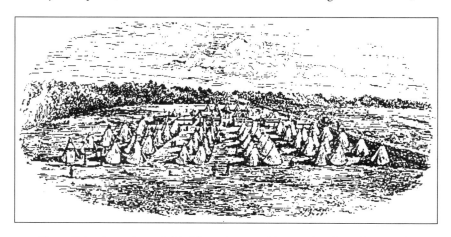

**Camp Schouler at Lynnfield, Massachusetts. From a sketch made in 1861.**

company attended a meeting. ... The exercises ... consisted of speeches by several gentlemen, and fine singing by ... a male chorus. ... Major Henry Merritt of the 23rd Regiment mustered the company into service. ... The ceremony [was] witnessed by a large audience."[60]

Company F spent its first few days on Winter Island "obliged to cook for ourselves. ... Our beds were only straw on hard board bunks."[61] As in all wars, bad language developed among the soldiery; on Winter Island, it was reported, the expletive "Gosh all hemlock!" popped out of a soldier who dropped a gun on his toe.[62]

The Salem newspapers were supportive of Company F: "The *Salem Gazette* ... editorially asserted that 'no single event has occurred in our city in reference to the present war, which is more cheering to every patriot than the enlistment of this organization of our young men. ... We are called, indeed, to lay our most precious jewels upon the altar now.'"[63] Thereafter Company F was known in the regiment as the "Jewels." A few days later the *Salem Gazette* wrote: "Those who have enlisted [in this company] are young men of fine appearance and quick intelligence. ... The company contains a considerable number of superior vocalists who will doubtless do their full share in maintaining a 'sunny side' to the realities of camp life."[64]

On October 18, 1861, Company F began its journey to war; the company, eighty-seven strong, marched through a cold drizzle to the neighboring city of Peabody, where the soldiers took a train to Lynnfield. Camp Schouler at Lynnfield was an organizing camp for several new military units.[65]

Fred Osborne marched off to Lynnfield, leaving home to put the world aright.

CHAPTER FOUR

# The Burnside Expedition

After the battle of Bull Run, Ambrose Burnside was promoted to brigadier general and was stationed in the Washington area.[1] He became a friend of President Lincoln, who liked this gentle, straightforward man and enjoyed visiting Burnside's camp.

Ambrose Burnside was, at thirty-seven, "a tall, rather stout, energetic man with large features and dark-socketed eyes.... He made up for his premature baldness with a fantastic set of whiskers ... from in front of his ears, down over his chops ... a half-ruff of facial hair standing out in contrast to his shaven jowls and chin.... [He was] casual in dress — low-slung holster ... knee-length jacket, and wide-brimmed ... hat ... likable ... for his hearty manner and open nature."[2]

General Ambrose Burnside proposed to President Lincoln in September of 1861 that he lead an expedition to attack Richmond from the south, to open a second front against that city.[3]

Richmond, the capital of the Confederacy, was a major Union target. Only one hundred miles south of Washington, it was under threat of attack throughout the war. "On to Richmond" was the early cry of the Northern public; the Union army had been on its way to capture Richmond and end the war when it was stopped at Bull Run.

The mission of the Burnside expedition was to bring a force against Richmond from the south, through North Carolina, while the Union Army of the Potomac pressed down from the north. The expedition would cut off war supplies to Richmond, tear up the railroads coming up to Richmond from the rich farm lands of the Carolinas, and capture the coastal and river ports in Albemarle and Pamlico sounds. President Lincoln and his new general-in-chief George McClellan were enthusiastic about the plan.

The first major amphibious landing in our military history,[4] the expedition would involve amassing infantry and artillery forces, loading them on to sea-going transports, assembling naval gunships, and launching a sea voyage of the assemblage of ships to the landing point on the North Carolina coast. The amphibious landing on the Normandy beaches in June 1944 would copy this operation on a much larger scale eighty-two years later.

Fred Osborne knew early on that he would serve under General Burnside: a Salem newspaper of October 7 printed a recruiting poster which promised that Company F would be in "General Burnside's Brigade."[5] Soldiers from the New England coast, who were knowledgeable about water and boats, were requested for this seacoast operation by General Burnside. Governor Andrew, a friend of General Burnside's,[6] arranged for several Massachusetts regiments, including Fred's Massachusetts 23rd, to be included in the Burnside Brigade.[7]

In October and November of 1861, the Massachusetts 23rd was at Lynnfield. Its campground was the lawn of the county seat of D. P. Ives, Esq. The rank and file were housed in tents, and Company F had the special assignment of installing wooden boards to serve as floors in the tents. Reveille was a new experience. So was the military caste system; officers were in a separate class, an idea new to young men used to living together as equals.[8] Fred made a special issue of officer privilege in his letters.

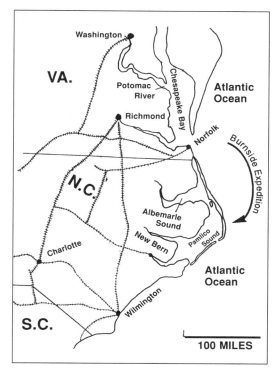

***Top:*** **General Ambrose Burnside.** ***Bottom:*** **Route of Burnside expedition**

Company F soldiers remembered Lynnfield for thin straw beds and scanty blankets, for company drill and battalion drill, sliding about on ground muddied by the freezing of nightly frost and the melting of morning sun.[9] The record says nothing of training the men to fire guns.

On October 26, Stephen B. Ives came to the Lynnfield camp and gave "over one hundred bibles to the men of Company F."[10] Ives was publisher of the *Salem Observer* and an officer in the Bible Society of Salem.[11] Ten years later Fred Osborne would marry Ives's daughter Cornelia.

On October 28, Governor John Andrew visited the camp and "witnessed battalion drill, after which he made a short address to the regiment."[12]

In early November, the regiment was ready to leave except for equipment yet to arrive. Finally, the missing knapsacks, haversacks, canteens, dress coats, and blankets came and the Massachusetts 23rd was ready for war. "Our last Sunday at Lynnfield saw the camp thronged with visitors.... It was a day of farewells, and although the members of Company F were light-hearted and full of hope, to the friends whom they were to leave behind it was a day of sadness; with many, deep foreboding."[13]

On November 11 they were aroused at four in the morning to get ready to take the train to Boston. Boston residents cheered them on State Street and fed them on Boston Common, all in the rain. A thousand men, wet to the skin in the cold November rain, the Massachusetts 23rd headed for New York in steamers.[14]

In New York they marched up Broadway, paying a salute to Mrs. Lincoln and singing a Massachusetts version of "John Brown's Body." They were ferried across the Hudson to Jersey City and boarded a train to Philadelphia.[15]

At Philadelphia, on November 14, 1861, Company F went on board the small steamer *Star* and set out for Annapolis, where infantry units were assembling for the Burnside expedition.[16] Having left Salem only 30 days before, the men of Company F, had had precious little training in the arts of war.

The Company F historian wrote: "The first part of the sail was exceedingly pleasant, but with the going down of the sun came a pouring rain which rendered us anything but comfortable.... It was Company F's fortune to be assigned to the upper deck.... On our arrival at Annapolis ... we landed and marched at once to the Naval Academy."[17] Company F was housed in a deserted museum building on the Naval Academy grounds.

Fred Osborne wrote home on November 16 (we do not have his letter of the previous day that he mentions):

> Annapolis
> Nov. 16, 1861
> Dear Mother:
> I wrote yesterday but as the conveniences did not amount to much I could not say all that I wished to.

When we came from the boat Thursday night it was raining very hard indeed. My overcoat was wet through, and I felt very tired. They marched us into a brick building and Co. A and our company were quartered in the same room. The men were so fatigued that they unstrapped their blankets, rolled up and went to sleep on the floor.

In the morning we had time to look around. It still rained hard and everything looked dull and miserable. As our breakfast did not come along until late I went out and bought some hot oyster soup and it went well, warming me right through.

I should think Annapolis might be a very pretty place in Summer but now the grounds that were used by the Naval Academy, which 6 months ago were green with grass are now trodden and trampled until they look like the rest of the street. About the only people to be seen are darkies and soldiers.

The Mass 21st [is] being quartered close to our building and [is] guarding the houses used by the Naval School and the Magazine. I tried to get a look into the magazine but as the ordnance sargent was not to be found I had to go without.

There are a great many brick houses used by the soldiers, but of their use before then I could not find out. Some of them were probably dwelling houses. It was impossible to get out to look around as the city is under martial law, and if the pickets catch anybody roaming around the city without a pass they put them in the guardhouse. The streets here are in a miserable condition, the mud being 6 or 8 inches deep and of a nasty yellow color.

We had dinner about 4½ o'clock and before we got through the order to pack up was given. The men strapped their knapsacks on, and we started for the college buildings about a mile distant. The streets we passed through were filthy and muddy so we marched on the sidewalk.

The College buildings are of brick with [a] good deal of fancy work. In front is a green running the whole length of the buildings surrounded by a fence inside of which the guard is mounted.

Our quarters are a large hall in the second story, which we share with Co. D. It is pretty cold here and my feet are almost frozen as I am writing. I bunk in with a fellow named Winchester. We sleep two together for the [sake] of being warmer.

This morning I bought a large piece of corn bread all buttered of an old negro woman who was outside selling it.

I should like to be at home for Thanksging. I wish you could send me something good to keep Thanksgiving with.

If you see John Margati tell him I am much obliged to him for his postage stamps. Give my love to Aunt Jane and all the rest, to those who made the stockings and mittens.

Yours,

Fred

Tell me what Nate says about me. Forward Ben Gray's letters if there are any.

If you send anything, unless you hear from me, direct at Co. F, 23 Reg't Mass, Annapolis.

Aunt Jane was a sister of Fred's mother's who lived with the Osborne family and helped to run the household. Nate was Nathan Osborne, Fred's older brother, a captain in the regular U.S. Army.

## *Down the Coast*

Burnside's troops waited at Annapolis until early January 1862 while he arranged for ships for his expedition.

Ambrose Burnside had to provide his own ships to take his troops and supplies to the Carolina coast. The navy and the army were in two different departments in Washington; there was no joint command. The navy would provide gunships to bombard coastal forts in this amphibious operation, but the army had to find it own ships to transport the soldiers.

So General Burnside spent that winter hunting for ships, buying or leasing whatever floating transportation he could find. He needed ships for 20,000 soldiers, supplies for three months, coal to refuel the steamers, horses, artillery, and ammunition.

The fleet that General Burnside put together was made up of schooners and brigs and barks, side-wheel steamboats, propeller steamboats, canal boats, ferries, freighters, passenger ships, whatever he could lay his hands on. His ships had to draw little water because only shallow-draft vessels could keep off the bottom in the sounds and rivers of the Carolina coast.

**A New York ferry converted to a gunboat.**

While they were waiting, General Burnside's troops spent their time drilling and keeping clean and getting familiar with their muzzle-loaders. There wasn't much ammunition, so actual firing of the guns was rare; "in most instances the regiments [only] went through the motions of loading and firing."[18] Bayonet drill was also skimpy. "By the time the expedition was ready to leave most of the regiments were still deficient in training."[19]

At Annapolis the soldiers had their first experience with slavery. Maryland was a slave state, and farms using slave labor surrounded the military camps. Sometimes slaves even escaped into the camps.

According to historian Richard Allen Sauers, "The major problem with the escaped slaves occurred when their owners came to the camps and demanded the return of their property.... The soldiers refused to permit the slave owners to search the tents. In one case, a slave who had been beaten by his master ... sought refuge with the 25th Massachusetts.... The owner and the sheriff arrived to search for the slave.... After they left, the slave was secreted aboard a northern-bound mail train."[20]

Fred's regiment, the 23rd Massachusetts, was put in Brigadier General John Foster's brigade; Foster's brigade also included the Massachusetts 24th, 25th, and 27th and the Connecticut 10th. John Foster, was well liked by his troops; a West Pointer, and an engineer, he had been with Major Anderson on Fort Sumter nine months earlier when the Confederates bombarded it.

Governor Andrew was one of many visiting dignitaries to review Foster's brigade, and because Washington was only twenty-five miles away, Secretary of State William Seward, Secretary of the Navy Gideon Welles, and Secretary of War Simon Cameron also came by.[21]

On January 6, 1862, the troops at Annapolis were ordered aboard the transports. The Massachusetts 23rd regiment left camp at 10 A.M. and marched to the docks "with about an inch of snow on the ground, and the thermometer eighteen degrees above zero."[22]

According to Sauers, "When the 23rd arrived at the Navy Yard their ships were not [at the dock].... The regiment formed into a hollow square and the men [lit] small fires to keep warm. Finally, about 6 P.M., the ... ships ... docked and the men were able to board."[23]

Fred Osborne was now on the schooner *Highlander*. This sailing ship was "originally the *Claremont*.... [It had] a centerboard [retractable] keel ... [was] built in New Jersey in 1858, for the southern pine [lumber] trade."[24]

William Welch, a soldier from Maine in Company A of Fred's regiment, described the *Highlander* in these terms:

**General John Foster**

She is very commodious between decks, the tallest man can walk up-right; she has wooden bunks along the sides, with beds of straw or seaweed, with passageways thirty inches wide on either side of the vessel; all the bunks were three tiers high....

About five hundred of our regiment are on board this schooner, some between decks, and as many more in the lower hold. My company, A, are fortunate in being between decks, and my bunk, numbered 169, is on the starboard side, upper tier, and near the main hatch, decidedly cool, but healthful.

Forward between decks on the starboard [side] is the galley, with large coppers for cooking the rations of the soldiers, and smaller ones for messes for the [officers'] cabin. On the port side forward is the sink for use of the men, and as it is the only place that smoking is allowed below, it is generally filled with smokers.[25]

Private Welch also described Burnside's fleet: "The harbor at Annapolis is full of vessels of all sizes, kinds and descriptions: huge side wheelers, capable of carrying a thousand men; propellers, old North river hay droghers, looking top heavy; ships, barks, brigs, schooners, down to little tugs, a formidable looking lot."[26]

Joseph Denny of the Massachusetts 25th was also on the *Highlander* and described its departure:

On the morning of January 9th, 1862, at 8 o'clock, the expedition, comprising one hundred and seventeen vessels, moved out of the harbor of Annapolis. It was the grandest sight ever seen before upon this side of the Atlantic. The steamer *New Brunswick*, having on board the Tenth Connecticut Volunteers, led the way, followed in two lines by the remainder of the fleet. From all the vessels and steamers the most enthusiastic cheers were heard, mingling with the music of a dozen or more regimental bands. It was a beautiful morning as the fleet sailed so grandly into the waters of the Chesepeake.[27]

The fleet moved down Chesapeake Bay, steamboats towing the sailing vessels. According to Private Denny: "[The] destination was unknown even to the officers of the fleet.... The sailing masters had only one instruction —'Follow the leading vessel'; and the master of the leading vessel moved under sealed orders.... [The first] envelope ... directed that it should be opened when Fortress Monroe was in sight — opened it read, 'Go to Hampton Roads and anchor.'"[28]

Newspapers in the North and in the South had been speculating for weeks on the destination of the Burnside expedition. There being few military secrets in the Civil War, Burnside's activities at Annapolis were thoroughly reported by war correspondents, who roamed the camps at will. Guesses at where the expedition would strike ranged from New Orleans to Yorktown.

The Confederacy was in some dread, feeling very threatened by the Burnside expedition: "Magruder is in a frenzy at Yorktown" reported Joseph Denny.[29]

General Magruder, at Yorktown with 20,000 Confederate soldiers, "(is) convinced that the destination is against him.... [He] has made all preparations to run.... [He] has telegraphed [Jefferson] Davis to know whether he shall burn the city and flee."[30]

Denny noted that "Beauregard was watching for it at New Orleans,"[31] and the *New York Times* wrote that at Norfolk "the rebels are all alive in anticipation of an attack"[32]

The Burnside expedition continued down Chesapeake Bay; Private Welch of the Massachusetts 23rd recalled: "[the *Highlander* was] towed along at five knots an hour. It came up foggy during the afternoon and compelled us to anchor before midnight. We started [up again] Friday, 10th, in the forenoon, arriving at and anchoring in Hampton Roads before 3 P.M."[33]

At Hampton Roads, the skipper of the lead ship opened his next envelope. The instructions said to "head for the Atlantic, turn south, and then open the final envelope."[34] The double line of ships, with their cargoes of 20,000 soldiers and of horses and coal and cannon, left Hampton Roads and moved out into the Atlantic heading south.

The final envelope told the lead skipper that the destination of the Burnside expedition was Hatteras Inlet. The expedition was to enter Hatteras Inlet, attack Roanoke Island, then New Bern, then Fort Macon.

General McClellan had said in a January 7, 1862, letter to General Burnside:

> Your first point of attack will be Roanoke Island and its dependencies.... Having completed your arrangements in regard to Roanoke Island, and the waters north of it, you will please at once make a descent on New Bern ... and the railroad passing through it.... You will at once ... take the steps necessary to reduce Fort Macon ... [to] seize and hold Raleigh ... [and] the railroad passing through Goldsborough.... A great point would be gained by the ... destruction of the Wilmington and Weldon Railroad.

Thus the work list for the Burnside expedition. Now to get the fleet down the coast, through Hatteras Inlet, and into Pamlico Sound.

After dark on Saturday, January 11, 1862, the fleet got out into the Atlantic. On Sunday a storm came up, Private William Welch, of the Massachusetts 23rd, on the *Highlander* schooner reported:

> [We were] still in tow of the *Hussar* [steamship], and to help along, made sail on the schooner.... The wind came out dead ahead, freshening every minute. We had to take in all sail; as we went along the sea was getting higher and higher, the boat was rolling heavily and pitching into it finely, and we making barely a knot an hour. About 4 o'clock P.M. ... we were hailed from the *Hussar* and told to cut the hawser. Captain Dayton, master of the schooner, gave orders to make sail. First, we reefed the mainsail, then double

reefed the foresail, and loosed the jib, and when these sails were set, one cut severed the hawser, and we were off on our own hook....

By this time all the sailing vessels had been dropped by the towing steamers and left to their own resources.... We had sailed from Fort Monroe with sealed orders, to be opened when well out to sea, which, when opened, were found to direct us to make for and enter Hatteras Inlet.

About the time we cut loose from the *Hussar*, we didn't care where we went to. There were five hundred or more of us on board a schooner, very badly adapted for the situation, for she had no center board, it having either been lost out of her, or so cramped in her as to be unmanageable, and she rolled and pitched about so that nearly every man was sick.... Off Cape Hatteras a squall struck us, blew the flying jib out of the bolt ropes, and nearly capsized us; [we took down all sail] except the mainsail, that stuck badly, and the captain of the schooner ran up the rigging, jumped on to the gaff and started it down. With everything down we lay nearly an hour, the boat rolling fearfully and throwing some of the boys out of their berths.... After a while we wore ship and stood in shore, and about 3 P.M., Monday, 13th dropped anchor ... about one and a half miles from shore and four or five from Hatteras Inlet.... We had had a fearful experience, and were in great danger, and so had all the fleet.

I had been on deck nearly all the time, making myself useful.... It was my first appearance at sea, and I wanted to see all that I could of it. I sat on the windlass and felt the bow of the schooner go down, down, till it seemed that she would go over end ways, and then I saw the stern go down, and the waves, several mountains high, apparently coming in top of us, and I wanted to go home.[35]

The *Highlander* anchored off Hatteras Inlet for two days, then signaled for a pilot and a tugboat to take the schooner through the inlet and into Pamlico Sound.

The schooner was taken under tow but, according to Private Welch: "We are hardly well underway when we see a ship's boat ... capsized, with men clinging to her.... Our boats are lowered at once ... [we pick up] eleven men ... [and take] them on board the *Highlander*.... Two of the men are dead.... They had [taken a small boat] in [to shore] to report the arrival of their vessel, and were swamped by the breakers.... On our left we see the steamer *City of New York* ashore and breaking up. She was a total loss.... We see the propeller [steamship] *Zouave* sunk.... She was also a total loss.... Astern of us is a schooner on a bar in a sinking condition, flying signals of distress."

General Burnside's ships were now outside Hatteras Inlet. The typical winter storms off the Carolina coast had taken their toll of the motley fleet and the storms continued.

Getting the ships through the Inlet and into Pamlico Sound would take three weeks. General Burnside would later say that it was the most trying time of his career.

## *Getting Through Hatteras Inlet*

The element of surprise that General Burnside had carefully arranged, to keep the Confederates from moving troops to reinforce the point of attack, was now at risk because of the delay in getting his ships through Hatteras Inlet. General Burnside later recalled:

> Great anxiety [had been] manifested to know [the expedition's] destination, but the secret had been well kept at Washington.... Mr. Lincoln afterward told me one public man was very importunate, and ... almost demanded that the President should tell him where we were going. Finally, the President said to him, "Now, I will tell you in great confidence were they are going, if you will promise not to speak of it to any one." The promise was given, and Mr. Lincoln said, "Well, now, my friend, the expedition is going to sea!" [36]

Burnside took the occasion of this anecdote to say of the president and the pressures on him: "No man has ever lived who could have gone through that struggle as he did.... His heart [was never] stirred with a feeling of enmity or resentment.... He was actuated by the simple desire ... to maintain ... the government at all hazards."[37]

At Hatteras Inlet the winter storm raged on. Some of the shallow-draft ships entered the Inlet and anchored in Pamlico Sound, but most ships could not get through the Inlet. Contrary to expectations the Inlet had a clearance at high water of only about six feet, and most of the ships drew eight and nine feet of water.

General Burnside, in the little steamer *Picket,* was everywhere among the ships urging the captains to try to get their vessels through the Inlet. The *Picket,* not exactly seaworthy, was buffeted by the storm, as General Burnside later wrote: "Everything on the deck that was not lashed down was swept overboard.... Men, furniture, and crockery below decks were thrown about in a most promiscuous manner."[38]

Some of the steamers were able to force their way through the Inlet, dragging on the bottom, smoke streaming out of their stacks, side-wheeler paddles spinning, throwing water in all directions. Finally they got clear and into the Sound. Some of the sailing vessels, bottoms scraping on the sandy bottom, were towed through the Inlet by the steamers.

Private Denny of the Massachusetts 25th described the scene:

> General Burnside ... on board the little *Picket,* with his yellow belt, blue shirt, slouched hat and high boots ... stood like a sea-god in the bows of his puffing and whistling little steamer, encouraging those disheartened, and always asking affectionately after the welfare of the men.... He had a living faith that success would attend his efforts ultimately ... and when his troops saw the firm determination resting upon his countenance, they had faith too. There was not a thought of failure.[39]

Several steamers ran aground and the civilian captains who commanded some of the rented ships resisted putting their ships at risk in struggling through the Inlet. According to Private Denny:

> Finally, Burnside determined to make an issue with the master of the largest transport, which was the *New York*. Captain Clark was notified that he "must put his steamer [through the Inlet] ... at once." Clark refused. "Very well," said the General, "the steamer shall go [through the Inlet] ... or be lost in the attempt." Clark refused. A file of soldiers came on board, arrested Captain Clark and conveyed him away in a small boat. Our troops looked on and some one said — "that means business," and another remarked, that "the general had got his back up," and still another offered to "bet ten to one that the *New York* would [go through the Inlet]." ...Burnside insisted that his order must be obeyed, or the captain should hang at the yard-arm! And that settled the matter.... Men don't like to hang by the neck ... so [Captain] Clark promised to make an attempt to [get through the Inlet].
>
> The next day ... [lightened] of all troops and freight ... the *New York* ... getting up a full head of steam, went gaily [through the Inlet] without touching bottom.... This success was greeted with hearty cheers from the troops.[40]

For their safety, to get them away from the breakers near the shore, the supply ships carrying coal and water were sent out to sea. Drinking water thus became a problem when the delay in getting through the Inlet stretched into days and then weeks. Private William Welch was on the *Highlander*, along with Fred Osborne and others in the Massachusetts 23rd: "We got so ravenous for water, that once as General Burnside was passing us, in the *Picket*, we swarmed up the rigging, and all hands, as one man, called for water! water! I can't say that it made General Burnside feel any better, but it helped us a great deal."[41]

The gentle Burnside later recalled, "Much suffering resulted from this [shortage of drinking water].... A flag of distress was hoisted on many

The steamer *New York* lying at a wharf in 1862.

of the vessels…. On one of these dreary days I for a time gave up all hope, and walked to the bow of the vessel that I might be alone. Soon after, a small black cloud appeared in the angry gray sky, just above the horizon, and very soon spread so as to cover the entire canopy, and in a few moments a most copious fall of rain came to our relief."[42]

General Burnside sent a messenger, a Mr. Sheldon, to President Lincoln to report his difficulties. "The president grew thoroughly discouraged as he listened to the endless obstacles Burnside seemed to face, finally remarking it was 'all a failure … they had better come back at once.' Not at all, Sheldon assured him, for despite the repeated impediments General Burnside was progressing surprising well, finding his way around every problem. At this Lincoln brightened."[43]

Ingenuity finally got the biggest ships through the Hatteras Inlet. General Burnside explained the scheme which they developed to get those ships over the shallows:

> The current was very swift … which proved to be much in our favor….
> Large vessels were sent ahead, under full steam, [and grounded] when the
> tide was running out, and then anchors were carried out by boats in advance
> [of the ship], so as to hold the vessels in position. The swift current would
> wash the sand from under them and allow them to float, after which they
> were driven farther on by steam and anchored again, when the sand would
> again wash out from under them. This process was continued for days, until
> a broad channel of over eight feet was made, deep enough to allow the pas-
> sage of the fleet into the sound.

By February 4, General Burnside was finally able to say, three weeks after arriving at Hatteras Inlet, "the entire fleet … had passed into the sound … and orders given for the advance on Roanoke Island."[44]

## CHAPTER FIVE

# The Battle of Roanoke Island

Years later military historians would marvel at General Burnside's remarkable amphibious operation.[1] While Lincoln's other generals were dilly-dallying, the gentle-natured Burnside set up this daring enterprise to open a second front against Richmond.

With no military precedent from which to learn, Burnside had to invent the strategy and improvise the equipment for an amphibious landing. He had to arrange for boats and cannon and troops, he had to oversee the complex movement of men and war materiel to get them to the battle site; and he had to devise the battle strategy for landing on an enemy shore. Good reason for military historians to admire this man.

Now the expedition was getting ready for the attack on Roanoke Island.

## February 1, 1862

The North had enjoyed little good news to this point because the war had not gone well. If General Burnside could take over the Carolina coast and put pressure on Richmond and Norfolk, the Northern newspapers would love it.

Fred Osborne had been on the schooner *Highlander* for a month. Leaving Annapolis on January 6, he had come down the coast in the mighty storm, waited on the *Highlander* while it struggled to get through Hatteras Inlet, and, still on board, waited longer, weeks, for the rest of the fleet to get through the Inlet.

Colonel Thomas Edmands, of the 24th Massachusetts, wrote of this time:

> Life on the transports was weariness and vexation.... Measles broke out on some of the vessels whose crowded condition defied proper sanitary precautions, and many poor fellows were carried to shallow graves scooped in the sands near [Hatteras Inlet].... The real hard work of the Burnside

Expedition — the hardest of all — was done right here. The obstacles over-
come were greater, and required more persistent pluck and patient endurance
than any of its subsequent victories.[2]

Private Denny of the Massachusetts 25th remembered getting ready for the
battle: "Orders were issued in regard to landing. The troops were to land ... with
three days' cooked rations. The company cooks went ashore ... and prepared the
three days' rations." Rowboats were to carry the troops from the ships to the
beaches. "Certain ... men were detailed ... as oarsmen, and when the waters
would permit, the vicinity of the fleet was alive with small boats filled with soldiers, practising with the oars."[3]

Burnside's troops, from the record, did not practice landing on an enemy
beach. Debarking thousands of soldiers from small boats and establishing a beachhead under enemy fire was left to be worked out in the actual landing.[4]

## February 5, 1862

Twelve thousand soldiers were aboard the transports. Steamers towed the
sailing ships up Pamlico Sound, and gunboats escorted the troop ships.

From the deck of the schooner *Highlander*, Private Welch of Fred's regiment
described the scene:

> At last, the last thing to get ready was ready, and ... we started for Roanoke
> Island. It was a splendid day; the water was very smooth; the wind was
> light, and it was comfortably warm.... Way ahead, as far as one can see,
> are gunboats; nearer, is another line of gunboats, then comes our line of
> transports, the steamer *New York* towing schooners *Highlander, Skirmisher,*
> and *S.P. Bailey;* the steamer *New Brunswick* towing schooners *Recruit* and
> *E. W. Farrington*; steamer *Guide* towing schooners *Sea Bird* and *Emma*; and
> on the flanks sail the ... gunboats ... acting as a guard for the fleet.[5]

Another soldier, Private James Stone of the Massachusetts 21st, on the big
steamship *Northerner*, wrote: "It was a handsome sight, eighty ships in all ...
gun-boats, and ... other ships carrying the troops, baggage, provisions, ammunition."[6]

Private Denny of the Massachusetts 25th reported: "The *Pilot Boy*, with
General Foster on board, took the lead of the transports, followed by the *New
York*, with the Twenty-fifth Massachusetts, the large fleet making a beautiful display, as it cut through ... waters ... as smooth as glass. At five o'clock, P.M., the
fleet anchored eight miles below Roanoke Island, and in view of its southerly
point."[7]

Almost three hundred years earlier, Sir Walter Raleigh had established a
colony on Roanoke Island. That was in 1585, before the Pilgrims landed in Massachusetts. Virginia Dare, who was born on Roanoke Island in 1587, became

famous as the first English child born in the New World. The colony disappeared mysteriously before 1590, however, leaving no clue as to its fate.[8]

Now, in 1862, Roanoke Island was a key element in the Confederate defense of the area below Richmond. According to historian Shelby Foote, the Union capture of that island would expose the Norfolk Navy Yard

> to attack from the rear. This would be worse than bad; it would be tragic, for the Confederates [depended heavily on the Norfolk Navy Yard to build ships to attack Union shipping and to defend Confederate ports].... The focal point for [the defense of Norfolk], as anyone could plainly see, was Roanoke Island.... It was like a loose-fitting cork plugging the neck of a bottle called Albemarle Sound. Nothing that went by water could get in there without going past the cork.[9]

Another observer noted that if the Confederates lost Roanoke Island and control of the Carolina coast, "an advance might be made on Richmond.... An effective [northern] army in North Carolina [could] intercept and hold the railroad[s], and by cutting off ... supplies ... oblige the (confederates) to abandon Virginia."[10]

Henry Wise, the Confederate general in charge of the defense of Roanoke Island, had taken command on January 7, only two days before Burnside's expedition had sailed away from Annapolis. General Wise has been called "one of the Civil War's greater anomalies." Not a military man, he was a former foreign minister to Brazil and a former governor of Virginia. Before war broke out, he "had been an ardent ... Unionist ... [but now] the pugnacious Wise was a fervent Confederate."[11]

When General Wise had made his first inspection of the island, he had seen a weak defense against an attack from the south; there were no fortifications on the southern part of the ten-mile-long island. General Wise made vigorous but vain requests to the Confederate high command for more guns and more men. He said later: "It ought to have been defended by all the means in the power of the government. It was the key to all the rear defenses of Norfolk. It unlocked two sounds ... eight rivers ... four canals ... and two railroads. It guarded ... supplies of corn, pork and forage. It should have been defended at the expense of 20,000 men."[12]

General Wise got little help, but he did try to stop Union forces with a fortification across the narrow part of the island halfway up from the southern tip. That fortification and the three coastal forts built of turfed sand facing the ship channel in Croatan Sound were to be his main defenses. Fort Bartow had nine cannon, Fort Blanchard, two miles up the shore from Fort Bartow had four cannon, and a mile further north was Fort Huger, out-fitted with twelve cannon.

General Burnside needed to learn something about the island to plan his attack; in this war, detailed maps of enemy territory were usually not available to either Union or Confederate generals. There seems to have been very little

known about Roanoke
Island, but General Burn-
side did have one good
source of information: "A
young negro, who had
escaped from the island on
our arrival at Hatteras Inlet, had given me most
valuable information as to
the nature of the shore of
the island, from which I
had determined that our
point of landing should be
at Ashby's Harbor, which
was nearly midway up the
shore."[13]

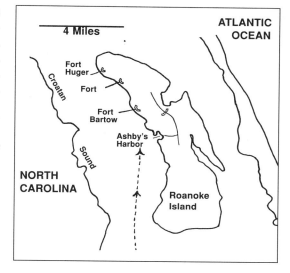

The fleet anchored
within sight of the southern
tip of Roanoke Island on Wednesday, February 5, 1862. Then fog settled in and
kept the fleet immobile all through the next day. On Friday morning, February 7,
the weather cleared and the fleet moved into Croatan Sound.

Burnside sent his topographical officer, Lieutenant W. S. Andrews, into
Ashby's Harbor in a small boat to see if troops could be landed in surf boats.
According to one historian, Lieutenant Andrews "made soundings, surveyed the
approaches, and actually set foot ashore" before a Confederate detail arrived.
"Andrews made good his escape and rowed back out to Burnside ... convinced
that there was sufficient water available for the approach.... Burnside ordered ...
[his generals] to prepare to land."[14]

At about 11 A.M. Burnside's gunboats began to fire on Fort Bartow, which
overlooked Ashby Harbor, to put it out of action before his troops landed on the
beach.[15]

Private Welch, who was with Fred Osborne aboard the schooner *Highlander*,
reported: "During this fight the most cheering sight was the movements of the
little sloop *Granite*. With an off-shore wind she sailed back and forth in front of
... [Fort Bartow], and in passing each time gave them a shot with her thirty-two
pounder. She behaved splendidly ... the bombardment continued all day."[16] Fort
Bartow was silenced.

According to General Burnside's account:

> Orders were given for the troops to land. The ground in the rear of Ashby's
> Harbor was cleared [of enemy troops] by shells from the naval vessels, and
> our large surf-boats were lowered [from the troopships], rapidly filled with
> troops, and towed up in long lines by [steamships] ... until they came near

to the shore of the harbor, when each of the surf-boats was cut loose and steered for the shore. There was no obstruction to their landing. In less than an hour 4000 troops were ashore, and before nightfall the entire force was landed.[17]

General Burnside was pleased: "I never witnessed a more beautiful sight ... as the steamers approached the shore at a rapid speed each surf boat was 'let go,' and with their acquired velocity ... reached the shore."[18]

Private Welch gave this report of the landing:

> A few shells from the *Delaware* and *Picket* quickly drove the enemy away [from the beach], and the landing of the troops was unmolested. General Foater, on the *Pilot Boy,* General Reno, with the *Union* and *Patuxent,* and General Parke, on the *Phoenix,* each steamer towing boats filled with men, landed in about twenty minutes over 4000 men.... There was hardly a second between the landing of detachments from the regiments of the ... Twenty-third, Twenty-fifth, and Twenty-seventh Massachusetts. My company [Company A] landed after dark, on, it seemed to me, a quaking bog. I had hardly started from the boats, making for a fire up on the shore, when my right leg went into a bog hole up to my hips. I got out of it, and managed to reach dry land ... I soon found my company, and proceeded to make my bed with my chum. We were in a cornfield.... We pulled up the stalks, placed them lengthwise between the rows; placed one rubber blanket under us, got up back to back, and pulled the other blanket over us, and went to sleep. We didn't go to sleep — for just then it commenced to rain, and up we got, and I commenced wandering, which continued all night ... I finally crawled into a dog kennel that stood in front of ... [a] dwelling house, and thought I had secured dry lodgings for the night, but soon was roused up and out by a strange voice that said, "that's my house." I guess it was his ... and I got out of it, and again wandered. As soon as it was daylight we got ourselves together and prepared to start off.[19]

Starting off from camp in the morning, Fred Osborne and Private Welch and the rest of the Massachusetts 23rd regiment followed the Massachusetts 25th up a road from the harbor toward the center of the island.[20]

This section of the island was all bog and swamp. Up the center of the island ran a road that was elevated on a dirt causeway which had been built through the swamp. Confederate officers believed the swamp on each side of this causeway was impassable by infantry.

To stop the advance of Union forces, General Wise had built a fortification across this road, a breastworks containing a battery of three cannon. Trees had been cut down in front of this fort for a distance of several hundred yards to expose enemy infantry making a frontal assault.

The Massachusetts regiments came along the road from Ashby's Harbor and

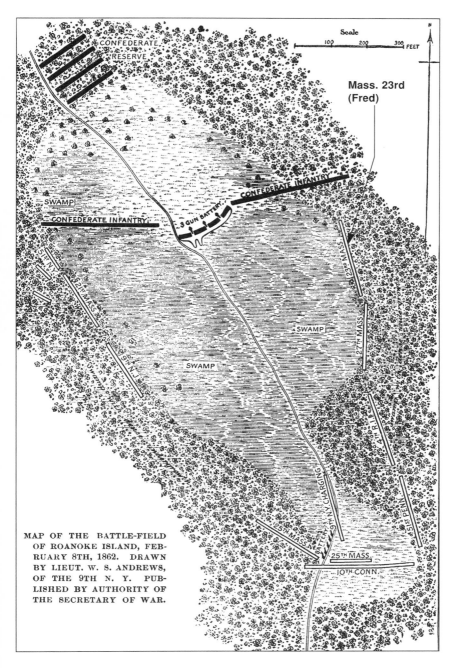

Map of the battle of Roanoke Island

turned onto the causeway road. When they looked up the road toward the north, they saw the breastworks and the Confederate cannon and infantry guns behind the breastworks began to speak.

Private Welch of the Massachusetts 23rd described the encounter:

> We marched along about a mile or so [from Ashby's Harbor] when we heard firing. Soon we came to a clearing and saw the Twenty-fifth in action ahead of us, with skirmishers ahead. We fell into column, by division, behind them, advanced when they did, and halted when they did. We were just in range of the bullets and their song was quite audible.
>
> The enemy had a three gun battery at the further end of a road through ... a swamp.... They had cut down trees some sixty or eighty yards across, and five or six hundred yards down the road, making an oblong cleared space ... [in front of the cannon].... These three guns completely covered the road ... and were firing ... all the time ... [showing] their determination to keep the road clear at all events.... They had about 800 men at the battery, deployed at either side ...and reckoned to hold the fort if we insisted on coming up the road, the marshes on either flank being considered impassable.[21]

General Foster decided to outflank the breastworks; he sent regiments out into the swamp on the right and on the left to work their way, out of sight, around the ends of the fort. It was now eight o'clock in the morning.

According to Private Welch:

> We were ordered by the right flank across the fire of the guns, into the woods and swamp to try and flank the enemy. We ... went across the fire, and here lost several men killed. We ... passed through the woods ... came to an open morass, and skirted the woods to our left, keeping close to them, made as fast as we could for the enemy. We were seen as soon as we emerged, and fired on, but kept going. We were some three hours getting through this swamp...."
>
> Our regiment [the 23rd] got far enough ... to open a raking fire ... on their flank.... While we are doing this the 25th Massachusetts in front has been relieved by the Tenth Connecticut. The 21st Massachusetts, 51st New York, and 9th New Jersey have ... pushed along on the right of the enemy ... and the 51st New York is being thrown still further to the left.... When the charge is made ... it was at this time that the 9th New York [a flashy Zouave regiment led by flashy Colonel Rush Hawkins] came on to the field.[22]

Lt. Colonel Edmands continued the story:

> The fight had now lasted three hours and a half.... The men ... [under] a heavy fire of infantry and three field pieces in the battery had worked their

**A Union assault on a three-gun battery. (From a wartime sketch.)**

way, inch by inch, wading at times waist deep in bog, mud, and water, through the morass, and were getting to firmer ground on which they could secure footing for assaults on the flanks of the breastworks.... [When the 9th New York was] ordered to charge the battery in front over the narrow causeway ... the 9th New York ... with a cheer rushed forward in column of fours — the road would admit no wider front — and made a gallant charge; the regiments from the right and left, rising on the firmer ground they had gained from the morass — deemed by the Confederates impassable — simultaneously charged with an answering cheer, and the battery was overwhelmed, front and flanks. Its defenders ... broke and ran.... No sooner had the battery been captured than the Union troops ... vigorously pressed to the northern end of the island to which the enemy had retreated, and in a short time the Confederates were all prisoners.[23]

Fred Osborne described his first battle in a letter to his mother:

Feb. 20, 1862

Dear Mother

We left the Schooner the 7th in the evening with three days rations in our haversacks and forty rounds in our cartridge boxes. The gun boats had been up the Sound all day, having gone ahead of the Fleet in the morning. We were in sight of them all day. About noon they engaged with the Rebel batteries. The firing lasted until night.

When we landed it was perfectly still. We had seen the fight to be sure but we did not know whether they had been beaten off or not. And did [not] know what we should meet when we did land.

The Steamer *Pilot Boy* had a deck of our reg't and was towing a string of boats besides. We were landed in a place all hummocks, salt grass, mud holes, etc. We could see the fires of the boys on the other side of the mud which was before us. Falling and stumbling round for about an hour, we got on terra firma, most of [us] wet with mud and water to our knees. We spent the night shivering round the fires. It rained all night, and we were miserable enough.

In the morning we marched up the road towards the woods where the Rebels were supposed to be. After getting through another mud hole, we heard firing ahead and orders came to hurry up the 23rd to support the 25th which had engaged the enemy.

At a turn of road where there was a place clear of trees, they had established the Hospital. The litters and the attendants standing round made a fellow feel kind of uncomfortable.

We pushed ahead and found the 25th had engaged the rebels who were in the woods on the edge of a clearing. At first it appeared they had no artillery as we could hear nothing but musket and rifle balls whistled past us. The rebels kept retreating through the woods and our colonel rec'd orders to deploy his Reg't to the right of the 25th to outflank the Secesh. We went right into a swamp where the water was about knee deep. When we had got pretty well in, we turned and marched by the right flank. The bullets, shell, grape shot, and cannister now began to fly about our ears in good shape.

Only one fellow was scared, he told the Captain he thought he had better go to the rear. He did not feel well. But it was no go.

We now turned and advanced by the left, which would carry us out of the swamp, but we encountered a close network of vines and brambles. We tried in vain to break through it and at last the officers had to cut through it with swords.

We pressed ahead then advanced by the right, the firing continuing brisk as ever. And the shells now began to fly pretty lively. We rushed ahead and just as we were getting out of the swamp and were in a puddle up to [our] waists, we heard a cheering and when we got out, found the rebels had a masked battery of four cannon and the 9th [N.Y.] Reg't "Hawkins Zouaves" charged on it and drove them out.

There were four smooth bore heavy guns and a howitzer. There were five rebels in the battery, four dead and one wounded and one dead outside. The Zouaves and the 24th went right down the road after the rebels. Some of the boys found revolvers, knives, shoes etc. in the fort, but I was not among the lucky ones. There was a rebel Lt. dead in the rear of the battery. The name on his clothes Richard Colt "Miss Legion."

After staying at the battery about two hours, we marched down the road. It was strewed with knapsacks, blankets, and equipment. The arms we saw were either broken or thrown into ditches. Everything looked as though they were well frightened. We could not pick up much as the Regiment before us had got everything. The 24th had come on to two villages of Rebel Barracks in the woods and the Col. surrendered without firing a gun. By this battle we got 10000 [word unclear] of arms, 3000 Prisoners and stores [of] flour, rice, pork, lard, sugar, molasses, etc. And as the whole Island is given up, we get 51 cannon.

The Secesh are miserable looking chaps, they average larger than we do, but do not look half so rugged, and are great braggers. Excepting one Company, the "Richmond Blues" who were dressed in a gray uniform faced with black, you don't find any two dressed alike. Tell Tuvvy [Fred's brother Orville] most of the officers of the Southern Chivalry are rascally looking scamps and as to their being better looking than our officers, as Tuvvy said the English papers used to say, is not true. They prefer to fight behind trees and masked batteries.

They say they thought that swamp [was] impassable, and when they saw us coming through, their Col. told them to run and they did. They must have carried their dead by some means for the woods were full of them when they were attacked. There was a mule dead in the battery, and I think they had more, and so carried their dead off. Some of the boys saw 40 in a ditch. I saw 4 new made graves myself.

Preparations are being made for exchanging these prisoners. It will be a bad thing, for the Lea and Miss. troops and Ben McCulloughs Riflemen are a set of villains.

This letter was written in my bunk, in the Rebel Barracks. Our Regiment was four hours in the swamp on the day of battle. I never got cold though I was wet to [the] waist till next morning.

Enclosed is a Rebel letter and proclamation. I write in a great hurry as the mail goes by six o'clock in the morning. Direct your letters same as before. Excuse bad writing. Write soon and often.

Love to all.

F.M.O.

The rebel letter and the proclamation were not found among Fred's letters. Fred mentioned in an admiring way the frontal charge on the Confederate cannon by the "9th N.Y. Regiment 'Hawkins Zouaves.'" The Zouaves got their name and uniform from a French infantry unit made up of Algerian recruits that was characterized by colorful oriental uniforms and precision drilling.

The commanding officer of this regiment was Col. Rush Hawkins, a flamboyant leader whose style often got him in trouble with his superiors and

**Uniform of Hawkin's Zouaves of the 9th New York Regiment**

with his colleagues. At the critical stage of the battle of Roanoke Island, Col. Hawkins and his Zouave 9th N.Y. charged the cannon battery. In his description of the action, he reported: "I had made up my mind to face to the front and make an effort to charge the [breast] work ... I ordered my bugler to sound the charge.... A great cheer went up.... Major Kimball ... was heading ... a direct charge up ... the center of the field ... directly to the sally port covered by a 24-pound howitzer.... All entered the [breast]work pell-mell together ... and soon the whole front of the breastwork was covered with a sea of red fezzes."[24] (The red fez was the uniform hat of the Zouaves.)

After the surrender of the rebel forces on Roanoke Island, the rebel barracks was named Camp Foster in honor of General John Foster, whose brigade [which included the 23rd Massachusetts Regiment] had much to do with the Union victory.[25] Emmerton, the regimental historian, watched Burnside congratulate General Foster; he was so touched that he longed for Edouard Detaille, the French painter of Napoleon and his armies, who was known for his accurate portrayals of battles and military life, to memorialize the scene:

> Shortly after our arrival [at the rebel barracks] General Foster came over, on horseback, to announce the surrender of all the enemy's forces. Have always thought the scene memorable and have wished that Detaille had been near to fix it with his magic pencil:
> Scene: The parade between the smoking embers of the barracks and the shell-torn officers quarter.
> Time: Early dusk brightened by the glare, from across the sound, of the burning battery at Red-stone point, fired by the enemy on his retreat.
> Enter: General Foster. A complacent pride in his achievement sitting as easily on his manly features as he on his captured horse.... Gen. Burnside, the commanding general, reaching up to pat the back of his successful subordinate and looking as if he would like to kiss him in his joy.[26]

Fred Osborne, four months from his Salem home, had been in his first battle. He was sitting in these Camp Foster quarters on February 20, 1862, when he wrote to his mother.

The battle of Roanoke Island was the first major victory for the Union and caused great jubilation in the Northern press. General Burnside was toasted as the hero.

CHAPTER SIX

# The Battle of New Bern

For some days, camp life on Roanoke Island was routine. Foraging, generally very closely controlled by the Union officers to protect the natives of each occupied area, was allowed on the island to a limited extent. But the natives were poor, and the soldiers did not have the heart to take much from them. In one case, "a family with ten children was found sick, naked and hungry. Company G of the 23rd furnished rations and contributed two bags of clothing."[1]

In late February, General Burnside began to get his expedition ready for the attack on New Bern. They would use steam-powered gunboats and sailing ship troop transports as in the attack on Roanoke Island.

New Bern was an important Confederate port some miles up the Neuse River from Pamlico Sound. Port facilities and railroad connections were critical to the Confederacy, as military analyst Richard Ward notes, "The denial of ... the waterway and the railhead of New Bern was paramount ... in ... [the] scheme for cutting the flow of supplies to [Richmond]."[2]

A strategy to capture New Bern had to deal with the forts along the Neuse River, which protected the city against an enemy coming up the river. General Burnside, representing the army, and Commander Goldsborough, representing the navy, had to work out this strategy together. Burnside and Goldsborough made up the informal joint command used throughout the North Carolina coast campaign because the army and the navy reported separately to Washington. The plan was for Burnside's men to land on the western bank of the Neuse River some miles below New Bern. They would then work their way toward New Bern along the riverbank, attacking the forts from the land side. The ships would fire on the Confederate batteries from the river.[3]

On March 6, 1862, Fred's company boarded the *Highlander* for the expedition to New Bern. Twelve thousand men on troopships waited at anchor at

62

Roanoke Island for four days, held up by the raw northerly wind. On the eleventh they got underway down Pamlico Sound and reached Hatteras Inlet about dusk. Private Derby of the Massachusetts 27th described the scene at Hatteras Inlet:

> Our hearts were gladdened by the arrival of the steamer *Suwanee* with a large mail from the North.... The 12th was a faultless day, not a breeze disturbing the long, smooth swell of Pamlico [Sound].... At an early hour, the fleet was moving ... the gurgling of water at the prow alone disturbing the stillness of the hour. Half a mile in advance of the transports ... the navy moved in line of battle, covering the fleet of sixty vessels which ... was ploughing the waters in the rear. The decks were covered by men basking in the sun, re-reading letters from home ... at 2 P.M. we entered the Neuse River.... Our approach ... [was] signalled [to] the enemy above, by means of fires along the northern bank, the black smoke rising upward like wierd fingers of fate....
>
> As night set in, the sky was heavy with threatening storm.... At nine o'clock we reached ... Slocum's Creek, fifteen miles below New Bern, and anchored for the night. No signal-light [from a lighthouse] threw its rays over the scene, but dark, grim and silent as the abode of death, the fleet rested on the waters. Night deepened into ... darkness and storm, the only sound being the driving rain upon [the] deck or the half-hourly toll of the night watch.[4]

## *Up the River Toward New Bern*

Colonel Rush Hawkins of the 9th New York Zouaves later wrote: "The next morning was as unpleasant as a cold penetrating rain and dark sky could make it, but notwithstanding ... at 6:30 ... the troops began to disembark, the majority going in small boats, while others in their eagerness for the fray jumped from the transports, which were fast on the mud bottoms, and, holding their cartridge-boxes and muskets over their heads, waded to the land ... 13 regiments of infantry [and] 8

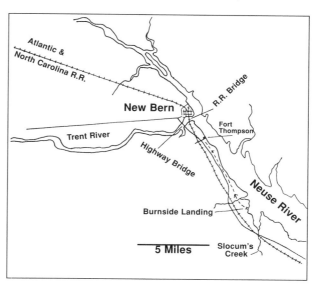

pieces of artillery."[5] The gunboats proceeded up the river, shelling the riverside forts, while the infantry started north along the bank of the river toward New Bern, fifteen miles away. "Each man carried on his person three day's rations, 40 rounds of ammunition, an overcoat, and rubber blankets."[6]

## The Attack on Fort Thompson

Of the several forts along the riverbank, only Fort Thompson gave serious trouble. To stop Burnside's advance on New Bern, the Confederate army made its stand at Fort Thompson, a long fortification which extended from the main fort on the bank of the Neuse River westward over a mile, across the highway and the railroad. The extended fortification consisted of earthern breastworks with rifle pits for infantry guns and numerous cannon.

Burnside's men came up along the highway and along the railroad tracks and bivouacked in a pine forest just before reaching Fort Thompson, on the evening of March 13. According to Private Derby: "Campfires were burning in all directions, some of them running to the top of the resinous trees.... The men lay about on beds of brush, and were covered with rubber blankets for protection from the rain. About two o'clock a cloud seemed to burst over the bivouac, deluging it with a flood which awakened the sleepers, most of whom found themselves lying in pools of water. At half past five, the 14th of March, the reveille roused the troops."[7]

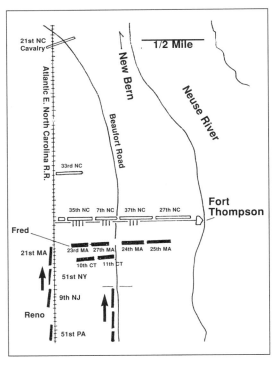

The Battle of New Bern, March 14, 1862. From a Confederate sketch map.

Burnside's men formed a line of battle to attack Fort Thompson. As it turned out, the battle of New Bern was resolved by this Union attack on Fort Thompson. The Union gunboats shelled Fort Thompson from the river while Burnside's troops attacked from the land side.

The Confederate troops gave in and retreated toward the city of New Bern, which lies at the intersection of the Neuse and Trent rivers. The main highway from the south enters New Bern by way of a bridge over the Trent River; as Burnside's army worked its way up the riverbank toward the city, the rebels burned this highway bridge.

Fred Osborne was in the front line with the Massachusetts 23rd and told the battle story to his mother in his next letter:

Newbern

Feb 19, 1862

Dear Mother:

We, that is the expedition, left Roanoke Island the 6th, and all went aboard the same vessels as before, going down the Sound the 12th. The Highlander led them all off, going up the Neuse River to Newbern.

The gunboats went ahead and shelled the woods on both sides to find out if there were any masked batteries along the shore. We were not fired upon however, and about three o'clock the afternoon of the 13th we were landed about sixteen miles from Newbern.

As soon as our regiment had all landed, the Colonel fell us into line and we started for Newbern. About a mile from the landing, barracks were discovered in the woods. Some of the boys who were ahead of our regiment told us that they had been occupied by rebel cavalry but they had cleared out before any of our troops had come up. The barracks were full of every kind of provision.

We were marched 10 miles that afternoon and night until 10 o'clock. The road was mud and water about a foot deep. Some of the boys thought that they couldn't see anything as tough as Roanoke, but when they had to lay in the woods in the rain that night when they felt so tired and miserable they began to open their eyes. I slept on a rubber blanket with another over me with my feet to a fire.

They started us early the next morning and after marching about three miles, the regiment ahead of us engaged a rebel battery. Burnie was riding up and down the road with his aides giving orders and hurrying the regiments up. Our regiment brought into line in front of the centre of the battery.

We commenced firing at once and the fire along the whole line was very sharp. The 23rd gun was the only artillery we had at first and none of the others came up until Capt. Dayton had used up all his ammunition. After our boys had fired a few rounds we had orders from the colonel to fall back. We were in a thin pine woods and the shells and balls from the battery made the splinters and bark fly and dropped the whole top of [a] small pine tree right on some of our heads.

Soon after we fell back we had orders to cease firing, lie down and fix bayonets ready for a charge. They then brought a Conn Regt right in front of us. We heard cheering all along the whole line and the Col. ordered us up and forward.

The space between the woods and battery was swampy and filled with brush and felled trees so if we had charged them we should have been all cut up by Genl Reno on their right. The battery was clear of the rascals when we got in excepting 1 live one and one or two dead ones. The battery was 2¼ miles long and mounted forty guns, a few of them rifled.*

We then left the battery and went on bound for Newbern. A short distance from the battery, The Col saw a man standing on the piazza of a house about 8 or 10 rods from the road. He ordered Lt Bates with 10 men to go to see what he was. Lt. took 10 of us from the right flank and went down; we found he was a rebel surgeon, took him prisoner and carried him to Genl Burnside. He told the Genl that he belonged in New York but he gave evasive answers to all the questions concerning the forces of the rebels or the number of their dead and wounded. The Genl talked like a true gentleman to him and so did our Col but some of the boys said that [when] we left him a Lieutenant blackguarded [him]. I should [like] to have thrashed him for the rebel himself was a gentleman and the best looking man I have seen amongst them.

We then marched ahead and as the rebels had burnt the bridge across the river to Newbern we had to go over to the city in boats. The Darkies seemed tickled to death because we had got there. The rebels had run and left their encampments all pitched so we moved right in and have good quarters.

The report of killed and wounded on our side is not made out. It is said that 1st Brigade, Genl Foster, lost 490 wounded, 90 killed. Our company has 5 wounded, none killed. Our wounded are Sam Brooks, Lou Robbins, Bill Pinkham, Ed Cummings, Ez Brown.

There were three or four batteries along the river which were taken by the gunboats. The rebels thought the place couldn't be taken. We took on Regt N.C. troop [writing not clear] and today 50 cavalry came in and surrendered themselves.

I received your letters today but none of our papers have come yet. It is said that Genl Foster is appointed Military Governor of N.C., and the first Brigade is to stop at Newbern. I hope it is true.

Give my love to all and write often. When I got your letter I thought your picture was in it instead of those combs. I am very glad you sent them but I was disappointed when I opened it. I wish you would send it.

Fred.


The spelling of New Bern was unsettled in Civil War times. Fred often spelled it Newbern and others, especially military writers, spelled it New Berne. The modern spelling is New Bern.

As Fred had hoped, General Foster's brigade stayed at New Bern. Fred's Company F of the 23rd Massachusetts, part of that brigade, began a period of military occupation of the New Bern area.

---

*A rifled gun has spiral grooves cut in the bore to impart a rotation to the projectile which makes it travel in a straighter line, making it a much more effective weapon.*

## CHAPTER SEVEN

# Life in New Bern

The battle of New Bern was a tonic to the North. The headlines in the *New York Times* read:

ANOTHER GLORIOUS VICTORY

NEWBERN, N.C. CAPTURED BY GEN. BURNSIDE

Precipitate Flight of the Rebel Army[1]

The Massachusetts legislature passed the following resolution: "Resolved, That the thanks of the people of Massachusetts are ... gratefully tendered, to the officers and soldiers of the Twenty-first, Twenty-third, Twenty-fourth, Twenty-fifth, and Twenty-seventh Regiments ... for their heroic deeds at the battle and victory of New Berne. In the hands of these men the honor of Massachusetts will always be safe."[2]

The slaves of New Bern welcomed their deliverers as Private Derby of the Massachusetts 27th noted: "As we landed at the Newbern wharf, a darkey woman, whose white hair betokened great age, came dancing forward with [the] exuberance of joy, and grasping ... [me] with both arms, exclaimed, 'Bress de Lord, Massa! Ize ben prain fur uze dese forty years! I taut uze nebber comin tall! But uze come at las! Bress de Lord. Bress de Lord!'"[3]

In the weeks following the battle of New Bern, the 23rd Massachusetts regiment was on picket duty on the railroad to Goldsboro. Camped on the railroad ten miles northwest of the city, Fred's regiment was on the frontier of Union-held territory. Picketing was a dangerous assignment, with enemy sharpshooters in the surrounding woods presenting a constant hazard.

Fred wrote home about his camp life:

Newbern

Apr 19th 1862

Dear Mother

I received your papers and the package yesterday. Mother I am very much obliged to you indeed for thinking so much of me and looking out so much for my welfare, but you trouble yourself too much. I have just cleared out my knapsack for it is so warm here that it is very hard to carry ever so little in them, and so you see I shall either have to throw them away or send them home.

One of the boys lost some of his things on Roanoke Is. He had one pair of them, but as for towels Mother I have two that have never been used. You may think from that I do not wash much but we all do every chance we can get.

The boys liked the ginger very much indeed. You said in your letter a little box. I expected to find a box about an inch square, but was very agreeably disappointed. Some of the boys did not ever see any before.

If I had known that you had been a going to send I should have told you a pair of suspenders, a black silk neckerchief and a new military cap, for the ones we get out here from the quartermaster are not worth much. But don't send anything till I write and tell you to. The reason is because we are not stationery and may be sent from here at any time.

We are 10 miles above Newbern on the railroad in the direction of Goldsborough. The rebels do not dare come down. We are engaged in building a bridge which the rebels burnt.

One of the Co. H boys shot one of a rebel cavalry picket who came

down to fire on our picket. Twelve of them left their horses in the bushes and came down and fired on our men, then turned to run when four of our boys who were on the post fired and shot one and wounded another. He, the dead one, was tall and slim, dressed in dirty ragged clothes looked just like the rest of them we seen.

The 3rd New York Battery have got two guns commanding the railroad, a Brass 32 lb pounder and a six pounder rifled Parrot gun, both of which were taken at Newbern.

Some darkies who came down from Kingston say that the Rebel Gen Branet who commanded at Newbern was coming back to take the city, but [when] he found we had advanced 10 miles, he concluded he wouldn't. The troops under him, some of whom were at Newbern, say that as soon as we come up they shall leave, but there is a South Carolina regiment which hasn't been into a brush yet and they are spoiling for a chance to get at us. They can beat us three to one, but the 3 is on their side I suppose.

I walked down to the city, 10 miles, two days ago and looked all round to find a place to have my picture taken, but couldn't. There is[n't] any place at all. I hope somebody will set up.

I guess I shall have to send some of your things home, Mother, to tell the truth the rags and bandages that I have got would half fill my knapsack, as it is. I do not beleive I could carry it on my back five miles.

The weather is getting very warm indeed. We do not drill at all during the middle of the day.

The other night the camp was alarmed and the long roll beat; the men turned out, but it turned out that some contrabands were coming down the railroad and the N. York boy who was on Picket fired and took to his heels and run. We turned in [and] were not disturbed again.

When I was down to the city, Jim Farley and I went into a restaurant and had the best dinner I have had since I left home. Beef Steak, Ham, Baked Fish, Oysters, Lettuce, Biscuits, Butter and Coffee Sweet Potatoes, only 50 cts each. We both ate a half dollars worth, I can tell you, for we had just walked 10 miles.

I see by the papers Sam Brooks is dead, poor fellow, and Sam Hooper, two of the most rugged fellows we had in the company.

The Comic Monthly you sent me was very laughable. We havn't received any letters at all lately, nothing but papers.

It is reported that a mail is down in the city, which we shall receive this afternoon.

You may expect to see a part of your bundle coming home again, for I shall have to throw it away, as all of us can not carry what we have got already.

Give my love to all, Father, Mother, Aunt Jane, Mary Ward, Lizzie, Jennie, Cousins and everybody. We have pickled cucumbers which makes me think of you Aunt Jane and Mary Barnard out in the barn making them. Why doesn't Nate write?

Write often.

FM Osborne

Tell Tuvvy that I suppose he is just having a very hard and disagreeable time packing away the furs. Tell him to look on the bright side, better times coming if I get home.

FM Osborne

Don't let Father get hold of that. After you have read it scratch it out.

Yours

FM Osborne

Mother you may send the suspenders and handkerchief as you can send them by mail but no matter about the Cap. Whoever gets the suspenders tell them to buy a good pair.

Fred mentioned his knapsack problems three times in this letter. The knapsack of a Civil War soldier was typically "packed with such items as underclothes, stationery, photographs, toothbrush, razor, soap, books, letters, and a mending kit known as a 'housewife.' Mess equipment, comprising a metal plate, knife, spoon and cup — and sometimes a light skillet — was usually divided between knapsack and hooks attached to the belt. In winter an overcoat ... was ... tied above the knapsack.... The weight of all this equipment ranged ... from forty to fifty pounds. Most Yanks eventually found means of reducing the load.... The process of becoming a veteran was ... one of shedding." There was a "tendency to get rid of overcoats and dress coats. Another item which disappeared at a fairly early stage was the knapsack, its contents — considerably reduced — being rolled into the blanket."[4]

The Nate of Fred's letters was his brother Nathan who was ten years older. Nate had enlisted as a captain in the 13th Infantry of the regular army in the summer of 1861, a few months before Fred joined Company F. Nate was initially assigned to Jefferson Barracks, Missouri, near St. Louis, but was soon sent to St. Paul, Minnesota, to set up a recruiting office for the 13th Infantry regiment.[5] He was still in St. Paul at this time but joined William Tecumseh Sherman a few months later to fight under General Grant at the battle of Vicksburg.

Mary Ward Osborne, Lizzie [Elizabeth] Osborne, and Jennie Osborne were Fred's sisters. Mary Barnard was a servant.[6] Tuvvy was Orville Osborne, one of Fred's older brothers. Fred's comment about Tuvvy packing away furs referred to his working in the family fur store on Essex Street.[7]

The "contrabands" mentioned in this letter referred to the former slaves who were now freedmen but had no means to support themselves. In their desperation the contrabands would take what they could to survive.[8]

## Military Occupation of New Bern

Fred had been in New Bern for two months and spring in North Carolina had advanced into May when he wrote home again.

New Bern

May 11th 1862

Dear Mother

We have left the encampment up in the woods and are now doing patrol duty in the city of Newbern, having taken the 25th Mass place.

The 25th were very mad indeed when we came down and they had to go up in the woods on picket duty. The 21st tried hard to get the chance, but Col John Kurtz was ahead of them.

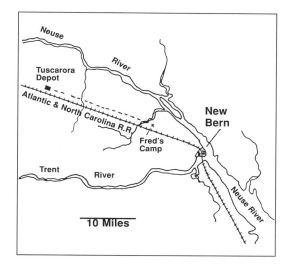

A day or two before we left the woods we went on a scout after the Rebs. I was one of the advance guard and had to skirmish through the woods ahead of the main body. It was about as bad as Roanoke swamp. Every rod or two we would go in up to our waists and tumbling over logs and stumps looking out for Rebs and keeping your powder dry. When we first started off we thought those who had boots were lucky but we came to a stream we had to cross and in we went and the short ones went in up to their waists.

The night before we started we had a thunder storm and the way the lightning flashed and the thunder roared was enough to kill any one who is afraid of such things. But we went up and met the 27th who had gone up the country by another road, and then advanced on to the Tuscarora depot but couldn't find anything of them. The 17th went still further up but they couldn't catch them.

The Rebs are all cavalry. We have now got a Reg't of Cavalry who were with Banks at the Battle of Winchester and as soon as they get on picket they will fix the Rebs.

The other day the pickets of the 10th Conn shot a Cap't and 5 men of the Rebs who came down to snoop our pickets.

Now we are in the city we have to keep all brushed up, clean boots blacked and musket shining.

I hope that we shall be able to keep the position but we cannot unless the boys are very particular indeed. The Reg't is so small that we have to go on duty every other day.

The boys who were at the hospital are all getting along finely.

We live in a house Mother and have the gas and it seems a good deal like home but the only furniture we have is our knapsacks. I suppose you will be glad to hear that we have got into the city.

From the appearance of things there is a move to be made very shortly.

There isn't as yet any place where I can get my picture taken but I am in hopes that somebody will set up soon.

**Company F quarters in New Bern. Sketch by a Co. F soldier, June 30, 1862.**

Some of our boys who have been sick are to have furloughs for 60 days. I received the suspenders and kerchief all right and they were just what I wanted. Tell Tuvvy that I am in hopes to be home before long and see him.

Love to all. How is Steve? I haven't heard much about him. Remember me to my friends.

Yours

FMO

I have written to Rob.


Fred used two versions of the spelling of New Bern in this letter. Settled by the Swiss, the city was named for Bern, Switzerland.[9] It was an important city from early colonial days with "a thriving seaport trade with New England and the West Indies through Pamlico Sound."[10]

Fred's mention of a possible move to be made refers to the expectation that the Burnside expedition would drive into the interior of North Carolina. The destruction of railroads and an attack on Raleigh were still unfinished business according to Burnside's instructions from General McClellan.

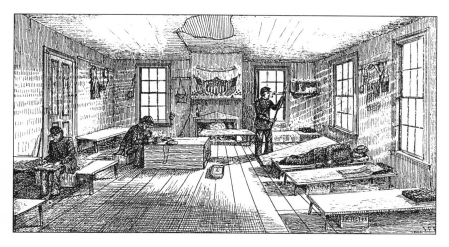

**Room in Company F quarters. Sketch by a Co. F soldier.**

The Confederates had just abandoned Norfolk, which they couldn't hold after Burnside took Roanoke Island. Norfolk was abandoned on May 8, just three days before Fred wrote this letter. The Burnside expedition was having its effect on the Confederacy.

The Col. John Kurtz mentioned in Fred's letter had been the commanding officer of the 23rd Massachusetts regiment since its birth in Salem. He was a 43-year-old baker from Boston when he enlisted.[11]

Fred inquired about "Steve," who was his brother Stephen, 33 years old and working in his father's fur store in Salem.

Two days later Fred wrote again:

Newbern

May 13th 1862

Dear Mother

A gentleman from New York has set up a saloon for taking pictures and I should have sent one by this means, but he hasn't begun to take cards yet. As soon as he does I will have some taken and will send them.

It is said that an advance movement is to be made in a few days.

The cavalry that have come out here within a few days have caught the Reb who rode the White Horse and made so much trouble for our pickets.

I think likely the bearer of this will call on you. He is the same fellow who was injured at Roanoke by the bursting of a gun.

Yours

FMO

Give my love to all my friends.

FMO

Fred's messenger was Alvah Tibbetts of Company F. When he enlisted, Private Tibbetts was 18 years old, a farmer from Hamilton, a small town near Salem. At Roanoke Island he received "an ugly wound … in the forehead from the breech-pin of a piece which burst in his hands."[12] Later, in 1863, he was taken prisoner at the battle of Drury's Bluff; he died in the infamous Confederate prison at Andersonville, Georgia and was buried at Andersonville, No. 4634.

The repeated interest Fred showed in having his picture made by the new art of photography is understandable because photographs were a great comfort in those times of separation. The daguerreotype, the first photographic system, was invented in France about 1840 and it generated a new American business, portrait photography.

The complicated daguerreotype method was soon displaced by a new technology, the "wet collodion" process. This relatively simple system provided cheap portraits on paper and had replaced the daguerreotype before the Civil War. Entrepreneurs set up "saloons" everywhere for making portraits. The Civil War was a boon to the commercial development of photography; pictures of soldiers were in demand by the folks at home, and homesick soldiers wanted pictures of family and friends. The "carte-de-visite," a little portrait, the size of a visiting card was a popular form.[13] This is probably the "card" that Fred referred to in the above letter.

In Fred's next letter we see his first negative comments about the army. He was against the enlistment of his older brother Steve.

Newbern

May 27th 1862

Dear Mother

I have written once since the date given in your letter, and sent it by one of the sick ones who went home on a furlough and I suppose it has reached you by this time. I have been very neglectful not to have written oftener, but we are on duty so often and have to keep all our clothes so clean we do not have as much time as we used to.

Bill Cook had a letter from Sam Foster saying that Steve was coming out to join our company. I don't know as it is true but just tell [him] to take the advice of one who has been through the mill and stay at home or do anything rather than get into the army. When a fellow gets a commission it is a different thing. I will not state my many reasons for saying this but you tell him to stay at home.

It is getting very warm and plesant here now. The trees and everything are getting out green, and the fruit is all formed on the trees.

I suppose that there will be a move made here shortly.

The cavalry have had one or two skirmishes with the Rebs and beat them pretty well. Co. I of the 16th Mass Regt went out in a scout and were returning without an advance guard out when they fell into an ambuscade and 3 were shot dead and 5 wounded. The whole company is Irish and that accounts for it in some measure.

The Bull Run prisoners are being exchanged and 400 of them [are] aboard the boats in the harbor and are to start for home tomorrow. The Salem boys are amongst them. Charlie Adams is also released.

All the gunboats have been ordered up to Washington in the state.

There is a report here that the President has called for 100,000 more men. If it is true perhaps it will put an end to the hopes of some of getting home the fourth of July.

I shall not think anything about it or believe we [are] going till I find myself on the way. It is better for anybody to think so than to be setting a time and thus disappointing themselves.

The boys who are in the hospital are getting better. George Wilkins is on duty and William Cook and Si Crocker are getting better. I have been well all the time myself.

Give my love to all by friends.

These Bull Run prisoners have been staying up to Salisbury in the state. Charlie Adams says that they have had very rough times and nothing to eat but bread and water. He says you don't know what it is to be a soldier until you are taken prisoner. Give my love to Father, Sisters, Brothers, Aunt Jane, cousins and everybody. I shall send my picture in a few days. I shall probably send the check for my money in a few days for we have been paid off again up to the 1st of May.

Don't let Steve come out.

Yours

FMO

The Bull Run prisoners being exchanged were from the first Battle of Bull Run, July 1861. Charlie Adams had been taken prisoner in the battle of Newbern. Now 22 years old, Adams had been a farmer in Marblehead, a town next to Salem, when he enlisted. He was acting as a messenger for General Foster when he was captured by the rebels.[14]

Fred's mention of a "move to be made shortly" refers to the possibility that the Burnside expedition would implement its strategy of a second front against Richmond and its plan to interrupt supplies to Richmond from the Carolinas. Colonel Thomas Edmands of the Mass 24th described this part of the campaign:

> Burnside was anxiously awaiting the arrival of wagons, locomotives, and cars, promised him ... [for] the final act of his expedition, namely, the destruction of the Wilmington and Weldon railroad, the capture of Wilmington and the threatening of Raleigh.
>
> All through April and May he waited, fortifying Newbern ... but still no transportation came. Without it he could move no further from his base than rations could be carried on the men; nor was the country ... such [that] he could forage sufficient supplies ... without transportation. Thus he was bothered and ... restricted; but by the aid of steamers he could send forays to various points on the sounds and up the rivers to keep the country stirred up and in a state of fear.[15]

Fred's comment that "gunboats have been ordered up to Washington in the state" refers to one of Burnside's forays to keep things stirred up. Washington was a river port on the Pamlico River with access to the Atlantic via Pamlico Sound.

Aunt Jane, often mentioned in Fred's letters, was his favorite aunt. She was his mother's older (by two years) sister. Aunt Jane was 51 at this time and lived with the family in Salem.[16]

From his modest pay of $13 per month Fred was able to send money home. Historian B.E. Wiley has described the army pay procedure in these terms:

> Every other month soldiers were mustered for pay.... Muster exercises ... included a review and inspection.... The muster proper consisted of calling the names on the company roll.... When a soldier heard his name he replied "here," brought his gun snappily to the "carry" position, and then dropped the butt to the ground and held it in the position of "order arms." After the mustering officer had accounted for every man on the roster he forwarded a copy of the muster roll to the Adjutant General in Washington. Soldiers were not paid at the time of the muster, but information was provided on which payments were made based.... Pay was commonly tardy, sometimes more than six months.... A paymaster's arrival [produces] more joy in camp than is ... produced in heaven over the one sinner that repenteth.[17]

Fred's comment "The whole company is Irish" tells us of his prejudice, the Boston-area prejudice, about the Irish. The Union recruited poor Irish men from Ireland to serve in the army. The Confederacy thought that this was unfair; Ambrose Dudley Mann, a noted Confederate diplomat, went to the Vatican, according to his biographer, "to obtain the aid of the Pope in checking the Federal recruiting ... of Irish Catholics.... Altogether the Northern cause won large numbers of recruits from Europe, mostly in Ireland and Germany, and it would have been worth a whole series of successful campaigns to the Confederacy if this enlistment of foreigners could have been frustrated."[18]

On occupation duty in New Bern, Fred was waiting for the next move of the Burnside expedition. General Burnside's campaign had been successful so far, and his men believed in him and were ready for the next challenge, the next victory. William Marvel, his biographer, has said: "The men under him gave him their unqualified faith. To them he was invincible; wherever Ambrose Burnside went, victory was sure to follow." It appears from his letters that Fred Osborne was a convinced follower.

## Waiting for a Move

General George McClellan and General Burnside were good friends and they were in contact at this time; McClellan and the Army of the Potomac were attacking Richmond from the east, coming up the peninsula between the York and James rivers. History would call it the "Peninsula Campaign." Burnside and McClellan had the notion of a joint campaign, McClellan moving on Richmond from the east and Burnside coming up through North Carolina from the south. When McClellan won the battle of Williamsburg and moved closer to Richmond and Norfolk was abandoned by the Confederates, Burnside thought the time had arrived to take the offensive in North Carolina, but according to biographer William Marvel, "he found himself hamstrung by a dearth of transportation. Wagons, locomotives, and railroad cars he had ordered … had not been delivered. The infantry reinforcements he requisitioned had manifested themselves only in four regiments…. He must have wagons, and the two dozen he might have mustered were not sufficient for an ammunition train."[19]

Burnside and McClellan kept talking, but a move by Burnside was still delayed. In the meantime Fred Osborne again wrote home:

> Newbern
>
> May 30th 1862
>
> Dear Mother
>
> It is very still out here now. There isn't any forward move to be made just yet. The report is that Burnside has had orders not to move until he hears from McClellan again.
>
> We have heard this Gen'l Banks has been defeated with loss of five thousand prisoners. Afterwards the report was that only his advance guard was driven in.
>
> There was a report that Gov Andrew had refused to raise the four regiments that the President called for from Massachusetts on the ground that he didn't think the President was doing right in not supporting Gen'l Hunter's proclamation. I hope it is not so for there would be trouble arise out of it.
>
> Gov Stanley has arrived and will go up to Raleigh in a few days. You can see knots of Secesh standing round and walking the streets all talking about the new Governor.
>
> Last night the Rebel pickets on the other side of the Neuse river shot a young darkie through the hand. Two black boys having finished their work on the other side of the river were crossing over to the city in a boat when they were hailed by some men on the shore. They didn't get the boat round quick enough so one of the men fired and shot this boy through the hand. The boys went back again and found about thirty Secesh cavalry on the shore. The Rebs found out all they could from the boys concerning our troops. They then took all the boats they could find and went off telling the boys to stay there till they got back which would be in about an hour, but the boys had another boat hid in the marsh and they took that and came over to the city.
>
> There are lots of turtles here and you can see them in the streets for sale. They lay them on their backs so they cannot run off. They are caught

down to Beaufort on the beach. They look different from common turtles and instead of claws they have great flippers.

Burnie is flying round from Newbern to Roanoke, from there to Beaufort and then up to Washington and all round, impatient because he cannot move forward. He has sent a splendid peacock home to his family. He goes round in a slouched hat, trousers in his boots, a blue flannel blouse and a yellow sash twisted round his waist, and from the looks of some lieutenants you would think that they had the command of the army.

In this letter I send the check for my money. The check is made out in Steve's name or order, but if he is out here by the time this reaches you somebody else will have to draw it, and whoever draws it, if you want to use the money take it Mother. I know you must need it.

Give my respects to all my friends. I suppose you have seen Mr. Tebbetts by this time. Remember me to Father, Brothers, Sisters, Cousins, Aunts, and everybody.

Yours

F M Osborne

I havn't received any letter from Jennie yet. I received your last one [in] the mail before last. What does Jim have to say now days and where are David and John? Give my love to Caddie, Hannah Lee and Harriet Eliza. Louis Emilio sends his respects.

Jennie was Fred's sister, and was two years older.[20] Fred's letters were written to his mother and to Jennie, with whom he had a close relationship.

Luis Emilio lived across the street from Fred when they were youngsters; one of the original members of Company F, he later rose to the rank of captain.[21] Governor Andrew chose Luis Emilio to be an officer in the first colored regiment, the Massachusetts 54th; all the officers were white men. The Massachusetts 54th soon achieved fame, proving the fighting qualities of colored soldiers.[22]

The Mr. Tebbetts referred to the father of Andrew Tebbetts, a sergeant in Fred's company. Sergeant Tebbetts had been wounded in the battle of Roanoke Island, and Mrs. Osborne may have planned to see Sergeant Tebbett's father concerning his son's progress in recovering from that wound.

The 23rd Massachusetts saw much of the former slaves in New Bern. "Every expedition [of the regiment] to the interior ... was the sign for great numbers to come in ... possessed with the single idea of personal freedom, they took no thought of how they were to be supported. Some of them seemed to have no idea that the change meant anything but a new and, they hoped, a kinder master. A young mother brought a cart-load of her black pickaninnies to the lines, and, when asked to whom the horse and vehicle belonged, had no answer but 'To you all, Massa.'"[23]

The surgeon of the regiment, Dr. James Emmerton, wrote that the freedmen "were, of course, of all shades of color. Mental development was, as a rule, in direct ratio of the proportion of white blood." This unhappy comment was somewhat balanced by his report on the "intense eagerness of some twenty or thirty blacks, of all ages from ten to fifty years, to learn to read" in a school set up by Captain Whipple of Company F. With no books and no equipment, Captain Whipple taught them orally and found them "waiting for school to open one [or] ... two hours before the appointed time." Some of the freedmen who were learning to read worked in lumber operations; "grown men ... had each his spelling book which was speedily whipped out and zealously studied at every break ... in [their work]."[24]

The General Banks to whom Fred referred was the Union general, Nathaniel Banks, who was out in the Shenandoah Valley, trying to drive the Confederates out of that prosperous crop region. Stonewall Jackson, coming up the valley, was carrying out a strategy by General Robert E. Lee to threaten Washington from the west and frighten President Lincoln into thinking that Washington might be attacked.

Lee, entrenched at Richmond, was under threat from McClellan who had come up the peninsula to within a few miles of Richmond. Lee "wrote to Jackson urging an immediate attack (on Banks) ... to prevent him from going ... to ... the peninsula ... whatever movement you make against Banks do it speedily and ... drive him back toward the Potomac and create the impression ... that you design threatening (Washington)."[25] Lee believed that Lincoln, if he felt that Washington might be attacked would keep reinforcements there and not send them to McClellan outside Richmond.

On May 25, 1862, Stonewall Jackson bloodied General Nathaniel Banks's nose at Winchester. Lincoln had earlier promised McClellan that he would get substantial reinforcements from the Washington area; with Banks routed and Washington [he believed] threatened, Lincoln telegraphed McClellan: "Do the best you can with the force you have."

Lee's strategy had worked; McClellan did not get the troops he wanted, and he was stalled outside of Richmond.[26]

The Governor Stanly mentioned by Fred represents an interesting and complex aspect of President Lincoln's attempt to manage matters in the captured portions of the Confederacy and reflects the basic nature of the Civil War.

Until late May 1862, New Bern and other occupied sections of North Carolina were under martial law; General Burnside could and did jail "those who challenged his authority."

Lincoln relieved Burnside of this civil responsibility and made Edward Stanly the military governor of North Carolina. Governor Stanly established his headquarters in New Bern on May 26, 1862, four days before Fred wrote this letter. Edward Stanly had been born in New Bern in the mansion that Burnside was using for his headquarters, so Burnside moved to another building.

Lincoln knew that there was considerable Union sentiment in North Carolina; the state had been slow to secede and in fact had been the last of the Confederate states to do so. He hoped to get North Carolina back into the Union.

The success of the Burnside expedition in North Carolina was encouraging disloyalty to the Confederacy; for example, "the mayor of Washington, N.C.

welcomed Burnside's troops as liberators."[27] Lincoln wanted to capitalize on these changing loyalties. By making Edward Stanly the military governor, Lincoln was trying to develop and solidify the Union sentiment in the state and eventually to get an elected government which would return the state to the Union.

Edward Stanly, "tactless and explosive in temperament," wasn't quite the right choice for the job. North Carolinians didn't like him and saw him as something of a traitor. Governor Stanly "made a steamboat tour of Union-held towns around the sounds, exhorting true patriots" to join the Union forces; "his appeals echoed in profound silence. Most of his … constituents curled their lips at a man they thought a traitor, a man who had gone over to the Union side."[28]

As military governor, Edward Stanly had to deal with an important issue of the Civil War: former slaves and what to do with them. At New Bern he returned escaped slaves to their masters in an attempt to convince North Carolinians that the North was not trying to do away with slavery. Abolitionists were angry, but Lincoln defended Governor Stanly because his priority was to get North Carolina back into the Union.[29]

Edward Stanly had been in the U.S. Congress for several terms and had made enemies in Washington, particularly Charles Sumner, the passionate abolitionist from Massachusetts. Edward Stanly did not last long as the military governor; in less than a year, General Burnside asked Washington to remove him.[30]

In his letter to his mother, Fred commented: "Gov. Andrew … didn't think the President was doing right in not supporting Gen'l Hunter's proclamation." Governor Andrew and other abolitionists were very unhappy with President Lincoln when he countermanded General David Hunter's proclamation freeing the slaves in his military command area. General Hunter had issued a proclamation on May 9, 1862, declaring all slaves in South Carolina, Georgia, and Florida to be free. He took this measure to help in the organizing of Negro soldiers. John Andrew, governor of Massachusetts, thought this a capital idea and was not pleased when President Lincoln would not support it. It was contrary to Lincoln's war strategy, however; he asserted that the war was being fought to save the Union, not to abolish slavery. At this time Lincoln was especially trying to mollify the border states on the slavery issue so that they would stay with the Union.

In a letter to Lincoln, who had just called for more regiments from

**General David Hunter**

the states, Governor Andrew tried to influence the president: "If the President will sustain General Hunter, recognize all men, even black men as legally capable of that loyalty the blacks are waiting to manifest, and let them fight, with God and human nature on their side, the roads will swarm if need be with multitudes whom New England would pour out to obey your call."[31]

General David Hunter was one of the president's special friends; he had been with Lincoln on the inaugural train when it left Springfield, Illinois, for Washington back in February 1861. But on May 19, 1862, President Lincoln declared General Hunter's proclamation void, thus alienating Governor Andrew and other abolitionists.[32]

## CHAPTER EIGHT

# Still at New Bern

Newbern

June 8th 1862

Dear Mother

I received your letter night before last, but had heard that Steve was coming out about a week ago. I suppose you have received my letter which says so much against his coming, but if he has started there is no help for it.

There isn't much doing out here now. The troops are mostly lying still, but the marine artillery and the 24th Mass had a skirmish up to Washington [N.C.] at the rebels and drove them back. Our loss was 12 killed and some few wounded. The rebs lost 150. Six of the 24th who were killed were buried here in the city this afternoon. I do not know what company they belonged to, nor their names.

The 17th are encamped just above the city and close to the battery. I have not had a chance to go up to see them yet.

I will send my picture as soon as I can get a pass to go out round the city.

The recruits havn't arrived yet, but it is time that they were here.

I suppose Steve looks the same as ever. Bill Cook told some of the boys that my brother was coming for Sam Foster wrote him that Steve was coming, so some of the boys got hold of it and began poking fun at me and asking about him. I am sorry that he is not going to join our company for some reasons and glad for others. It is just Steve's style to come out here and not join a Salem company. If he joins Co. G Capt. Raymond, he will get into a good company where there is a good set of fellows and the NCO [non-commissioned officers] deserve the name of men more than the NCO of Co F.

I hope Steve had his teeth fixed before he started for if he didn't he will suffer enough. I havn't been troubled with mine at all. Has Steve got anything for me or wouldn't he fill his knapsack up with everything? I do not believe he will like this dirty city though; he had rather be out in the woods.

So they have got the bold Sammy Foster to keep garrison at Fort Warren. That is a fine place for such chaps as he. And they have got to stay there 3 months. If I was there, when I got out, I should feel as if I were coming out of jail.

I am glad Steve didn't go there. Where is [word unclear] now; has he gone to Fort Warren too?

I received the postage stamps and wish you would send me some more three cent ones as I am almost out. I haven't received any letter from Jennie yet. I suppose Caddie calls and laughs at Ov as much as ever doesn't she. How is Father and how did he like to have Steve come off too? Tell Tuvvy to keep a good heart for if when the Osbornes all get home again we will have a good time.

Young men are pretty scarce in Salem about this time I guess. How do the gals come on without them to beau them round or is there a home guard there yet?

What does Jim say about the war now, is he Secesh or not? When did you hear from Nate? I haven't heard from Nate but once but I suppose he has enough to do besides writing. Mother, you will have more than you can attend to, to write to four great boys all the time. Jim doesn't say anything about coming home does he? Where are David and John? Give them my respects if they are at home. Is Dave married yet?

Aunt Jane has been making lection cake I suppose or is the time for it past?

Give my love to Father, Aunts, Uncles, sisters, Tuvvy, cousins, and everybody.

Yours

FMO

The record shows that Stephen Osborne enlisted on May 14, 1862. He joined Company G of the 23rd Mass Regiment.[1] As Fred pointed out, Company G was not a Salem company but came from Beverly, a nearby town.

Company G was commanded by Captain John Raymond, a farmer from Beverly, who seems to have had Fred's approval. Later in the war he proved to be a strong leader in battles at Drury's Bluff and at Cold Harbor and, near the end of the war, in the siege of General Lee's army at Petersburg. John Raymond was seriously wounded in each of those battles. He earned a promotion to major and then to colonel.[2]

The Bill Cook Fred mentioned was seventeen-year-old William Cook of Company F, who had been a student in Salem before enlisting. William Cook was "discharged for disability" three months later; the nature of the disability was not given in the record.[3]

The Jim that Fred refers to in this letter is believed to be his brother James Osborne. James Osborne was a sailor and was listed as a mariner in the Osborne household in the 1850 Census when Fred was 5. In this letter Fred mentions Jim twice, inquiring whether he might be "Secesh" and whether he might be coming home. Jim is apparently one of the "four great boys" his mother is writing to.

The fact that Fred asks his mother if Jim is "Secesh"—a rebel or a secessionist—gives us an insight into the liberal intellectual and political climate in the Osborne household. Nate and Fred decided early on to fight to save the Union, and Steve had just come to that decision, but Jim may have sided with the South.

The Osborne household must have been open, even encouraging, to varied intellectual opinions. Salem encompassed many elements: abolitionist lecturers at the Salem Lyceum, business people who were against war because it was bad for the textile mills, antislavery firebrands like William Lloyd Garrison and Governor John Andrew, and supporters of the vague but powerful notion that the Union—Lincoln's "last best hope of earth," the great American experiment in democracy—must be saved. The defenders of the Union relished the oratory of Daniel Webster, the great constitutional lawyer whose speeches gave Abraham Lincoln much of his inspiration for the defense of the Union.[4] Webster was the great enemy of secession, who cried out for the Union: "While the Union lasts, we have high, exciting, gratifying prospects spread out before us.... God grant that ... my vision ... never may be opened ... on the broken ... fragments of a once glorious Union."[5]

All of these strong voices had to be sorted out, and Fred and his brothers had to come to their own decisions about what part each would play in the war.

Fred wrote: "So they have got the bold Sammy Foster to keep garrison at Fort Warren." Fort Warren, in Boston Harbor, held Confederate military and civilian prisoners during the Civil War. It received international attention during the war for the Trent Affair, which involved a British ship, the *Trent*. Captain Charles Wilkes of the Union navy became famous overnight when he put a shot over the bow of the *Trent* on November 8, 1861, and removed James Mason, Confederate commissioner to London, and John Slidell, Confederate commissioner to Paris. Mason and Slidell were on their way to Europe to attempt to persuade England and France to declare war against the Union, but they ended up as prisoners in Fort Warren.

Captain Wilkes received a hero's welcome when he came back to the United States shore. Gideon Welles, Lincoln's secretary of the navy, wrote to Wilkes: "I congratulate you on the great public service you have rendered in the capture of the rebel emissaries.... Your conduct ... was marked by intelligence, ability, decision, and firmness." The House of Representatives had a special medal struck for him. Historian Peter Parish wrote: "Wilkes's deed excited such an astonishing ... response because ... it ... slaked the popular thirst for bold, decisive, aggressive action at the end of a dismal year ... [for the] Union war effort ... [and it gave] a sharp twist to the tail of the British lion."[7]

England and France threatened war while Mason and Slidell were being held at Fort Warren. At the end of the year, the day after Christmas 1861, Lincoln had them released.[8]

"Aunt Jane has been making lection cake I suppose" is a reference to "a kind of fancy cake, associated with the celebration of elections."[9] The *Yankee Cook Book* says: "Election cake ... originated in Hartford, Conn. [about 1850], and was served to all who voted the straight ticket."[10]

One recipe for election cake contains 6 lbs. flour, 2 lbs. sugar, 1 lb. butter, 12 eggs, 1 quart of milk, 1 pint of yeast, mace."[11]

Fred wrote again in late June:

New Berne

June 25th 1862

Dear Mother

I received yours and Jennie's letters by the last mail, also the papers. Steve hasn't got his [letter] yet for I have been a little sick and not able to go out and as the boys have not been on guard near there, I do not like to ask them to go so much out of their way. He will get them tonight or in the morning.

Last Friday the sword got up for Burnie by his friends in R. I. was presented to him. Genl Mauran and Staff of R. I. arrived with the sword while Burnie was up to Norfolk, so they surprised him [his aides used to have good times while he was gone] and last Friday they had a review of all the troops in a large field the other side of the river, and they presented him the sword. I didn't go over for I was on duty. That afternoon it rained hard here in the city while across the river it didn't even sprinkle. Burnie didn't make any speech at all.

This morning six regiments were [word unclear] marching and had three days rations. There is to be a move made somewhere very shortly. They are getting all the wagons ready.

Yesterday a woman shot with a revolver into a crowd and shot one dead. The guard immediately arrested every person in the house and carried them to jail. Now [that] our Colonel is Provost Marshall things are going to be carried on [word unclear]. The old provost marshall was not strict enough.

I have received a letter from Sam Foster. I suppose they will be sent to Washington before long.

It is about time Thom Harris went. I should think he might feel cheap enough now they have all gone but him. You say he has [word unclear] Geo Hogan and is lugging him around. I don't think you [would] catch me, if I was such a big [word unclear] lubber as he is, going around with George who looks like a ghost. I should be afraid people wouldn't think much of me. Or is he after a chance in the 33rd Reg't?

Steve has been on guard two or three times and has got pretty well broken [in]. He will stand it [word unclear] I guess.

Last night I sent Father yesterday's paper. It contains Gov. Stanly's speech.

I hope Jim will come round entirely after a while for if he doesn't come home I may go out and see him.

Nate is in the same place I suppose. I wish I was under his command or any other than the one I am now as far as company is concerned.

Give my love to all my friends, and Jennie must excuse me for not answering her now but I do not feel able to write any more. I will try and send the picture when I answer hers.

Ruthelia's brother has seen some of the hardest service of the whole war. He will have something to tell. I guess that he can write a more interesting letter than I.

There is a story about that Gene Foster was taken prisoner while on his way to Beaufort in the [word unclear]. I do not think it is true.

Write soon and often. Tell Lizzie to write for if there is anything that gives a fellow the blues it is to have a mail come and he gets no letters.

[no signature]

Fred's comment on his feeling unwell, "I have been a little sick and not able to go out," might have been related to the typhoid fever epidemic occurred during the occupation of New Bern. One of General Burnside's burdens was the loss of men to that epidemic; many of his men were sick in barracks or at home on sick leave or had died from the "fever." The Massachusetts 23rd, particularly, was "reduced in strength because of typhoid fever."[12]

Nate was still at St. Paul, Minnesota, on recruiting duty for the 13th Infantry regiment, U.S. regular army.

A Burnside move against Richmond from North Carolina continued to be an option under consideration in Washington. In early June, Secretary of War Stanton asked Burnside to come to Fort Monroe to make plans for such a move, and President Lincoln asked Burnside to come on up to Washington from Fort Monroe for more talks.[13] McClellan was stalled outside of Richmond, and Lincoln was trying to get him to move more aggressively, perhaps with help from Burnside. Some troop reinforcements and railcars and wagons came in to New Bern, but no orders to move. Burnside had 14,000 men, and "wanted to be off."[14]

The presentation of the sword to General Burnside that Fred mentioned was an occasion for his troops to show him their affection. William Marvel, Burnside's biographer, describes the scene in this way:

> The Tiffany sword ordered by the Rhode Island general assembly was finally ready, and a small delegation headed by Adjutant General Mauran traveled down from Providence to make a formal presentation, which they carried off despite the embarrassment it caused the modest Burnside. The deputation was no little vexation to him.... Nevertheless, on June 18 the entire Burnside expedition trotted out ... and formed a hollow square. Every man not detailed for guard duty wore his parade best. The brigades came to attention, and just as the 4th and 5th Rhode Island regiments escorted Burnside onto the field the rainshower ended, a rainbow stretching behind the procession as though to form a triumphal arch. Battery F of the 1st

Rhode Island Artillery thundered a salute. General Mauran made the presentation, Burnside thanked him with a little speech characteristically throwing all the credit on the officers and men under him, and fifteen thousand soldiers raised a deafening cheer.[15]

Fred's comment that "It is about time that Thom Harris went ... or is he after a chance in the 33rd Reg't?" indicates something special about the 33rd. The Massachusetts 33rd regiment was organized about that time, in 1862, and perhaps Fred believed that Thom Harris hoped to get a preferred place in it. It turned out that the Massachusetts 33rd became a storied regiment, serving in several of the famous Civil War battles, including Chancellorsville, Gettysburg, Chattanooga, and Atlanta. It was with Sherman on his march through Georgia and the Carolinas at the end of the war.[16]

## Burnie Makes a Move

In late June, 1862 Fred Osborne was still at New Bern with General Burnside's army. McClellan was outside of Richmond, trying to bring off the capture of that Confederate city. Lincoln and his staff were looking at the options for using Burnside's army: Bring his forces directly to McClellan to help him take Richmond or go ahead with the original objectives of the Burnside expedition — take over Goldsboro and the railroads in North Carolina and put pressure on Richmond from the south.

Burnside's view of his options appeared in a dispatch to Washington: "I can place 7000 infantry in Norfolk ready for transportation to ... [McClellan, outside of Richmond] ... in five days, but with no wagons, camp equipage, artillery, or cavalry; ... or I can move on Goldsboro at 60 hours' notice with 10,000 infantry, 20 pieces of artillery, and 5 companies of cavalry."[17] General Burnside clearly wanted to move on Goldsboro, but that was not the move he was to make.

President Lincoln was worried about McClellan, who had been beaten at the battle of Gaines Mill outside of Richmond on June 27. McClellan, always complaining that he was outnumbered by Confederate troops, wrote to the secretary of war: "I have lost this battle because my force was too small.... I again repeat that I am not responsible for this ... I ... feel that the government has not sustained this army. If you do not do so now the game is lost. If I save this army now, I tell you plainly that I owe no thanks to you or any other persons in Washington. You have done your best to sacrifice this army."[18]

General Robert E. Lee, who was maneuvering his Confederate army to save Richmond, had 85,000 men against McClellan's 100,000, but McClellan was convinced that Lee had 200,000 and that he was greatly outnumbered.

President Lincoln decided that McClellan was in serious trouble. He wrote to General Burnside on June 28, the day after the battle of Gaines Mill: "I think you had better go, with any reenforcements you can spare, to General McClellan."[19]

General Burnside "began crowding his troops onto transports at Newbern." He took two of his three divisions to help McClellan, leaving General Foster's division (and Fred Osborne) to continue the occupation of New Bern.[20]

> Newbern
>
> July 10th 62
>
> Dear Jennie
>
> I received yours by Ad Paine some time since but havn't answered it before for the same old reason, we have to go on duty every other day and it takes most of our time to keep our arms and equipment in good shape, and battalion and dress parade, *and the musquitos* nights. We do not have any extra time so if I do not write often you musn't think I am sick.
>
> Burnie has gone up to Richmond with 10,000 men. We havn't heard anything from them so I guess Mac [General McClellan] isn't going to let them write until he does something. Burnie carried the second and third divisions with him.
>
> Last Thursday Lieut Emmerton, a sargent, [a] corporal and ten men of our company were detailed as guard to a squad of prisoners from the different regiments who were put in jail for different misdemeanors and were sent to Fort Macon to serve their sentence out. One poor fellow has got to work out the rest of his three years without pay.
>
> We started Thursday morning and got to Beaufort about noon. The bands were playing and they were firing a salute for the Fort [Fort Macon] for the news had just come that Richmond [was] taken. We then went to the Fort. It was a very different place than I expected it was, and much smaller. Your could see where gun shot struck it during the bombardment by the new brick work that has been set into the walls. I couldn't get anything worth remembering it by, we were in such a hurry. We got aboard of the boat and went back to Morehead City and put up for the night with some of the 5th Rhode Island.
>
> Friday morning, the 4th [of July], we started and got back to Newbern about noon. The bells were ringing, flags flying and the city was free for everybody, and all the guard's duty was to arrest anybody making a disturbance. But it didn't seem anything like the fourth.
>
> In the afternoon I went up to the 17th and took supper with Capt Kenny. He sent his respects to Father and Mother and all the girls.
>
> One of our boys, Ed Whittredge died this week. Ed was taken sick some days before I was when I was sick about a week. I wrote to you about it. He staid at the quarters about 10 days and as he did not get any better he went to the hospital. I didn't get a chance to go and see him and last Sunday I was going when I heard he was so sick that nobody could see him and day before yesterday he died. We didn't any of us expect it. Ed was one of the

best fellows in the company and as heavy and rugged a one. He slept next to me ever since we had been in the city. All I have got to remember him by is his pipe which he left with me.

Two men were discharged this week.

Lieut Emmerton has started for home on a furlough and I do not much expect that he will come back again for he isn't well at all.

You must excuse me for not sending my picture for I am waiting for Charlie [word unclear] to get started as I believe he is going to take cards. Dear Mother, I wish that you would send me out two shirts. Some of the boys have had some sent out. They are either very light flannel or wool and cotton and are much better to have out here as these thick flannel ones are very uncomfortable and it is almost impossible to keep [them] clean. The wool from them gets on to your body and with the sweat and dust makes a very nasty mess. Plaid or something of that sort is better than plain. Do not get a very light color as that will show the dust too soon. Geo Walker or some other furnishing store probably has just what I want.

And I want Tuvvy to get me a pair of light neat looking boots and then have a half sole put on to them. The size for my foot is eight. Tell him I do not want a clumsy heavy boot for it is too hot to have a very heavy boot. Tell him not to let Buswell or who ever he gets them given him but let him get what he thinks I would like. If they were to find out what he wanted them for, they would try and palm something on to him by saying that it [is] just what he wants.

And then enough cambric to line a pair of trousers as these woollen ones are very uncomfortable to wear next to you. It is so hot that under-clothes are out of the question.

A shirt that will fit Ov will about fit me, I guess, but should be a little longer. I do not weigh much more than I did when I left home so I guess that my neck and wrists are not much bigger than his, I suppose, though they could shrink some when they were washed. I guess though a little mite large for him would go for me.

If those boots I left at home are not worn out, if Ov didn't take them, why send them instead of new ones. I guess, though, he will have to get the new ones for I suppose he wore those out last winter. I guess, though, he had better go to Barlow's and get a good pair of the army shoes that lace up in front, that is if Barlow has got any he made himself, size 8 and very high on the instep. I suppose, Mother, if Capt Whipple [commanding officer of Company F] has a box coming out about the time you get those ready, you had better send them in that as it is more likely to come safe.

And as pay day is almost here, whenever I send my money you take the pay for them out of it. Send them as soon as you can, Mother, and mind and make a square and compact bundle so as to pack well. If there isn't a box coming for the Capt when you get them ready, send it by itself in a small wooden box as soon as possible.

I suppose Jennie would know my taste for a shirt as well as anybody so let Tuvvy bring some home for you all to look at.

Give my love to all my friends.

Yours

FMO

Now I [am] sweat[ing] as much as if I had sawed a cord of wood. If there is any little nice thing you can send, why put it in.

FMOsborne

Jennie's letter had been brought to Fred by Ad Paine, a Salem youth coming back from sick leave. He had been wounded at the battle of New Bern. He did not recover his health and was discharged on August 11, 1862.[21]

The celebration of the fall of Richmond (the news had just come that Richmond had been taken) while Fred was at Fort Macon, was considerably premature, but a rumor had spread that McClellan had taken the city.[22] This rumor may have derived from McClellan's success in the battle of Malvern Hill, fifteen miles from Richmond. That battle on July 1, 1862 had capped off what became known as the "Seven Days," seven days of running battle between McClellan and Robert E. Lee outside of Richmond. On the seventh day, Lee attacked McClellan's forces on Malvern Hill and was repulsed in a Union victory. But McClellan did not follow up, did not drive Lee back toward Richmond; instead he retreated to his supply base on the James River while Lee's army recuperated. This was the end of McClellan's Peninsula Campaign to capture Richmond.[23]

The damage to Fort Macon caused by Union bombardment, mentioned above in Fred's letter, occurred during the capture of the fort by Union forces in March of 1862.[24] Fort Macon, commanding the entrance to Beaufort Harbor from the sea, was the third major objective of the Burnside expedition (after Roanoke Island and New Bern).

Ed Whittredge whose death Fred discussed was John Edward Whittredge, a 21-year-old farmer from the town of Hamilton, near Salem.[25]

Lieutenant Emmerton, who took Fred to Fort Macon and later, Fred wrote, went home on sick leave, was George Emmerton, a 26-year-old Salem merchant who was married and had two daughters. His health didn't improve, and he resigned a month after Fred's letter, on August 7, 1862.[26]

"Geo Walker, or some other furnishing store" was a reference to Geo. Walker, "Shirt and Collar Manufacturer,"[27] a store at 152 Essex Street, the main shopping street in Salem. Also on Essex Street, at No. 145, was John Barlow, "Boots and Shoes,"[28] where Fred asks Jennie to get him a pair of boots. Stephen Osborne's fur store was nearby, at 191 Essex Street.

Fred wrote again four days later:

Newbern

July 14th 1862

Dear Mother

The city is very quiet now so many troops having left with Burnie. Gen'l Foster is here with first division, and the 23rd still keep this position in the city as patrol guard. The last we heard from Burnie he was encamped at Newport News with 30,000 men.

The people who ran away from here when we took the place are gradually coming back and before cold weather comes again I suppose the greater part will be back. I hope they will for the city is very dull now.

We have had some very hot days and soon it will be hot right along. The darkies say that there will be two months of hot weather yet.

By the papers the loss of life before Richmond is tremendous. Major Richmond went up the country a week ago and got a Richmond paper of this month and that admitted their loss up to that time to be 60,000.

Don't think anything of what I said about company officers, but a fellow can't help spitting out once in a while for sometimes they get a little too bad.

Howard Hambler has come from the hospital to his quarters but isn't strong enough to go on duty. Harry Thomas is well and sends his respects. Si Crocker and Geo Wilkins are both well and on duty. They all send their respects.

Thom Harris is pretty sick then. I am very sorry for what I said, for I didn't know he was unwell. If they call for 15,000 more troops from Mass he and Tuvvy will have to look out for themselves and get a doctors certificate or they will draft them. Tuvvy mustn't come anyway for two in the ranks is enough. Give him my respects and tell him to look out for himself. He is out of a bad scrape anyway.

How is George Hogdon getting along. Does he get any better. Ad Paine has gone home with his discharge. Frank Caird has got back again amongst us, jolly as ever.

A detail of 5 men from each company of the 23rd is to be made for the purpose of manning the fire engines of the city of Newbern. The machines are all out of order and if there happened to be a fire there wouldn't be any very affective(sic) means of putting it out.

One of our boys was detailed last week as Brigade Forage Master. A very good chance, 40 cents a day extra pay. Alec Munroe was the lucky one. It was through the influence of the Brigade wagon master that he got it.

How are all the Salem folks, same as ever I suppose. Give my love to all my friends, Father, Aunt Jane, Mary, Lizzie, Jennie, Uncles, Aunts, cousins and everybody. I want Tuvvy to send his picture and if you have a card of Nate's send that.

How is Aunt Jane, well I suppose. Tell her that the figs that grow here taste a good deal like bananas and I often think that I wish I could get some home.

Geo Osgood has just caught a little mouse and we put him in a tumbler. It made me think [of] Jennie when she used to have them in a box.

When you get this Mother, if you havn't sent the things I wrote for, put in some cotton stockings.

My love to all. Will send another paper when one comes out that is worth sending.

F Osborne

Fred wrote that "the last we heard from Burnie he was encamped at Newport News with 30,000 men." General Burnside had taken two of his divisions from New Bern (leaving General Foster's division) to help McClellan at Richmond. But McClellan retreated to his supply camp on the James River and didn't need Burnside at the moment, so Burnside set up camp at Newport News to wait for developments. Additional troops were added to his force while he was at Newport News, but Fred's figure of 30,000 men seems high based on the historical record.[29]

General Burnside, with his special reputation for Union victories, received accolades from soldiers and civilians as he traveled around the East: "After an interview with President Lincoln [near Newport News] ... he proceeded to Baltimore ... [where] he ... collided with a mob of admiring soldiers. A dash to New York on railroad business led to a similar demonstration on the streets of Manhattan."[30] Burnside was an officer of the Illinois Central Railroad, which was the reason for the New York trip. Burnside and McClellan had worked together as officers of that railroad before the war.[31]

The George Osgood to whom Fred referred was George E. Osgood, 20, who was a Salem saddle maker when he enlisted in the original Company F. He was wounded in the battle of New Bern.

Fred's comment "By the papers the loss of life before Richmond is tremendous" referred to the "Seven Days" of running battle between Generals Lee and McClellan, June 25 to July 2, 1862. The Union forces lost 19,749 killed and wounded, and the Confederates lost 15,849.[32] A bloody business: twenty percent of both armies dead or writhing on the battlefield.

Fred wrote again in late July:

Newbern

July 25th 1862

Dear Mother

I have received yours of the 15th, but havn't had time to answer it until now. There isn't much new here excepting that the citizens have commenced the game of firing on the sentries from houses in the night. Last night on one post where it has been repeated several times a man fired on the guard twice with a revolver. Two of the sentries returned it with their rifles and then chased him, but it was so dark and he being acquainted with the yards and gardens round there he got off. They have arrested one man and got him in jail. It is hard to do it but they had ought to take everyone they catch and shoot them. That would stop it as quick as anything. If it goes on in this way it will be worse than living on picket. Johnny Kurtz [commanding officer of the 23rd Mass] gave orders to the sentinels if they [are] fired at from a house to bang away right into it, and no matter who is hit.

We havn't heard anything from Burnie yet. I suppose he is at work somewhere though. I think that he will give them a good thrashing if he gets the chance.

I should like to see the flag man and drummers going round the streets. A fellow that enlists now unless he has had a good reason for staying at home must feel nice to be drummed out before they could get him to go.

Did you receive that letter of mine relative to the things I wanted you so send to me? If you didn't I wish you would send me a pair of these lace up army shoes such as those I brought out with me when I started from home. I shall want eights and they must be very high on the instep. Tell Ov to get a good pair.

Also two fancy plaid thin flannel shirts. I suppose Geo Walker keeps them. Do not get very flashy ones or bright colors for when you wear them the sweat makes them look worse than ones without so many bright colors. And some cotton stockings and cambric or sassnet enough to line a pair of trousers and some postage stamps and good buff envelopes. If Captain Whipple has a box coming out, send them in that if not send in a box by Adams Express.

I shall send the check for Tuvvy to draw my money in this letter and you can pay for the things out of that and Mother take what is left if there is any.

All the boys are well. I believe Geo Wilkins has been sick, a little cold or something. It kept him off duty two or three days.

The Lt Col has gone home on a furlough and the Major has got the command of the regiment. He is going to be more strict in regard to cleanliness. Every man has got to have two pairs of trousers so that he can keep one pair clean all the time and he is going to visit the quarters several times a week without giving the men any notice of it. Some men were spoken of by him to the orderly saying that they were not as clean as they should be and every man that doesn't look as clean as he should will be sent to his quarters to clean up. I hope they will put it on to some of the dirty ones.

Give my love to Ruthelia, Hannah Lee, Hattie, Caddie, and Sisters, Cousins, aunts, Uncles and friends. All the boys send their respects.

Fred M O

All write as soon as possible. Send those things as soon as possible. I suppose though you have received the other letter before now and perhaps they are now on the way.

A further incident of the kind of shooting at soldiers by the local people that Fred described was reported in the regimental history: "Col Kurtz, as Provost-marshal, entered the house whence the shot came and ordered the inmates to vacate, in order that it might be pulled down. A woman, tearfully protesting her innocence, came out with several children and took refuge with a neighbor. The soldiers removed her furniture, discovering some concealed arms. Then, with a will, they pulled and tore, till house, out buildings and peach-orchard were levelled and a neighboring field of tall corn, too good an ambush to be left standing, was pulled up."[33]

The 23rd Massachusetts Regiment continued in its assignment of maintaining law and order in the New Bern area. Fred wrote to Jennie in August:

Newbern

August 6th 1862

Dear Jennie:

I don't know as my letter will interest you much as there isn't anything at all going on here. Do you know whether it is true that Capt Whipple's and Capt Brewster's families and Lieut. Bate's Mother and sister are coming out here? That is the report but I do not know whether it is true or not.

The orders are very strict now concerning guard duty. One of our company was court martialed today and lost a month's pay just for leaving the guardhouse without permission. That was Charlie Bate's doing. There is not another lieutenant in the regiment mean enough to do it.

Capt Tibbets, Sue's uncle, is here in the city. His vessel put into Beaufort for repairs and he is stopping up here. He looked the same as ever. The other morning just before we marched on to line for guard mounting he came up and asked for Eben Perkins. The old man stepped out and shook hands with him, said a few words and right about face marched to his place in the ranks again. I havn't seen him to speak to yet and don't know as I shall.

I am glad you got those boots, for next time he can fit me I suppose. I guess that everything will suit for you know my taste pretty well. I expect to receive the box by the time you get this letter. Did Mother receive the letter with the check in it. I have sent it.

That long man that goes to the 1st Baptist Church has turned out just as I thought he would, all show.

Have they drummed up any recruits yet, or will they have to draft. Some of the recruits [who] just come out here received $150 clear of pay and bounty. If they can't get men at that they will have to draft. I am sorry for Thom and for what I said. Give him my respects.

I should like to see the cadets coming out here, that Gus Brown for instance. I suppose that they think they are doing some service there in Fort Warren.

I should like to have some of the boys guard those Secesh prisoners about a week just to see if they would be as saucy as they are now to the Cadets. If they would prick one with a bayonet it would stop the whole of it.

I wish you could see a specimen of a Newbern lady sitting at her window with her snuff stick in one hand and snuff box in the other, and have to walk up and down past her for about two hours. It is very pleasant, and all that are not snuffers are darkies, so between it all there isn't a dozen ladies in the whole place.

I wish you would send me some postage stamps. I havn't but two left. Why doesn't Lizzie answer my letter. Give my love to all my friends. How does Liz Borden get along? I havn't heard a word about her since I have been out here or as to that about any of the girls. Poor Eliza Saul. I never thought she would go into consumption.

Love to Mother, Father, Uncles, Aunts, Cousins, Sisters, Brothers.

Yours

Fred Osborne

Write soon and tell Lizzie to write.

The Eben Perkins to whom Fred referred was a Salem sailor when he enlisted; he was 27 years old at this time."[34]

Fred had heard that some members of officer's families might be coming out; the practice of allowing families of officers in camp was special in the Civil War.

Fred's mother heard from him three weeks later:

Newbern

August 31 '62

Dear Mother

The reason I havn't written you for some time is that I have been out of postage stamps for some days and they are an article that it is very inconvenient either to buy or borrow.

I have been off duty for a week or ten days now, not exactly sick for I can poke about a little but the least bit of work tires me all out, in fact I am completely used up and shall have to lay off till I am built up again. My complaints are pains and weakness throughout my whole body, in fact I am good for nothing for the time being and that lame old shoulder aches once in a while.

Dr. Emmerton (that is Corporal Emmerton [who] has got his commission as Ass't. Surgeon) has been ordered to Roanoke Island and another one from the Potomac has taken his place. This one understands his business and is right after the boys.

Now don't be alarmed because I am a little sick.

Everything here goes on the same as ever. Genrl Foster has gone on an excursion with his family and is going to visit all the places in N.C. under his command.

All the bands of the Reg't are to be discharged and sent home. Most of them here including ours have been mustered out of the service. When they are gone I shall live in a house again, for after the new recruits came the house was so full two tents were pitched in the yard, and some of us put into them. But the Capt has engaged the Band Quarters when [they] are empty and probably we shall go into them.

Lieut. Bates is in command of the company and he is a very mean officer. He is coming down on the boys so as to make them all sit at one table and have all the rations thrown in together so that the hogs will get whole and small eaters come out short. It won't bother me much for when I am well I can keep my end of the stick up.

I suppose that you have heard of Lou Emilio's promotion to a corporal. If he conforms to Bates's ideas he will be a thundering mean one. Andrew Tebbets has also been appointed corporal. More promotions will have to be made by and by for there has got to be two more sergeants.

Mother if Barlow has not got those boots too far along tell him that I want them sewed and have a thick sole so that when it is worn down I can have a tap put on out here. If he hasn't commenced on them and you havn't ordered them you needn't till I write again.

How is it Mother that I havn't received any letters in the last two mails. I didn't have one.

Give my love to Father, Aunt Jane, Mary, Lizzie, Jennie, Caddie, Tuvvy, Hannah Lee, Hattie, Ruthelia and all my numerous uncles and cousins.

Can Jennie have her picture taken as large as yours and Lizzie's. That other is too small. My picture would look too peaked. Excuse [the] bad writing, my hand is not very steady.

This will come by Capt. Whipple.

Yours

FMO

Write often.


The Lieutenant Charles Bates whom Fred criticized was a Salem young man and a lieutenant in the original Company F when it was formed in the fall of 1861.

This is the third letter in which Fred mentioned being sick. Sickness in the military camps of the Civil War was common and of a great concern to officers because sick soldiers couldn't march and couldn't fight. The spread of disease in the high human density of military camps was understandable in those times before antiseptic methods were developed; the germ theory of disease was some years away.

Fred seems to have held on cheerfully while waiting to get well. He made no effort to get a sick furlough. In Fred's war to save the Union, it turns out, however, that he sacrificed his robust health. The residue of camp sickness stayed with him after the war, and he struggled with poor health the rest of his life.

The regimental bands mentioned in Fred's letter had been given special notice a few months earlier in the *New York Times*. The *Times* war correspondent had traveled with the Burnside expedition down the North Carolina coast, through Hatteras Inlet, and up Pamlico Sound to Roanoke Island. The correspondent was on the *Highlander*, Fred's ship; his comments on the bands appeared on the February 10 front page:

> The New England troops excel in the music faculty and in every regiment from Massachusetts, Connecticut or New Hampshire, music teachers or good singers abound, and many an otherwise tedious evening has thus been beguiled by the elevating influence of music. In this respect no regiment, perhaps, is more favored than the Massachusetts Twenty-third composed chiefly of Salem, Marblehead, Danvers and Boston men. Many of the officers were members of the best musical societies, and leaders or pillars in their church choirs at home.... (Music was a great comfort) ... on board the *Highlander* during many of the boisterous nights we have been anchored in this Sound, while the storm howled without.

It is not surprising that new shoes were again a subject in Fred's letter. Civil War infantry marched twenty and thirty miles a day, and comfortable shoes were a high priority. Union soldiers were usually able to get good shoes, but this was not the case for the Southern soldier. As the war went on, supplies of all kinds became a problem for the South, and Confederate soldiers often marched with worn-out shoes or no shoes at all.

## CHAPTER NINE

# Lincoln, Burnside, McClellan, and the Emancipation Proclamation

## Summer, 1862

Fred Osborne, who was on patrol duty, watched the war from New Bern. His favorite general was in the thick of things.

President Lincoln ranked Ambrose Burnside high on his list of generals. In July, when McClellan was still outside Richmond, Lincoln asked Burnside to take over McClellan's army. Lincoln was impressed with Burnside's energy and depressed by McClellan's lack of it. Burnside, discomforted by the idea of replacing his friend, argued that McClellan was the better general, and gently turned down the president's offer.[1] McClellan remained at the head of the Army of the Potomac, but Lincoln marked the modest Burnside for greater things in the future.

In early August, Burnside was holding his 12,000 troops on board ships off Fort Monroe, waiting for an assignment. McClellan was outside of Richmond, testing Lincoln's patience with inaction.

In August came the second battle of Bull Run. The Union general in this battle was John Pope, whom Lincoln had brought on from the West to head up the Army of Virginia. Pope was an arrogant man, and his men and his officers learned early on to dislike him heartily.

Pope was camped with the Army of Virginia on the Rapidan River, fifty miles from Richmond and the same distance from Washington. His orders were to protect Washington from "danger or insult" and to capture Richmond, rather a large assignment.[2]

General Robert E. Lee decided to go after Pope. Lee and Pope collided at the second battle of Bull Run on August 29 and 30, 1862. General Pope was beaten; his army broke and retreated back toward Washington, a result similar to the first battle of Bull Run. The Union losses were 14,462 killed, wounded, and captured out of a total force of 63,000; the Confederates lost 9,474 killed, wounded, and missing out of a total force of 54,000.[3] McClellan and Burnside were not active participants in that battle. After the battle, General Pope was dismissed.[4]

General Robert E. Lee then decided to go north, to invade Maryland and threaten Baltimore and Philadelphia. Washington went into a panic. Lincoln organized a new army to drive Lee out of Maryland, and he asked Burnside to take charge of it. According to William Marvel, Burnside's biographer, "President Lincoln called [Burnside] to the White House.... He wanted Burnside to lead that new army. McClellan's old friend once again declined.... He could not manage so large an army, but McClellan could. He seemed quite stubborn, so the president sighed and released him."[5] McClellan was given the new army, and Burnside was made one of his top generals.

McClellan, with the new army, marched north into Maryland to find General Lee. The Confederate and Union armies met at the battle of Antietam on September 17, 1862. According to the historian Peter Parish, it was "the bloodiest single day in the whole war ... fiercely contested ... confused and chaotic."[6]

Although Burnside was ready the next day to go after Lee's weakened forces, McClellan was not so aggressive and allowed Lee's army to withdraw. Antietam was declared a Union victory.

McClellan was heavily criticized for letting General Lee escape with his wounded army. Abraham Lincoln was unhappy and made a visit to Antietam to see McClellan. A month later he removed McClellan.

At Antietam, where one fourth of the soldiers in the contending armies were lost, little was decided. Little was decided in battle after battle in the Virginia theater: Winchester, Cedar Mountain, Harpers Ferry, Fredericksburg, Malvern Hill, Gaines Mill, First Bull Run, Second Bull Run, Seven Pines, Drewry's Bluff, and many others. Thousands of men, Union and Confederate, were lost, but no permanent advance was made, no cities were captured. Hundreds of thousands of dead and wounded were buried or sent to the hospital or home as invalids. They were replaced by volunteers or by the draft; regiments were thus replenished and the regiments went into battle again, losing men again, to be replenished again. The carnage in the Virginia theater was almost beyond belief. In his letters, Fred wrote about friends killed and wounded, buried or sent home, about recruits arriving to fill up the depleted regiments. Fred accepted it and didn't object to the carnage. No one objected to the carnage.

The bloody battle at Antietam, which was viewed as a Union victory, gave President Lincoln the political opportunity to deal with emancipation. He had not wanted to free the slaves, at least not until later. He was trying to cajole the border states into staying with the Union, and he knew that freeing their slaves would precipitate strong feelings against Washington. But the abolitionists were impatient; to them the war was about freeing the slaves, and they were increasingly unhappy with Lincoln because of the delay. Lincoln had not wanted to take action on freeing the slaves when the war was going badly, fearing that it would appear a desperate measure, but the battle at Antietam freed him to act.

Two years after the Emancipation Proclamation, Lincoln said to a British visitor:

> Many of my strongest supporters urged Emancipation before I thought … the country ready for it … had the proclamation been issued even six months earlier than it was, the public sentiment would not have sustained it…. We have seen this great revolution in public sentiment slowly but surely progressing, so that when final action came, the opposition was not strong enough to defeat the purpose.[7]

On September 23, 1862, President Lincoln issued his Emancipation Proclamation, declaring that on January 1, 1863, "all persons held as slaves within any State … in rebellion against the United States, shall be then, thenceforward, and forever free."

The Proclamation freed only those slaves in the rebellious states, and Lincoln was initially criticized because he did not free all slaves. But the public soon saw that when the war was won, all the slaves would be free.

Lincoln's Emancipation Proclamation was big news for Union soldiers as well as for the Northern public. Not all soldiers gave a high priority to freeing the slaves; saving the Union was the main issue for many. Fred's letters indicate that he agreed with President Lincoln about freeing the slaves: "Save the Union" had the higher priority.

Fred was probably not suffering the North Carolina heat and swamps to free the slaves. He had learned, as he was growing up, only eighty years after the Declaration of Independence, when the American experiment in democracy was still active in the public mind and was still discussed, that the United States was unique in the history of man. Having studied the wars and governments of history in grammar school, Fred was sophisticated in his judgment of American democracy; it was special, fragile, and worth any sacrifice.

Fred Osborne was in the war to save the Union. When Lincoln countermanded General Hunter's emancipation proclamation and a report circulated that the enraged John Andrew, the abolitionist governor of Massachusetts, was threatening not to raise more troops because of Lincoln's action, Fred wrote in his letter of May 30, 1862, that he hoped the report about Governor Andrew was not true. Fred was more interested in recruiting troops than in an emancipation proclamation.

## November 1862

The war wore on. In November of 1862, Lincoln dismissed McClellan and gave his command, the Army of the Potomac, to Ambrose Burnside.

Fred wrote to his mother on Thanksgiving Day:

Newbern

Nov 27th 62

Dear Mother

The 23rd Regt has left the city and gone into camp on the southern side of the Trent River. This camp was occupied by the 21st Mass before they left with Burnie. The 17th Mass has taken our place in the city.

Their ranks were so thinned by sickness that those in authority thought it was time for them to see the sunny side of a soldier's life (for a soldier doing patrol in the city of New Berne is a gentleman contrasted with one doing picket duty).

Two of our companies, A and G, are on picket about six miles from camp and Co E are in the Block House which is a little nearer the city than our camp. Steve is on picquet with his company [Co G] and as I havn't seen him since we left the city I don't know how he is, well though I'll bet.

We left the city last Saturday so that now our camp begins to look quite neat.

Our Colonel (John Kurtz) has resigned on account of some difficulty with Colonel Amory of the 17th. In losing him we lose the best officer we ever had and the command will be given either to Lt Col Elwell who is at home with a broken arm or Maj Chambers. Their isn't much choice between the two, and it is my opinion that now Col Kurtz has gone harder feelings will exist between officers and men than were before. Probably there will be some promotions made now amongst the commissioned officers.

The boys don't regret leaving the city very much. They have been lying still so long that they are ready for anything. There is a report that the 23rd is to leave Newbern and go to Texas with Banks but no reliance can be placed in it.

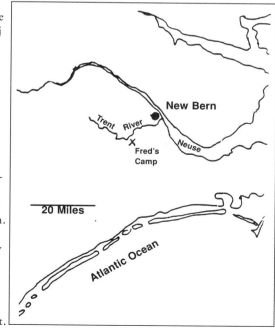

The 43rd and 45th are encamped pretty near us. Some of them are in barracks. We are in tents now. I don't know wether barracks are to be built for us or not.

I havn't had a letter from home for three or four mails. I received my shoes all right. They fit me splendidly and are well made. Have you sent the shirts yet or havn't you got them done.

It is Thanksgiving today. We are to [have] Turkey and Plum Pudding and vegetables and as like a home dinner as possible. I ate my last Thanksgiving dinner in Annapolis. It doesn't seem as though I had been in the service a year. I suppose Aunt Jane is flying round amongst puddings and pies, putting them on the front of the stove to warm just before dinner, down cellar for a pitcher of cider, and Aunt Hariet, Hannah Lee, and Harriet, Eliza, Aunt Hannah. After supper a kind of a family gathering. After all [have] gone to bed, Tuvvy sitting by the fire in the parlor.

Send Etta's picture.

Give my love to my friends and send some good pictures.

[signature smudged]

Colonel John Kurtz had been provost marshall in New Bern (as well as colonel of the 23rd Massachusetts regiment in which Fred served) since June 1862. He was "hurt by a severe reprimand from his superior officer for neglect of an order which, through negligence of the messenger, he had never received, resigned, and was honorably discharged."[8] Col. Kurtz returned home and in February of 1863 he was appointed chief of police of Boston.

## December 1862

Ambrose Burnside, Lincoln's new general in charge of the Army of the Potomac, had Lincoln's approval for a plan to capture Richmond — "if you move very rapidly."[9] The plan was to organize the army immediately at Fredericksburg for the march on Richmond, fifty miles to the south.

But General Robert E. Lee attacked Burnside at Fredericksburg before the Union army could get underway. General Burnside, trying to get his campaign toward Richmond organized rapidly, had been held up waiting for supplies. His army had waited day after day while General Lee massed his forces and, on December 13, 1862, at the battle of Fredericksburg, Burnside's Army of the Potomac was attacked and badly beaten. Burnside lost 12,500 men. As historian Peter Parish has noted, "For the North, Fredericksburg was perhaps the most humiliating and inexcusable defeat of the war, and its shock waves reverberated through … the whole country."[10]

Ambrose Burnside offered to resign, an offer which President Lincoln resisted but finally accepted.[11]

## *The Goldsboro Expedition*

General Foster, who was left in charge of North Carolina operations when Burnside went north in July 1862, decided to make the long-awaited move on Goldsboro. He had just finished tidying up his empire of Union holdings: New Bern, Roanoke Island, Plymouth, Washington, North Carolina and a corridor along the railroad from New Bern down to Beaufort. This sketchy web of Union positions was held together by water communication, around the sounds and up the rivers. Since all the Confederate ships had been destroyed at the battle of Roanoke Island, it was easy to get to these isolated holdings.

General Foster, a West Point engineer by training, "set himself to protect New Bern by a complete system of earthworks, which rendered the place defensible by a minimum number of men ... and ordered the same to be done at the other points in North Carolina held by [Union] forces."[12]

Confederate forces constantly probed for weakness around each of these Union positions, threatening to drive out the intruders. In New Bern, Fred often served on picket duty in outpost camps to detect any Confederate force which might be moving on the city.

With his positions in North Carolina well fortified, General Foster was ready for the long-awaited advance on Goldsboro. According to William Marvel, reinforcements for the expedition had arrived at New Bern: "principally ... nine month troops from Massachusetts, the 3rd, 5th, 8th, 43rd, 44th, 45th, 46th, and 51st regiments."[13] Historian Peter Parrish writes that "Foster ... was ordered to make an expedition to Goldsborough.... The expeditionary force consisted of twenty regiments of infantry ... a regiment of cavalry, and forty [cannon].... There were in all between eleven and twelve thousand men.... The expedition started on Thursday, the 11th, December, 1862."[14]

Fred recounted the experience to his family in his next letter.

New Bern

Dec 23rd 1862

Dear Mother

You must excuse me for not having written before, but for the last ten days I have been on an expedition. Last Thursday the 11th, the whole force stationed here under command of Gen'l Foster left this city and took the Kinston road.

There were four brigades of infantry and light batteries and eleven hundred cavalry. All the force was taken from the city but the heavy artillery, and the picket and provost duty was done by the convalescent ones.

We came across some of their pickets the first day and continued driving them. The cavalry did this and shot several of them. On the 12th just before we went into camp at night five hundred of the Reb cavalry formed a line of battle to oppose us, but before the first Brigade could be got into line

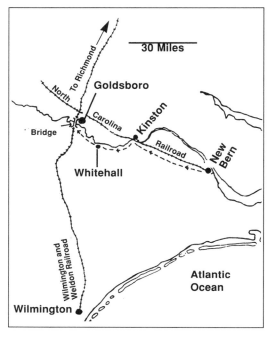

of battle, the Rebs left. That night the pickets fired six shots but there was no alarm.

The 13th, as we began to near Kinston, the advance had to be more vigilant. There were two companies of infantry with two pieces of artillery on one of the roads to Kinston, the one they expected us by, and in the middle of the afternoon they began to shell the woods in the direction they supposed we were advancing. In the meantime we were coming on to them from another direction and our cavalry came upon them so suddenly that they ran and left one piece of their artillery without spiking it, and the cavalry caught some of them.

We made a halt about the middle of the afternoon on a kind of a plantation and had just began killing our pigs and chickens and making our beds for the night when it was forward and away we went through a mud hole, got all wet, then turned in to a wet swampy corn field and spent the night.

The next day we reached the river at Kinston. The Rebs formed a line of battle some distance from the river and we had to drive them. Our regiment supported the 85th Pennsylvania, an old regiment that has fought on the peninsula under McClellan. We had to advance through a swamp (rather Roanokey only we were not in it so long) and so we couldn't see much of this regiment in front of us because the brambles were so thick, but when we got on to the edge of the swamp and the 85th should have advanced into the field, they hung back and tried to come through our ranks. Their Colonel and an aide were the only officers of their regiment that I saw.

The Colonel had the right wing in line ready to charge but the left wing wouldn't stand up to it. The Rebs formed a line of battle where we could see them but we had no orders so we could neither charge nor fire. They fell back and soon after we drove them over the bridge into the town and then the artillery shelled them out.

Our regiment was on the left of the road. The fighting on the right was much heavier as the Rebel breastwork was built on that side. Before the artillery was done shelling two companies of the Rebs, who didn't have time to get across the bridge and were down under the bank amongst the trees and bushes, couldn't stand the firing and came out and surrended. Afterward two companies of the 23rd [word unclear] surrendered to our Major.

One of the Rebs tried to set the bridge afire but caught afire himself and was shot by our men. In this battle the 45th Mass and 10th Conn suffered the most. We took a Rebel Colonel prisoner. He was wounded in the foot.

The town of Kinston is much prettier than Newbern. It is more modern. There are not so many black nigger shanties.

We left the next day, burning the bridge behind us, and started for Whitehall. The General didn't expect much resistance here but the Rebs had burnt the bridge and got the river between themselves and us as usual.

They had their sharpshooters hid in the trees and under brush and in some old buildings. Our artillery commenced the fight and we were ordered up to support the 17th. I saw three men of that regiment behind a tree. That is all I saw. We advanced on to the bank of the river and began giving it to them. That is, what we could see of them as they jumped about from one stump to another.

Hiram Almy and Charlie Manning were shot dead before we had got into position and Oliver Saunders, George Nourse, Wadleigh Hinckley and Ellison wounded. All of the wounded ones but Saunders were recruits. The regiment lost 66 killed and wounded, more than any other in the expedition.

As we didn't cross the river we had no chance of seeing what kind of a place Whitehall was.

When we marched out from the river back into the field singing rally around the flag it made some of the 9 months boys open their eyes and when they saw us fill up cartridge boxes to go in again if called on, they thought we were something. The Major and General Amory were very proud of us.

We left the battlefield and marched for Goldsboro. All we fought at Whitehall for was to drive the rebs from their position in order to get to Goldsboro, for unless we passed Whitehall and their batteries we couldn't get to Goldsboro. We camped that night five miles from Goldsboro. The next morning we marched and the river was between us and Goldsboro as usual (though of course we knew it before we started). We burnt the railroad bridge and tore up the track so as to prevent their sending reinforcements north. That was the chief object of the expedition. The artillery shelled the woods some and then we started for home.

After the greater part of our force left and got down the road, seven regiments of rebels crossed the river on a foot bridge that Foster knew nothing about, and charged the force that was left in the rear. There were two batteries in the rear and they double charged their guns with grape and cannister and piled the Rebs up in heaps. They broke and ran and they didn't trouble us again.

Tell Jennie I will write to her as soon as I can.

My clothes are down to the city. I shall get them again.

FMO

Excuse me for ending so abruptly but I had to run to get it into the office in time. Love to all.

FMO

Historian J. Lewis Stackpole recounts the action at Goldsboro, one of the most important railroad centers in the South: "On Wednesday, the 17th, the advance reached the railroad near Goldsboro…. [General Foster's men] steadily drove back the enemy and … set fire to the railroad bridge which was thoroughly consumed. The troops then took up and destroyed several miles of the rails."[15]

The expedition to Goldsboro was originally intended to capture and hold Goldsboro and then go on to Raleigh. But its mission was interrupted at Goldsboro when General Foster learned "that Burnside had been defeated at Fredericksburg, and that [Confederate] reinforcements were on their way to intercept [Foster]."[16] Foster hurried his army back to New Bern as soon as the critical railroad bridge at Goldsboro was destroyed.

The town of Whitehall cannot be found on the map of North Carolina today because in 1951 it changed its name to "Seven Springs." The 1980 Census gives a population of 166, of which 153 were white and 13 black.

The battle at Whitehall was a vicious one for Fred's Massachusetts 23rd regiment. The regiment, unprotected, traded fire with the enemy across a narrow but unfordable river. One participant in the battle reported:

> The regiment came marching … through the fringe of woods on the river bank … so near that officers … discharged their revolvers across the river at the enemy. [The regiment] stood there, at give and take, till many had fired their forty rounds, till ten had been killed and fifty-two wounded, stood, in spite of the dangers of short-timed shells and boughs lopped from the trees by our own batteries in the rear, till recalled, and marched, in accurate line, up the bloody slope, singing "Rally round the flag, etc.[17]

**View of Goldsboro, North Carolina. From a wartime sketch.**

On the day after Christmas, Fred wrote to Jennie:

Newbern

Dec 26th 1862

Dear Jennie

I received your letter the day the regiment returned to camp from up country. That was Sunday morning. I kept up with the company all the way up and back until the last day when my feet were so lame that I got aboard one of the wagons and rode all day. The regiment encamped about nine miles from the city. I asked the wagoner if he would carry me into the city (the teams were all going in) as it would save me the trouble of walking in in the morning. He said he would, but he carried me five miles farther and then made me get out and I crawled into the city the best way I could.

After I had got into the city I went to the old colored lady who lives back of the house where our company quartered in the city. Staid there all night, had a good breakfast in the morning and found that there were more than a dozen of the boys came in the same way.

About noon all of us went over to camp. You had ought to have heard those nigs talk and see them open their eyes when we told them about the fight. How they would chuckle when we told them how the artillery piled the Rebels up at South Goldsboro, and the folks at home couldn't be any more glad to see us back, than these darkies were to see us again. And when they would seem to feel so much for those who were shot, it seemed like getting home again in one sense of the word.

On the road up the country and back, at every halt and at every chance the boys would get they would be after turkeys, chickens, pigs and every-thing that was eatable. And there was a captain on Gen. Amory's staff who was appointed to look out for all property on the road to see that it was not molested and it was a perfect fight between this Captain his guards and the soldiers of the other regiments (his guards were all from the 45th). The boys would go to a house and get everything that they could carry off when the old gray headed Captain would be after them on horseback with his revolver drawn, drop everything you have or I'll shoot you, and then there would be a rush and some would get off with their plunder and others have to leave it where it was.

The Dutch Major of the 17th is another object of hatred. He would be behind the Brigade that his regiment belonged to with his revolver drawn, driving up those that couldn't keep up. There are reports round of our regi-ment having a Colonel and the Dutch Major is one that has been designated as one of those likely to get it. If he does it will spoil the 23rd Regiment.

Hiram Almy and Charlie Manning, the two boys who were killed in our company, were not buried until the day after the fight because the Rebels fired on everybody who went near the riverbank, and I guess that it was some time before the bodies were all got out of the woods. The wounded men of our company are all getting along well.

Going on that expedition and being so successful made things look bright for a while, but now the prospect is blacker than before. Gen'l Foster is in Washington and I see by the papers that all the Generals are there holding a grand consultation. If they don't do something soon all their consultations will avail them nothing.

And this story of their being short of provisions doesn't amount to anything for if there was anything in it pork, meal, lard, flour, etc. would not be so plenty in N.C. as it is.

Steve was on the Expedition and in both fights and was well all the time. I haven't seen him since for his company is on picquet at the ferry about two miles from camp.

I received the bundle. Everything was all right and the shirts fitted me splendidly, and stockings I was very glad of for I used up two pair on the march.

Tell Aunt Ann that I am ever so much obliged to her for the slippers; they were just the things to put my lame feet into. Steve hasn't got his yet but I shall send them to him at the first opportunity. Steve has sent that money, I suppose, for he said that he was going to before we left the city.

I hope that Nate will get better. I should like to have him at home and Steve and I there too (it would be one man and two dogs).

I should like to see that couple I used to get laughed at but when George Perkins hitched up with her the chaps used to hoot him engagement ring it will have to be returned I guess somebody at home there won't agree and it will smash. I am glad that I am not in the poor boy's place. He will get in places perhaps where he can't write so often (then she will be like the cavalry man that told me his sorrows; he had written his wife sixteen letters to her one).

Lu Emilo has got a picture of Sue and it is [a] good picture, the nose is on the rise just a little.

If Wendell Upham cannot see through [word unclear] it is about time for him to go to some one that he can. Has George Austin been married to Annie Perkins. I heard that he had.

A picture of Kate is just the thing. I want lots of pretty ones to fill up.

Mother had better send the pies soon, as there is no knowing how soon we may be off on another transfer.

We have been paid off for two months and I have sent home $15.00. The check for it will probably be in this letter. It is written in Mother's name so she will have to sign it.

Tell Tuvvy his cap was a nice one and just the style that is going here. My love to Father, Mother, Aunt Jane, Mary Ward, Lizzie, Aunts and Uncles, Cousins, and friends.

F Osborne

I wish you would send me some postage stamps and writing paper and some good steel pens. I cannot send that check by this letter. The money is going by this mail and they want it to arrive before the check.

In this letter, Fred commented about "one man and two dogs." The one man is presumably his brother Nate, an officer, and the two dogs are Steve and

Fred, two privates. Nate, a captain in the 13th Infantry of the regular U.S. Army, was stationed at Indianapolis, Indiana, where he had been transferred in September 1862 to serve as a mustering and disbursing officer.[18] At Indianapolis, Nate contracted typhoid fever. The post surgeon reported: "I have examined this officer, and I find that he is laboring under ... an attack of typhoid fever, contracted on or about 16th September, 1862 at Indianapolis ... and that in consequence thereof he is, in my opinion, unfit for duty." Nate was given sick leave to go home to Salem.[19]

Fred was impatient with the generals who were having a conference in Washington. According to historian J. Lewis Stackpole: "Foster was called to Washington ... [where he] was ordered to take ... [an] expedition to South Carolina, and cooperate with Admiral Dupont in the projected attack on Charleston. This was especially gratifying to [General Foster], because he had been with Major Anderson at ... [the] surrender ... [of Fort Sumter in Charleston Harbor, in April, 1861]."[20]

When we next hear from Fred he is getting ready for the expedition to South Carolina to attack Charleston.

## CHAPTER TEN

# The Battle of Charleston

## January 1863

Fred was at Camp Pendleton, near New Bern, where he had been since November when his regiment left patrol duty in the city. The regimental historian described Camp Pendleton in this way: "Pitched on the sandy plain [near] ... the Trent River ... the regiment was provided with a new set of Sibley tents, and, the space being ample and level, the camp made a fine appearance."[1]

A soldier's tent was always a subject for discussion. Sibley tents, which seemed to please the regimental historian, found a less enthusiastic response from a soldier who wrote that they were "cumbersome, conical [structures] ... in which eighteen men lie upon the ground with their feet toward the center."[2]

In his next letter, Fred was concerned about the regiment's new commanding officer. His November 27 letter had reported that Colonel John Kurtz, who had been their respected and admired commander since they left Salem, had resigned. Col. Kurtz's second in command, Lieutenant Colonel Andrew Elwell, a Gloucester clothier before the war, had been kicked by a horse and was on sick leave with a broken arm.[3] Major John Chambers, in temporary command of the regiment since Col. Kurtz had resigned and Elwell was on sick leave, was Elwell's competitor. Major Chambers had been a well-known printer who was once toasted, at a gathering with General Burnside, as "the printer-soldier of Massachusetts."[4]

Camp Pendleton

Jan 4th 63

Dear Mother

I received your letter this afternoon. Lt. Col Elwell and Adjutant Emmerton came on the same boat. Major Chambers will not like Elwell's

**Camp Pendleton, with Sibley tents at left.**

coming back very well for he has been counting on the Colonlcy of the 23rd pretty strong.

We have been brigaded again. We are now in the third brigade, with the 9th New Jersey, 8th and 3rd Mass.

Steve's company has come in from the ferry. They were relieved by a company of the 51st Mass, the brigade that regiment is in being detailed to do all the garrison duty of the city.

Steve is well and looks tip top. He came in to see me the same evening that he got into camp. He has written home lately he says. I gave him the slippers that Aunt Ann sent him, not having had a chance to get them to him before.

I am going to have another picture taken and send it to you, and you must have some cards taken from it, that is if there is anybody wants my mug, for it costs too much to have them taken here. Such ones as that I sent to you are a dollar. The only ones any cheaper are these things about half an inch square and you cannot tell how anybody looks by them at all.

I have sent one to George Smith. You can see it by getting Tuvvy to ask him; I shall send you one just like it. There isn't anybody here that takes photographs or I should have them instead of these tin ones.

Caddie's picture is a splendid one, and I am ever so much obliged to her for it. Your must have some cards taken so that I can return these favors. I hope [word unclear] and Ruthelia's will get here soon for there is no know- ing how soon we shall leave Newbern for another raid.

My pictures that I have had taken are the best ones in the company. I don't know the reason, but not another fellow in the company has taken as clear and true as I have.

Have you sent the box? If you have it will reach here before we leave unless we start very suddenly.

I have heard that some of the 50th put into Port Royal on account of the leaky conditions of their vessels. They are having it rough in the beginning.

The peninsula brigade under Genl Wessell are a funny looking set. They havn't been paid for six months, and most of the officers are as poor as the privates and they all look equally dirty.

Give my respects to my friends and everybody.

Yours

FMOsborne

I have sent Father a Newbern Weekly in this mail.

Tell Caddie it brought the smiles all over Steve's face when he looked at her picture.

Historian J. Lewis Stackpole sheds light on Fred's comment "The peninsula brigade under Genl Wessell are a funny looking set." According to Stackpole,

> There arrived [at New Bern] a brigade commanded by General Wessells ... from the Army of the Potomac.... They were pointed out to soldiers ... as exemplars [which] it would be well for them to imitate, and General Wessells was always referred to as that old veteran, the old reliable Wessells. As a matter of fact, Wessells was a superannuated army officer with little ability, and his men shone but dimly even when compared with fresh levies from Massachusetts. They were ill disciplined, and had a habit of straggling, which, when they became aware of firing at the front, amounted to positive genius.[5]

The "peninsula brigade" had served under General McClellan whose reputation for producing well-disciplined soldiers would be tarnished by this account.

Camp Pendleton

Jan 12th

Dear Mother

I sent you this letter in care of Lt Bates, he having resigned his commission.

I had a picture taken this morning but it was such a miserable one I will not send it.

I have sent my shoes home again in a box. I burnt them on the last expedition and there isn't a shoemaker here that can fix them. You can let Rice fix them or not as you please. At any rate don't send them until I write for them.

We are under marching orders and shall leave Newbern tomorrow probably for Beaufort to go aboard transports for Wilmington N.C. or Charleston S. C.

This was written in a great hurry and you must excuse me for not writing before.

Yours

F M Osborne

Fred had said earlier, in his letter of August 31, 1862, that Lieutenant Bates was "a thundering mean" officer. Fred seems to be on better terms with Lieutenant Bates now, perhaps because of his resignation, for which the record discloses no reason.

The burned shoes sent home by Fred were probably a casualty of sleeping with his feet toward the campfire.

Fred told his mother they would soon be leaving for Wilmington, North Carolina, or Charleston, South Carolina. Wilmington had been the objective for the expedition for a time, but it was abandoned in favor of Charleston.

The decision to attack Charleston was made in Washington in early January 1863. General Foster and his army were to make an expedition by water, south along the Atlantic coast to South Carolina, and get ready for a joint army-navy attack on Charleston. Army-navy amphibious operations had been given a boost by the highly successful Burnside expedition, where cooperation between General Burnside and the navy officers was exemplary.

Charleston was an emotional target for a Union attack. South Carolina had led the secession of Southern states, and the first ordinance for secession had been passed in Charleston. Confederate soldiers had fired on Fort Sumter, in Charleston Harbor, to start the war. "As Boston was ... the cradle of American liberty, where the Union was nurtured, so Charleston, in later days, came to be ... the nursery of disunion," said Charles Rodgers, a Union naval officer at the battle of Charleston. "No city in the South was so obnoxious to Union men as Charleston. Richmond was the objective of ... our armies, as its capture was expected to end the war, but ... it was to ... Charleston that the strong feeling of dislike was directed, and the desire was general to punish that city."[6]

At Camp Pendleton, outside of New Bern, on January 12, 1863, "The expected order came for a movement.... Rations were prepared for the men's haversacks, and the officers bought their private stores.... Tents were struck and packed ... the regiment bivouacked ... for an early start."[7] On January 13, the Massachusetts 23rd "marched to [the] railroad, embarked for Carolina City, pitched a camp on the sandy plain ... and waited."[8]

They waited a week at Carolina City for sea transport. Carolina City is not on today's map of North Carolina. The city had been laid out in 1855, before the Civil War, by the North Carolina Corporation to be the terminal port of the Atlantic and North Carolina Railroad (connecting to New Bern and on to

Goldsboro). The opening of Morehead City (which became the terminal port rather than Carolina City) and the Civil War brought about its death. The Union army camped there for three years.[9]

On January 20, Fred's regiment boarded the transport ship *James Morton* in Beaufort Harbor. Held on board, the men waited for days; "These were lively times in Beaufort Harbor. The huge fleet was in all the variety of gun-boats, store-ships and transports ... the latter ... crowded with soldiers."[10] On the *James Morton*, according to one soldier's memory, the men occupied their time with "wrestling, smoking, fighting, sewing, dancing, swearing, climbing, gambling, writing, eating, washing, singing, working, ... reading and 'flouring the niggers.'"[11] Research has not uncovered the meaning of the last expression.

After many days of delay, the *James Morton* got underway on January 31. After it arrived at Port Royal, South Carolina, the regiment stayed on board for more days before being landed on St. Helena Island on February 11.[12]

There were two Beauforts in Fred's letters: one near Morehead City in North Carolina and one near Port Royal in South Carolina.

> St. Helena Island
>
> Port Royal Inlet
>
> Feb 14 63
>
> Dear Mother
>
> I received your letter today. I havn't written to you since we left the camp at Carolina City.
>
> We went aboard the transport James Morton at Morehead City the 20th of Jan. The fleet laid in Beaufort Harbor a few days waiting for fair weather. We left there and started for Port Royal. We had a pleasant passage.
>
> Nothing of interest happened excepting one of the boats on the Wilmington Blockade overhauled us and found out our business before we could keep on.
>
> We anchored in the inlet and it was some time before we could land. The Weehauken and another Monitor have been in here since we came in, and the New Ironsides came in.
>
> We are now in the 10th armee corps. When we left Beaufort we were in the 18th.
>
> Foster wanted to take command of all the forces and have Hunter under him, but Hunter looked upon Foster's troops as re-inforcements and Foster inferior to himself. They couldn't agree and Foster couldn't use any of Hunter's boats to land his men. Hunter put a gunboat on the blockade to keep Foster's boats from running out but two of them got out and Foster has gone North to settle it some way.
>
> This island is a poor place. There isn't hardly any wood or water that is fit to use. The water is muddy and dirty and the wood is small growth so

that it is hard work getting enough to cook with.

Genl Hunter was going to bring his nigger brigade down from Beaufort for Foster's brigades to take pattern by. The boys used some of the nigs pretty rough and Hunter didn't like it pretty well.

Hannah Lee's picture is a splendid one. It looks just like her. I am ever so much obliged to her.

Today is Valentine's Day. I suppose that there will be a good many young ladies have there vanity stirred up by nonsense on a pretty piece of paper.

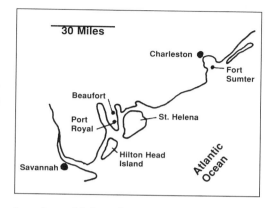

**Locations of Osborne's Regiment, February–April 1863**

I got the box when I was on board the vessel. Everything was real nice. Nothing spoil[ed]. The candy made me think [of] lying awake and watching the stocking. I got the paper and stamps both. I will write more next time.

Love to all

F Osborne

Eben Perkins had the picture of Mr. Brook's daughter, Annie I believe it is. I told Eben if he wrote to Mr. Brooks to send him my respects. If he writes I will answer it to the best of my ability only don't say anything to him. If he writes let it be of his own accord.

Steve keeps about half shaved, clips them with the scissors. I had a good [mind] to send for a razor to scrape my phisog but I guess I will wait until we get [word unclear].

The use of the word *phisog* as slang for *face* lingers in New England today and is believed to be derived from *physiognomy*.

The navy, under Admiral Samuel DuPont, was accumulating ships for the upcoming attack on Charleston, as is indicated by Fred's comment to his mother about this gathering of naval firepower.

The Wilmington Blockade boat mentioned in Fred's letter was part of a blockade squadron set up from Texas to Florida to New Jersey by the Union navy to block Confederate ports. The blockade was set up by President Lincoln in the first days of the war to keep cotton from going to Europe and war supplies from reaching the Southern states so that the Union could strangle and starve the Confederacy into submission.

The "Genl Hunter" mentioned by Fred is the General David Hunter who had in May 1862 issued an emancipation proclamation freeing the slaves in his command area — South Carolina, Georgia, and Florida. General Hunter was in charge of the infantry in this expedition against Charleston; his opposite number, in charge of the navy, was Admiral Samuel DuPont. General Foster and his troops reported to General Hunter. Fred's remark, "Foster wanted to take command of all the forces and have Hunter under him," suggests that General Foster was not happy to be under Hunter. J.A. Emmerton's regimental history records this disagreement: "Gen. Hunter issued an order assuming that our force was a reinforcement to his command, and subject to his orders. The discontent ... at this ... found expression in protest and ... revolt among the ... officers. Some of these were put in arrest."[13] Peace was obtained by a reassignment of officers, the particulars of which are not revealed in the record.

## March 1863

Fred Osborne was on St. Helena Island, forty miles south of Charleston, waiting. Preparations for the attack on Charleston seemed to be moving very slowly.

> Camp Russell
>
> St. Helena Island
>
> Mar 17, '63
>
> Dear Mother
>
> I wrote last time the boat went but instead of sending them in the mail I gave them to Lu Emilio and he missed the boat. By the time this reaches you he will probably have arrived.
>
> Last Saturday I was over to Hilton Head. It is a regular government station. The houses having been all built since our forces took possession. There is a fort, a large house used as Headquarters, Hotel, Post Office, and the rest of the buildings are long low storehouses with white-washed roofs. They look as though it had been snowing.
>
> Most of the storehouses are full of army grub, and if we have got to masticate all the hard tack there is there before we are discharged we shall stay the rest of our three years.
>
> Three days ago was the anniversary of the Battle of Newbern.
>
> The officers have introduced the stocks as punishment for the men who receive a sentence at the hands of a regimental court martial. The boys refused to go into them at first and wouldn't come out of the guard tent when their names were called. One of the new lieutenants undertook the knock down drag out business and went into the tent to pull them out but was knocked down and kicked out himself by the prisoners and both the sergeants of the guard were knocked down. The Colonel doubled the guard and finally they succeeded in quelling them. But they couldn't very well stop their tongues and they kept them agoing as fast as they could. If an officer came within sight or hearing he had all his shortcomings laid out before him

as loud as they could howl. For a time the officers were afraid of mutiny throughout the regiment. The Colonel sent twenty of them over to the Fort and it has been quiet ever since. It showed them that there is such a thing as pressing a volunteer too hard.

Nate will be on his way to his regiment by the time you get this.

I suppose that in the regulars it would be a heavy penalty. As it is I guess they will fare hard enough. This dept comes nearer the regular service than the Dept. of N. C.

Did you receive the letter with one enclosed for Nate? If you did I should think it was time I heard from him. There was a mail yesterday but I didn't get any letters. The one before that I got yours and Jennie's and Lu Emilo has got the ones I sent in answer and one for Nate.

Did Nate say anything about getting me a chance in those new regiments. I didn't know but that he would try without my writing. He knows about how well I would like to get out of this, at least he ought to. The getting home is worth as much as the commission. I think your letter said his furlough was up the 20th of this month.

It seems to me that there are a great many commissioned officers at home on furloughs. The whole army are lying still and they might as well be at home, I suppose, as with their regiments. The Capt of Co K of our regiment is home. Capt Whipple as still at Newbern.

My love to Father, Aunt Jane, Mary Ward, Lizzie, Jennie, Aunts, Uncles, cousins and friends.

If the draft goes into effect it will start stay-at-homes, but I see if a man has $1000 he is clear. It is about as just as the rest of the laws.

Tell Tuvvy to send me his phisog.

FWOsborne

Write often.

Fred's comment about hard tack indicates that it may have been getting a little wearisome. Hard tack was "a hard biscuit ... made of flour and water without salt";[14] the name is derived from *tack*, which means "food, especially coarse food."[15]

Fred Osborne was getting tired and homesick; it seems that he would even have tried to get a commission if it meant getting home: "The getting home is worth as much as the commission." With over a year of camps and marches and battles, and no furlough home, Fred was a bit worn down.

As the months dragged by, Fred's letters were becoming less disciplined in grammar, less careful of vocabulary, less a reflection of the cultured Salem that nurtured him, the milieu of the lyceum and Hawthorne and Emerson that he had left behind long months ago. Army living, of course, never did promote refinement.

Fred referred to his letters being carried home to Salem by Lu Emilio, who was returning to Salem at that time because he had been selected to become a commissioned officer in the 54th Massachusetts Regiment, a black regiment being organized at that time by the governor of Massachusetts. Governor Andrew was a dedicated abolitionist and wanted to demonstrate the value of black soldiers,[16] but in his history of Fred's regiment, Dr. J. A. Emmerton reported unenthusiastically: "While we were in South Carolina the orders were issued which resulted in reinforcing our army with 300,000 disciplined colored soldiers. Of the 66 men selected from the army for commissions in the 'Corps d'Afrique' forty-eight were from Massachusetts and of these, four were from the 23rd, all original members of Co. F.... The service was not popular. It required no little moral courage to gratify ambition by way of a commission in the 'nigger regiments.'"[17]

But Lu Emilio, one of the original soldiers in Company F (and Fred's boyhood neighbor on Oliver Street), seemed to thrive on this opportunity. He had been selected under the severe requirements set up by Governor Andrew for the officers of this black regiment: "Young men of military experience, of firm anti-slavery principles, ambitious, superior to a vulgar contempt for color, and having faith in the capacity of colored men for military service. Such officers must ... be gentlemen of the highest tone and honor." The regiment became famous.

Emilio wrote the history of that regiment: *A Brave Black Regiment, History of the Fifty-Fourth Regiment of Massachusetts Volunteer Infantry 1863–1865.*[18] His book, which was published in 1891 and republished in 1894, 1968, and 1990, has won critical praise. The book gave publicity to the first African-American to win a Medal of Honor, Sergeant William H. Carney. On the medal are inscribed his words: "The old flag never touched the ground, boys." A movie called *Glory.* was made about the black Massachusetts 54th regiment. *Glory* starred Matthew Broderick, Denzel Washington, and Morgan Freeman and it won an Oscar for Denzel Washington.[19] Vincent Canby, writing in the *New York Times* said, "*Glory* ... the beautifully acted, pageant-like movie that tells the story of the Massachusetts 54th ... is the first serious ... movie about the Civil War ... in years.... [It can be compared with] *Birth of a Nation* ... [and] *Red Badge of Courage.*"[20]

The story of this black regiment is also told by Peter Burchard in his book *One Gallant Rush,* in which he recounts: "When ... [the Massachusetts 54th] marched through Boston on their way to war, the tough and implacable William Lloyd Garrison stood on [a balcony] ... weeping for joy as the Negroes of the Fifty Fourth passed by."[21]

A television special, "The Massachusetts Fifty Fourth Colored Infantry," produced by David McCullough and shown on Public Television in 1994, presents a sensitive and powerful history of the black 54th.

Fred Osborne and the rest of the 23rd Massachusetts had now been on St. Helena Island for six weeks, waiting to attack Charleston, which was forty miles away. The men were beginning to get restive, and impatient with the delay. Fred's next letter was an unhappy one, which was unusual for this cheerful, positive young man.

Camp Russell

St Helena Island

Mar 25th 63

Dear Mother

We were reviewed by Genl Hunter this morning. The review was in a field close to our camp so we didn't have far to march. All the troops on the island were there. Hunter had all his gold lace on as usual.

It is reported that some of the troops on this island are under marching orders and also that Genl Burnside is on his way to take command of this Dept.

If Genl Hunter doesn't have any more force than he has got now he will not make a very big thing of attacking Charleston or Savannah.

The Stocks have fallen into disuse I guess for I havn't seen them lately. The last time they had them out the boys kicked them pretty well to pieces and I haven't heard anything about them since.

Have you got the letters I sent by Emilio or hasn't he arrived in Massachusetts? If you havn't, I sent for a black silk neck kerchief, a pair of suspenders, and a half a yard of the same flannel as my shirts are made of. Though you have the letter by this time, it was in Jennie's letter.

I sent one letter to Nate before I sent the one by Emilio. Did he get them both? Nate has left home before this time I suppose.

I have got your letter in which you say he tells me to keep dark. That was the last one I received from home.

By the papers I should think that they were having fine times in Salem. Concerts, Theatres, Parties, and everything else.

The Conscription Act doesn't affect the younger people so they can

**Camp Russell on St. Helena Island. From a sketch made in April 1863.**

carry their merriment on without interruption. That is a foolish law. Half of the army now in service are under twenty and most of the older men are not so tough as the young ones. There are a set of small boys in Co A and they are the toughest ones in the Regt.

The War Dept seems to try to put this thing through by lying still. They might as well do that as fight for they won't accomplish much.

The men are discouraged. It is best to keep on a bright face as long as possible but it looks blue enough now. The men who have families are the most discontented as this withholding the pay put their families in a unpleasant position.

As for myself I will keep kicking as long as there is hope. But I hate to hear some who are running the government [down] and moaning over being cheated out of so much of their rations and keep it going all the time when if they held the position themselves the men wouldn't fare half as well as they do now.

Genl Hooker is putting the army through a thorough reform and kicking out the discontented ones. He had ought to hang them. It is no use of being miserable now, but if I was out of it I would tell what I think of it.

I hope the next mail I shall hear from Nate. Tell Lizzie to write; she hasn't written for a long time.

My love to Father, Aunt Jane, Mary, Lizzie, Jennie, Tuvvy, Eliza, Caddie, Hannah Lee, Hattie, Ruthelia and Aunts and Uncles.

Yours

F M Osborne

As Fred indicated, Ambrose Burnside had been offered the North Carolina command by President Lincoln. After the Union defeat at the battle of Fredericksburg, Lincoln tried to find a place for General Burnside, whom he still liked and admired. But Burnside didn't want to replace General Foster, his former subordinate, in North Carolina, so he accepted a command in Kentucky, where the action was heating up at the time.

Fred commented that the Conscription Act should extend to younger men. The Conscription Act specified a minimum age of twenty for the draftee; it was given in the *New York Times* of February 19, 1863, provided that "all able-bodied male citizens of the United States ... between the ages of twenty and forty-five years ... shall be liable to perform military duty ... when called out by the President for that purpose."

Until early 1863, the Union army was all volunteer, but battle carnage such as occurred at Fredericksburg and Antietam required replacements at a faster rate than could be supplied by the stream of volunteers.

The Conscription Act provided an escape for wealthier men: "a drafted man could avoid enlistment either by providing a substitute or by paying a ... fee of $300."[22] Historian Shelby Foote notes: "Large numbers of men from the upper classes ... went to the expense of hiring substitutes (usually immigrants who were brought over by companies newly formed to supply the demand, trafficking ... in flesh to an extent unknown since ... the slave trade)."[23]

Fred's comment "The men are discouraged" probably reflects a reaction to three weeks on shipboard followed by more weeks in a confined camp. The Company F historian, Private Herbert Valentine, described the situation in these terms: "Long confinement ... is always demoralizing, and possibly those in authority making no allowances for existing conditions did not deal with the difficulty in the wisest way. The men were instructed to remain in company streets [of the camp], and orders for roll-call every two hours ... the guard house, the buck and gag were ... utilized in ... punishment ... even a row of stocks. Measures such as these ... injured the good name of the regiment.... The regiment was, in drill and discipline, the peer of any ... in service.... Never ... in camp or field, did it refuse duty, however difficult or dangerous."[24]

Another soldier remembered these unhappy times on St. Helena Island writing: "[There] occurred the most marked difficulty between officers and men in the history of the regiment.... Infractions of discipline were met by new, and, the men thought, excessive punishment. Men were sentenced ... to knapsack and log drills ... the buck and gag and, in that condition, exposed to public view at dress parade ... finally, a row of stocks."[25]

The "buck and gag" was a particularly distressing punishment. The "buck" consisted of "tying the wrists together, passing the arms over the bent knees, and inserting a stick over the arms and beneath the knees."[26] The "bucked" soldier was then gagged. This punishment was also used at the infamous Confederate prison at Andersonville, Georgia.[27]

General Joseph Hooker, whom Fred mentioned, was a handsome and controversial soldier; President Lincoln had chosen him to replace Burnside as the head of the Army of the Potomac after the battle of Fredericksburg. After that battle and after Lincoln had chosen Hooker to replace Burnside, the Commmittee on the Conduct of the War, a powerful congressional committee, looked into that Union defeat in which 12,500 Union soldiers were lost, causing great consternation in the public and press. That committee concluded that some of Burnside's generals did not give him proper support during the battle and that some generals were prepared more for failure than for victory and behaved accordingly. One of these generals was Joseph Hooker.[28]

"Fighting Joe" Hooker took over the Army of the Potomac with a vengeance, made extensive reforms, improved rations, cleaned up unsanitary camps, and bolstered morale. Fred apparently heard about it. Perhaps Fred also heard about Joe Hooker's reputation for drink and good times; one report had it that Hooker's "army headquarters became a place to which no self-respecting man liked to go, and no decent woman could go. It was a combination of barroom and brothel." Hooker's name "entered the language as the ... slang word for prostitute."[29]

Fred's comment that the Union force under General Hunter was too small to attack Charlestown successfully is a sentiment repeated by his brother Steve in his letter of May 13, 1863. Steve indicates that their mother had a similar opinion on the strategy on attacking Charleston. (Steve's letter can be found after Fred's letter dated April 19, 1863.)

As commander of the Department of the South, General Hunter, was the top officer in the Port Royal area. Fred's comments in his letter of February 14, indicate that General Hunter had some black regiments in his command. Lu Emilio had at this time just returned to Massachusetts to be an officer in the black regiment, the 54th Massachusetts. General Hunter requested that the regiment be sent to South Carolina, and on May 28, having completed their training, the men of the 54th Massachusetts started on their trip to South Carolina. The 54th would make its reputation in the fighting around Charleston.

At the time of this letter, Nate was at home in Salem on sick leave, recovering from the typhoid fever he had contracted at Indianapolis. In Nate's military file is a handwritten letter requesting active duty:

> Brigr Gen'l L. Thomas
> Adjutant Gen'l U.S. Army
> Sir:
> Having been on detached service ... I feel that valuable opportunities for acquiring a more practical knowledge of my profession than I possess have passed, and that my relief from duty would not be disadvantageous to the interests of the Union, and it would result in benefit to me. I hereby respectfully make application for an order relieving me from Mustering service at Indianapolis and directing me to report to the Head Quarters of my regiment at Newport Barracks directly upon the expiration of my leave of absence
> I am, Sir, Most Respectfully
> Your Obd't Servant
> Nathan W. Osborne
> Capt. 13th Infantry

This letter was handwritten; all documents in Nate's lengthy military file were handwritten until just before his death in 1895, when typed documents began to appear in his file. Typewriters did not come into common use until the 1890s.[30]

In a synopsis of his military career found in his military file, Nate said: "I ... was ordered to join my regiment ... opposite Vicksburg. My first participation in Active Operations was in command of H Company, 1st Battalion, 13th Infantry when the 15th Army Corps ... moved ... against Vicksburg ... with Gen'l Grant. Subsequently ... I was actively engaged wherever the 15th Army Corps was ... until we stood before the defenses of Vicksburg."[31] The 15th Army Corps was commanded by General William Tecumseh Sherman. Nate served with Sherman in the siege of Vicksburg, Mississippi, one of the most important Union actions in the Civil War. It opened up the Mississippi River and cut the Confederacy in two. Grant's campaign against Vicksburg was, said a pleased President Lincoln, "one of the most brilliant in the world."[32]

At the end of March 1863, Fred Osborne was still waiting on Hilton Head Island for the battle of Charleston.

## The Battle of Charleston

The Battle of Charleston was planned as an army-navy joint operation. According to the battle strategy, the navy would knock out the Charleston Harbor forts with the fire power of ironclad gunships and the army, coming overland, would take the helpless city.

Charleston Harbor was ringed with forts to protect the city from attack from the sea. Right after the capture of Fort Sumter in April 1861, the Confederates had heavily fortified Charleston Harbor. An enemy ship coming into the harbor could have as many as 69 cannon trained on it.

But the Union navy had convinced itself that ironclad gunships could knock out those shore batteries and remain unharmed. To understand the enthusiasm of the Union navy for ironclads we must go back a year, to the spring of 1862 when the new ironclad fighting ships were making naval history.

The new ironclads, those warships with hulls covered with thick iron plates to ward of cannon fire, caused great excitement in March of 1862; the world saw a new kind of naval warfare in the historic battle of the *Monitor* and the *Merrimac.*

The pokey Union navy, bound to tradition and resistant to change, was late in building ironclads. The Confederates, left with almost no navy and thus no traditions to throw off, waded in and built the first ironclad, the *Merrimac.*

In the spring of 1861, just weeks after the firing on Fort Sumter, the construction of the *Merrimac* was underway. A scuttled steam battleship that had been burned and sunk when the Union abandoned the Norfolk navy yard was raised and outfitted with iron plates.

News that this Confederate ironclad was under construction at Norfolk startled Washington into action. The Union navy advertised for plans for an ironclad battleship.[33] John Ericsson, a genius of naval armament, submitted plans for a strikingly new type of gunship; it was iron-plated, had a rotating tower containing two large cannons, and a flat iron deck just at the water line to minimize exposure to cannon fire.

Navy people were less than enthusiastic about John Ericsson's ironclad design but, after some insulting treatment of Ericsson,[34] the navy staff "finally let him go ahead with a contract which stipulated that he would not be reimbursed in case of failure,"[35] and construction was begun at Brooklyn, N.Y.[36] Ericsson's iron-clad would be called the *Monitor*.

It was a race against time for the two iron-clads, the Confederate *Merrimac* under construction at Norfolk and the Union *Monitor* being built at Brooklyn, N.Y.

On the afternoon of March 8, 1862, the *Merrimac* was launched out of the Norfolk navy yard into Hampton Roads. Several Union warships were lying at anchor in Hampton Roads, among them the *Cumberland* and the *Congress*.

The *Merrimac* moved on these two wooden warships, which were helpless against the ironclad. In a few minutes naval warfare was changed forever: "In this battle all things passed away, and the experience of a thousand years of battle ... was forgotten.... Iron-clads were in future to decide all naval warfare."[37]

After destroying the *Cumberland* and the *Congress*, the *Merrimac* withdrew, planning to finish off the rest of the Union ships in the harbor the next day.

That evening President Lincoln received the news in the White House, some miles up the Potomac River from that scene of destruction. In an atmosphere of panic, he called a cabinet meeting. His secretary of the navy, Gideon Welles, later described that cabinet meeting: "There was general excitement and alarm.... The most frightened man [in the room] ... was the Secretary of War [Edwin Stanton]. The *Merrimac*, he said, would destroy every vessel in the service, could lay every city on the coast under [siege].... He ran from room to room ... swung his arms.... The President and Mr. Stanton went repeatedly to the window and looked down the Potomac — the view being uninterrupted for miles — to see if the *Merrimac* was not coming [up the river] to Washington."[38]

President Lincoln got better news the next day when the Union's *Monitor* arrived at Hampton Roads.

The construction of the *Monitor* had been completed in a hurry: "The mechanics worked upon her day and night up to the hour of her departure."[39] The *Monitor* started from Brooklyn on March 6, 1962, towed by a tugboat, on the dangerous ocean passage to Hampton Roads. "It was at once evident that the *Monitor* was unfit as a sea-going craft."[40] After a tenuous trip on the open sea, the *Monitor* arrived at Hampton Roads on the evening of March 8, after the *Merrimac* had retired. The *Monitor* crew could see the "fine old *Congress* burning brightly.... Soon a pilot came on board and told of the ... disaster to the *Cumberland* and the *Congress*, and the dismay of the Union forces.... [Then] the *Monitor* anchored [for the night]."[41]

The next day, March 9, 1862, the historic battle of the *Monitor* and the *Merrimac* was joined. When the *Monitor* was first sighted by the *Merrimac*, "she appeared but a pygmy" an officer on the *Merrimac* recalled later.[42] But the *Monitor* was very maneuverable, and the two cannons in her rotating turret could fire from any position. The *Merrimac*, a long, massive ship, "unwieldy as Noah's ark," took "thirty to forty minutes to turn."[43] The two ships circled each other for six hours cannon fire bouncing off their armored sides.

With little damage to either ship, the *Monitor* finally withdrew from the

***Top:*** **The *Merrimac*, the Confederate ironclad; *bottom:* The *Monitor*, the Union iron-clad.**

battle. The *Merrimac* did not pursue; it returned to Norfolk. The winner of the contest was judged to be the *Monitor*, which had stopped the *Merrimac*, halting the further destruction of the Union fleet.

President Lincoln and the Union navy were so pleased with the *Monitor* that copies of that ironclad, given the generic name "monitor," were hastily ordered to be built.

The Union navy became enamored of the monitors. In fact, "The Navy Department was [said to be] suffering from an affliction [called] 'iron-clads on the brain.'"[44] Assistant Secretary of the Navy Gustavus Fox became a booster. He told "a congressional committee that the monitors ... could steam into southern harbors, flatten the defences, and emerge unscathed."[45]

When Charleston became the target of a Union expedition, Mr. Fox was enthusiastic about using monitors "to reduce Charleston ... (and then) to move on to Savannah, then send them down to the Gulf to give Mobile the same treatment. Iron-clads were trumps, according to Fox."[46]

When the battle of Charleston, which was to be a joint army-navy operation, was about to get under way in April, 1863, Gustavus Fox, the assistant secretary of the navy, was so sure that the ironclads would knock out the forts in Charleston Harbor and render the city helpless that he didn't want to share the

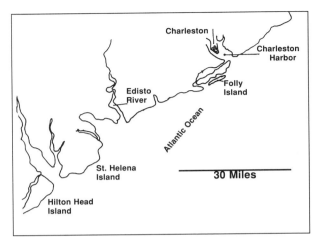

**South Carolina Coast**

glory with the infantry. He warned Admiral DuPont, "I beg of you ... not to let the Army spoil it." Mr. Fox "wanted the show to be all Navy, with the landsmen merely standing by to ... pick up the pieces when the smoke cleared."[47]

Fred Osborne and the Massachusetts 23rd regiment went aboard transports at St. Helena Island on Easter Sunday, April 5, 1863, and moved up the coast to anchor in the mouth of the Edisto River, fifteen miles from Charleston. There they waited to take their part in the upcoming battle.[48]

General Hunter landed 12,000 more men on Folly Island, five miles from Charleston harbor, and waited for the naval bombardment.[49]

On Monday, April 6, the day after Easter, nine brand-new monitors dropped anchor outside of Charleston harbor, ready to "bring their great 15-inch guns to bear on the Confederate forts."[50]

The next day, April 7, 1863, "the iron column started forward, the nine ships moving in single file, slowly and with a certain ponderous majesty ... *Weehawken* in the lead, followed by *Passaic, Montauk, Patapsco, New Ironsides, Catskill, Nantucket, Nahant,* and *Keokuk.* [The column passed] Morris Island in an ominous silence as the rebel cannoneers ... held their fire ... as the ships approached the inner [harbor] ... bands on the parapets [of the forts] struck up patriotic airs — and the guns began to roar."[51]

*Weehawken*, the lead monitor, was "under the muzzles of guns whose projectiles were already hammering [it] like an anvil" when it "spotted a rope obstruction dead ahead ... [and] swung hard to starboard ... to avoid becoming entangled in the web.... The result was that the whole line was thrown into confusion by the abrupt necessity, confronting each ship in rapid sequence, of avoiding a collision with the ship ahead."[52]

All the monitors now began to take a beating. "When the Confederate guns ... were turned upon the iron-clads, the sight was one that no one who witnessed it will ever forget; sublime, infernal, it seemed as if the fires of hell were turned upon the Union fleet," remembered Rear Admiral C.R.P. Rodgers, chief of staff to Admiral DuPont.[53]

"The shots literally rained around [the monitors] splashing the water up thirty feet in the air, and striking and booming from their decks and turrets ... smokestacks perforated, turrets jammed, decks ripped up, guns knocked out of action ... [but] the only effects on the [forts] ... was ... pock marks and discolorations," reported a journalist looking at the forts through his glasses.[54]

At 5 o'clock, after the shore guns had been pounding the monitors for several hours, Admiral DuPont gave the order to retire: "Make signal to the ships to drop out of fire. It is too late to fight this battle tonite. We will renew it in the morning."[55]

But Admiral Dupont found that five of the nine monitors were too badly damaged to fight the next day. The *Keokuk*, for example, was "riddled like a collander, the most severely mauled ship one ever saw."[56] DuPont decided to call a halt, to terminate the attack on Charleston: "We have met with a sad repulse; I shall not turn it into a great disaster."[57]

General Hunter, with his 12,000 men waiting on Folly Island, proposed to Admiral DuPont that the army and the navy establish a beachhead on Morris Island, at the outer edge of Charleston Harbor, and try to attack the city from that position.[58]

But the admiral had to tell General Hunter that the battle of Charleston was over. President Lincoln, he had just heard, had decided that "the opening of the Mississippi River [was now to be] considered the principal objective to be attained.... You are to send all the iron-clads ... immediately to New Orleans.... We cannot clear the Mississippi without the iron-clads."[59]

The battle of Charleston ended thus. Ironclads were no match for the forts on the shore and the infantry never played a part in the battle.

Fred Osborne had spent three months on St. Helena Island to no purpose. We next hear from him when he is back at New Bern.

## CHAPTER ELEVEN

# The Battles of New Bern and Little Washington

## April 1863

Fred was back in New Bern and ill with dysentery. Acquired on tropical St. Helena Island during that futile campaign against Charleston, Fred's dysentery tortured his intestines for the rest of his life. That affliction, that intestinal misery, kept Fred from any career he might have had, indeed from any regular work, in the years after the war.[1] It was a heavy penalty to pay for his willingness to go to war to save the Union.

The Massachusetts 23rd was now off on a new expedition but Fred was left in camp on sick call. The regiment had gone to rescue General Foster, who was besieged by Confederate troops at Washington, North Carolina.

The Confederate army was trying to throw the Union out of North Carolina, and Washington was one of the targets. New Bern had been attacked a month ago while Fred was still on St. Helena Island in this effort to dislodge the Union force.

The Confederate government had developed a sudden fear that Richmond might be attacked by General Foster's army coming up from North Carolina. The Confederates remembered General John Foster and his "smashing attack on Roanoke Island," and worried that he might bring his army north against Richmond.[2]

General James Longstreet, later to become famous at the battle of Gettysburg, was put in charge of the campaign to get General Foster's army out of North Carolina. Longstreet assigned the campaign to eliminate Foster's Union army to General Harvey Hill, who put together a substantial Confederate army of some 20,000 men at Goldsboro.

In March 1863, just before Fred got back from St. Helena Island, Longstreet ordered General Hill to make an attack on New Bern. General Hill told his men: "Soldiers, your brutal and malignant enemy is putting forth efforts unexampled in the history of the world.... He is maddened with the thirst for vengeance.... He is pushing forward to ... plunder your property and lay waste [to] your homes."[3] His army headed for New Bern: "On the evening of March 13 the main body of Hill's command drove in the [Union] pickets.... [The] next morning, the 14th, [the Confederate] army ... attacked a [fort] on the north side of the Neuse [River] opposite the town." When the Union commander

**Confederate General Harvey Hill.**

declined to surrender the fort, "a heavy fire was opened on the fort, which proved quite ineffective, owing ... to his guns and shells working badly.... Union gunboats on the Neuse River soon drove the enemy away."[4]

That was the end of the Confederate attack on New Bern. The historian J. Lewis Stackpole has noted: "The whole affair was weak and ineffective to the last degree. The day was the anniversary of the [Union] taking of the town, and there can be no doubt that Hill seriously hoped to recapture it."[5]

In his next letter Fred mentioned that Confederate attack on New Bern: "the Rebs [had] made an attempt to attack New Berne but a few shells from the gunboats put them to flight." He did not seem to be impressed by their effort.

General Hill was off to a poor start in his campaign but he boasted to Longstreet that he was going to "clean out" North Carolina.[6] His next move was against the Union-held town of Washington, North Carolina.

Fred mentioned the battle of Washington in the two following letters, one to his mother and one to Jennie, both written on the same date.

New Berne

Apr 19th '63

Dear Mother

After three months knocking round in South Carolina we have arrived back just where we started from but are not encamped in the same spot. We are on the fair ground in about the same place we were after the Battle of New Berne.

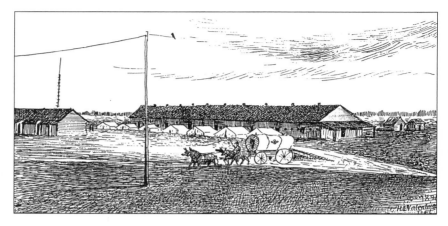

**Barracks occupied by the Massachusetts 23rd Regiment, fair ground, New Bern. Sketch by a soldier in Company F.**

As soon as we got back here or rather the next day the regiment was ordered up the country. The Doctor said that I must stay in camp. I have had the dysentery a short time while we were aboard the transports. There I had no chance to stop it so it got better hold of me than it would if I had been on shore. But I am getting better fast so don't get worried a bit.

We left St Helena Island the fifth of this month and went on transports to Edisto River about fifteen miles from Charleston. We laid there a few days aboard the vessels and then went back to Hilton Head. We went into camp there and staid one day, then packed up, went aboard the transports again and came up to Morehead City where we arrived the 6th and then came on the [railroad] cars to New Berne.

The people were all glad to see us again and cheered us. The regiment marched down to Gen'l Foster's quarters and were cheered by his wife and aides.

The Gen'l had just got out of a scrape up to Washington. The Rebs had him and his force of 1500 men surrounded but didn't like to come in and get him as they had him penned up 15 days and then they lost him after all, for he ran their blockade in a steamer. She has some shot put through her but he got off safely. That is the reason the boys had to go off again so soon. He has sent most of his force up there and if they make a stand there will be some hard fighting.

Last 14th of March, the anniversary of the battle of New Bern, the Rebs made an attempt to attack New Berne but a few shells from the gunboats put them to flight.

The nigs say that the Secesh women in the city were baking and cooking up all their good stuff for the 14th, they were so sure the Rebs would come in.

There is a report around that Jeff Davis made the remark [that] the

Yankees must be cleaned out of N.C. Gen'l Hill says give me 40,000 men and I will do it, so I suppose he has undertaken it for the Rebs are getting very bold.

You must excuse me Mother for not writing more and going into the details but it is very warm and I am not strong enough for my hand trembles so much.

Give Kate my congratulations on the great event of her life and tell her I should like to be there to give them myself. I suppose it will [not] be Kate much longer but Mrs. Burton.

Yours

Fred Osborne

Love to all.

Nate told me to write to him at Indianapolis. I received that letter the night we struck camp at St. Helena. Your letters since then say he has gone to Vicksburg so you must tell me where to direct his mail.

In the regimental history of the Massachusetts 23rd, Dr. Emmerton reported, "Very little of satisfaction or credit accrued to the regiment from its trip to South Carolina."[7] But Fred was not inclined to complain of the fruitless expedition. He also did not complain in his letters about the miseries of life on a barren coastal island, which others described as "three months of idleness much of it spent on the crowded transports.... The life on shore was an alternation of pouring rain and blinding sand-storms, of broiling sun and shivering sea breeze."[8]

The "scrape up to Washington" which General Foster had "just got out of" according to Fred was an adventure that his brother Steve had been a part of. After returning from South Carolina, the "regiment was ordered up the country" as Fred put it, to rescue General Foster, who was under siege at Washington, North Carolina. Steve, in Company G of the Massachusetts 23rd, went on the expedition, while Fred stayed in camp on sick call.

Struggling with his illness, Fred wrote two letters on April 19th, the one we have just seen and one to Jennie:

New Berne

April 19th '63

Dear Jennie

We are back at New Berne again just as you were wishing in one of your letters some time ago. But the boys didn't get much rest out of the transfer from S.C. for they were hurried off up the country the next day after we arrived. I am left behind as you will see by Mothers letter. I should have been well enough to have gone but for living on those transports where I could get nothing to eat, for the disease having nothing to work upon, worked on me and took all my strength away.

The Hunter Expedition against Charleston seems to have been a failure for, just as our Monitors got to work well, Comm[ander] Dupont had orders to draw them off. He wanted to continue the action but his orders wouldn't let him and the Rebs ceased firing at the same moment. This incident makes some think that there is something at the bottom of it which has something to do with a cessation of hostilities but that doesn't seem probable as the war is carried on in this State livelier than ever.

The 24th Mass and 10th Conn are still in S.C. They are in camp at Edisto River, the place where we laid previous to our return to Hilton Head. I hear that they have picquets firing with the Rebs every day. All the troops that Foster carried with him into S.C. have not returned, only the 1st Brigade Gen'l Heckman. The reg'ts are 81st N.Y., 9th N.J., 23rd Mass, 98th N.Y.

After we had sailed from Hilton Head, orders from Hunter to stop us came down to the Dock, but too late, we were gone.

Companies A and K of our regiment were aboard a sailing vessel. They started in tow of a steamer but it was so rough they had to cut loose. The steamer got in soon after we did but the ship was blown off and the two companies didn't get here until yesterday so they didn't go with the expedition (to Washington, N.C.).

A week ago today the 23rd was in camp at Hilton Head. Today they are up somewhere about Washington, N.C. so you can see how quick they get moved round sometimes.

New Berne has been fortified considerably since we left it. The woods have all been cut down on the South side of the Trent River and the camps are all enclosed by breastworks and new batteries have been thrown up and there are huts thrown up that they used last winter instead of tents.

Steve is well and has gone with the regiment. He sent home his money (we were paid at Hilton Head) to the Beverly Bank, $50. I think he told me if I wrote before he did to tell you so that Tuvvy might get it or send for it. He didn't say anything about any receipt so I don't know wether he has got one or whether it can be got without one. I sent mine by the usual way and should have send the check before but couldn't write. It is made out to Father or order but Ov can draw it as well.

Give my love to Aunt Jane and tell her I am ashamed of myself for not asking more about her but I don't hardly know what to say. Now some fellows would fill up six or seven sheets with what they have seen for this three months but I couldn't. I can't write long letters.

Give my love to Father, Mother, Aunt Jane, Mary, Lizzie, Tuvvy, Aunts, Uncles, Cousins and Nieces. Congratulate [word unclear] for me.

Tell Mother to use the money for herself or do what she wants to with it. I received the handk[erchief] and suspenders all right. Geo Wilkins and all the corp are well and send their respects.

I cannot send as much money as Steve for he lives on soldiers fare and I indulge in some extras which he gets along without.

Nate's advice is very good but no more than I should know enough to do myself.

Yours,

Fred.

Fred had the impression that Admiral DuPont was ordered to stop his attack on Charleston, and he related this order to a hopeful rumor that the war might be ending. The historical fact is that Admiral DuPont decided to stop the fight because his ironclads were badly damaged.[9]

The 24th Massachusetts and 10th Connecticut were still in South Carolina, as Fred reported, because General David Hunter had wrested them away from General Foster. General Hunter had tried to take over General Foster's regiments when they came to South Carolina for the battle of Charleston. When Foster objected, Hunter wrote to the War Department in Washington: "The conduct of General Foster ... [was] disrespectful and insubordinate and tending to incite mutiny." He threatened to arrest Foster.[10]

The War Department stopped Hunter from arresting Foster but did little else. The historian J. Lewis Stackpole wrote: "In General Foster's conduct there [was nothing] to blame or criticise.... The mistake the War Department made was in not turning Hunter out and putting Foster in his place. Hunter remained."[11]

Hunter kept those two regiments, the 24th Massachusetts and 10th Connecticut, of Foster's brigade, not allowing them to return to New Bern. Fred's regiment feared that Hunter might also keep it in South Carolina. The regimental historian wrote, "[The prospect that] we might ... be transferred to [General Hunter] ... hung over us all the time." When they left the dock for North Carolina, "thinking that General Hunter might ... countermand [our] departure ... [our commanding officer] ordered all steam ahead.... A steamboat did pursue us for that purpose."[12] But, as Fred wrote, "too late, we were gone." General Hunter was relieved of his command two months later.[13]

One letter from Stephen Osborne was found among Fred's letters. It discusses activities of this time, late April 1863, and is presented here. Steve, in Company G of Fred's regiment, recounts going on the expedition to rescue General Foster, who was besieged at Washington, North Carolina. General Foster had rushed up to Little Washington (so-called to distinguish it from Washington, D.C.) on March 30, 1863, to fend off the attack by General Harvey Hill. After the battle of New Bern, General Hill had moved his army to Little Washington, the next objective in his campaign to "clean out" North Carolina.

Foster had 1100 men at Little Washington; Hill had 14,000. General Hill "erected batteries [of cannon] up and down the river ... and made a thorough blockade.... General Foster ... strengthened the fortifications and erect[ed] new ones.... His troops worked like beavers." wrote historian J. Lewis Stackpole.[14]

"[General] Hill summoned the town to surrender.... Foster sent back word: 'if they want Washington, come and take it!' The siege continued for a fortnight."[15]

General Foster sent to New Bern for a relief expedition. As Stackpole points out, however, in New Bern: "the management of affairs might fitly be termed ludicrous.... General Prince ... [was] designated to take command of the relieving column.... [He] took [a] steamer to the mouth of the river, looked at the [Confederate] battery, thought it was too strong, became sick at his stomach ... and returned to Newbern.... [Inexperienced] General Spinola ... was ... [then put in command] of the expedition.... So, to the surprise of every enlisted man in the Department ... Frank Spinola, who up to this time 'had never set a squadron in field nor the division of a battle knew' went out to the relief of Washington."[16]

Steve wrote to his mother about that expedition:

> Carolina City, N. Carolina
>
> May 13 1863
>
> Dear Mother:
>
> You have written twenty letters to me, while I have sent but eleven to you. By my memorandum book, the last one of the eleven was sent Feb. 21, from St. Helena Island, S. C. The letter previous to this, was sent from the ship J. Morton; and the one before the last above, from Camp Pendleton. It is my impression that you never received the ninth and tenth. The tenth acknowledged the receipt of the new year's present; and the other contained an account of our first two expeditions. This filled 22 pages, and would have been longer but our departure from Camp Pendelton forced me to give it an abrupt conclusion.
>
> Fred, in his letter to you a few days ago, mentioned that I had sent $50.00 to the Beverly Bank, I would rather have sent it directly to Salem; but it was difficult to do so at that time. Orville would do me a great favor by doing such an errand as he did on a former occasion. It was necessary for me to make the money payable to some one; therefore I used his name.
>
> A sudden stop was put to the expedition to Charleston, partly caused, it was said, by the disagreement of Hunter and Dupont; but the true reason was, no doubt, the force was too small to attack a place of such strength. I think that you are not the only one who believes it strange that this effort was so disproportioned to the end which was in view.
>
> We left the vessels, stopped a day or two at Hilton Head, then went to Newbern, and were once more placed under the command of Gen. Foster. A day and night only were spent in camp, after this, the 23d., with others, received marching orders. They left Newbern, went up the Neuse, landed on the opposite side of the river. After a halt of about an hour and a half, the march was commenced. The roads, as usual, were miserable; but the men pressed on till evening, and then went into bivouac.
>
> On the next morning, the troops moved forward upon the road towards Washington, N.C. They marched all day and stopped at night on and

around a farm on the Washington road. Places from which rebel soldiers had been driven were passed during the day, but the enemy were far off; and the evidences of a precipitate departure were scattered around.

I was called up in the night, and went out, with others, as scouts. The guide of the party was not well informed; he missed his way, and led the men five or six miles in a wrong direction. We traveled about all night, up hills and down hollows; among stumps, pits and gullies; through clay mud and water; but no enemy was seen, and no satisfactory information was obtained.

At daylight, the party retraced their steps and waited in the road for their regiment to come up. By sunrise the column was seen advancing up the road; and the scouts fell into the ranks.

The troops advanced towards Washington; but were soon ordered to countermarch; they went back, countermarched again, made several halts, formed a line of battle once; and were finally ordered to rest in the woods. The 23d. were placed near the 9th New Jersey. There they staid till the next afternoon, when they went on board the steamer Phoenix, for Newbern.

The 23d. arrived in Newbern at 10 o'clock on the next night. They staid there but three days and are now at "Camp Dale," on the same ground that they occupied on January last.

We are resting here, but do not know whether the rest will be of long or short duration.

Fred and I are well. I received your letters of Apr. 7 and May 3.

From S. H. O. (Stephen H. Osborne)

The siege of Washington continued. General Foster finally decided that he must escape and head up a relief column himself. Historian Stackpole reports: "At daybreak on [April] 14th, General Foster ... ran the [Confederate] batteries [on the river banks], the Steamer *Escort* which carried him being struck by artillery 47 times and her pilot, Padrick, killed by a rifle shot."[17] Fred mentioned that incident in his letter to his mother, saying, "The Gen'l got out of a scrape up to Washington.... The Rebs had him ... and then they lost him ... for he ran their blockade in a steamer."

At about this time the siege ended when Hill withdrew his 14,000 men, "General Hill never once tried an assault ... [because of] the unwillingness of his men [to attack Foster's] fortifications."[18] The battle of Little Washington was over.

In their letters, Steve and Fred treated their mother as an intelligent and respected confidant. Steve agreed with his mother's opinion that the Union force was too small for the attack on Charleston. Fred assumed in his letters that his mother readily understood what he was describing; there was never a "you wouldn't understand what we men are going through" coloration. Mary Osborne was a strong, knowledgeable, perhaps adventurous, woman. She had come over from England, where her father had been an English sea captain.[19] A sea captain of her father's time, in the age of sail, lived an exotic life of constant danger.

Growing up in that seafaring tradition, Mary Osborne could understand and appreciate the hazardous lives of her sons: James a mariner and Nate, Steve, and Fred in the war.

In Fred's next letter, we begin to see a longing for home and talk about a furlough. His letters, once energetic and sparkling, became a little ragged; he was wearing down. We have just seen in Steve's letter that energy and enthusiasm we once saw in Fred's writing in the early part of the war.

But Steve was sixteen years older than Fred and a soldier for less than a year; his trials were yet to come. Wounded in battle, he would spend painful months in hospitals, and he would be captured by the enemy and see the inside of a Confederate prison. Steve also became worn down by the war.

## May, 1863

Fred had seen a year and a half of camps and battles and was burdened with sickness and longing for home. Victory seemed a long way off.

The war was not going anywhere. In the two years since it started, the Union armies had made almost no progress against the Confederacy and had taken very little Confederate territory. The soldiers saw no prospect of victory, of going home.

Fred was irritable and out of patience. His testiness showed in his next letter, written from camp at Carolina City, North Carolina. On arrival at the "City," the soldiers found "three houses and a barn," not the exciting metropolis "engendered by its name."[20] A coastal town near Morehead City, it was a jumping-off point for troop movements by water. The Massachusetts 23rd regiment was waiting here, ready to be sent off to some trouble spot.

> Carolina City
> May 7th, 1863
> Dear Mother
>
> You write about my getting a furlough. In the first place I am well again and then I should as soon think of shooting myself as ask for one. If a man is to have a furlough he has nothing to say about it. The surgeons manage that, and if a man asked for one, if he was dying they would put him on duty saying that he was playing it to get home.
>
> I am afraid, Mother, you think that asking for a thing [means] getting it. A private is a dog, plenty of kicks and cuffs. If they would give us more of what belongs to us and less of what doesn't we should do very well.
>
> This is the second time you have written about a furlough. Don't write again about it. It shows you at home have no conception of the petty games that are played to cheat the private out of his dues. If a man asked for a furlough, they would think he was insane and then I wasn't so very sick after all. You mustn't worry so.

**Company F Quarters, Camp Dale, Carolina City. From a sketch by a Company F soldier.**

I saw by a paper the other day that Nate's reg't had been into it but it must have been before he reached it as the paper [is dated] April 7th.

Why don't the girls write? I havn't had hardly any letters except from you and Steve hasn't had any for two or three months.

I see by the papers that most of the two years troops' time is out. There are thirty odd regts from N.Y. that will go home this month and next. The government doesn't seem to take any measures to fill their places.

The Hawkins Zouaves who came out with us in the old Burnside Expedition have been mustered out. They had only about 176 men [out of an original complement of 1000] for duty.

Orders were read to us on parade tonight to the effect that every box and package belonging to an enlisted man shall be opened and searched before it comes into his hands. I suppose it is to prevent liquor being brought into camp.

And our drill tactics are to be changed. We are to adopt Casey's method, also that the brigade shall drill skirmishing particularly. So I suppose we will lie inactive [for] some time.

Capt. Whipple has resigned and is probably home by this time. It was on account of ill health.

You must excuse this letter Mother but I don't like to have you worry so much.

I wish you would send me 3 yds of silicia to line a pair of pants for it is getting so warm that I shall soon have to leave off underclothes and the pants are coarse and rough.

Tell the girls to write. Next time I will try to write a more agreeable one. Do write to Steve and I will see that [he] answers them. Direct to Newbern, Camp Dale.

My shoes that I sent home so long ago will get there soon I suppose. The box has been in Newbern all the time that we were down [in] S.C. One of the boys found [it] at Newbern and started it off. Tuvvy can carry the shoe that is hurt to Rice and see if he can fix it. If he can, you may send them to me again. If not, they are good for nothing.

Give my love to Father, Aunt Jane, Mary, Lizzie, Jennie, Tuvvy, Caddie, Hannah Lee, Hattie, Ruthelia, Aunts, Uncles and friends.

Have you received the check for the money? I sent it in Jennie's letter I think and Steve's, I wrote you about.

Yours,

F M Osborne

Fred displayed irritation in this letter to his mother, the one instance in all of his letters when his distress and frustration betrayed him, allowing regrettable comments to escape into his letter.

Fred's comment that "our drill tactics are to be changed" reflected the new thinking in military circles on the best way to use infantry.[21] Instead of massed troops, a more flexible style was emerging using "skirmishers" as a part of the main attack plan. Fred wrote, "We are to adopt Casey's method." "Casey" was Brigadier-General Silas Casey whose book, *Infantry Tactics for the Instruction, Exercise, and Manoeuvres of the Soldier, a Company, Line of Skirmishes, Battalion, Brigade, or Corps d'Armée*, had just been approved by President Lincoln and his secretary of war for use by Union troops.[22]

General Casey recommended that two out of the ten companies in a regiment should be assigned as skirmishers: "picked men, possessing the highest qualifications, marksmen as well ... shall be used as skirmishers."[23] The elite youths, the best, would go first into battle.

Fred commented on the resignation of Captain George Whipple, who had been the commanding officer of Company F since its inception as the Union Drill Club of Salem. An older man, he was warmly regarded by the men in his company.

When Captain Whipple left North Carolina he took home a dog which had an unusual history. In this somewhat informal war, the commissary of Company F had brought his dog to war with him. Herbert Valentine, the Company F historian, wrote: "Curly, Commissary Chapple's dog, ... attracted much attention as, covered by her red blanket, she marched demurely by her master's side on the way through Boston and New York."

According to Valentine, in North Carolina "Curly strayed away into the rebel lines and was gone several weeks.... One day word came in from the rebels that a dog with the name of 'Chapple' on the collar was in their possession, and they were willing to exchange her for some tobacco." The trade was made, and

Curly was restored to Commissary Chapple. "Twelve pups [were] born to her on the night before the battle of Roanoke Island. Captain Whipple took one of Curly's pups home with him in 1863, calling him 'Roanoke.' Curly followed the fortunes of F for three years and lived some time after the war."[24]

The "silicia" in Fred's request to his mother for "3 yds of silicia to line a pair of pants" was likely a misspelling of "Silesia," which was a thin linen cloth of a type once made in Silesia that was used for lining clothes.[25]

Two weeks later Fred wrote again from Carolina City:

Camp Carolina City

May 22

Dear Mother

There is nothing going on here at all. We lay in the tents nearly all day as it is getting very warm. The reveille is beaten earlier now than before and we have a drill before breakfast soon after sunrise, and another and dress parade towards night so that we don't have to be out in the sun so much as before.

Our [Company F] chaplain is [now] with the regiment and holds services every Sunday.

Lt. Woodbury of Co. G will be back from Massachusetts next week and it is reported he is to be our Captain.

Elwell has got the Colonelcy at last and Chambers the Lt Colonelcy. Chambers has gone home on a furlough.

I wish you would buy for me the three volumes of Casey's Tactics. It is a new work and is to be adopted throughout the army. They are small books. You can send them to me in any way you think the best. Mail would be the quicker but I suppose it would cost considerable but you can send them any way you think the best.

I got your paper by the last mail but no letter.

Have you heard from Nate lately?

Hooker hasn't done any better than any of the rest and I suppose he will be superseded.

Give my love to Father, Aunt Jane, Mary, Lizzie, Jennie, Tuvvy, Caddie, Ruthelia, Hannah Lee, Hattie, Aunts, Uncles, and friends.

You must excuse this short letter but I cannot find anything to write about.

Geo Wilkins, Howard Hamblet and the rest of the boys are well and send their respects.

Has anything turned up yet in regard to Nate's effort for me?

I see by the paper that Father is one of the gentlemen in the Harbor Defence committee, I think it is called.

Steve is well and sends his love.

F M Osborne

Mother, will you send me some Postage stamps? I am nearly out again.

Be sure and get the right tactics. It's Casey's that I want.

May 23rd I received yours and Jennies letters.

Today there has been some talk about furloughs but there hasn't been anything yet.

I am glad that Nate thinks so much about me. Coffee without milk being a deprivation to him, coffee with milk is a luxury to me. Generally speaking a commissioned officer lives as well as at home.

I can write no more.

F Osborne.

A long-running competition, mentioned in Fred's January 4, 1863, letter, had by this point ended with Andrew Elwell getting the command of the Massachusetts 23rd regiment and John Chambers taking second place. Andrew Elwell, a clothier in civilian life, was a major in the original 23rd Massachusetts regiment. John Chambers, who had been a printer in civilian life, was adjutant in the original regiment; he died of battle wounds a year later.[26]

The "Casey's Tactics" that Fred requested from his mother was a soldier's manual based on French army practice. In fact, the standard U.S. Army infantry manual had been, up until Casey's manual was approved, an English translation of a French manual on infantry practices.[27] Both Union and Confederate armies were quite dependent on European military methods in the Civil War, which may explain the brutal use of foot soldiers against heavy artillery.

Casey's *Infantry Tactics* taught soldiers the detailed particulars of every movement on the parade ground and on the battlefield. As a case in point, Casey taught the loading and firing of the muzzle-loading rifle: seventy-three different movements which had to be repeated for every shot. Standing in full exposure to enemy fire as he made these seventy-three motions to reload his rifle, the young soldier had to demonstrate steady nerves and courage to a remarkable degree.

A training manual was definitely needed, because infantry soldiers received little training in the Civil War. There were very few professional officers to do the training. Most officers were amateurs because only 440 West Point graduates were available to the Union army,[28] and there was little organized effort to prepare these amateur officers to train the soldiers. They pretty much had to prepare themselves: "These amateur officers ... spent hours pouring over ... the tactical manuals ... emerging from their tents to try to transfer paper precepts to the parade ground."[29]

Historian Russell Weigley has written: "The shortcomings of training no doubt help explain high casualty rates in the early battles of the War. Soldiers ... learned little but parade-ground drill.... Regiments frequently lost fifty per cent in one battle and occasionally more than eighty per cent."[30] We have seen that Fred's letters mention almost nothing about rifle training. As late in the war as April 1864, Major General George Meade, commander of the Army of the Potomac, paid belated attention to shooting skills. He issued an order authorizing the expenditure of only ten bullets per man to teach the men to use their rifles.[31]

Fighting Joe Hooker, who was championed by Fred in his letter of March 24, 1863, has lost his lustre: "Hooker hasn't done any better than any of the rest and I suppose he will be superseded." General Hooker, President Lincoln's choice to replace Burnside as the head of the Army of the Potomac, was arrogant, as this quotation shows: "My plans are perfect. May God have mercy on General Lee, for I will have none."[32] But in Hooker's first fight, the battle of Chancellorsville, May 2, 1863, Lee outgeneralled him in style. The Union lost, 16,792 killed and wounded. Hooker was replaced six weeks later.[33]

Fred's inquiry, "Has anything turned up yet in regard to Nate's effort for me?" indicates that Nate was looking for a special place in the regular army for Fred; the historical record does not reveal the particulars of this expectation by Fred. But what could Fred have been looking for in some other military situation? Only relief, it would seem, from his present life, from near despair about where he was and what he was doing.

A month passed before Fred wrote again to his mother. His regiment was still in the same place, still waiting.

## CHAPTER TWELVE

# Better Times

### Early summer, 1863

The Union was about to enjoy two badly needed victories: Vicksburg and Gettysburg.

Nate was in the fighting at Vicksburg. Almost impregnable, Vicksburg was situated on high cliffs overlooking the Mississippi River and was protected by extensive fortifications, but President Lincoln had given General Ulysses S. Grant the difficult assignment of taking Vicksburg.

The capture of that city had been General Grant's objective for an extended time. Beginning in late 1862, Grant had made a number of false starts, trying to get his army into a favorable position to attack the highly fortified city. Now, in April 1863, his army was still hovering around the city without making an attack.

The public and the press were becoming critical of Grant: "He had apparently wasted ... months in futile and fanciful attempts to find the magic key to Vicksburg's defences," according to historian Peter J. Parish.[1] "Newspaper reporters with the army wrote dismal stories [about Grant's efforts].... President Lincoln was under great pressure to remove [him]," wrote another historian.[2]

Grant finally settled on bringing his army down the west side of the river, crossing at Grand Gulf, and coming at Vicksburg from the east. His army was now at Millikens's Bend on the Mississippi River above Vicksburg, where it had been for some time waiting for a definitive move on Vicksburg.

Nate, in the 13th Infantry regiment of General Sherman's Fifteenth Corps, was involved in a feint at the Confederate stronghold at Haines Bluff to draw off Confederate forces while Grant's army was crossing the river at Grand Gulf. In Nate's military records, we have his statement that "My first participation in Active Operations [on rejoining his regiment after his sick leave] was in command of 'H'

142

Company, 1st Battalion, 13th Infantry, when 15th Army Corps, to which the Battalion was attached, moved up the Yazoo and made a feint against Haines Bluff at the end of April 1863 simultaneously with General Grant's movement on Grand Gulf."[3]

Sherman, in his memoirs, recalled:

> [Grant] proposed to cross over ... [at] Grand Gulf ... and he thought I could put in my time usefully by making a "feint" on Haines Bluff.... Of course I answered him that I would make the feint ... and I did make it most effectually ... [moving up the Yazoo River in] all the old boats I could get [good boats were reserved for Grant's crossing at Grand Gulf], taking ten small regiments [including Nate's 13th Infantry] ... to make a show of force [at Haines Bluff].... We afterward learned that [the Confederate general] Pemberton ... had previously dispatched a large force ... to Grand Gulf ... when he discovered our ostentatious movement up the Yazoo, and recalled his men, and sent them up to Haine's Bluff to meet us.... [These] troops ... marched sixty miles without rest ... [and arrived] completely fagged out.... This diversion ... completely fulfilled its purpose ... leaving Grant to contend with ... [only] a minor force ... [at] Grand Gulf.[4]

Grant took his army — except for Sherman's Fifteenth Corps which was feinting at Haines Bluff—fifty miles down the west side of the Mississippi and across the river at Grand Gulf on May 1, 1863.[5] Six days later Sherman's Fifteenth Corps followed behind Grant down the west side of the river and, on May 7, 1863, crossed at Grand Gulf.[6]

Now that he was across the river, Grant's strategy was to eliminate all Confederate armies which could support Vicksburg from the east and to control all the roads and railroads out of Vicksburg. With the Mississippi River controlled above and below Vicksburg by the Union navy, Grant would then have the city completely in his grip. His first big target was Jackson, Mississippi, sixty miles away, a regional railroad center which delivered supplies to Vicksburg.

Grant's army left Grand Gulf on its way to Jackson, Grant and Sherman traveling together. They arrived at the outskirts of Jackson on May 14 and got into a fire fight with rebel troops guarding that city. The rebels retreated, leaving Jackson to Grant's men.

While Sherman spent the next two days tearing up railroad tracks and destroying an arsenal, a foundry, and a cotton mill, Grant [on May 16] borrowed a division (which included Nate's regiment) from Sherman and headed for Champion Hills, twenty miles away, where a battle was underway. The rebels were beaten at Champion Hills and withdrew toward Vicksburg. Grant's army followed, driving the rebel army ahead of it.

Nate's regiment rejoined Sherman's corps, which reached the Big Black River on May 17 and found rebels on the other side of the river, firing at them. A battalion, probably including Nate's company, jumped on some artillery horses,

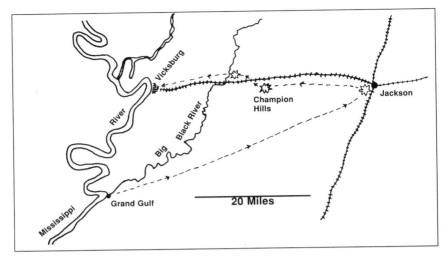

**Movement of Grant's Army, May 1863**

swam the river, drove the rebels away, and built a pontoon bridge for the rest of Sherman's corps to cross the river.[7]

Sherman reached Vicksburg on May 18. In the synopsis of his career found in his military file, Nate wrote: "We stood before the defenses of Vicksburg on the evening of the 18th of May, 1863.... I was in the assault on the defenses of Vicksburg on the 19th of May, 1863 and in the skirmishing and night advance to determine the strength and preparation of the enemy."[8]

Grant's army found the Vicksburg fortifications too strong to assault successfully. Grant set up a siege, cutting off rebel soldiers and private citizens of Vicksburg from access to the Mississippi River or to any roads leading out of the city. General Sherman said in his memoirs: "By May 31st the city of Vicksburg was completely beleaguered.... The fate of ... Vicksburg was merely a question of time."[9] Grant's army waited for the city to surrender all through the month of June 1863.

Fred wrote to his mother in late June:

> Carolina City
>
> June 19th, 63
>
> Dear Mother
>
> I received a letter from you the night before last and have just got time to answer. I suppose you are about tired of waiting to hear from me. I havn't written for some time.
>
> Nate had a rough time for the first battle. I should have liked to [have] seen Nate's letter. I could then tell what kind of a place he got into. From your account I should think whoever sent him ahead so without any support

didn't know much. I am glad he got out of it without losing any more than he did. I should think that he got into a very tight place.

He cannot sympathize with me in everything, Mother. If it is ever his fortune to get in as I do, with forty ounces of lead dragging down one shoulder, and four or five pounds of hard tack on the other, a pack on his back of overcoats and blankets, then he can, but as long as he wears a sword he never will.

You needn't write him this but as a general thing officers have but little thought for their men. The fighting isn't the worst of this. The hard marches, the starvation, [the] bad usage are all to be thought of when anybody wants to sympathize with a private. I don't [know] as it is right in me to write this, but I am afraid Nate is like most [of] them. His men are things.

We are having much better times now than we ever had. Our new Captain has drawn all the back ration money, and we have salt fish and potatoes, cheese, pickles, flour, and each has had tobacco, note paper and envelopes, blacking for every tent, white gloves for all the men, and he buys things right along.

We are to have plum duff for dinner today. It is the first pudding I have seen since I left home excepting the thankgiving dinners and pay-days when the tents crew put in and we have one good meal always.

How much of the ration money should we have seen if such officers as we have had all along had drawn it? Each man would have had a sheet of emery paper and perhaps a box of blacking to a tent and perhaps not so much.

He is a gentleman and has won the respect of the men.

If Hayward had drawn that money it would have furnished his table instead of ours. That is saying a good deal but I believe it.

Now today some of the boys are stockading the Captain's tent. He had ale and lemonade for them. Some people would say that he set a bad example, but all is if anybody didn't want it they could leave it alone and some of the boys have orders from the doctor to drink ale. A private cannot get it without an order. Almost anything is better than some of the water out here.

Send my love to Nate and I congratulate him on his luck in getting out safe.

Love to Father, Aunt Jane, Mary, Lizzie, Jennie, Tuvvy, Caddie, Ruthelia, Hannah Lee, Hattie, Aunts, Uncles and Mrs Burton.

Yours,

F M Osborne

The furloughs have been drawn again and I didn't get one.

I have got my books.

Tear this up. This letter is letting off some of the mad that I have had pent up. I have let off too much lately. In my last letter I am afraid you will think I am getting downhearted.

Steve is well.

Fred was critical of Nate's superiors who, he deduced from his mother's letter, didn't support him properly in a battle. Fred was right in his assessment. The battle in question was the assault on the rebel defenses at Vicksburg on May 19, 1863. The 1st Battalion, 13th U.S. Infantry, was assigned to make the assault, and Nate was the commanding officer of one of the seven companies which made up the 1st Battalion.[10] General Sherman, in his memoirs, describes that battle:

> General Grant believed that the morale of the Confederates had been so severely shaken by the battles at Champion Hills and [at] ... Big Black [River] that ... on the 19th he ordered an assault made at two o'clock in the afternoon. This was a direct frontal attack on intrenched Americans, hence the hardest task ever set for men to do.... At the appointed signal the line advanced.... My troops reached the top of the parapet, but could not cross over. The rebel parapets were strongly manned, and the enemy fought hard and well.... My loss was pretty heavy ... falling chiefly on the Thirteenth Regulars [Nate's battalion].... We, however, held the ground.... The battalion lost 77 men out of 250 engaged.[11]

A soldier of Nate's battalion who was in the assault wrote:

> In our minds the picture of that desperate assault is more deeply engraven than any other event in our eventful lives.... The hill-sides were so irregular ... gullies and ravines ... [that it was] impossible to preserve ... a line of battle.... [We were] exposed to a ... sweeping fire of artillery and musket ... but the flag steadily advanced, and each man ... strove to keep within its shadow.... Amid exploding shells, and ... grape and canister, the little band made its way. No sooner did the flag go down with one of its bearers than it was seized and borne ... onward by another. Rapidly the ranks were depleted, until ten, twenty, forty per cent of the whole battalion had fallen; still no order came to halt, and the broken column pressed bravely onward. Not more hopeless was the Charge of the Light Brigade....
>
> Regiments to the right and left, composed of troops as heroic as any the war produced, unwilling to breast the deadly leaden storm, stopped and took ... shelter ... but the flag of the Thirteenth steadily moved onward and upward; nor did it halt until it floated from the rebel parapet.[12]

At the rebel parapet, the battalion was not supported, according to another member of the battalion: "Our colors were the first and only ones planted on the rebel works, but we could do nothing as the other regiments would not follow."[13] In his letter to his mother, Fred said: "Send my love to Nate and I congratulate him on his luck in getting out safe." Nate was indeed lucky to survive that slaughter.

Captain Nathan W. Osborne was honored by a promotion to Brevet Major for "Gallant and Meritorious Service in the Siege of Vicksburg."[14] "Brevet" was a title "conferred by the President of the United States by and with the consent of the Senate for distinguished conduct ... in the presence of the enemy."[15] Nate had brought honor to the Osborne family for his heroism in one of the most famous Civil War battles.

The next day Grant withdrew his men from the rebel defenses and began the long siege of Vicksburg. But the assault on the rebel fortification at Vicksburg lives on in the memories and glories of the 13th U.S. Infantry. A military board "after careful examination ... of the evidence ... decided unanimously ... the Regiment ... shall have inscribed on its banner, FIRST AT VICKSBURG.... The board find the Thirteenth U.S. Infantry entitled to the 'First Honor at Vicksburg,' having ... planted and maintained its colors on the Parapet, with a loss of 43 per cent ... its conduct and loss ... unequalled in the Army."[16]

Fred was delighted with the new captain of his regiment, Henry Woodbury, who was promoted to captain and commanding officer of Company F on May 8, 1863. Captain Woodbury took over the responsibility for company supplies from Lieutenant Charles Hayward, who had clearly frustrated Fred. Lieutenant Hayward had been sent to Morehead City to supervise the building of fortifications in early June 1863.[17] In August, 1863, he got the choice job of recruiting in Massachusetts, although it turned out to be less than fun when he had to deal with recruits who were "nearly all ... bounty jumpers of the most objectionable type."[18] Captain Woodbury was a shoemaker before the war; he would make a praiseworthy record as a leader in battles to come, including the bloody affair at Cold Harbor where he was wounded.[19]

Fred mentioned that some of the men were "stockading" the captain's tent; this was a procedure to reinforce a tent with wooden stakes.[20]

Carolina City

July 1st 63

Dear Jennie

This is probably my last day in this camp as there are orders for five companies to report to Little Washington and F is one of them.

The story is that we start tomorrow. We don't know yet wether the other companies will stop here or not.

Most of the nine months troops have left New Berne for Fortress Monroe. Three companies of the 8th are at Morehead waiting for transportation. I saw Capt Kenny this morning. He was in the [railroad] cars bound for New Berne. I didn't have time to say anything to him.

Genl Lee has been getting up quite an excitement by his raid into Maryland and Pennsylvania.

It stirred up the people some by the way Old Abe called for more troops.

You must send all the pictures you can get hold of. Perhaps it will be some time before I get home and you will get tired of waiting so you had better send what you can.

This letter I send by Corporal Woodbury who is coming home on a furlough. He wanted one so I wrote this. You must excuse the shortness.

I guess he can give you a good description of me. You seem to want a minute one.

Love to Father, Mother, Aunt Jane, Mary, Lizzie, Tuvvy, Caddie, Ettie, Aunts, Uncles, Cousins, and Friends and Mrs Burton.

Tell Tuvvy to send me out a slouched hat by this Corporal, that is if he has a good chance. Tell him to send a good light one in weight and one that will wear and put two pair of home knit socks in it.

Yours.

F M Osborne

Don't let Father pick out the hat. Let Tuvvy get one to suit him and I guess it will me. Direct to New Berne as before. Make the package small as possible, if too large omit the slouched hat.

I suppose the Corporal wanted to see you as much as anything else. You have had one [soldier] already to see you.

Please send 2½ yds of the same kind of Silica as before for another pair of pants as one pair of mine gave out suddenly. Send it by the Corporal with the other things.

I suppose you think I am old ladyish having my pants lined.

The proud display of pictures of his sister Jennie had, it seems, stimulated romantic thoughts among some of his soldier friends. Corporal Josiah Woodbury had been a Salem leather worker in civilian life and had been a member of the Salem Drill Club along with Fred. Five years older than Fred, he was three years older than Jennie. Corporal Woodbury was apparently not related to Captain Henry Woodbury, the new commander of Company F.

Despite these romantic events, Jennie, when the war ended, married a boy from her neighborhood, David Saunders, who lived on the next street when they were growing up.[21]

In this letter to Jennie, Fred mentioned her desire to know what he looked like at that point. Fred had been gone from home for two years, time for the memory to fade, for the details of a loved one's appearance to become uncertain. Always close but now separated by the war, Jennie and Fred were changing, maturing, becoming young adults. Jennie had seen her brother leave home a boy of sixteen. She must have wondered how he had changed, now a young man of eighteen, marked by privation and killing.

Photographs were hugely important to soldiers and to family members left behind to refresh fading memories and to keep up with changes in the teenagers who became soldiers and in the siblings back home. These were the big years in their lives, when they began to know who they were and what they could do. Remote from their families, from the usual support and care, they needed the comfort that photographs could give them.

Fred's request for a slouched hat probably reflected his wish to copy General Burnside's famous hat style.

Fred's comment about people being stirred up by Lincoln's call for more troops noted the public reaction against the draft, the Conscription Act of March 1863. The draft was not popular; there were protest meetings and riots in many parts of the Union, as historian Shelby Foote notes: "This rash of draft disturbances ... broke out in the ... summer [of 1863] ... [in] Boston and Newark ... Albany ... New York, and ... Pennsylvania ... New Hampshire ... Milwaukee. By far the greatest ... [riot] was the one that exploded in New York City.... Lincoln [sent] troops ... to deal with the situation.... Streets were swept by grape[shot] ... houses were stormed at the point of the bayonet ... [until] the miserable wretches ... confessed the power of the law."[22]

Fred's expectation that Company F would be ordered to report to Little Washington was not borne out. The Massachusetts 23rd regiment was ordered to return to New Bern on July 2, 1863.[23]

## July 1863

Fred Osborne was in camp in New Bern waiting for action. He would soon hear the great news of Union victories at Vicksburg and at Gettysburg. Sherman would call the victory at Vicksburg in which Fred's brother Nate figured "the most important enterprise of the civil war."

The siege of Vicksburg ended on July 4, 1863, with the surrender of that city by the rebels. In his memoirs, General Grant recalls that on July 3

> About 10 o'clock A.M. white flags appeared on ... the rebel [earth]works....
> Soon two persons were seen coming toward our lines bearing a white flag....
> It was a glorious sight to officers and soldiers ... and the news soon spread....
> The troops felt that their long and weary marches, hard fighting, ceaseless watching by night and day, exposure to all sorts of weather ... and, worst of all, to gibes of many Northern papers that came to them saying all their suffering was in vain, that Vicksburg would never be taken, were at last at [an] end and the Union sure to be saved.[24]

On the afternoon of July 3, Grant worked out the terms of surrender with the Confederate general behind the parapets; the terms were unconditional surrender, similar to terms Grant would eventually get, after many hard months, from General Robert E. Lee at Appomattox Court House.

According to General Grant, on the next day, the Fourth of July, "at the appointed hour the [rebel] garrison of Vicksburg marched out of their [earth]works and formed a line ... [and] stacked arms.... Our whole army ... witnessed this scene without cheering.... The two armies began to fraternize.... I myself saw our men taking bread from their haversacks and giving it to the enemy they had so recently been engaged in starving out."[25]

General Sherman wrote in his memoirs:

> The campaign of Vicksburg, in its conception and execution, belonged exclusively to Grant. His success at Vicksburg justly gave him great fame at home and abroad. The President conferred on him the rank of major-general ... the highest grade then existing. After the fall of Vicksburg ... the Mississippi River was wholly in the possession of the Union forces, and formed a perfect line of separation [of the Confederacy]. Thenceforth, they could not cross it save by stealth and the military affairs on its west bank became unimportant.[26]

The Vicksburg campaign was, according to Sherman, "probably the most important enterprise of the civil war — [resulting in] ... complete control of the Mississippi River, from its source to its mouth — or, in the language of Mr. Lincoln, the Mississippi went 'unvexed to the sea.'"[27]

After the city surrendered, General Joseph E. Johnston's Confederate army still had to be dealt with. Johnston's army, a few miles to the east at Big Black River, had been a threat to the rear of Grant's army as it gripped the city.[28] Grant had expected Johnston to try to lift the siege of Vicksburg, as he recalls in his memoirs: "[In late June] positive information was received that Johnston had crossed the Big Black River for the purpose of attacking our rear, to raise the siege."[29]

Grant respected Joe Johnston, who was later recognized as one of the South's best generals. Grant told Sherman that Johnston was the only Confederate general that he feared.[30] It turned out that Johnston had already given up on Vicksburg, and he did not make an attack.[31]

Immediately after the city capitulated, Grant recalls, "I notified Sherman ... to take the offensive against Johnston ... to drive the enemy from the state."[32] General Sherman proceeded at once to move against Johnston.

In his career summary in his military file, Nate wrote: "[After] the surrender on July 4th, 1863 I moved with Gen'l Sherman's command upon the Confederate Commander Joseph E. Johnston and joined the pursuit beyond Pearl River after the bombardment and evacuation of Jackson Heights."[33]

On July 5, the day after Vicksburg surrendered, Sherman started the march against Johnston. Johnston withdrew from the Big Black River and "was in full retreat for Jackson"; over the next several days, Sherman's army followed Johnston toward Jackson. General Sherman wrote: "The weather was fearfully hot.... Johnston ... had caused cattle, hogs, and sheep to be driven into the ponds of water, and there shot down ... dead and stinking carcasses [spoiling the water]."[34]

By July 11, Johnston was bottled up in Jackson. According to Sherman: "We pressed close in and shelled the town from every direction.... The weather was fearfully hot, but we continued to press the siege day and night ... and on the morning of July 17th the place was found evacuated."[35] General Johnston had been driven out of Jackson, driven "beyond Pearl River" as Nate put it.

But Joe Johnston would be heard from again; a year later he would be the chief obstacle to General Sherman when Sherman began his Atlanta campaign and the march to the sea.

The siege of Vicksburg ended on the Fourth of July, a Saturday; the battle of Gettysburg took place at nearly the same time. Lee's army was making its first invasion into Northern territory, working its way from Maryland into Pennsylvania. The Confederate army was spread out for miles, the leaders near Harrisburg.

President Lincoln urged the Union army to attack: "The animal must be very slim somewhere. Could you not break him?"[36] The Union army probed the Pennsylvania countryside looking for Lee.

General Lee knew that the Union army was pursuing him, but he was operating blindly because his cavalry scouts under Jeb Stuart, who normally kept him well informed of enemy movements, were off on a raid, miles away.

Neither army wanted a fight except on its own terms, on its own choice of battle site. That the battle took place at Gettysburg was an accident; it came about because of the scarcity of shoes in the Confederate army. Confederate soldiers often marched without shoes even on snow and ice.

On June 30 the Confederate general Johnston Pettigrew was dispatched to chase down a rumor that there was a supply of shoes in Gettysburg; he marched his brigade ten miles over hilly country to that small town. When he encountered a few Union soldiers near Gettysburg, he returned to camp with the news, but his commander, General Henry Heth, didn't take those few Union soldiers seriously. He believed that the main Union army had not had time to catch up with them, and he wanted the shoes so he said, "I will take my division tomorrow and go to Gettysburg and get those shoes."[37]

The next day, July 1, 1863, General Heth's soldiers marched to Gettysburg: "They came, three-deep and booming; Heth was on his way to 'get those shoes.'"[38] When he reached Gettysburg, General Heth encountered a substantial Union force under General John Buford, who gave the Confederates a fight and called for reinforcements from the nearby Union army. To support Heth, General Lee brought the rest of his army into Gettysburg and the battle was underway. The battle of Gettysburg went on for three days. It ended on July 3, when General George Pickett's 4600 men made the infamous charge, the bloody and futile uphill charge into Union cannon.[39] When the battle of Gettysburg was over, fifty thousand soldiers, Union and Confederate, lay dead and wounded. The next day, the "debris of rotting horseflesh and manflesh — thousands of fermenting bodies ... in the July heat" covered the battlefield.[40]

President Abraham Lincoln would come to that battlefield in November and dedicate the Union burial ground with a brief address. Historian Garry Wills notes that "Out of all these senseless deaths ... [Abraham Lincoln] would transform the ugly reality into something rich and strange." Lincoln's words, which began, "Four score and seven years ago," struck a chord in the people of the North. The Gettysburg Address "became a symbol of national purpose, pride, and ideals."[41] On July 5, 1863, General Robert E. Lee took his army back to Virginia, never to invade Union territory again.

The Confederacy had, on almost the same day, taken two severe beatings, at Vicksburg and at Gettysburg. The war, though it continued for nearly two more years, was never the same; the South could not win. William Tecumseh Sherman, perhaps the most perceptive general on either side, wrote: "The capture of Vicksburg ... fatally bisected the Confederacy ... and it so happened that the event coincided ... with another great victory which crowned our arms far away, at Gettysburg, Pennsylvania ... and the two ... should have ended the war; but the rebel leaders were mad, and seemed determined that their people should drink of the very lowest dregs of the cup of war."[42]

Fred was now in a camp above New Bern. On July 2, 1863, when the battle of Gettysburg was taking place, Fred's Company F and four other companies from his regiment had been ordered from Carolina City to Washington, North Carolina, but the orders were changed en route and they were sent to New Bern and then to Camp Stevenson, which was north of New Bern along the Neuse River.

At about the same time, Steve's company, Company G, and three other companies from the regiment were ordered to New Bern and then on an expedition to Trenton, North Carolina (some twenty miles west of New Bern) to establish a base for cavalry raids on the Confederates.[43]

Fred wrote his mother from his new camp.

New Berne

July 9th '63

Dear Mother

We are now in camp at Fort Stevenson way up above the city and very near the Neuse River.

We broke camp at Carolina City the 2nd [of July] and the four companies that were going on the [other] expedition went up on the train in the morning. The rest of us did not go up until night. We got into New Berne about ten o'clock.

Instead of going to Washington as we expected, we went into the barracks on the Fair Ground [at New Bern]. We staid there that night and the next day, the 3rd. That night we had a little dance in the barracks. I danced three or four cotillions.

The next morning, the 5th, the troops started [on the expedition to Trenton, N.C.]. Steve's company was one to go and the same morning we were ordered out to this Fort.

I wrote Jennie a letter and sent it by one of the furlough boys [Corporal Woodbury]. It is reported that the steamer [carrying Corporal Woodbury] is taken by the pirates but I don't know whether it is true or not.

That letter told just where we expected to go when we left Carolina City. I wrote this one thinking that you would receive the other. I sent for some things to come out by him. If he gets there safe you can send the Silicia and stockings but never mind the hat. I have one. If he doesn't get home and you will know by the time you are ready to send an answer to this I will write and tell you what to send.

What promotion is it that Nate is trying for? I should like to know how high he is flying. If he gets it I may possibly stand a chance.

Steve is well and stood the march first rate. His letter will probably tell you all about the expedition. All I know is what I have heard. Lt. Col. Chambers was wounded in the shoulder by a shell. I don't know whether it is very dangerous or not.

Geo. Wilkins's company was not on the march either. I don't know whether the companies will remain as they are or the regiment be joined again. We are having a pretty easy time here. I don't suppose that they will let us stay here though.

When we first came here we stationed a picquet at a bridge just above the camp but yesterday morning the 9th NJ relieved us and today we didn't have but one man on duty.

I read that piece in the Wizard about the water. The old preacher frightened them with his denunciations of the poison.

You must excuse me for not writing more.

Love to Father, Aunt Jane, Mary, Lizzie, Jennie, Tuvvy, Aunts, Uncles, Cousins and Friends.

Yours.

F. Osborne

In mentioning that "pirates" might have captured the ship on which Corporal Woodbury was traveling, Fred was presumably referring to Confederate ships which preyed on Union shipping. In Fred's next letter, we find that his worry was groundless because Corporal Woodbury made it home safely.

Steve, in Company G, went on the Trenton expedition; Fred reported that he "stood the march first rate." That expedition brought back to New Bern, as the spoils of war, "an extraordinary train [of] … all the horses, mules, asses, bulls and steers, all the wagons, carts, coaches, carryalls and buggies, all the negroes, negresses and pickaninnies in a wide stretch of country."[44]

The wound sustained by Lt. Col. Chambers, according to the record, was caused by a shell fragment and was serious but not dangerous. George Wilkins, of Company A, had been a young blacksmith from Salem when he enlisted; he died of battle wounds ten months hence.

New Berne

Aug 1, '63

Dear Jennie:

I received yours by Corporal Woodbury this morning.

Last night we got back from an expedition to Winton on the Chowan

River. When I wrote my last I was at Fort Stevenson. We left there the same day and came to the barracks [at Newbern] where we [had] stopped before. [We] had just got settled when about a hundred men were detailed from the Reg't and sent down to work on the same battery at Morehead that we worked on before. We staid there two weeks and came up a week ago last night.

The next morning at three o'clock we went aboard the steamer Utica and Sunday afternoon landed at Winton on the Chowan River. It is one of those rivers that run up from Roanoke. There were the 9th N.J., 17th Mass., 25th Mass., 81st N.Y., Belger's R.I. artillery battery and the 23rd, and that night 2000 cavalry and a regular battery came down from Norfolk, Va. by land.

As soon as we landed the 17th and 9th went up the road and about three miles up drove the Rebs out of a breast-work. The 16th had three or four wounded.

The town of Winton was burned last year by the Hawkins Zouaves and there are only one or two houses left. The next day we were ordered 2½ miles to a cross road to do picquet. I staid there one night.

The next night I was all turned in and going to sleep, when it was: "Fred Osborne with his equipment." I went out and got on the same horse with an old Secesh and went off through the mud and rain to his house. It seemed somebody had been robbing him and I was sent as a safety guard.

I staid there two days and nights. [I] lived with the family and had the best room in the house [with] a bureau and looking glass, and a feather bed which I couldn't appreciate. It was too much of a soft thing. When I first laid on it I sank down out of sight. I soon got out and slept on the outside and then I tossed round all night.

The planter's name was John Vann. He was a very pleasant man. I smoked with him and drank a very little brandy. I should have had more but they stole it most all from him.

A Captain that was on [General] Heckman's staff was there once or twice and we all talked and smoked [and] had a good time generally.

The family lived first rate. They had] chicken, ham, all kinds of vegetables, corncake, biscuit, [and] buttermilk [at] every meal. They cannot get coffee and they use a substitute made of corn, burnt and ground. It was much more palatable than some of the coffee we get in camp.

I should like to have Tuvvy see the place. It was a regular plantation, [a] low house with a broad piazza and a large yard with splendid great trees in it not set out regularly but thrown in anyway, some close together and everyway.

Mrs. Vann was a timid woman and the clank of a cavalryman's sabre would make her nervous. She used one of mother's expressions. She said her heart turned over.

I never thought I should sit at a table and have a little nig with a fan of peacock feathers to keep the flies away.

Altogether it was the best time I have had since I left home.

You are getting to be quite a cavalier. You would make a better cavalry-man now than I would.

This letter will come by another Corporal (Jakie Hiltz, the Captain of our tent).

The furloughs have been drawn again and I was not lucky.

I hear the 54th has been in a fight. I had a letter from Lu last night. He was there on St. Helena.

Love to all

Steve is well.


"Jakie Hiltz" was Jacob Hiltz. A Salem mariner before he became one of the original members of Company F, he left the company in November 1863 when he received a promotion into another regiment.[45]

Fred's comment that "the 54th had been in a fight" and that he "had a letter from Lu last night" was a reference to Luis Emilio and the black 54th Massachusetts Regiment. Lu Emilio left Fred on Helena Island and traveled to Massachusetts, in the spring of 1863, to help train the black soldiers. He returned to South Carolina that summer with the 54th Massachusetts regiment to take part in an attack on Charleston. It was that attack to which Fred referred.

The country watched to see how black soldiers would do in battle. On July 18, 1863, Union troops, including the Massachusetts 54th, made a night attack against Fort Wagner, a heavily fortified Confederate installation in Charleston Harbor.

The Union general in charge later admitted that the attack was a hopeless assignment: "The storming of a position strongly held by both artillery and infantry ... [was] an operation attended with imminent peril.... The best troops can seldom be made to advance ... [against] the fire of ... artillery supported by [rifles] ... yet this was the work we had set out to do."[46]

Valor did not suffice, however: "Although the troops went gallantly forward ... and gained a [forward position] ... the enemy forced a withdrawal.... The repulse was complete and our loss [was] severe."[47]

Although the attack failed, the black 54th regiment made history. That regiment lost 281 men out of 600; even when forty percent of their comrades were down, the soldiers of the 54th kept moving forward. They showed that black soldiers could fight. Captain Luis Emilio, commander of one the companies in the battle, later said in his history of the regiment: "It was a supreme moment for the Fifty-fourth, then under fire as a regiment for the first time. The sight of wounded comrades ... and the screaming shot and shell flying overhead, cutting the branches of trees ... the dark line stood stanch, holding the front at the most vital point. Not a man was out of place."[48]

Historian James McPherson wrote in the introduction to the 1969 reprinting of Luis Emilio's regimental history: "The attack on Fort Wagner was for black men what the Battle of Bunker Hill had been for Yankee revolutionaries in

1775.... The desperate courage of black troopers on the parapets of Fort Wagner, even in a lost cause, disproved the smug assumption of many whites that the Negro was too servile and cowardly to make a good soldier."[49] General Grant, after Fort Wagner, said: "By arming the Negro we have added a powerful ally."

Fred's Twenty-Third Massachusetts was having a much quieter time in North Carolina, and his next letter spoke mainly of photographs.

New Berne

Aug 13th 63

Dear Mother

George Osgood, another of our boys is coming home on sick furlough and I have had two pictures taken and send them by him as I think they will not be so likely to get broken as they would in the mail.

I want you to have some photographs taken from them and send a dozen out to me as the boys have a mania for having each other's mugs.

I sent fifteen dollars by express. You [will] probably get it at the same time you do this letter. Those are very good pictures of me indeed but the ears are rather small.

We had a battallion drill last night. The first one since June 3rd.

That money is directed to you so if the Post office clerks don't know it is yours, you keep a look out for it.

Love to all.

F Osborne

Corporal Woodbury told me that the picture he saw of me didn't look like me at all.

Fred Osborne

George Osgood was a Salem saddler when he joined the original Company F with Fred. He served mostly on a gun crew.[50]

Fred wrote a letter to his mother and a letter to Jennie on September 1, 1863:

New Berne

Sept 1st 63

Dear Mother

I came in this morning from two days picquet at a covered bridge about a mile and a half above camp. It isn't really picquet duty such as we would have at any of the outposts, but the railroad is picqueted the whole length, that is, as much of it as [is] in our possession. The duty of these picquets on the railroad is to see that no one passes with [out] a proper pass.

Co[mpany] B, I and G went across the river this morning with two days rations. I suppose they are going to Swift Creek but it is not known.

How are the conscripts coming on? I suppose it will take some time for them to get enough as nine out of ten are rejected. They had better come soon and the duty will be lighter. There [are] only about a dozen of Co F on duty now. I came off this morning, go on again tomorrow.

Charleston will have to give in soon I guess. They [put] up a cannonade that would batter down anything.

The papers say that Lu Emilio has been promoted to Major.

I am sorry you didn't like the pictures. I think they are the best ones yet. I didn't look stiff and prim as I should if I had wore a coat and necktie. The picture was just as I am, careless. I never wear a coat excepting when I am obliged to and that hat in preference to a cap. The reason you didn't like the neck was because I wore my shirt open at the throat.

I don't believe Capt Raymond said that about Steve, and then there are plenty of old members that havn't got above private yet.

How do you like Corporal Hiltz's side whiskers. Has Henry Lufkin been to see you yet. He went from here in the same boat with Osgood. I suppose he has been to the house by this time.

I should like to be one [of] that battalion that is to be raised for the garrison of Fort Lee or [Fort] Pickering.

Tom Perley flies high if he thinks of going out with a commission. I hope he will get it if he wants it. I expected Tom would come home something more than he went out. He is such a wonderful youth.

I guess that most of them have got enough of it. Some of the boys's letters say that they hated their officers. I havn't heard from any of them yet, but doubtless they will write soon.

My love to Father, Aunt Jane, Mary, Lizzie, Jennie, Tuvvy, Aunts, Uncles, Cousins and friends.

F Osborne

Fred wrote that Company G had gone across the river, probably to Swift Creek, because his brother Steve was in Company G. Swift Creek was a Union camp about ten miles up the Neuse River from New Bern.[51]

Fred predicted that "Charleston will have to give in soon." Fort Sumter, the central fort in Charleston Harbor, was bombarded by Union forces for seven days, from August 17 to August 23, and reduced to rubble. According to Emilio's account: "With Sumter in ruins ... General Gillmore [the Union commanding officer] ... expected that the navy would run past the [remaining] batteries into the harbor.... The Navy Department thought otherwise, declining to risk the vessels in the attempt."[52] Charleston escaped capture once more.

Although Fred said he read in the papers that Lu Emilio was promoted to major, the record shows that this was not the case. He was promoted from first lieutenant to captain (and commanding officer of Company E in the black 54th Massachusetts Regiment) on May 22, 1863, and retained that title until his discharge in March 1865.[53]

Fred had heard that Steve's commanding officer had said something derogatory about Steve: "I don't believe Capt Raymond said that about Steve." Capt.

Raymond was Captain John Raymond, commanding officer of Company G, Steve's company.[54]

Henry Lufkin, an original member of Company F and a leather worker in civilian life in Salem, was discharged for disability on August 14, 1863.[55]

Fred was referring to two forts on the Salem seacoast when he wrote: "I should like to be one of that battalion that is to be picked for the garrison of Fort Lee or Fort Pickering."

New Berne

Sept 1

Dear Jennie

There is so little going on here that it is hard to fill up one sheet and then it is uninteresting enough. It seems strange that there is more excitement at home now than here.

I hear that they are to raise a battalion for the garrison of the forts on Salem Neck. Is it to be composed of invalids or able bodied men?

The papers state that the 1st Battalion of the 2nd Reg't Heavy Artillery is ready to leave for New Berne. The first advertisements of that reg't stated that it was to garrison the Forts in Mass[achusetts]. It may be the same with the Fort Pickering battalion.

I should like to see Wm [last name not clear] very much indeed. His friend has got a regular Pad name. I hardly think Bob will take the commission, that is if he is well situated now.

The 50th have then arrived at last, they didn't make as much of a show as I thought they would.

Has Thom Harris been to the house yet? Mother says Tom Perley has. Have they got enough of it or are [they] coming again? There were some others in the company that I knew. They are all well, I believe. Are they to have that party that was to come off when they got back?

I am sorry Mother didn't like my pictures. They were good ones and looked exactly as I do excepting being better looking.

Have all the furlough boys been to see you? I sent letters by George Osgood, Henry Lufkin and Corporal Hiltz and told all the rest to go [to see you]. I don't suppose they will.

The drafting and getting the conscripts into camp is slow business. I guess Hayward sports around considerable. Has he made any long prayers yet?

Is Geo. Perkins going to be married?

Geo. Hogdon has been a corporal some months.

I hope Mr. and Mrs. Burton will not be at home as much when I get home for I hate cooing.

Ruth and Hannah Lee will get to be quite good sailors and you will get to be a regular horseman. I shouldn't dare to ride with you.

I am so used to taking things coolly that it comes natural now.

I hope Kate will send her picture soon.

My love to Ettie, Caddie, Ruth, Hannah Lee, Mrs. Burton.

Yours,

F Osborne

I hope those cards will take well.

I guess by this time you have received that box I sent last winter.

F M O

Fred's comment about conscripts: "The drafting and getting the conscripts into camp is slow business. I guess Hayward sports around considerable," refers to First Lieut. Charles Hayward, who had been sent to Boston to train conscripts.[56] Not one of Fred's favorite officers, Lieut. Hayward had been mentioned in Fred's June 19, 1863, letter; Fred was unhappy because Lieut. Hayward was stingy with supplies for the men's comfort.

George Hogdon, in Company A, was a clerk in Salem before he enlisted in the 23rd as an original member of the regiment.[57]

Fred was still in New Bern two weeks later when he next wrote home.

*CHAPTER THIRTEEN*

# To Newport News, Virginia

## September 1863

New Berne

Sept 15th, '63

Dear Jennie

I send this letter by Anton Bauer. He is one of tent three and, where we have been in camp, I have always had my place next to his, ever since we left Camp Pendleton last fall for South Carolina. He has been in the hospital for some two months and is now discharged. He is a real good fellow and one of my best friends. I shall miss him very much. Everybody liked him throughout the company.

I am getting better fast. In fact I haven't been very sick. An attack of fever which most of the boys have had. Some have the chills with it, but I was lucky enough to escape without them.

The furloughs have been drawn but I was not one of the lucky ones.

You may be surprised to see him come in citizen's clothes, but he told me he should doff the soldier's clothes as soon as he got in Old Salem.

Have you received those shoes that I sent home last fall? The boys have got theirs. I paid my share of the freight at this end. If you have got the shoes, and they can be repaired have it done and send them out to me. If not I will write what I want, for I shall have to have some kind of boots or shoes.

If not too much trouble I wish you would draw fifteen dollars of my money and send it to me for I have by some means or other got [to get] out [of] a situation I haven't been in for some time. Send it by one of the furlough boys [George Osgood] if he hasn't started for here. If you can't send it that way or think the express is quicker send it that way. Get it here the quickest way you can. That is my object in sending for it, to have it right off. I am almost ashamed to send for any, I have sent so little home, but get it here as soon as you can.

Steve is well and on duty. He got through his [illness] without going to the Doctor. He hasn't been to him yet and don't want to.

How many pictures are you having taken? I hope they will take well.

Anton Bauer is a German. You will see by his conversation he is a foreigner and I suppose will want to know what nation he is [from].

Love to Father, Mother, Aunt Jane, Mary, Lizzie, Jennie, Tuvvy, Uncles, Aunts, cousins and friends.

Fred Osborne


Anton Bauer, who carried this letter home to Jennie, joined Company F in July 1862. He was 23 years old and was married and living in Salem when he enlisted. He had been a tailor in civilian life. The record shows that on September 14, 1863, the day before Fred wrote this letter, he was discharged for disability; the disability, presumably the reason that he was in the hospital, was not identified.[1]

Fred was ill again, but in his characteristic way, he discounted his difficulties. Camp illness was devastating in the Civil War, in that time of primitive sanitation. Far more men died of disease than of battle wounds.

Fred had been patiently waiting for his shoes to be repaired. Letter mail seems to have been fairly promptly handled, but packages were more problematical. Shoes were, of course, very important to the soldier. Fred did not complain about having to look after his own footwear. Although shoes were issued to the men, replacement or repair may have been up to the soldier to a great extent.

Fred missed out again in the lottery for furloughs, but he didn't dwell on his bad luck.

Fred was out of money, perhaps in debt to his friends. Perhaps he had borrowed money to spend on food. We can imagine that he was often hungry; army food was limited and Fred, at eighteen, was feeding a growing body. He did feel guilty about his extravagances; in an earlier letter he had commented that Steve spent less and sent more money home. Steve was, of course, an older man, mature in his habits and in his physical growth.


New Berne

Oct 8th 63

Dear Jennie

I received yours of the 29th yesterday morning but didn't have time to answer till today.

Yesterday we moved from the barracks we have been quartered in to the ones recently occupied by the 9th N.J. Most of the carpenters in the regt have [been] at work upon them for about a week. Some like these better than the old ones, but they are not as near the river and so not as convenient.

About three weeks ago one hundred men were detailed from the Reg't to [go to] Hyde County as an escort for a foraging party. I was detailed as one, but as they had more than the required number, one was taken [back] from each company. I was the lucky one in F and so got clear. It wouldn't have been much any way as they went in a steamer. They were gone two days and nights.

I think that it is a flam calling the nine month men veterans. Some of them saw hard service but most of them had easy times.

I received the money you sent in just the right time. I got it about ten days ago I guess.

Geo Osgood came back again from New York, I guess, for he hasn't got out here yet.

I will [have] another picture taken and see if I can get one you will like better.

I am glad you liked Anton Bauer. Did you have a chance to see his wife? She is a French lady. I only have seen her picture. He had it out here with him.

That School Ship is full of visitors all the time.

I should judge we havn't been on the salt water for some time since last winter.

I have seen Dick Matthews some. His brother Ferd was out in this company. He died a year ago last summer when we were in the city.

Herbert Valentine is in Salem I suppose.

Have you seen the Corporal and private that are home from this company? The Corporal you have, for he lives in Salem.

I hope Andrew Tebbetts will get a chance in one of those Forts, but it will be rather dull business. There will be any quantity of ladies round there examining the works and asking foolish questions. That wouldn't be very dull though.

I am first rate now and Steve too. He is on guard today.

I don't know wether to have a mate to that shoe made or not. If my foot is any bigger it would be better to have a new pair but I guess I will run the risk and have it made.

I want a pair of shirts too. No need of making them like the others. [I would like to] have dark flannel. Make them long and big enough in the neck and wristbands. No bosoms on them.

Nate has got just where he wanted to be. I guess he will have an easier time than in his reg't.

I can't guess your puzzle. You will have to send the answer.

Don't send the shirts until you hear from me again. I may possibly draw a furlough then they would get here just as I got home. You mustn't think I am coming just because I wrote this because my chance is the same as ever.

With this letter you will probably get a long roll wrapped in brown paper. It is a roll of the whole company from the time we left Lynnfield up to now. A fellow handed round a sample and we subscribed for them. You can have it framed or not as you like. I suppose you would have hard work finding a place to hang it. It is a very good thing to keep a chap's old acquaintances in his mind.

Love to Father, Mother, Aunt Jane, Mary, Lizzie, Tuvvy, Ettie, Aunts, Uncles, Cousins and Friends.

Yours

FMOsborne

Send the other four pictures. They will be to give away.

Fred's comment that "it is a flam calling the nine months men veterans" involves a use of the word *flam* to mean "lie or deception" that is not heard today.[2]

Ferdinand Matthews (the "Ferd" mentioned by Fred) had died at New Bern June 10, 1862. He was an original member of Company F, single and living in Cambridge, Massachusetts, when he enlisted at the age of 18.[3]

Herbert Valentine was to become the historian of Company F. He was a Salem photographer when he enlisted at the age of 20 in 1861.[4] Private Valentine made a number of sketches of camp life, some of which are presented in this text. He wrote the history of Fred's company, *The Story of Co. F, 23d Massachusetts Volunteers in the War for the Union 1861–1865.*

The corporal who was "home from this company" was probably Corporal Jacob Nagel. He had been in the Salem Union Drill Club and had enlisted in Company F when he was 34 years old. He was married and worked as a tailor before he enlisted. He was discharged for disability in March 1863.[5]

Fred had asked in his letter to Jennie on September 1 if the battalion for the forts on Salem Neck was to be composed of invalids or able bodied men. He must have heard from Jennie that invalids would be used because, in this letter he hoped that the invalid soldier Andrew Tebbetts would have a chance to serve in one of the forts. Private Tebbetts had been discharged for disability a few days before Fred wrote his letter. A Salem man, he was a 34-year-old leather worker and a married man when he joined the original Company F in the fall of 1861. He was wounded after the battle of Roanoke because he was assigned to discharge captured muskets and one blew up in his hands.[6]

Fred's comments about shoes and shirts being large enough reminds us that he was an adolescent who was still developing. Feet, neck, and wrists were larger than when he left home two years ago. His mother and his sister wanted those pictures to see how much he had grown and how much he had changed, perhaps to see the man who was replacing the boy they had sent away.

His mother and Jennie knew from his letters that Fred was changing in other ways. They saw the letters becoming careless in grammar, becoming a little less civil. They were the letters of a tired, worn-down youngster who was getting desperate to see his home again, but all the while was trying to keep up a front to his mother and sister.

Fred wrote that "Nate has got just where he wanted to be. I guess he will have an easier time than in his reg't." In his career summary in his military file;

Nate stated: "[In late July or August, 1863, following the siege of Vicksburg and after driving General Johnston out of Jackson, Mississippi] I [left] the command of D Company and transferred to the Staff of the 3rd Division, 14th Army Corps, as Ass't Commissary of Muster and moved with the Division to Helena, Arkansas ... and afterward to Memphis, Tenn."[7]

But Nate soon came back into action. In his career summary he wrote: "[I] was transferred ... [back to General Sherman's] 15th Army Corps [camped, at that time, outside Vicksburg, at Big Black River[8]] in September, 1863, and I moved across the country to the relief of Chattanooga." A Union general, William Rosecrans, had got himself into trouble at Chattanooga; his army had become trapped in that city. As General Sherman explained in his memoirs,: "The whole country seemed paralyzed by this unhappy event; and the authorities in Washington were thoroughly stampeded [into some kind of action].... The Eleventh Corps ... and the Twelfth Corps ... were sent [to Chattanooga] by rail [from Virginia].... Orders were also sent to General Grant [on the Mississippi] ... to send ... reinforcements ... toward Chattanooga."[9]

So in September, 1863 at the time that Fred wrote this letter, Nate was with General Sherman, on the move "across the country to the relief of Chattanooga." The 13th Infantry traveled five hundred miles by steamer from Vicksburg to Memphis and one hundred miles by rail to Corinth and finally made a three hundred and fifty mile march to Chattanooga. The historian of the 13th Infantry described in these terms the march from Corinth to Chattanooga: "On [September] 16 ... [we began] ... a forced march of three hundred and fifty miles ... one of the longest in history.... [Rosecrans's] Army was in danger, and must be rescued".[10]

Fred's next letter was from a camp at Newport News. The camp was situated on a headland overlooking Hampton Roads, the scene of the great naval battle of the *Monitor* and the *Merrimack* ironclads back in March of 1862, 18 months earlier. Fred's regiment was getting closer to Richmond and closer to the crescendo of battles around Richmond which would bring the war to a close.

Newport News, Va.

Nov. 1st, '63

Dear Jennie

I have knocked round considerable since I last wrote you. In the night of the day that I last wrote you, a hundred men from the reg't (ten from each company) were sent on an expedition to Elizabeth City and Edenton. I was one of them.

We went aboard the Jersey Blue transport [ship] at night. The expedition consisted of one hundred infantry, two hundred and fifty cavalry and two pieces of artillery.

We reached Elizabeth City two days after we started. The infantry took possession of the town, picquetted the four roads leading out of it and posted the artillery on the two main roads.

The cavalry then went out to see if there were any Rebs around. Cap't Kent had a guard on his quarters in the city and I was on that.

The cavalry came in that night having been twenty two miles. They didn't find anything. The cavalry broke open some stores and there was considerable poultry knocked over.

The next day the cavalry started overland for Edenton and we embarked for the same place.

At Edenton we found a detachment of the troops who came from Plymouth [N.C.]. We relieved their picquets and then they left on their boats for Plymouth.

So there was nothing there but [our] one hundred men, the cavalry not having got in.

I left the picquet I was on, and went down to a house some distance from the post. There was a lady, her daughter, and two little boys there.

The Mother talked Union, but the girl she launched out against the Yanks, but as I let her have her own way (and had the Yankees cowards, beaten in every battle, and it was them who brought on the war), I got along first rate with her.

She was handsome and just like all other women wanted her own way in everything.

She knocks everything, yet when I first went there she wanted to know if I wasn't afraid to come out there, and told of two of the 11th Penn(sylvania) who were shot close to the house by the rangers (that is the name the guerillas have given themselves). I supposed at the time that they were not far off, as what sent me down there first was seeing two men cross the road.

At all events I should like to go there again. I wished at the time the rangers might come out. She could see what the Yanks were made of.

We left Edenton that night when the cavalry got in and arrived in New Bern two days after. The [regiment] was gone to [Newport News], Va., and all our things with it.

We went to Morehead [City] that day and two days after that embarked for Va.

When we got to the Reg't [at Newport News] they were in shelter tents (dog kennels, that you can't stand up in), but now we have got larger tents.

The furloughs were given out this time and so of course I didn't get one. It may come some time.

I suppose you havn't sent my things yet. You can send them now. Send over just what I sent for and ask Father to get me a good rubber blanket. The ones we draw are good for nothing, in fact I have the one I got in Lynnfield [Massachusetts].

Do have more of those pictures taken. The boys are all in love with them. They are much better ones than some of them have, and I will have a good one taken and send it to [you] and you can have some from it for yourself.

You had better scare me up some pictures of the fair lasses for I can't get them for myself, as you told me I must when I come home.

I shall send a letter by one of the boys, I guess.

Did you like the company roll? You will have to puzzle your brains for a place to put it.

I should think Nate would write home oftener than he does.

Love to Father, Mother, Aunt Jane, Mary, Lizzie, Tuvvy, Aunts, Uncles and Cousins, Caddie, Fannie, Ethel, Hannah Lee, Hattie and friends.

Yours

F Osborne

Tell father to get a good large one and as light a one as he can.

Fred's first stop after the trip up the sound was Elizabeth City: "We reached Elizabeth City two days after we started." That city, one of the few Union holdings in North Carolina, had been captured in 1862 during the battle of Roanoke Island. A soldier in Fred's regiment described the operation:

> An expedition ... was organized [in October, 1863] for the purpose of breaking up a nest of bushwhackers, who had their head-quarters in the swamp to the north of Elizabeth City ... and made forays upon the so-called Union men of the neighborhood.... [The expedition] under command of Colonel Mix, of the 3rd New York cavalry, [was] made up of a squadron of cavalry, a section of artillery, and about one hundred of the 23rd under Capt. W. L. Kent of "H" [Company]. Having landed at Elizabeth City ... Capt. Kent was ordered to hold the town, with the artillery and the infantry, retaining ... [everyone] who came in, and permitting none to pass out.[11]

In his report, Capt. Kent said:

> We picketed all the roads and, for two days, hived all the small farmers, old women and boys who came in, making it very unpleasant for all, who, without exception, came to me and offered to prove that they were good Union men and women. The cavalry pushed out into the swamps, and, at the end of two days, we received orders to embark for Edenton to meet Col. Mix. We took all the horses that had come into town.... We reached Edenton next day.... The mayor entertained us very handsomely ... [then] we started for New Berne. Our transport, little more than a tug, was ill-adapted for so many men.... Charles Wheeler, private of "I" [Company] was missing [the next morning].... We supposed he had walked overboard. When we arrived at New Berne, we learned that the 23rd had started for Virginia. [We] took cars for Morehead [City] and rejoined the regiment en route for Newport News.[12]

Fred's use of the term *guerrillas*, to refer to the rangers is interesting since *guerrilla* was a new word in Fred's time. It was first used to describe the guerrilla warfare in Napoleon's Peninsula Campaign in the early 1800s.[13]

Fred wondered why Nate wasn't writing home oftener, but he was pretty busy at this time, early November of 1863. Nate was traveling to the relief of Chattanooga with General Sherman and the 15th Corps. Sherman stayed close to Nate's 13th Regiment while traveling and in battle; the general was the commanding officer of the 13th Regiment at its inception at the beginning of war.

Sherman's wife and two sons and two daughters were traveling with the general. At Memphis his son Willie suddenly became ill with typhoid fever. Willie, his first-born son and namesake, was to General Sherman "that child on whose future I based all the ambition I ever had."[14] Unfortunately, the boy sank rapidly from the fever and died. In his memoirs, General Sherman wrote: "I had watched with intense interest his development, and he seemed ... to take an interest in my special profession.... We were with him [at his sickbed] ... and, helpless and overwhelmed, saw him die."[15] Nate's regiment, the Thirteenth Infantry, acted as an escort for Willie's casket in the military funeral for Sherman's son. That night, after the funeral, General Sherman was moved to write a letter to the commanding officer of that regiment: "I cannot sleep tonight till I record an expression of the deep feelings of my heart to you, and to the officers and soldiers [of the regiment] ... for their kind behavior to my poor child.... I realize that you all feel for my family the attachment of kindred, and I assure you of full reciprocity."[16] Sherman and his men continued on toward Chattanooga, where three weeks later, a major battle would be underway.

Newport News, Va.

Nov. 3rd '63

Dear Mother

We are getting to be quite comfortable here. Most of the tents are stockaded and some of them have underground stoves (the same as we had in Annapolis).

There are six reg'ts in all now that came from N.C. The 25th Mass, 27th Mass, 23rd Mass, 98th and 81st NY, and 9th NY, and one battery of the 3rd NY Artillery.

It is said the 17th Mass, 3rd NY Cavalry and more artillery are to come.

There has been two reviews since we have been here, one by Gen'l Heckman, the other a grand review by Gen'l Foster. The old chap looks about the same as ever. There is a rumor circulating that he is to go the Dept of Washington and that Gen'l Butler is to have the command here. If so we shall have another grand review to go through.

Did you send my note paper. I haven't seen anything of it yet though it may be at New Bern.

I don't know as I shall send a box. There is something about having the Provost Marshall inspect [it], which bother I can clear by sending a package by one of the furlough boys.

Where is Hayward? Cap't Raymond has been back some days. I should have thought he would come at the same time.

I shall send home my [Casey's] tactics which you will see are not thumbed much. My pack has got to come down as much as possible and those I can do without.

In the next company a fellow is playing a violin. The tune carries me to Salem, on a hall floor, scraping and bowing at some fair damsel.

It is going to be a gay winter, North. They don't think much about the war. This call for 300,000 will bring out some of them. It will have to be a draft without any $300 clause in order to get them.

I am going to send home the boys pictures as fast as I get them. You see we exchange all round and I am in hopes your curiosity to see the company's mugs will induce you to be more prompt in sending mine out. I have you some seven or eight now to send. They will probably come with this letter.

Why doesn't Lizzie write?

If I could come home I would stir them up so that they write more. I was disappointed when I got back from that ten day jaunt and found not a letter for me.

Love to all.

Fred Osborne

A picture once in a while is a good preventative of the blues.

Don't parade these pictures where everybody will see them.

The historical record does not reveal the reason for moving Fred's regiment from New Bern to Newport News. It seems likely that this move was not part of any overall war strategy. There was no grand strategy for Union army movements. The war was fought pretty much ad hoc; for nearly three years now, the war had been a catch-as-catch-can, aimless kind of operation. That would not change until the coming March when President Lincoln would put General Grant in charge of the Union armies. Grant then developed the first grand strategy for fighting the Confederacy.

Fred mentioned reviews by General Heckman and by General Foster. General Charles Heckman commanded a brigade of four regiments, including the Massachusetts 23rd; he had moved his brigade up from North Carolina.[17] General Foster, who until recent months had been in charge of Union forces in North Carolina, was now commanding officer at the huge Union military base at Fort Monroe. Fred's camp at nearby Newport News apparently came under General Foster's command. Fred's supposition about a change in command was correct. General Ben Butler, the flamboyant former Massachusetts politician, did replace General Foster as commander of Fort Monroe, arriving on November 11, 1863, eight days after Fred wrote this letter to his mother.[18]

What Fred meant by the "Dep't of Washington" is not clear. A month later, on December 11, 1863, General Foster replaced General Ambrose Burnside as commander of the Army of the Ohio. General Burnside, located at Knoxville, Tennessee, asked to be replaced after his successful participation in the battle of Chattanooga.[19]

Fred's comments on their tents, here and in the previous letter, parallel comments recorded in Private Valentine's history of Company F:

> The men were [at first] provided with "shelter tents".... They put no high value on them.... [They] not only could not stand up in their tents but even had to crawl out, in order to get off coat and boots, to go to bed ... [but] ... about two weeks after our arrival, we received "A" tents which, by stockading and flooring, the men proceeded to make habitable for winter. For heating, a hole about two feet deep was dug in the centre, and a cast-off camp kettle, with the bottom knocked out, was inserted. A flue, made of old stove-pipe, ran under the floor to the outside, where the upturned section was steadied with bricks.[20]

Fred's campsite at Newport News was on a bluff overlooking Hampton Roads,[21] the busy ship channel where the James River empties into Chesapeake Bay. Hampton Roads was the site of the battle between the *Merrimac* and the *Monitor*. From his camp on the bluff, Fred could look out and see the partly submerged wreck of the *Cumberland*. One of his friends in Company F wrote: "A short distance offshore, the wreck of the *Cumberland* was visible ... a constant reminder of the terrors of that dread day and the service rendered by the gallant little *Monitor*".[22]

The Hayward to whom Fred referred was Lieutenant Charles Hayward of Company F, the subject of disparaging remarks in some of Fred's earlier letters. He had been wounded in the battle of Whitehall. He was now returning from Boston, where he had been sent to train some recalcitrant, bounty-jumping conscripts.[23] Bounty jumping was an abuse of the draft system. General Martin McMahon describes his experience with bounty jumpers in the Union army in Virginia in 1863 in these terms:

> The professional bounty-jumpers ... came in large numbers ... with the intention of deserting at the earliest opportunity and repeating the profitable experiment of enlisting for large bounties.... Their favorite time for leaving was during their first tour of picket duty, and it was found necessary to throw a cordon of cavalry outside our own picket lines. A gallows and a shooting ground were provided ... and scarcely a Friday passed during the winter while the army lay [idle] ... that some of these deserters did not suffer the death penalty.[24]

When he reminisced about dancing on a "hall floor," Fred may have been referring to Hamilton Hall, a popular place for dancing parties in Salem. In her book about Salem life in the 1800s, Caroline Howard King wrote:

> Hamilton Hall ... the harmonious proportions of the noble room ... entirely lighted by candles; candles in the central chandelier, candles in sconces, candles everywhere, shedding their soft, mellow ... light on the gay scene ... four beautiful old convex mirrors in richly carved frames hanging on the walls ... two large roaring woodfires ... square dances and country dances ... quadrilles

… the Spanish dance, a kind of slow half waltz … the Boulanger, an all round dance, and the Virginia Reel with which our balls always ended.[25]

Fred referred in this letter to the provision in the Conscription Act, passed in March 1863, that allowed a drafted man to avoid enlistment by paying a fee of $300.[26] The draft was unpopular and it was not a successful method of getting men into the army. Less than 7 percent of the soldiers in the Union army were draftees.[27]

Newport News, Va.

Nov. 30 '63

Dear Mother

I received your and Lizzie's letter last week but haven't had a chance to answer. As Howard Hamblet is discharged and is to be a sergeant in the 2nd Heavy Artillery, I wrote this note to send by him.

I received the box Saturday. Everything was right and real nice. Aunt Jane's gibralters were splendid and made me think of the times when she used to tell me to open my mouth and shut my eyes. I am ever so much obliged to all of you.

The furloughs are stopped and the men who do not reenlist are not to have any.

It isn't fair, now that half have had furloughs, to shut down on the rest; but their stopping them won't make any more re-enlist, as [a] man who would bind himself for three years more for the sake of thirty days furlough is a bigger fool than I am.

After the re-enlisted men have had their furloughs, the rest, who haven't had any and don't re-enlist, may have theirs, but the excuse will be your time is too near out. That is the way government treats her soldiers and expects a man to sell himself into slavery for one thousand dollars and thirty days furlough.

I believe ninety have re-enlisted in this reg't. The Colonel thought we would rush to enlist again like a pack of hungry dogs.

I suppose Nate has seen some fighting in these last battles of Grants. Have you heard from him yet?

This letter is a scrawl it is so cold my fingers are stiff. It has been raining for a few days but this morning it is cold enough.

I don't think you will see me before my last year is out. I know it will disappoint you, Mother, but one year more without a furlough is better than three with one.

Has Jim Miller recruited any men yet? I should think that bounty would catch some of them.

Who is this Cap't Richardson who is in command of the Fort on the neck? How is Jerry?

This letter is kind of blue but you must excuse it. I wanted it to be plain and to the point.

Love to Father, Aunt Jane, Mary, Lizzie, Jennie, Ov, Caddie, Laurie, Ethel, Mrs. Burton, Aunts, Uncles, cousins and friends.

Yours

Fred Osborne

Seeing Howard will be almost as good as seeing me.

Howard Hamblett, who carried this letter to Fred's mother in Salem, had been a sixteen-year-old Salem farmer before he enlisted in Company F along with Fred, in the fall of 1861. As Fred notes, he was discharged from the regiment at this time to be promoted to sergeant in the 2nd Massachusetts Artillery. He was later promoted to 2nd Lieutenant and then to 1st Lieutenant. He served until the end of the war.[28]

The gibraltars that so delighted Fred were hard candies popular in New England in the 1800s. One authority says that gibraltars were "hard white candy flavored usually with peppermint or lemon."[29] Gibraltars figure in several literary works. Nathaniel Hawthorne had a special fondness for them; in a letter to his sister Louisa, he said: "I send Susannah's Gibraltars. There were fourteen of them originally, but I doubt whether there will be quite a dozen when she gets them."[30]

"No account of Salem in the old days would be complete without mention of 'Salem Gibraltars,'" said Caroline Howard King in her book on life in old Salem, "They were first made by a Mr. Spencer, an Englishman who came to Salem in 1826, and were sold in the streets by his mother, whose funny old cart and quaint personality were familiar objects there early in the last century. I have often seen her in her queer old-fashioned bonnet."[31] Mrs. Spencer's wagon is now on display at the Essex Institute in Salem.[32]

**The Gibraltar Woman**

In a recent article on gibraltars, W. L. Francis said: "The fame of Mrs. Spencer's Gibraltars spread around the world, as Yankee sea captains took with them this most indestructible sweet. They are still known in some far corners of the world — the Japanese royal family have them mailed regularly. Jackie Onassis stopped to pick hers up, but her chauffeur went in and got them for her."[33] Mrs. Onassis's secretary, responding to a 1994 letter from the author, wrote that Mrs. Onassis did not remember the incident.

The candy operation started by Mr. Spencer was sold to a Mr. Pepper, whose Pepper Company, the "oldest candy company in America," continues making gibraltars today.[34] It is situated across the street from the House of Seven Gables in Salem and a few blocks from Fred Osborne's old home on Oliver Street. The recipe for gibraltars is said to have remained unchanged for 150 years: "Pure cane sugar, cream of tartar and natural flavoring, either peppermint or lemon, are stirred in a copper pot. Not a moment too late, the sticky stuff is pulled on a hook like taffy, rolled flat and cut with scissors into diamond shaped pieces."[35]

Gibraltars were also popular in London in the 1800s; Henry Mayhew, cofounder of *Punch* magazine, wrote a report on London street vendors in Dickens's time in which he described the way gibraltars were made for the street trade.[36]

Reenlistment became a big issue at this time, November 1863. A thirty-day furlough was offered as a reward for reenlisting for three years. "In all, upwards of 200 men reenlisted [in the 23rd Massachusetts Regiment] and were furloughed to Massachusetts."[37] But Fred was not interested. His three-year term was up in October, 1864, ten months away, and a furlough, however much he craved it, could not induce him to enlist for three more years.

Fred asked if Nate had fought in Grant's recent battles. Nate was indeed in the fighting at the battle of Chattanooga. President Lincoln had ordered General Grant to come over from Vicksburg and take charge of the Union forces around Chattanooga. And Grant did take charge. He fired General Rosecrans, who had let his army become trapped in Chattanooga, and he put General George Thomas, one of Rosecrans's best officers, in command of the trapped army. Grant wrote in his memoirs: "I [telegraphed] Thomas that he must hold Chattanooga at all hazards.... A prompt reply was received from Thomas, saying, 'We will hold the town till we starve'.... It looked, indeed, as if but two courses were open: to starve ... [or] to surrender."[38]

But Grant had Sherman on the way to Chattanooga, and he had a good man in General Thomas. Grant surveyed the situation and set up the Union attack. The Confederate forces occupied Missionary Ridge, overlooking the city. Grant's objective was to drive them off that ridge and free Chattanooga from the siege. Sherman's troops had the assignment of attacking the north end of Missionary Ridge.

Nate, in Sherman's 15th Corps, had arrived at Chattanooga on November 18, 1863, after the historic march from Corinth. The battle took place on November 23; we have seen that Fred, well tuned to the news, mentioned the battle in his November 30 letter to his mother.

At midnight on the day before the battle, Grant gave orders to ... Sherman to attack at daylight. in his memoirs, Grant describes the battle:

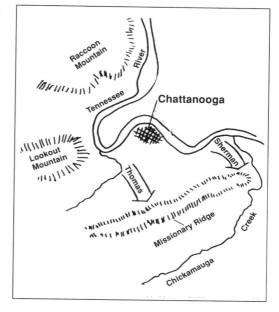

The morning opened clear and bright ... Sherman was out as soon as it was light enough to see.... The ridge is steep and heavily wooded.... The troops advanced rapidly ... and carried the end of the ... rebel [earth]works.... Sherman now threatened [the Confederate] flanks.... From the position I occupied I could see column after column of [Confederate] forces moving against Sherman.... Every Confederate gun that could be brought to bear ... was concentrated upon him.... Sherman's condition was getting ... critical.... I now ordered [General] Thomas to order the charge [of divisions which had been held in reserve].... Our men drove the ... rebel ... troops.... I watched their progress with intense interest.... The fire along the rebel line was terrific.... Cannon and musket balls filled the air.... The pursuit continued ... and soon our men were climbing over the Confederate barriers.... The retreat of the enemy was precipitate.[39]

Historian Peter Parish reports: "The defeated army did not stop until it was many miles away," and he notes that the Confederate general Braxton Bragg said later that his defeat was caused by a "panic which I have never before witnessed [that] seemed to have seized upon officers and men."[40]

The battle of Missionary Ridge, as it became known, was over. Bragg's losses were heavy, 6667 men, while 5824 Union soldiers were killed or wounded.[41] It was one of the turning points in the war. Chattanooga "was now ... 'a gateway wrenched asunder,'" and the "road lay open into the heartland of the South."[42] In the summary of his military career, Nate said modestly: "I moved [with General Sherman] to the relief of Chattanooga ... [and] participated in the battle of Missionary Ridge."[43]

Fred spent Christmas of 1863 at Newport News.

## CHAPTER FOURTEEN

# Fred Osborne's New General, Ben Butler

## January 1864

Back in the spring of 1861, the North had believed the war would be finished quickly with 90-day soldiers, but now, almost three years later, the war was still grinding on. In fact soldiers like Fred who had enlisted for three years were now being asked to reenlist for three more years.

President Abraham Lincoln was discouraged, because his generals had made little progress against the Confederacy. With the exception of the Mississippi River, little Confederate territory had been wrested from the South. Hundreds of thousands of Union soldiers had been killed and wounded with little result. The public's war motivation, a complex mixture of preserving the Union and eliminating slavery, was weakening, and a peace sentiment was developing.

Fred Osborne was in camp at Newport News, Virginia. His regiment had been there, out of action, since October, perhaps an indication of a less than aggressive war effort.

Fred wrote to his mother for the first time since November:

Newport News Va

Jan 10th 64

Dear Mother

For a few days we have had regular northern weather. The snow fell about an inch and half deep. The officers of the cavalry and one of the batteries had their horses on two big sleds. They were riding round all the afternoon, and today I saw a fellow with a pair of wooden skates on.

Capts Center, Hart and Woodbury have got their ladies out here. So now there are five in camp (Mrs Lt Col Chambers, Mrs Maj Brewster).

Part of the reenlisted men started for home this morning. The rest are to go tomorrow. They didn't seem joyful enough for a crowd who were starting for home. They are to go by boat to New York then to Boston. They carried their arms and light firearms and will probably get some duty at home. Most of the officers are to go. I don't know as they will come back to the Reg't. They may recruit up at home and go to some other Dep't.

I don't know what they will do with the remainder of the regiment. The camp will probably be broken up within a week.

The box arrived safely. I was very much pleased with the hat and the shoes. The Cuba honeycomb was splendid.

The officers who had their ladies here were building a shanty to live in but as everything is uncertain they suspended operations on it.

Hurt my leg while in a scuffle. It has been pretty lame but now is nearly well. The chords of my knee were strained. It was my left leg.

The camp seems deserted enough and tomorrow it will be more so.

The report is that we go to Norfolk to do duty with those of the twenty seventh who did not reenlist. These men reenlisted as veteran volunteers so it is a matter of uncertainty of wether they will be the twenty third reg't and we are transferred to some other [regiment] or we form the reg't and they make a new organization. When this reenlistment fever is all over I suppose I shall be at a loss what to write about.

Genl Butler is about to get the control of exchanging prisoners in his own hands so that matters will be conducted in a more straightforward manner than heretofore.

Most of the boys who reenlisted are sick of their bargain. They begin to look farther ahead and see the other three years they have to go through. I am sorry for them but they are gone. It will lengthen the draft.

Love to Father [writing too faded to be read]

This is rather a dry letter but it will let you know where I am. Tell Tuvvy he couldn't have suited me better as to a hat.

F M Osborne

Fred accepted the idea that officers had special privileges and did not seem to resent officers having their wives in camp: "Capts Center, Hart and Wood-bury have got their ladies out here. So now there are five in camp (Mrs Lt Col Chambers, Mrs Maj Brewster)." Addison Center, captain of Company C, was an artist from Gloucester, Massachusetts, when he enlisted in the original 23rd Massachusetts regiment. Carlos Hart, captain of Company K, was a jeweller from Foxboro, Massachusetts, when he enlisted in the original regiment. The record says that he had two sons, three daughters, and a second wife.

Captain Henry P. Woodbury had been the commander of Company F since his promotion in May 1863. Major E.A.P. Brewster had been a surgeon living in Salem when he enlisted in the original 23rd Massachusetts regiment; before he was promoted to major in August 1863, he had been the captain of Company A. Lieu-tenant Colonel John G. Chambers was a printer from Medford, Massachusetts who had seen army service in the Mexican War. Fred had mentioned him in an earlier letter when he was promoted to lieutenant colonel and became the commanding officer of Fred's regiment. Mrs. Chambers later had reason to feel thankful for those days in camp with her husband. Four months later, on May 16, he would receive multiple wounds in the Battle of Drury's Bluff, and she would become a widow when he died in the hospital.[1]

"The Cuba honeycomb was splendid." The nature of this delicacy remains a mystery; research has failed to uncover a description of Cuba honeycomb.

"Hurt my leg while in a scuffle." Fred played down his injury but it became a serious problem later and kept him out of action.

In his comment "General Butler is about to get the control of exchanging prisoners in his own hands," Fred identified two subjects which received much newspaper comment during the Civil War: Ben Butler and prisoners of war. Ben Butler's name was often in the headlines; he was a hero in the North, a villain in the South. Prisoners of war were a painful but popular subject; most families, including, it would turn out, Fred's family, had a soldier in an enemy prison.

## General Benjamin Butler

In December 1863, just before Fred wrote this letter to his mother, General Butler, had been appointed commanding general of the Department of Virginia and North Carolina, which included Fred's camp at Newport News and all other Union forces around Richmond. His headquarters were at Fort Monroe. General Butler was perhaps the most aggressive and the most colorful of the Union generals. He was originally from New Hampshire, and his mother ran a factory boardinghouse in Lowell, Massachusetts, in his youth. He became a criminal lawyer, made a fortune from shrewd investments, and married an actress. One biographer noted: "His talent for biting epigrams, and his picturesque controversies made him one of the most widely known men in politics from 1860 till his death."[2]

A Democrat when the Democratic party was strong in the South, Butler had attended the Democratic Convention at Charleston, South Carolina in April 1860 and outraged Massachusetts when he voted to nominate Jefferson Davis for the presidency.[3] But when the Southern states seceded, Ben Butler made a sharp turn, had himself appointed brigadier general of the Massachusetts militia, and immediately began getting troops ready for war. On April 17, 1861, only five days after the firing on Fort Sumter, General Butler had headed south from Boston with his 8th Massachusetts on his way to save Washington, which had been isolated by secessionists who had burned the bridges and destroyed the railroads around the capital. It was Ben Butler's troops that rebuilt under fire the railroad to Baltimore, connecting Washington to the outside world. "Thereupon began one of the most astounding careers of the war," one historian has said. "Butler was, until Grant took over, as much a news item as any man except Lincoln.... He moved in a continual atmosphere of controversy."[4]

General Butler served President Lincoln in several theaters of the war, making friends and enemies and headlines all the while. He won particular notice as the military governor of the important port of New Orleans. President Lincoln had given him that job in April 1862 when New Orleans was captured. In that job General Butler won the approval of much of the North.

Southerners had a quite different view of Ben Butler; they gave him the title "The Beast of New Orleans." As military governor he administered what would become known as "reconstruction" in New Orleans, giving freed slaves a place in that city's commercial life. The South did not like its first taste of reconstruction.

General Butler became especially hated for his punishment of a man named Mumford. Mumford, leading a mob, "pulled down a ... [United States] flag, trailed it on the ground through the streets, tore it to pieces, and distributed the pieces among the mob for keepsakes...." The flag had been flying on the U.S. Mint in New Orleans. Ben Butler ordered Mumford hanged for treason from a scaffold built in front of the Mint, the scene of his crime, before an ugly crowd of his sympathizers. "The fate of Mumford caused the greatest excitement throughout the whole Confederacy," General Butler recalled in his memoirs.[5]

The women of New Orleans gave General Butler a special kind of trouble, resulting in the famous "Woman Order." General Butler recalled in his memoirs: "Complaints of treatment from women ... came pouring in on me.... A soldier ... passing along quietly on the sidewalk ... a woman coming the opposite way would take great pains to hold her skirts aside as if she feared they might be contaminated.... One of my officers in full uniform, his prayer book in hand, on his way to church ... met two very well-dressed, respectable looking women.... One stepped across in front of the other and spit in his face.... Flag-Officer Faragut ... while going along one of the principle streets there fell upon him what first he took to be a sudden and heavy shower; but it proved to be the emptying of a vessel of water ... from the balcony above and not very clean water at that."[6]

General Butler knew that arresting women for such behavior would cause considerable excitement and commotion that might produce a riot; after some days of deliberation, Butler issued the following order, General Order No. 28: "As the officers and soldiers of the United States have been subject to repeated insults from the women (calling themselves ladies) of New Orleans ... it is ordered that hereafter when any female shall ... insult or show contempt for any officer or soldier ... she shall be regarded and held liable to be treated as a woman of the town plying her avocation.[7]

General Butler noted in his memoirs: "There was no case ... after that order was issued ... of insult ... against our officers or soldiers.[8]

In his farewell address upon leaving New Orleans, General Butler said: "[When I came here] I found you trembling at the terrors of ... [slave] insurrection. All danger of this I have prevented by so treating the slave that he had

not cause to rebel.... I found the dungeon, the chain, and the lash your only means of enforcing obedience in your servants. I leave them peaceful, laborious, controlled by the laws of kindness and justice."[9]

But because of his kind and fair treatment of the Negro population and his firm administrative style as the military governor, General Butler was reviled throughout the Confederate states to the degree that Jefferson Davis issued this proclamation: "I, President of the Confederate States of America … do pronounce and declare …

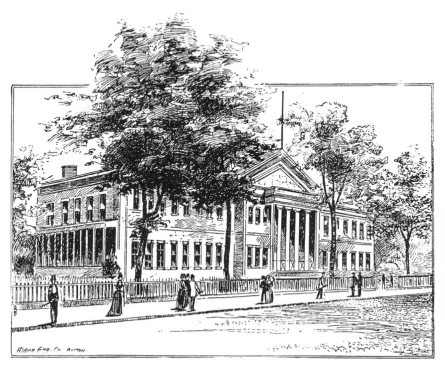

*Top:* General Ben Butler in 1856; *bottom:* The Mint at New Orleans

Benjamin F. Butler to be a felon … [and] an outlaw and … [an] enemy of mankind … [who] in the event of his capture … [is] to be immediately executed by hanging."[10]

Lincoln was particularly impressed by Ben Butler and offered him the vice presidency in the November, 1864 presidential election. General Butler declined, saying to Lincoln's messenger: "Tell him … I would not quit the field to be Vice-President, even with himself as President.… Ask him what he thinks I have done to deserve the punishment … of being made to sit as presiding officer over the Senate … to listen … to debates more or less stupid."[11]

President Lincoln then asked General Butler to be his secretary of war. In his memoirs, Butler recalls the occasion: "I replied … that I should hold no office except an active command in the army until the war had terminated." General Butler was resented by officers in the regular army because he was an amateur, not a West Pointer; he notes in his memoirs that Lincoln's offer to appoint him secretary of war caused an uproar because of "the opposition of the regular army."[12]

After the war, Ben Butler continued in the public eye, serving in the U.S. Congress for several terms. He was elected governor of Massachusetts in 1882. He ran unsuccessfully for the U.S. presidency in 1884 against Grover Cleveland.

Ben Butler figured in the only presidential impeachment trial in U.S. history. He led the impeachment proceedings against President Andrew Johnson. Republicans believed that Johnson was too sympathetic toward the Southern states during the reconstruction period after the war. When he removed Secretary of War Edwin Stanton, a Republican partisan, from office without Senate approval, Republicans saw an opportunity to punish Johnson and started impeachment proceedings. Ben Butler presented the case against President Johnson before the Senate: "I was ready at the appointed hour. When I entered the … chamber … the scene was almost appalling.… The … Senate chamber was full.… The galleries were also crowded.… I came as near running away then as I ever did on any occasion in my life … but I stuck to my post and addressed the Senate in a speech of two hour's length." The impeachment failed by one vote.[13]

## Prisoners of War

Fred had heard that President Lincoln had asked General Butler to sort out the prisoner exchange problem. Prisoners of war were a burden; housing and guarding and feeding thousands of prisoners was a drain on the war effort for both the North and the South. Prisoners were such a severe problem that sometimes captured soldiers "were simply paroled, i.e., placed on their honor not to participate further in the war.…"[14]

Northerners were scandalized by stories of captured Union soldiers starving and dying in disease-ridden Confederate prisons. Libby Prison in Richmond and Andersonville Prison in Georgia had particularly bad reputations; prisoners there were underfed and underclothed and they lived in their own refuse like ill-kept animals.

In January 1864 the South had 13,000 Union prisoners and the North had about 35,000 Confederate prisoners.[15] To deal with the prisoner problem, the North and the South agreed "[to] a cartel arrangement ... [to exchange prisoners], paroling any excess obove the actual number of ... men exchanged. The cartel operated ... under commissioners of exchange in Richmond and Washington."[16]

But the use of colored troops by the North became an issue in this prisoner exchange. The Confederates were outraged that the Union had made soldiers of former slaves; Jefferson Davis issued an order that captured colored soldiers could not be exchanged. The Confederacy took the view that captured slaves were recovered property and should be returned to their original owners.[17] Because of this disagreement, prisoner exchange had come to a halt.

Now, at the beginning of 1864, President Lincoln, who was worried about Union soldiers suffering and dying in Confederate prisons and eager to get the exchange of prisoners going again, turned to General Butler to straighten out the prisoner problem. Lincoln gave Butler the special title of "Commissioner of Exchange."[18]

An activist always, Ben Butler started off by sending 505 Confederate prisoners up the James River in a boat to the Confederate camp at City Point, offering them for exchange. After a "stormy session of the Confederate Cabinet in Richmond," during which cabinet members tried to figure out how to deal with the "Beast of New Orleans," the Confederates sent 520 Union prisoners in return.[19] Prisoner exchange was again in progress and continued, with some ups and downs, into the next months.

In his letter of January 10, 1964, in which Fred mentioned the topic of

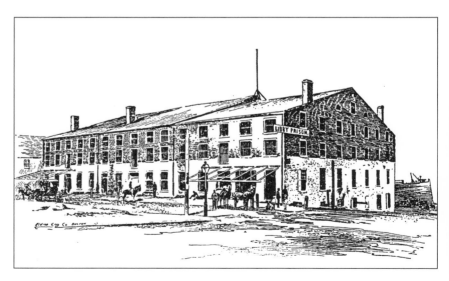

**Libby Prison**

prisoner exchange, he also raised the issue of reenlistment, commenting that some reenlisted men were leaving for home. The record shows that the reenlisted men of the 23rd regiment left on January 13 in a steamer for Boston for their promised furloughs.[20] Valentine described the reenlistment situation in his history of Company F: "While we were at Newport News efforts were put forth to secure the reenlistment of the men, and the necessary papers were distributed through all the regiments. Great efforts were made by our officers to induce re-enlistment, and the promised furloughs were alluring to many, but few were captured in Company F."[21] Company F, since it had few reenlistments, had few men on furlough, which is why Fred commented: "Col Chambers says that if we got into action we would show them that the fighting part of the 23rd is left out here."

Newport News Va

Jan 21st 64

Dear Mother

I received yours with Nate's enclosed this morning.

The reenlistments rage [is as] high as ever. About two hundred of the 25th put down their names yesterday and as many in the 9th. There are even more in our regt. The 18th NY [several lines too faded to read]. Col Chambers says that if we got into action we would show them that the fighting part of the 23rd is left out here. Steve hasn't enlisted yet [so] I guess that the Govt won't get either of us.

The box got out here all right. The shoes fit first rate and the hat was just what I wanted. The stockings would have been better if the feet were a little longer.

There are eight more enlisted in the Regt and before the first of March they will have more. I suppose the people at home will turn out and hail these men as defenders of their country who are ready to pour out their blood in its defence, but in reality [they should be seen] as the soldiers who are saving them from the draft. Because a man has been in a hard place for two years I can't see that it is any reason why he should stay three more. In fact the shirks at home had better come out and bear their share of the burden.

When these fellows come back the majority of the people will laugh and say they have got rid of them for three years more, and these same fellows who have gone home, are the ones who have run [down] the service and Government the hardest and a part of them never intend to shirk all they can. I don't believe they will bring back as many as they carry home. You needn't say anything about this. It is merely my opinion.

Do send me a few more of those pictures. The boys all keep at me and I don't have any peace. This one I send you is of the same style. You send me some and I will have a good one taken and send it to you.

Nate has said something about ambition to advance and a commission in a negro regt, but I shall stay where I am and then come home. You would like to have me an officer I suppose but I have got soldiering enough. He says if I have a taste for the military proffession. I don't think I have. He wants me to get it on my own exertions. I am not qualified to pass an examination. Some of them received their appointment without any.

Love to all

F M Osborne.

Fred's response to Nate's suggestion that he seek to be appointed an officer indicates that he was in the war to fight the secessionists, not to pursue a career in the army.

Fred commented in several letters about "the shirks," men who stayed home and didn't come out to fight for the Union. Many young men back in Salem apparently did not share Fred's feeling for the Union or his sense of duty. Fred was committed to the war, a commitment that had, for nearly three years of rough and dangerous existence, remained strong. In no letter did he lose faith, never did he comment that maybe it was a mistake. Now, however, with the war was not going well, going home was in the distant future and his resolve was indeed being tested.

Fred's next letter came from a new location. In January, 1864, Fred's regiment, now under General Ben Butler's command, left Newport News for a new camp, Getty Station, on the railroad a few miles west of Portsmouth.

On January 22, 1864, according to the Company F historian, Company F broke camp and in the evening went on board a steamer at the dock at Newport News, "finding cold sleeping quarters on the upper deck. Next morning early we left for Portsmouth, and about eight o'clock landed on the dock, taking [railroad] cars, after the usual delay, for Getty's Station, some three or four miles distant".[22] The Massachusetts 23rd regimental historian also wrote of this trip: "We reached Portsmouth soon after sunrise, loaded our effects on [railroad] cars and followed, on another train, to our ... camp near the railroad and just outside the fortified lines, some three miles from Portsmouth."[23]

The Union holdings in this area were sketchy; In his memoirs, Ben Butler recalls: "The Union forces were in occupation of the cities of Norfolk and Portsmouth and a line extending towards Suffolk."[24] Getty Station was on that line on the Seaboard and Roanoke Railroad, a frontier between Union and Confederate forces. The Union held Suffolk and Portsmouth and the railroad in between. Getty Station was apparently a stronghold on that railroad.

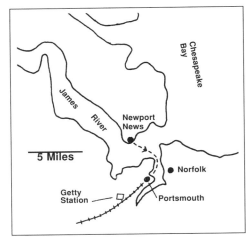

**Departure from Newport News**

The precise military situation around Getty Station, in February 1864, when Fred wrote home is difficult to deduce from the record. It does appear that Union forces were trying to clear this area and other areas south of Richmond of Confederate resistance preparatory to a major attack on Richmond.

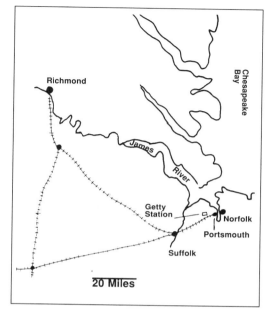

**Osborne's Location, February 1864**

Getty Station, Va

Feb 11th, 64

Dear Mother

I received yours of the sixth yesterday but won't excuse myself for the delay in replying as there isn't any reasonable one to give.

The Gettysville Theatre performed last night. The house (or shanty) was crowded. Mrs Heckman and some other ladies were present. There were more eyes watching them than the play. The programme was got up for something extra, but it wasn't as good as some they have had.

The invalid corps expects to leave tomorrow. They have been going for nearly a year but havn't got started yet. Their destination is Harrisburg Pa (I don't think they will go at all).

Do you hear anything regarding the boys at home? We don't know wether they will come back to us or not. Their thirty days are slipping away fast. If they don't come then probably they will not at all. I hope we shall see them again somewhere. They will have some tall times to tell about. Frank Bunker is one that went from our company.

The Rebels have drawn off from New Berne. They met with a pretty warm reception, rather more so than their General anticipated. Today's paper said that a Rebel band came out on the railroad in sight of New Berne and played Dixie and the Bonny Blue Flag then our band went outside the works and played the Star spangled Banner and Yankee Doodle. I didn't know before that they could raise a band in the Southern Confederacy.

My knee is doing very well though it won't get entirely well until the weather is more settled and Spring sets in. There have been some quite cold nights since I last wrote. It doesn't stop me from walking round but I limp slightly. So you musn't worry any more about it. If anybody asks about me tell them I am first rate but a little lame.

How long is it since you heard from Jim? Your letters havn't said anything about him for a long time.

The Draft is coming again and some are shaking already. It can't take any more of us. Three is about enough.

I should think Nate would have another furlough. He has seen some hard service.

Steve is well. Has he written yet? I stirred him up about it some time ago.

Lt Merritt of the 2nd Heavy Artillery was in camp yesterday. He doesn't look much different than he used to.

Love to all.

Yours

Fred M. Osborne

The Mrs. Heckman who was present at the theatrical performance was the wife of Brigadier General Charles Heckman. General Heckman, who served under Ben Butler, was in charge of a division assigned to defend the "Getty Line," the line from Portsmouth to Suffolk.[25] Fred's regiment was in General Heckman's division.

Fred referred to the Invalid Corps in this letter. Injured soldiers who could not serve in action were put in a separate organization, the Invalid Corps. Injured himself, Fred was a candidate to join that corps if he did not recover.

The Frank Bunker whom Fred mentioned was a nineteen-year-old clerk from Belmont, Massachusetts when he enlisted. He reenlisted in early 1864 and would be wounded at the upcoming battle of Cold Harbor in June 1864 and again at Petersburg in July 1864.

Fred's statement "The Rebels have drawn off from New Berne" refers to an attack on New Bern, which was at that point in General Ben Butler's department, on February 1, 1864, by the flamboyant Confederate general George Pickett.[26] Already famous for his bloody and futile charge up Cemetery Hill in the battle of Gettysburg, General Pickett won more notoriety here. After three days of ineffective skirmishing outside of New Bern, he withdrew his 4500 men, along with some captured prisoners. Among the prisoners captured were 53 natives of North Carolina who had joined the Union army. According to General Rush Hawkins, who had been in charge of recruiting these North Carolinians back in 1862, they had asked what would happen to them if they were captured by the rebels. "We assured them that the Government of the United States would protect them and their families to the last extreme, and that any outrage perpetrated upon them ... would be severely punished."[27] General Ben Butler recorded in his autobiography: "By ... [General Pickett's] order they were tried by court martial and twenty-two of them were hanged.... Their supposed offence was that they, being enrolled in the Confederate army, had enlisted in the Union army." Furious, General Butler, who knew that General Pickett had been a West Pointer and an officer in the U.S. Army before he switched to the Confederate army, continued: "Pickett himself deserted our army to take up arms in the Rebellion.... I referred the whole [matter] ... to General Grant."[28]

Grant's response to Butler at the time is not known, but Grant was involved in the case later. After the war, the Union held General George Pickett responsible for these hangings, and he asked for a pardon. Secretary of War Edwin Stanton and others wanted to try him, but General Grant interceded, saying: "General Pickett I know personally to be an honorable man.... His judgement prompted him to do what cannot well be sustained, though I do not see how good ... can be secured by his trial now. It would only open the question whether or not the Government did not disregard its contract entered into [with the North Carolina recruits]." Grant's recommendation was all-powerful, and nothing was done.[29]

Fred referred to the draft again in his letter. President Lincoln had in early February 1864 announced a new draft.[30] Lincoln believed that the draft was needed to build up the Union army, even though the draft was inefficient and hated. Replacements were needed for heavy battle losses. Also, the three-year enlistments of men who joined when the war started in 1861 were up. Half of the soldiers in the army were coming to the end of their three-year term that year and could head for home. Reenlistment was sweetened by the promise of a thirty-day furlough and a bounty of $400.[31] That $400 bounty was a substantial amount of money; it corresponds to $4000 in today's money.[32] Historian Shelby Foote writes: "And for pride, a man who reenlisted was to be classified as a 'volunteer veteran' and was authorized to wear on his sleeve a special indentifying chevron, a certificate of undeniable ... valor."[33]

In his next letter, Fred mentioned fights in his regiment that were caused by strong feelings about "volunteer veterans," whom Fred called "Vets."

> Getty Station, Va
>
> Feb 27th 64
>
> Dear Mother
>
> Yours of the twenty fourth was received this afternoon. I sat down to answer immediately.
>
> There is nothing going on here. It is the most quiet place we have ever been in.
>
> The monotony of camp life is enlived sometimes by the gunners of the Fort right back of us firing at a target. The last time they fired the gunner of the second gun smashed the target to pieces the first shot. His is the gun that always makes the best shot. Two thousand rounds of condemned ammunition was given out to the Forts. The firing will continue until that is expended.
>
> The Thirteenth N.H. and the Cavalry have bands. One or the other of them is playing every evening. Sundays on Dress Parade our regiment has the Thirteenth's band so we have music enough.
>
> Genl Heckman's lady and her two daughters are here with him most every day. I see them riding out with some of the staff officers.

The Invalid Corps left about a week ago. They are now comfortably situated in Harrisburg, Pa. A letter from one of them says they are invited to parties and all social gatherings. They are enjoying the sunny side of a Soldier's Life.

The Vets came into camp yesterday. There was a great outcry of wheat! wheat! from some of the chaff as soon as they were in hearing. That was relative to the remark in Col Prescott's speech, that those left behind were nothing but the chaff. A few of them looked pretty hard. Wednesday they had a free fight in the [railroad] cars, and some were pretty well beaten. One or two have got into the Hospital to quicken [recover]. The roughs smashed up the cars, threw the stores outdoors and broke all the windows. Probably there will be a bill brought against the Regt. The twenty seventh's bill for damages on the roads and boats was $4000. I shouldn't have spoken of this but only want you to see that Chaff is entirely the worst. Don't say anything about this. It will appear in the papers soon enough. There was quite an excitement for a short time, but everything has settled down into the old routine. You can tell a Vet anywhere you see him by the pretty clothes he wears.

Love to all.

Fred M Osborne

Steve is well. I am glad he has written.

The papers came all right. All you send comes safely through. I sometimes forget to say so in my letters.

Jim has gone to mining again I guess. He had better come home. Your boys are pretty well scattered.

The papers haven't said much about Genl Sherman's expedition so I can't tell exactly where Nate is.

I received Lt Millen's letter.

Don't let the draft take Tuvvy.

Did Father get the papers I sent?

I will enclose some of the boys's pictures.

Mail service in the Civil War was quite remarkable. Fred began this letter, written on February 27, with, "Yours of the twenty fourth was received this afternoon." He was reading his mother's letter which had been written in the Osborne home in Salem, Massachusetts, only three days before. Considering the transportation difficulties of war time, mail delivery was admirable.

"Jim" was James Osborne, Fred's older brother by fourteen years. Very little has been discovered about Jim, who was listed as a mariner in the 1850 Salem census. Fred indicated here that he was away from home and in some kind of mining activity.

Fred's military record discloses that the continuing trouble with his knee caused him to be hospitalized prior to his next letter. Since he still used the Getty Station dateline, the hospital was probably at that campsite.

Fred took a critical view of the Vets, "volunteer veterans": "You can tell a

Vet anywhere you see him by the pretty clothes he wears." The $400 bounty was a source of money for "pretty clothes." When Fred said, "There was a great outcry of wheat! wheat! from some of the chaff as soon as they [the vets] were in hearing," he was referring to the remark in Col. Prescott's speech that those left behind were nothing but the chaff. Fred reported bitter feeling between the "wheat," soldiers who had reenlisted, and the "chaff," those who hadn't. These terms derived from an incident which occurred when the reenlisted men, on their way home for their thirty-day furloughs, stopped at Boston to be honored. The historian of the Massachusetts 23rd describes the incident: "The furloughed men of several regiments, including the 23rd, were received in grand style in Boston ... lodged and fed on the best in the land ... marched through the ... streets ... addressed at Fanueil Hall. One of the speakers (a Colonel Prescott) called them the wheat and their non-enlisting comrades in camp, chaff."[34] The regimental historian chose not to report the bitter fighting between the "wheat" and the "chaff" that Fred described which occurred when the Vets returned to camp after their furloughs. In most Civil War histories, there is little mention of the dislike which developed between those who reenlisted and those who didn't.

Fred again wondered what Nate was doing as he campaigned with General Sherman. General Grant, trying to keep the war going in his part of the country in spite of the winter season, assigned Sherman to march his army east from Vicksburg for 150 miles to wipe out Meridian, Mississippi, a major railroad center and an arsenal for the Confederacy. The Meridian expedition also had the objective of paralyzing that part of the Confederacy so that Mississippi would not create problems during Sherman's upcoming campaign through Georgia.[35]

Nate, on the Meridian expedition, was taking part in General Sherman's first punitive campaign. Sherman believed that Southerners should have seen that their cause was doomed after the Union victories at Vicksburg and Gettysburg six months earlier. He blamed the leaders of the Confederacy for continuing a hopeless war. Sherman now wanted to give Southerners, including civilians, a clear understanding of the brutality of the war they insisted on continuing.

Sherman's army left Vicksburg on February 3, 1864, on the way to Meridian. He told his generals to "punish the country ... take freely the horses, mules, cattle, etc."[36] Sherman made good progress in spite of terrible winter roads and arrived at Meridian on February 14.[37] Meeting little resistance, he proceeded to destroy the city; he said, in his memoirs: "We at once set to work to destroy an arsenal, immense storehouses, and the railroad in every direction.... I was determined to damage these [rail]roads so that they could not be used again ... during the rest of the war."[38]

Sherman reported to Washington that he had "ruined 'a full hundred miles of railroad ... and (made) a swath of desolation fifty miles broad across the State of Mississippi which the present generation will not forget.'"[39]

One unusual aspect of the Meridian campaign was the thousands of slaves who attached themselves to Sherman's army as it marched back to Vicksburg.

Sherman reported, "We bring in some 500 prisoners, a good many refugees, and about ten miles of Negroes."[40] Historian John Marzalek described the procession of "long lines of fugitive slaves, estimated at five thousand to eight thousand.... 'They form a mournful curiosity,' an observer noted, 'with their lacerated backs, branded faces, and ragged garments....' [Shermans's men] saw negresses carry two children for two hundred and fifty miles and drag others who clung to their skirts." [41] Sherman's soldiers "felt compassion for sobbing and weary pickaninnies and wished to carry them."[42]

Sherman wanted Southerners to understand that they would be punished for continuing the war. Historian Lloyd Lewis describes Sherman's strategy: "While the word of his fearsome raid went up and down the Mississippi Valley, Sherman sent messages to his subordinates to heighten Southern fear of the Federal army.... He sent a paper to be read to civilians ... 'to prepare them for my coming.'" General Sherman's "paper" stated that:

> I believe this war is the result of false political doctrines ... [the] nonsense of slave rights, States' rights ... and such other trash as have deluded the Southern people into war, anarchy, bloodshed.... Three years ago by a little reflection and patience they could have had a hundred years of peace and prosperity, but ... now it is too late.

In this paper, Sherman outlined his policy of destroying Confederate property, excluding houses of noncombatants but little else.[43] Sherman hated carrying on this futile war and having his soldiers killed in useless battles, and he was determined to teach Southerners the brutality of war in order to make them want peace.

# Grant Takes Over

## March 1864

Fred was in the hospital. The reason is not entirely clear, but it was probably because of his damaged knee. He wrote the next two letters, one to his mother and one to Jennie, on the same day.

> Getty Station, Va.
>
> Mar 24, '64
>
> Dear Mother
>
> Yours of the sixteenth was received yesterday, but I had to defer answering until today.
>
> It has been quite stormy here for some days. It was cold and the snow fell to the depth of one foot. There were some quite large drifts. Yesterday it cleared up and now is thawing fast. The walking is miserable though I stay indoors most of the time.
>
> Today some companies are pitching into others with the snow balls. I saw F getting drove out of their company street. Then they rallied and the others had to leave. This has been the heaviest snow storm we have seen since the regiment left Mass.
>
> The Rebs haven't made any more raids on Suffolk yet. The next time the Nigs (2nd U.S. Colored Cavalry Regiment) go there it will be burnt, so their officers say, and all trouble put an end to.
>
> Last Monday evening the Gettysville Theatre played. It was the benefit of John Thornton the star actor. He is a member of Co F band.
>
> Dr Derby arrived from home yesterday. He had had a long furlough ever since the reenlisted men went.
>
> Four recruits left the regiment today for the Veteran Reserve Corps. They were seven hundred dollar men, but unfit for active service.

189

All the recruits that come from the islands in Boston harbor are unwell. They are worked too hard there, and every one of them have bad colds. One or two of every lot that comes are sent into the hospital.

Those soldiers whom you see wandering round not knowing what to do with themselves are the ones who have spent all their money and want to get out here again as they cannot enjoy themselves there without money. Some of ours were glad to go into camp at Mendham before their furlough was out.

One of the Vets of this reg't, who came back all rigged out in new togs, has sold everything, watch and all, and come down on the army doeskin. He is the same one who married a girl and three days after didn't know her. She got some of his money and gave him the slip.

It is strange Nate can't find time to write a little oftener but he knows best.

I am glad Ov is getting better. As soon as summer gets along he will go it first rate.

Steve never says anything about being discontented. He is no more so than the rest. For if a man said that he was satisfied out here I shouldn't believe him. It isn't natural for anybody to be contented with this life.

The Vets, some of them, are the most discontented. Some of the chaff keep at the Vets all the time asking them how many months difference there is in the time to serve. That makes them the worse. All they have to cheer them up is the hope that Grant will end the war. Then there are others who looked the matter in the face before they enlisted for another term and don't care, [are] happy go lucky.

I am not sensitive about being a private. It seems as though other people were. A good many haven't been even that yet.

Love to all. Love to Aunt Jane.

Yours,

Fred M. Osborne

Dr. Peirson is right about my knee. An injury of that kind always takes time to get well.

The town of Suffolk Fred mentioned was a major railroad center about twenty miles further west on the same railroad as Getty Station. Railroads converged at Suffolk to deliver food and goods north to Richmond from the rich Carolinas. Suffolk was under tenuous Union control, and the Confederates constantly threatened to take it back. Fred's regiment, the Massachusetts 23rd, responded to a Confederate attack on Suffolk in early March 1864, spending several days fighting off the attackers. General Ben Butler wrote in his memoirs: "On the 9th of March the Confederates made a demonstration upon our lines at Suffolk.... The movement of the enemy was handsomely met and repulsed." Fred was not with his regiment in that fight because he was in the hospital.

The Gettysville Theatre Fred referred to is described in the history of Company F: "[a] little log theatre ... built by a New York artillery regiment and frequently filled with good audiences drawn thither to witness plays performed by histrionic talent gathered from the various regiments of the division." John Thornton, who was born in Ireland, "played leading parts in dramas, and a soldier from a Rhode Island regiment did the same for comedies, while Corporal Phippen assumed female parts. Once they had a joint benefit and were honored with a 'splendid house that paid well.' 'Luke the Laborer' and 'Poynet Arden' were among the attractions, and 'Don Cesar de Bazan' was in course of preparation when the rehearsals were cut short by marching orders."[1]

George Derby, the regimental surgeon Fred mentioned, was a Boston physician when he enrolled in the original 23rd regiment in 1861. Dr. Derby seems to have been a special person, as the Massachusetts 23rd regimental historian remembers: "[He was] the courteous gentleman ... the genial comrade whose trained voice was ever ready to help in sacred melody or convivial song; ... on the battlefield ... the fearless surgeon, thoughtless of self; ... in garrison ... he gave us ... the lesson of his daily life. Of more value than ... pills or potions ... was his gentlemanly courtesy, his inflexible integrity. All this was invaluable to the younger men ... whose characters were forming amid the trials of war and the myriad temptations of camp." Dr. Derby was married on March 3, 1864, while at home, hence the long furlough mentioned by Fred.[2]

These comments about Dr. Derby in the regimental history tell us much about the underlying civility in the Civil War. Brutality there was, and hardship — but gentleness too.

The Veteran Reserve Corps Fred mentioned, was the former Invalid Corps, renamed because of complaints about the old name. The Veteran Reserve Corps was a success story. The Corps gave a place to semi-invalid soldiers, keeping them in the army instead of giving them discharges, using them for light duty and releasing able-bodied men for active duty. Some 60,000 men served in the Veteran Reserve Corps during the war.[3]

To his mother at home in Salem, Fred commented about "soldiers whom you see wandering around not knowing what to do with themselves." The reenlisted soldiers at home on their one-month furloughs often found themselves restless and ready to come back. As historian Shelby Foote notes: "After three years of life in the service, home was likely to be no great fun.... It fell considerably short of their expectations.... [One soldier said] 'I almost wish I was back in the army' and a furloughed soldier, barely a week after his departure, wrote to a comrade still in camp, 'Everything seems to be so lonesome here.... There is nothing going on.'"[4] Fred mentioned that one of the men who had reenlisted had sold his new clothes and settled for army doeskin. Doeskin was "a firm woolen cloth with a smooth, soft surface like a doe's skin"; it was used in Union army uniforms.[5]

The "Ov" whom Fred had heard was getting better was Orville Osborne, one of his brothers who was twenty three years old and was working in his father's fur store on Essex Street in Salem. Ov was also called "Tuvvy" in Fred's letters.[6]

In the 1860 Salem census, when Orville was 19, his occupation was given as "artist"; during the Civil War, he was a clerk in the fur store.[7]

Fred remarked how discontented many of the "Vets" were. Committed to three more years, the Vets were hoping for a shortened war. A great deal was expected of Grant by the soldiers and by the people. The Northern public had found a hero in Ulysses S. Grant. His victories at Vicksburg and at Chattanooga convinced the public that the Union had a general who could win. President Lincoln, who was disappointed in his other generals and his own attempts to manage the war, put Grant in charge of all the Union armies. The president sensed that a take-charge man was needed and that Grant was the man.

> Getty Station, Va
>
> Mar 24th
>
> Dear Jennie:
>
> Your letter by George Hogdon to here yesterday. I didn't see him. A fellow that met him brought them in to me.
>
> It has been very stormy lately. We all had to crowd around the fireplace in the hospital and smoke to kill time.
>
> Considerable snow fell today. The boys are having a snowball fight. The Jewels were getting beat when I saw them. Havn't seen any sleigh rides such as they had at Newport News.
>
> Last Sunday I saw a first Lieut of the 2nd US Colored Cavalry (formerly a corporal in Co F). He said the Nigs fought well and will put a stop to the Reb raids by burning and sacking Suffolk.
>
> The Gov't is going to make a big thing of the Veteran Reserve Corp. Four of the recruits that cost seven hundred dollars each were sent to join it today. I shouldn't be surprised if some of the Vets were put into it. There are a few that are good for nothing else.
>
> Last Monday evening the Gettysville Theatre played for the benefit of Jack Thornton the star actor. Jack is a little Irishman and was always known through the regiment by his spouting Shakespeare whenever he got a little enthusiastic. He belongs to our company.
>
> Dr Derby came back yesterday. He has had a long furlough, was married at home.
>
> Capt Woodbury received a box for the company. I believe it was from Capt Whipple. He said there were some books in it and told me to come down and look them over to see if there was anything to interest me. He said come wether he was there or not, but not knowing how his lady would like to have a private in her domicile I didn't go.
>
> Geo Hogdon used to have relatives in Braintree [near Boston], though he may have a sweetheart [there] too. I don't believe I can get anything out of him.
>
> Since I have been in the hospital I don't see hardly anybody.
>
> I should like to have been at the party. Who is it that lugs the adorable Margaret round to all the entertainments? Was John there too?

I have had only one letter from Luis Emilio since he left the company. I answered that. He never wrote again.

I heard about Hayward's marriage. All the scandal about our superiors finds its way out here double-quick through whose agency I don't know. If he is one of the most splendid men just twig [notice] that stiff leg; it is the right I think.

Sometimes I play cards considerable. I hope you are not acquainted with the noble game of bluff. You use one of the expressions of that game. The flush takes the stakes pretty often. The reason you ask is probably because I have sent no money for so long. Once in a while when the butter pail is empty we play all fours to see who shall fill it. That is about all the gambling there is done in F. If you can call it so. I never saw bluff playing in the company once or twice, and then it was stopped.

Havn't seen anything of that new game. It will find it's way out here soon.

You say yours is uninteresting. What is this?

Love to all

Fred M Osborne

Tell Tuvvy to cheer up.

Ask Jim Miller if he remembers a chap named Arthur Trussell who was in the nine months service with him. He is in our company and sends his regards to Jim.

George Hogdon, who brought Jennie's letter, was a Salem farmer and a member of the Union Drill Club in Salem before joining the original regiment in 1861. He rose to the rank of corporal and reenlisted in January 1864. Here he was just returning from his reenlistment furlough. He must have been close to Fred to go out of his way to bring this letter from Jennie. He never married and died at the age of 37 in 1880.

The "Jewels" engaged in the snowball fight were the men of Company F; the name came from an editorial in the *Salem Gazette* appearing when Company F was formed in Salem that referred to the young men as "our most precious jewels."[8]

The "Colored Cavalry," some of whom were used to protect Suffolk, were a special and substantial part of General Butler's army. General Butler had recruited colored soldiers in North Carolina and southern Virginia when he took over the command the previous November. According to historian Richard West:

> Butler pushed the enlistment of Negro soldiers, and sent out numerous Negro-collecting [expeditions] ... into the no-man's land beyond his fortified lines. "The recruitment of colored troops has become the settled purpose of the Government," reads his general order of December 5, 1863. It was the duty of every officer and soldier to aid in this recruiting, irrespective of personal predilection. He ordered ... officers to bring in entire families within his lines, affording them ... aid, protection and encouragement. General Butler recommended that Congress pay colored soldiers

on the same scale as white (white soldiers were paid $13 a month and black soldiers, $10): "The colored man fills an equal space in ranks while he lives, and an equal grave when he falls."[9]

Fred's remark that Captain Woodbury suggested he look over some books the captain had just received indicates that Fred was known for an interest in books. Captain Henry Woodbury, the commanding officer of Company F, had been a leather worker from Beverly, Massachusetts (near Salem). He would be wounded at the upcoming battle of Cold Harbor, June 3, 1884, a battle of particular ferocity. The Company F historian writes of this battle: "Company F, ... commanded by Capt. Woodbury ... clambered over ... [breast]works and moved ... up the gradual slope, under that terrible shower of shot and shell, until we came to a stand within a short distance of the enemy's works. So intense was the fire that the divisions in front seemed to melt away like snow falling on moist ground."[10]

Fred mentioned that he had had only one letter from Luis Emilio, who it will be recalled, lived across the street from him when they were boys. A year earlier, in the spring of 1863, Emilio had been selected to be the captain of a company in the black regiment, the 54th Massachusetts. The black 54th became famous for its demonstration of the fighting qualities of colored soldiers. Two of its well-known battles were the battle of Fort Wagner, in Charleston Harbor, and the battle of Olustee in Olustee, Florida. The battle of Fort Wagner, July 18, 1863, was one of several unsuccessful Union attempts to capture Charleston; the black 54th was sent on a suicide mission, leading a night assault against the fort. The official battle report describes the assault:

> The regiment advanced at quick time.... The enemy opened on us a brisk fire.... Exposed to the direct fire of ... [cannon] and musketry ... as the ramparts were mounted ... the havoc made in our ranks was very great.... The colors of the regiment reached the crest ... hand grenades were now added to the missiles against the men.... The fight raged here for about an hour when, compelled to abandon the fort, the men formed a line about seven hundred yards from the fort, under the command of Capt. Luis F. Emilio.... The other captains were either killed or wounded.... The regiment then held the front until relieved ... at about 2 A.M. The Union forces were finally repelled. The Massachusetts 54th lost 256 men, over a quarter of its complement.[11]

The battle of Olustee in February 1864 was an attempt, promoted by President Lincoln, to retake Florida from the Confederates. The fight went awry for the Union, the Massachusetts 54th taking heavy losses in brave fighting.[12]

That the black soldier could fight was demonstrated to all, including many skeptics, by the Massachusetts 54th. The regiment won national attention and was honored by a monument on Boston Common, a sculpture by August

Saint-Gaudens. Lincoln Kirsten, a respected commentator on the arts, has said: "Of all of Saint-Gaudens' work, it is the monument to ... the Fifty Fourth Regiment of Massachusetts Volunteers which magnetizes the most passionate admiration."[13]

Fred seemed intrigued by Lieutenant Charles Hayward, whom he had mentioned several times in his letters. Lieutenant Hayward had earned Fred's dislike when he was in charge of the regimental supplies; Fred apparently retained his dislike because he mentioned Lieutenant Hayward's stiff leg.

The Arthur Trussell Fred mentioned was a 20-year-old farmer from Hamilton, Massachusetts, who had joined the army early in the war as a nine-months soldier. At home on the farm after his nine-month term, he decided to reenlist. He reenlisted on February 16, 1864, and, a month later, was in Getty Station with Fred.[14]

Fred next wrote in April, 1863. He was still in the hospital. The war was about to enter its final stage; General Grant was getting the Union armies ready for a spring campaign against Richmond.

## Grant Devises His War Strategy

### April 1864

The final year of the war was getting underway. It would be a brutal, bloody year. President Lincoln had turned war operations over to General Grant. Lincoln had not met Grant before deciding to put him in charge of the war; he knew without an interview that Grant was his man.

Ulysses S. Grant devised a strategy for defeating a desperate Confederacy. Fred's regiment would play a part in those final battles. The Massachusetts 23rd was serving under General Ben Butler and Butler's army would, according to Grant's strategy, coordinate with Grant's army and with Sherman's army to snuff out the last flame of rebellion.

General Grant was a stranger in Washington when he arrived from the West to receive his new commission as general-in-chief. In his memoirs he describes this meeting:

> In my first interview with Mr.Lincoln ... he stated to me that he had never professed to be a military man ... but that procrastination on the part of commanders ... forced him into issuing [military orders].... He did not know but they were all wrong, and did know that some of them were. All he wanted ... was some one who would take ... responsibility and act.... Assuring him that I would do the best I could ... and avoid as far as possible annoying him or the War Department, our first interview ended.[15]

Grant took the president seriously; he kept his own counsel, and, for the rest of the war, did not disclose his military plans to the president or to the War Department or to anyone else in Washington. He set up his headquarters away

**General U. S. Grant**

from Washington, in Culpepper, Virginia, near the winter quarters of the Army of the Potomac.

Grant was surely modest in style, but he had absolute confidence that he would succeed in his new assignment. Adam Badeau, who later wrote Grant's military history, interviewed him at this time, asking him if he really expected to be successful in his new job: "He was perfectly certain of success.... He did not know, he said, how long it would take ... but of its eventual accomplishment no shadow of doubt ... crossed his mind."[16]

Surveying the military situation, Grant noted in his memoirs how little progress the Union had made against the Confederacy. "In the East the opposing forces stood in substantially the same relations towards each other as three years before, or when the war began; [Lee's army and the Union army] were [still] between ... [Washington and Richmond]. It is true, footholds had been secured by us on the sea-coast in Virginia and North Carolina, but, beyond that, no substantial advantage had been gained by either side."[17]

While his army was immobilized by bad roads in the spring of 1864, Grant devised a plan to end the war. Up until Grant took over, the independent generals of the Union army had attacked Confederate forces in the different theatres of the war in a haphazard fashion. In his memoirs, Grant set up a coordinated campaign such that all Union armies would engage the Confederates at the same time and keep them from moving reinforcements around. General Grant writes:

> Before [now] ... various armies had acted separately and independently of each other, giving the enemy an opportunity ... to reinforce [the army under attack].... I determined to stop this.... My general plan now was to concentrate all the force possible against ... [the two] Confederate armies ... the Army of Northern Virginia, General Robert E. Lee commanding ... [a few miles north of Richmond] confronting the [Union] Army of the Potomac, and the army under Joseph E. Johnston at Dalton, Georgia, opposed to Sherman, who was still at Chattanooga.[18]

General Lee was protecting Richmond, the Confederate capital, and General Johnston was protecting Atlanta, a major railroad center for the South and an entry into the deep South. Sherman learned about the overall strategy in a letter from Grant: "General: It is my design ... to work all parts of the army together ... Butler [will] ... operate against Richmond from the south side of the James River.... I will stay with the Army of the Potomac ... and operate directly against Lee's army, wherever it may be found. You, I propose to move against Johnston's army, to break it up and to get into the interior of the enemy's country as far as you can, inflicting all the damage you can against their war resources."[19]

As he outlined in this letter to Sherman, Grant expected General Butler to bring his army up along the James River toward Richmond while Grant, with the Army of the Potomac, came toward Richmond from the north. Fred's 23rd Massachusetts regiment would be in the action under General Butler.

Ben Butler and Grant got along well, though General Butler was not a West Point graduate. Ben Butler believed this was a definite advantage:

> The less of West Point a man has the more successful he will be ... all of the very successful generals ... stood near the lower end of their classes at West Point.... Take Grant, Sheridan, and Sherman.... All the graduates in the higher ranks in their classes never came to anything as leaders of armies in the war. The whole thing puts me in mind of an advertisement I saw in a newspaper in my youth. It contained a recipe for making graham bread out of coarse flour mixed with sawdust. The recipe ended as follows: "the less sawdust the better."[20]

During the month of April, the advance of spring was carefully noted by General Grant; as the roads began to dry up, he looked forward to "fixing a day for the great move."

Meanwhile, General Ben Butler kept things stirred up in his department. On April 13, 1864, a few days after Fred's last letter, the 23rd Mass regiment went on an expedition to feel out the strength of the Confederate city of Smithfield, on the south side of the James River, in preparation for the upcoming campaign against Richmond. Smithfield was a few miles from the 23rd Massachusetts encampment at Getty Station. Fred was in the hospital, but Steve, in Company G, went on the expedition. They took rail cars from Getty Station to Portsmouth, where they boarded a steamship and traveled up the James River toward Smithfield.[21]

They landed at 4 A.M. on April 14 and started marching along the Smithfield road. They met rebel skirmishers and pushed them back until the rebels made a stand. Steve was hit, taking a bullet in his left thigh. He was taken by boat to a hospital in Hampton, Virginia, where surgeons operated to remove the bullet.

Antiseptic surgery was unknown at this time, to Steve's disadvantage and to the disadvantage of thousands of other wounded soldiers. Antiseptic practice did not come about until after the Civil War; Joseph Lister published his work on antiseptic surgery, changing hospital practice almost overnight, in 1867, two years after the Civil War had ended.[22]

Probably because of the lack of antiseptic conditions, Steve developed gangrene and suffered prolonged misery from his wound. He spent months undergoing painful gangrene treatment, including "burning out with caustic fluids." It would be December 1864, eight months later, before he could leave the hospital and rejoin his regiment.[23]

In his next letter Fred, still in the hospital, has heard of Steve's injury.

Getty Station, Va

Apr 23rd

Dear Jennie

I have got to excuse myself this time. Yours of the thirteenth was received Saturday, but I haven't felt well until now. It is rather expensive keeping the shakes around. They will shake the beef off of you.

Serg't Porter who was wounded on the last expedition is dead.

Steve is doing well so far as I have learned. Probably you will hear from him by the time this reaches you.

The first and third brigades of the division have gone to Yorktown. Gen'l Stevenson is there with his brigade from the South. Probably there will be a concentration of troops there for some offensive movement in the direction of Richmond.

It is difficult to tell whether we will stay here this summer or not. One regiment of our brigade, the twenty-fifth Mass, left last night for Roanoke Island. Light marching orders and five days rations.

The Rebel Ram seems to be making quite a fuss down there in N.C. and the Rebs are threatening Plymouth.

The boys found quite a lot of letters on this last expedition. They were much better than any I have seen before. One chap named Joe had a sister living in Portsmouth. She gave it to him well for not writing oftener and told him how some of the gals took on with the Yanks. He had one [girlfriend] but had forsaken her on account of her intimacy with the Yankees. She told him not to believe the stories he heard about her, it was her sister that was disgracing herself by being acquainted with the Yankees. She told about these women who run the Blockade with the mails as though it was quite a common occurence. The Yanks were dogs with her.

You needn't worry about my marching to Richmond. If my leg isn't better I shan't march anywhere.

The order relative to the seamen in the army going into the navy has been read to the regiment. One hundred and twenty five are going as soon as they will let them. The regiment will be small enough.

Cap't Woodbury has sent Nan home. Mrs. Center is going to stay through thick and thin. Mrs. Brewster will too I suppose.

Has Lt. Miller left Mass yet? Does Mary Miller look anything as she used to? I suppose not.

[signature is illegible]

This is a little miserable letter.
Steve's address is Stephen H. Osborne
          Co G. 23rd Mass
          McClellan Hospital
          Hampton, Va.

Fred had mentioned having the "shakes" in a number of his letters; he had contracted dysentery a year earlier in the spring of 1863, when he was on St. Helena Island. Dysentery, that intestinal misery, stayed with Fred after the war and for the rest of his life. Dysentery, also called "bloody flux," produced symptoms of fever, depression, pain in the abdomen, diarrhea, and bloody discharge from the bowels.[24] Fred would pay this price into the future, long after the war was over, for his devotion to the Union cause.

The Thomas F. Porter whose death Fred noted was 23-years-old and came from Great Falls, New Hampshire. He fell at Smithfield and was taken, with Steve, by boat across the James River to a military hospital in Hampton, Virginia. The action at Smithfield was reported by Colonel Elwell, who was commanding the Massachusetts 23rd regiment:

> I proceeded by rail, with 16 officers and 389 enlisted men of my regiment, to Portsmouth at 5 o'clock P.M. on the 13 inst., ... and embarked on the steamer *John W. D. Pentz* and sailed up the James River, under convoy of the gunboat *Brewster*. I landed with my command about nine miles above Smithfield, at four o'clock on the morning of the 14 inst. I immediately took a line of march towards the town.... [We]came upon the enemy's pickets and drove them in. Continued on about two miles ... came upon the enemy concealed behind earthworks; after a short skirmish ... drove them out, with a loss ... of two men [Privates Osborne, Co. G, and Symonds, Co. C].... I had one sergeant dangerously wounded through the left shoulder [Sergeant Porter of Co. I].... The enemy's cavalry having begun to give me some trouble in my rear, and having no means to carry my wounded ... I deemed it proper to fall back to the James river.[25]

The regimental historian also writes of the Smithfield action: "The enemy's pickets ... made a stand in front of their [earth]works.... Co. 'G' was sent on their right flank.... Osborne ... [was] hit soon after the formation was made.... Sergeant Porter, with characteristic recklessness, exposed himself ... to the enemy's fire. He received two or three fatal wounds which his astonishing vitality resisted for hours. He died during the night."[26]

Fred noted the movement of troops to Yorktown. General Ben Butler was getting his army ready to move on Richmond in concert with General Grant, who was to come down on Richmond from the north. Butler was concentrating troops at Yorktown, on the peninsula; Fred's Massachusetts 23rd regiment would move to Yorktown on April 26, three days after Fred wrote this letter to Jennie.

Yorktown was a gambit by Ben Butler to mislead the Confederates: In his memoirs, General Butler wrote: "To divert the enemy's attention ... troops were concentrated at Yorktown."[27] Butler really planned to move his army up the south side of the James River, but he tried to convince the Confederates by his activity at Yorktown that he would come up the peninsula in his move toward Richmond.

Fred showed in this letter his attentive following of the news — the rebel attack on Plymouth took place on April 19 and 20 and it appeared in his letter to Jennie on April 23. The "*Rebel Ram*" generated country-wide headlines. It was a Confederate ironclad ram named the *Albemarle*. The style of ship called a "ram" was a Civil War phenomenon. The ram had been invented several years before the Civil War by a navy engineer, Colonel Charles Ellet. In the early months of the war, Colonel Ellet promoted the new ship to his navy superiors, but the conservative Union navy officials were not interested.[28]

A ram was steam-powered and ironclad and had a strong frame and prow. It was designed to drive its prow into the side of an enemy ship; most ships were relatively lightly framed and were thus vulnerable to a heavy blow at midships. The action of a ram is illustrated by the fight between the ram *Queen of the West* and the battleship *General Lovell*, as described by historians Johnson and Buel: "The two vessels came toward each other in most gallant style, head to head, prow to prow.... At the critical moment the *General Lovell* began to turn; and that moment sealed her fate. The *Queen* came on and plunged straight into the *Lovell*'s exposed broadside; the vessel was cut almost in two and disappeared under the dark waters in less time than it takes to tell the story."[29]

The Union navy, long-established and resistant to change, did not want to hear about the radical ram ships. But the Confederate navy, starting from scratch, was open to innovation and built several rams early in the war. A pamphlet disclosing the Confederate construction of rams was published by Colonel Ellet; it shook up the Union secretary of the navy, who ordered Colonel Ellet to begin the construction of rams immediately.[30]

The *Albemarle*, the ram that Fred referred to in his letter, was one of the early Confederate rams; it was built under a contract to Gilbert Elliott, a North Carolinian still in his teens. From a ship-building family, young Gilbert Elliott was already a veteran, having been captured by Union forces and exchanged back to the Confederacy. While in a Union prison, he had sketched new gunboat designs. Because of his youth he grew a beard to appear more mature to the Confederate officials when he presented his proposal to build the ironclad ram which would be named the *Albemarle*.[31]

Gilbert Elliott set up the construction project in a cornfield on the banks of the shallow Roanoke River, some sixty miles up the river from Plymouth. This site was protected from Union gunboats cruising in Albemarle Sound since they could not enter the shallow river at Plymouth. The *Albemarle* itself was designed for very shallow water so that, when construction was complete, it could come down the river and enter the Sound at Plymouth. Historian V. C. James describes her construction: "In the cornfield was assembled as much equipment as could be found: a sawmill, a blacksmith's forge, and an assortment of tools. Soon, men were cutting massive yellow pine timbers.... The *Albemarle* slowly took shape.... She was one hundred and fifty-two feet long, forty-five feet wide, with a depth ... of eight feet. Two propellers 'each powered by a huge steam engine with an eighteen-inch cylinder' would drive her.... Her yellow pine timbers were fastened with iron and [with] treenails [dry wooden pegs which swell when moistened]. Her prow, or ram, was of solid oak.... The carpentry moved rapidly."[32] But the thick iron plates, which required many holes for fastening them to the sides of the ship, were a problem; the drilling method used at the time for making holes in iron was very slow and was holding up the construction schedule. Peter Evans Smith, son of the owner of the cornfield, saved the day. He was a mechanical genius and later became famous for many inventions. He invented a speedy drilling method, "the first twist drill, a device that cut the iron out in shavings instead of powder."[33] Construction was soon back on schedule.

Rumors were plentiful in Union circles that a ram was being built up the Roanoke River which could attack Union ships and break the blockade along the Carolina coast. Union officials were agitated and considered what to do; there was a proposal to send a thousand Union cavalry in a sneak attack on the ram construction site. But Union officials, in the end, did nothing.[34]

Several months passed while the Confederacy made preparations for an attack on Plymounth; the *Albemarle*, the centerpiece of the attack strategy, was to come out of the mouth of the Roanoke River at Plymouth and lay waste to Union battleships while Confederate land forces overwhelmed the city. With Plymouth captured, the rebels planned to take Washington, North Carolina, and New Bern next.[35]

On April 19 the rebels began the land and sea attack on Plymouth. The

**Building the *Albermarle***

*Albemarle* came down the Roanoke River, emerged at Plymouth, and attacked Union warships in Albemarle Sound. It destroyed the wooden gunboat *Smithfield* and helped protect Confederate troop movements in the area by controlling the approaches by water to Plymouth. The city of Plymouth was taken by Confederate forces on the next day.[36]

Just how the letters Fred mentioned came into the hands of his friends is not clear, but they probably came from dead rebel soldiers. One of the captured rebel letters mentioned women who were running the blockade. The Union blockade of Confederate ports along 3000 miles of coastline was a gigantic enterprise. In the first days of the war, President Lincoln had ordered the blockade to be set up. From Virginia to Florida to Texas, the Union stationed 450 armed ships to keep seagoing commerce out of Southern ports.

Desperate for foreign trade, the Confederacy designed special ships to run the blockade and had them built in Europe. In *Civil War Naval Chronology*, there is a description of these ships:

> Over the months, blockade-running developed into a science, carried on by vessels built abroad especially for the purpose of slipping through the cordon of Union ships lying in watch off the Southern coast. These runners were long, low, side-wheel steamers ... their frames sharp and narrow.... They had feathering paddles and rakish telescopic funnels capable of being lowered close to the deck. Their hulls rose only a few feet out of the water, and were painted a light lilac color that simulated the clouds.... They burned a smokeless coal in their furnaces ... steam was released under water. In daylight they could scarcely be seen a matter of yards away.[37]

The "smokeless coal" used in blockade runners was a type of anthracite coal which burned with a blue flame and very little smoke.[38]

Running the blockade was a crucial aspect of the Confederacy's war efforts. Because the South had little industry, it was dependent upon supplies from abroad to keep it fighting. The Union blockade was, however, generally successful: "While munitions and supplies came pouring into the North from Europe, the South ... was almost shut off from overseas and had acute difficulty in ... supplying both Army and Navy." Civilians also suffered from "shortages in consumer goods causing fantastic prices: $350 for a barrel of floor ... $85 a yard for woolen cloth, etc."[39] In today's money $350 corresponds to $3500 and $85 corresponds to $850.

Fred's letter to Jennie was followed the next day by a letter to his mother.

Getty Station, Va
April 24th
Dear Mother
   Yours of the twentieth was received today. Probably by this time you have got my last.

**The Blockade Runner *A. D. Vance***

I saw a Salem Register the other [day]. It told more about Steve than I knew or have been able to find out.

It gave the Osbornes quite a puff.

I will see about those letters that were misdirected, though Father had better write to the Captain again for those [letters] may leave this dept., perhaps have already.

Steve's things have been sent to him. I should [have] thought he would have written. Perhaps they will not let him sit up. In a Hospital you have to do just as the Doctor says.

I should think you would feel sick, all the boys being afflicted so at once, but you must make the most of the two you have got with you. Steve and I havn't got much longer to stay.

Who did Father write to about Steve's coming home? I hope they will let him, and if they do you must keep him for good. He has done duty enough.

You mustn't worry about me for I shall probably be out of harm's way the rest of my term. The Doctor says I cannot do any more marching though you must keep it to your self for if people knew I wrote it they would think that I was glad of it.

There are still rumors of our leaving this place, and just as many the other way. Somebody has got to stay here, wether it will [be] us or not it is impossible to tell. If this regiment does go on the peninsula or the Potomac probably all the dead heads will go to the Veteran Reserve Corps. That will carry them farther North in the vicinity of Washington. Now you mustn't tell that to a single person.

How does Nate seem? Is his furlough until he gets well? I wish I could be at home.

Steve's wound was by a musket ball and just penetrated slightly so that the doctor extracted it right off. The boys say he stood it well. He takes everything cool.

Now don't worry a bit. Love to all.

Respectfully yours

Fred M Osborne

I have sent two blankets home. They will be left in the store. Nothing to pay, we are going to settle at this end.

According to his military records, Nate had been given 20 days of sick leave starting April 7, 1864. The nature of his illness is not indicated in the record.

The newspaper article Fred referred to was in the *Salem Register* of April 21, 1864:

### WAR ITEMS AND INCIDENTS

Capt. Nathan W. Osborne, 13th U.S. Infantry, arrived at his home on sick furlough last week. He was at the siege and capture of Vicksburg, the battle of Missionary Ridge, and other stirring actions in which Grant's army were engaged in the Southwest.

Mr. Stephen H. Osborne, a brother of the Capt., a private in Co. G., 23rd regiment, was wounded on the 14th inst., in a skirmish near Wren's Mills, in the vicinity of Portsmouth, Va. Capt. Raymond writes that the wound, though painful, is not dangerous. It was in the fleshy part of the leg between the left hip and knee. Mr. O. is at one of the General Hospitals at Hampton, near Fortress Monroe. A third brother is in Co. F in the same regiment.

Captain Raymond was Steve's commander, the captain of Company G of the Massachusetts 23rd regiment. Wren's Mills, just outside of Smithfield, Virginia, was an alternate designation for the action at Smithfield.

Fred's regiment, the Massachusetts 23rd, moved to Yorktown on April 26, 1864. When Fred next wrote to Jennie, he was with Steve in the McClellan Hospital at Hampton, Virginia.

McClellan Hospital
Hampton, Va

May 2nd '64

Dear Jennie:

I have forgotten whether your last was answered by me.

We have been dragged round some since I wrote to anybody. At Getty Station there was a great deal of surmising. Some had it that we were going to stay there, others that we should go to Yorktown. Every day each party would have some new yarn to substantiate their opinion, but last Wednesday evening put an end to all their supposition.

We struck camp and Thursday forenoon left Portsmouth for Yorktown. When we got there the Doctor found that all the disabled and sick would have to go back again. So the next afternoon back we went and at last brought up in ward five of this Hospital. Luckily I got in the same ward with Steve. He is doing well and takes it cool enough. He hasn't been up to walk around any yet but is getting better every day.

When the boys got to Yorktown they had to take whatever they wanted out of their knapsacks and have them sent back to Portsmouth to be stored. Some of the boys kept nothing but their blankets and overcoats so I imagine some of their friends will be worried at not hearing from them, but they can't expect to hear as often as formerly for the boys are right in for a peninsular campaign and I feel ashamed of myself for not being with them.

If Nate stays at home the Osborne's will not participate at all. They have done a pretty good share considering. I hope Steve will go home and then you keep him there. I don't know as I shall ever train with the twenty threes again. The Veteran Reserve Corps is dead ahead now.

The sick are coming down every day from everywhere. Something will have to be done to make room for them. Some have been sent North already. Don't think by that I am coming[home] for there isn't the slightest danger of it.

How did you like the last pictures I sent?

Did you go a-Maying yesterday?

Last night the parson and sisters of charity came in and sang one or two hymns. The parson spouted a while. They go through all the wards Sundays.

There is a Secesh in this ward. He is rather an old man. Was sentenced to be hung for shooting one of our men, but his daughter got him pardoned and he stays here. [He] has a guard at his heels when he goes out. The daughter comes in to see him every day.

How are your romance(s)?

Tell Nate that I think my illustrious career in the service will wind up in the Invalid Corps.

There are several regiments of [word unclear] infantry stationed here. One has a black band and another has white orderly sergeants.

Love to all.

Yours.

Fred M. Osborne

Steve sends his love to all and wants to hear from somebody.

My letters have followed the reg't; [I] can't tell how long [I] shall get them.

When Fred wrote on May 2, "Did you go a-Maying yesterday?" he was remembering that the previous day had been May Day. Fred referred to expected fighting on the "peninsula," the land enclosed by the James and the York rivers and running back from Newport News toward Richmond. This expectation was common among the soldiers and the public at the time but was quite in error and was a tribute to General Grant's control of information about his campaign to end the war. Grant was determined to use surprise to the maximum extent as a military weapon. After his first interview with President Lincoln, Grant recorded in his notes: "I did not communicate my plans to the President, nor did I to the Secretary of War."[40] Grant wanted General Lee to be misinformed about his strategy and especially to believe that the peninsula campaign of 1862 would be repeated. In that campaign, General McClellan had come up the peninsula toward Richmond; when they were a few miles from Richmond, the Union forces had been withdrawn and moved to Washington to protect the capital. Grant had different notions about an attack on Richmond.

Fred was in McClellan Hospital at Hampton, Virginia, and the Massachusetts 23rd was at Yorktown, ready for the big move on Richmond. It would get underway in two days, on May 4, 1864.

## CHAPTER SIXTEEN

# Grant's Campaign Begins

## May and June, 1864

President Lincoln, aware that the campaign would soon get underway, wrote a warm letter to General Grant on April 30, 1864:[1]

> Executive Mansion
> Washington, April 30, 1864
> Lieutenant General Grant,
> Not expecting to see you again before the Spring campaign opens, I wish to express, in this way, my entire satisfaction with what you have done up to this time, so far as I understand it. The particulars of your plans I neither know, or seek to know. You are vigilant and self-reliant; and, pleased with this, I wish not to obtrude any constraints or restraints upon you. While I am very anxious that any great disaster, or the capture of our men in great numbers, shall be avoided, I know these points are less likely to escape your attention then they would be mine. If there is anything wanting which is within my power to give, do not fail to let me know it.
> And now with a brave Army, and a just cause, may God sustain you.
> Yours very truly
> A. Lincoln

President Lincoln used the title "Lieutenant General," which had been especially authorized for Grant by Congress in December 1863 to rank him above all other officers in the Union army.[2] The rank of "general" was apparently not available in deference to the memory of George Washington, who was the last to use that title, but it was often used casually in referring to lower-ranking generals such as a brigadier general or a major general.

> Executive Mansion
> Washington, April 30, 1864
>
> Lieutenant General Grant.
>
> Not expecting to see you again before the Spring campaign opens, I wish to express, in this way, my entire satisfaction with what you have done up to this time, so far as I understand it. The particulars of your plans I neither know, or seek to know. You are vigilant and self-reliant; and, pleased with this, I wish not to obtrude any constraints or restraints upon you. While I am very anxious that any great disaster, or the capture of our men in great numbers, shall be avoided, I know these points are less likely to escape your attention than they would be mine— If there is anything wanting which is within my power to give, do not fail, to let me know it. And now with a brave Army, and a just cause, may God sustain you.
>
> Yours very truly
> A. Lincoln.

**Abraham Lincoln's handwritten letter of April 30, 1864**

On May 4, 1864, the campaign began. General Grant, General Butler, and General Sherman, in concert, got their three armies underway on the grand strategy to end the war.

In his memoirs, General Grant describes the beginning of his Richmond campaign: "Soon after midnight, May 4th, the Army of the Potomac moved out ... to start on that memorable campaign, destined to result in the capture of the Confederate capital ... [in] as desperate fighting as the world has ever witnessed...."[3] It was a massive movement, more than four thousand wagons of war supplies for 150,000 soldiers, wagons that would have formed a train sixty miles long if they had been all placed in a single line, according to Shelby Foote.[4]

Grant's Army of the Potomac first had to cross the Rapidan River in the face of Robert E. Lee's entrenched and fortified army that was waiting for him on the other side. Temporary bridges had to be built, and they had to be protected against enemy fire as troops and cavalry and wagons crossed. In his memoirs, Grant notes: "I left [camp] after all the troops had been put in motion ... crossed the Rapidan ... and established headquarters ... in a deserted house.... Dispatches were received announcing that Sherman ... [and] Butler had moved according to programme."[5]

Lee learned that Grant had crossed the Rapidan, and he moved to intersect Grant's army as it moved south. This was just what Grant wanted; Lee and Grant both wanted a fight. The next morning, May 5, 1864, they probed to find each other in a section of country called the "Wilderness." Speaking of the Wilderness, Grant writes: "The battle-field ... [of] the Wilderness ... was covered with a dense forest. The roads were narrow and bad. All the conditions were favorable for defensive operations."[6] Lee's was a defensive operation; Grant was on the offense.

Grant and Lee fought in the Wilderness for two days, May 5 and 6. The dense thicket of trees and underbrush reduced visibility so that fighting was all small scale; since the gunners couldn't see through the thicket, artillery was useless, as dangerous to friend as to foe. "It was desperate," wrote a Confederate survivor of the battle of the Wilderness, "wild yells ... [the] roar of musketry ... strewing the Wilderness with human wrecks.... The storm of battle swept to and fro, in some places passing several times over the same ground, and settling down at length almost where it had begun the day before."[7]

Grant on the battle of the Wilderness: "More desperate fighting has not been witnessed on this continent than that of the 5th and 6th of May. Our victory consisted in having successfully crossed a formidable stream ... in the face of an enemy, and in getting the army together as a unit."

But in the Wilderness Grant lost 17,666 men while Lee lost 7800. Historian Shelby Foote asserts: "What it all boiled down to was that Grant was whipped ... if he would only admit it by retreating."[8] But Grant did not retreat, he advanced. "What ever happens, there will be no turning back," Grant had said before the campaign.[9]

After the heavy losses in the Wilderness, Grant's soldiers thought they were in a retreat when they marched away from the battlefield; but the column turned south, in the direction of Richmond. "There were cheers and ... tossed caps, and long afterwards men were to say that, for them, this had been the high point of the war. 'Our spirits rose,' one ... would recall, 'we marched free. The men began to sing.... That night we were happy.'"[10]

On May 7, Grant quietly moved his army past Lee in a night march, trying to get to Spotsylvania. In his memoirs Grant explains this maneuver: "My object in moving to Spottsyvania was two-fold: first, I did not want Lee to get back to Richmond in time to attempt to crush Butler before I could get there; second, I wanted to get between his army and Richmond if possible."[11] Grant always wanted to get behind Lee, between Lee and Richmond, so that he could attack and destroy Lee's army in the open before Lee could retreat into his prepared entrenchments in Richmond.

But Lee got to Spotsylvania first; Grant and Lee fought the battle of Spotsylvania from May 8 to May 20 with the result that Grant was bloodied but not stopped. It was during the fighting at Spotsylvania that General Grant made his famous comment to the War Department: "Our losses have been heavy as well as those of the enemy ... [but I intend] to fight it out on this line if it takes all summer." Grant lost 18,399 at Spotsylvania and Lee lost about 10,000.

According to historian Shelby Foote, Grant was now "down to 56,124 effectives, less than half the number he had mustered when he crossed the Rapidan, twelve days before." Grant had lost 35,000 in battle casualties in the Wilderness and at Spotsylvania, but he "did not let his heavy losses ... deter him from his purpose ... which was to whip the rebel army."[12]

On May 20, Lee didn't show fight, staying within his lines, so Grant again edged past Lee's army, going around his own left flank, moving towards Richmond.

General Lee was not aggressive in pursuing Grant; the weak condition of his army limited him to fending off Grant's army, trying to keep it away from Richmond. Lee was trying to hold on; he was short of men, of food, of shoes, and of war materials. His cause was hopeless. A Confederate victory in the war was not possible. To fight on, to cause thousands of additional battlefield deaths, both Union and Confederate, had to be justified in the minds of Lee and Jefferson Davis by the hope that Lincoln would lose the coming election, in November 1864, and the Union would then sue for peace.[13]

Grant had now advanced into country for which he had no maps. This was often the case in the Civil War for Union armies fighting in Confederate territory. In his memoirs, Grant notes: "The country ... was new to us and we had neither guides nor maps to tell us where the roads were. Engineer and staff officers were put to the dangerous duty of ... reconnoitring ... to locate the roads."[14]

From May 21 to the end of the month, Grant worked his way down toward Cold Harbor. Lee's army was also edging down, staying to Grant's west. Lee was moving toward entrenchments that waited for him in Richmond, and Grant was trying to cut Lee off from those entrenchments so he could attack Lee in the open country.

At Cold Harbor, at the end of May 1864, a fight was building. Grant, needing replacements for his heavy losses at the Wilderness and Spotsylvania, called on General Butler. Butler sent 16,000 troops, including the Massachusetts 23rd, under General W. F. (Baldy) Smith. They came on boats down the James River and up the York River.

General Butler did not at all agree with this use of his men or with the strategy of having a fight at Cold Harbor, as he writes in his autobiography: "Those sixteen thousand men under Smith were of no earthly advantage to Grant.... If he had not had them ... he probably would not have made the fight at Cold Harbor. That fight was simply an indiscriminate slaughter of our men to the number of eighteen thousand, and more than three thousand were of the troops I had sent — and better officers and soldiers never stood in line."[15]

General Smith marched his men to Cold Harbor, arriving on June 1. Smith's men were in the fight on June 2 and June 3. Grant notes in his memoirs: "An assault was ordered on June 3 ... at half past four in the morning ... Smith's [men] gained the outer rifle-pits [of the enemy].... The ground over which ... [Smith's men] had to move was the most exposed of any.... An open plain intervened between the contending forces at this point, which was exposed both to a direct and a cross fire." Grant adds sadly, " The assault cost us heavily and probably without benefit to compensate."[16]

Although Grant was later not pleased with his decision to fight at Cold Harbor, he may have been influenced by the vision of Cold Harbor as the last battle of the war, the possibility of vanquishing Lee on the steps of the Confederate capitol. Major General Martin McMahon, who participated in the battle, later wrote that Grant's troops, now only nine miles from Richmond, "almost within sight of the spires of [that city]," thought that this would be the last battle of the war: "Every one felt that this was to be the final struggle.... Richmond was dead in front.... Promptly at the hour named on the 3d of June the men moved ... with steady, determined advance, and there rang out ... such a crash of artillery and musketry as is seldom heard in war." Lee's army was in a semicircle around Grant's men, firing at them from the front and side. Scouts had not been sent out to discover Lee's deadly position. Grant's men, including the Massachusetts 23rd, walked into a slaughter, as the historian of Company F notes: "Company F ... clambered over our works and moved steadily up the slope under that terrible shower of shot and shell." And after the battle, he reports, "Night came down upon the field with our dead and wounded lying where they fell ... the groans ... and moaning of the dying ... a windrow of dead and dying.... Our dead had to be buried ... where they fell."[17]

General McMahon wrote: "In the opinion of a majority of its survivors, the Battle of Cold Harbor never should have been fought."[18] Grant is quoted as saying, "Cold Harbor is, I think, the only battle I ever fought that I would not fight over again."[19]

Grant and the Army of the Potomac now moved away from Lee's army, which was intrenched close to Richmond, and they joined Butler at City Point on the south side of the James River. Grant now planned to attack Richmond from the south.[20]

During the month since May 4, when the joint campaign began, General Butler had been working on his assigned objective of coming at Richmond along the south bank of the James River, first establishing a base at Bermuda Hundred and City Point.[21] On May 4, twenty-five thousand men, including the Massachusetts 23rd, had embarked at Yorktown, had come down the York River during

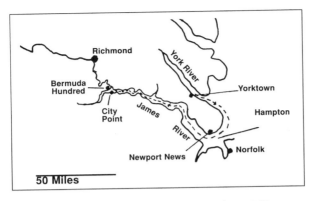

**Movement of Butler's Army, May 4–5, 1865**

the night, and had anchored in Hampton Roads. "At daylight of the 5th the whole ... fleet was assembled at Newport News and ascended the [James] river, led by the ironclads."[22] General Butler brought his army, consisting of the 10th Corps and the Eighteenth Corps, up the James River and captured City Point and Bermuda Hundred that day, May 5, and began to set up a base of operations. That evening he sent a telegram to General Grant: "Have landed at City Point.... Eighteenth and Tenth Army Corps are now being landed at Bermuda Hundred, above the Appomatox. No opposition thus far, apparently a complete surprise."[23]

According to historian Richard West: "Troops poured ashore unmolested.... Supplies grew in toppling pyramids [in] the village of City Point and [on] the shore line of the strategic Bermuda Hundred triangle.... The enemy's surprise had been complete.... In City Point and Bermuda Hundred, Butler confidently believed he held the key of Richmond."[24]

On May 5 and 6, when Grant was engaged in the battle of the Wilderness, Butler's men were digging a five-mile trench across the neck of the Bermuda Hundred peninsula; General Butler proceeded to fortify that trench, protecting the Bermuda Hundred triangle from landside attack. The Massachusetts 23rd anchored the southern end of that long fortification at a place called Cobb's Hill, which overlooked the Appomattox River. A member of Company F of that regiment remembers the early days on Bermuda Hundred: "Here, on a line running almost due north from Cobb's Hill, on the Appomatox, to the James River, the 'Army of the James' established itself.... Much of our off time was occupied with pick and spade upon the breastworks which were laid out along the line mentioned, and which later in the campaign served a good purpose in the protection of our base against frequent ... attacks by the enemy."[25]

A *New York Times* war correspondent rode that defense line with General Butler one day, and he reported in the May 9, 1864, issue of the *Times*: "[the weather was] insufferably hot, [the air] dense with dust raised by hundreds of cartwheels and thousands of horses .... [Butler's men] are enthusiastic and will go onward with eagerness at his bidding. I believe they have great faith in his leadership.... The cheering was hearty ... [for] the gallant old Massachusetts soldier."[26]

Richmond was twelve miles away; it was protected by strong fortifications at Drury's Bluff, a high cliff overlooking the James River. Butler sent General Baldy Smith and 30,000 men (including the Massachusetts 23rd) to attack Drury's Bluff and prepare the way to Richmond. In the dawn on May 16, in a dense fog, the Confederates counterattacked, driving off Butler's men. Fred talked about this battle in his next letter.

In late May, after this unsuccessful attack on Drury's Bluff, Grant ordered a contingent of Butler's men, including the Massachusetts 23rd, to come to Cold Harbor, as we have seen, to take part in that bloody battle.

Fred wrote his next letter from a hospital ship tied up at a Bermuda Hundred wharf. No longer hospitalized himself, he was serving as an aide to the ship's surgeon. Fred was now in the Veteran Reserve Corps, also known as the Invalid Corps.[27]

> Hospt Steamer Matilda
> Bermuda Hundred, Va
>
> June 5th 64
>
> Dear Jennie
>
> I have written home but once since I came here, as there has been no letters for me yet. I supposed you didn't get it. The last letter I received was at Getty Station. All that you have written since followed the regiment.
>
> I was sent here from Hampton about a month ago. The Post Surgeon sent me aboard this boat and Dr. Pratt, the surgeon here, kept me. I am now doing the writing in the office.
>
> This is merely a receiving institution. The wounded and sick are kept here until they can be taken to Fortress Monroe.

**A Union hospital ship**

I havn't been able to find out anything personal about the boys until within a few days. Geo Wilkins is dead and four or five of our company are taken prisoner. Poor Geo was killed the morning the Rebs came in on them in the fog. You heard of it before I did.

I saw a sergeant of Co K yesterday. He says the last he heard of the boys they were at Fair Oaks. The last time he saw them in line there were twenty five men and six officers. A great many are prisoners and more sick but where they have gone to I can't find out. There hasn't a sick man of the 23rd passed through this way. The boats must have taken them from up above.

There are thirteen of us detailed on the boat. The Doctor is a jolly old fellow and we have a good time. There is a barge close by us full of women (or four or five). It is a man and his family. The Old gal makes our bread for us.

Bermuda Hundred has got to be quite a place. There is a regular soldier's village, tents and shanties.

Most every night we can hear heavy firing, supposed to be Grant but as for knowing anything for certain it is out of the question.

The boats from Fortress Monroe get fired into once in a while down the river, but no regular attempt to stop communication has been made.

There is only part of the 10th Corps holding the works up here now, the rest having gone to join Grant.

Gen'l Butler is fortifying very heavily. The works are about six miles out from this place.

The black cavalry do all the duty at this station.

Our boat lies at the wharf all the time. Mr. Winchester, one of our company, is here with me. The Doctor is [a] queer fellow. He judges a man according to the amount of service he has seen. When he examined me, all he asked was how long have you been in the service, any fights, then said he guessed he would keep me.

The other night I got turned out of my domicile to make room for some secesh gals who came down from the front. There were sixteen of them large and small, old and young, and they drove me out of my room to make room for two damsels. Their children were howling and when they came aboard the squalling awoke every one. The next day they went home again. The shells drove them out of their house. There wasn't any bowing and scraping among the officers all rushing to see who should do something for them first.

How is Mrs. Wilkins? It must have been a hard blow for her.

Has Nate returned to his regiment yet? I hope not. He had ought lay back this campaign.

Where is Steve? He had ought to be at home.

Is Tuvvy better?

There must be lots of letters for me somewhere, but I can't get them.

Do you know what Dept Jim Miller is in? He has left the State by this time.

You can write me lots of news. It is so long since I heard from you. Did you receive the letters I wrote from Hampton, one to Mother and one to you? The rest of my correspondents must think I am a strange fellow, for I havn't even thought of writing anywhere except home. I should have written before but have been waiting for an answer to the other one.

I have had the chills and [word unclear] and Vc almost since I came here, but you can't find anybody that don't. One or the other of our crowd has to have them. We want to keep them in the family.

This is an uninteresting letter but it will let you know where I am and that I am in the land of the living.

How does the draft come on? Send me some scraps of news in the letter for a paper may not come safe.

My love to Father, Mother, Aunt Jane, Mary, Lizzie, Tuvvy, Caddie, and all the rest and write as soon as you can for we may leave at any time.

Yours

F M Osborne

Address: Fred M. Osborne
Bermuda Hundred, Va.
(Care of Surg. J. F. Pratt, Hospt. Steamer Matilda)

On April 27, 1864, Fred had been transferred to the Invalid Corps, also called the Veteran Reserve Corps.[28] Through this profound change in his army status, Fred had been removed from his regiment and was not active in the fighting going on nearby. He was no longer with the "Jewels," Company F, now down to a few men. He hadn't heard from Steve and didn't know where he was or how he was recovering from his wound. He hadn't heard about Nate to know whether he was in dangerous fighting in Sherman's new campaign, and he hadn't received any letters from home since he had left Getty Station back in April, six weeks ago. And Fred's dysentery must have made it hard to be courageous and upbeat. But, rising above all of his difficulties, he had written a cheerful letter to Jennie.

Fred reported to Jennie that he was helping with correspondence in the office of the hospital boat where he was recovering. In a receiving hospital like this one, transferred wounded soldiers on to other hospitals, each soldier's background had to be forwarded to the new hospital. Clear and legible writing was necessary because typewriters would not be invented for another forty years. Fred's education in cultured Salem made him a useful secretary, and his fifty-two letters home show that he wrote a neat script.

The battle of Drury's Bluff to which Fred referred in his letter was perhaps the most unhappy battle in the history of the Massachusetts 23rd regiment. The George G. Wilkins, who was killed in this battle was a private in Company A of Fred's Massachusetts 23rd regiment. He had been a Salem blacksmith and was 18 years old and single when he enlisted in 1861.[29] Fred's family must have known the Wilkins family because Fred asked about George's mother: "How is Mrs. Wilkins? It must have been a hard blow for her."

The battle of Drury's Bluff started on May 15, 1864, when Ben Butler's Army of the James approached under fire the fortification on Drury's Bluff, high up on the cliff overlooking the James River, eleven miles from Richmond. General Heckman's brigade, consisting of the Massachusetts 23rd, 25th, and 27th and the 9th New Jersey, found the approach to the fort hotly contested by the rebels. The brigade worked its way slowly to within a mile of the fort and then, as darkness fell, dug in on the open ground which sloped up to the fort and waited for the morning.[30]

The regimental history contains an account of the battle from General Heckman:

> At midnight the rebs moved out ... massing strongly ... and, just before daylight, rushed ... on our pickets, but, after a desperate struggle, were forced back.... Shortly after dawn, a dense fog enveloped us, completely concealing the enemy from our view.... [Rebel] brigades ... drove in our pickets.... My brigade swept instantly in line and steadily awaited their coming.... When only five paces intervened between the rebel bayonets and our inflexible line, a simultaneous scorching volley swept into the faces of the ... foe, smiting hundreds to the earth and hurling the whole column back in confusion.... Five times ... that magnificent rebel infantry advanced ... only to ... be driven back by those relentless volleys of musketry ... but they once more advanced ... and the Star Brigade ... vastly outnumbered, was, for the first time in its history, compelled to fall back.... I never at any other time experienced such musketry fire.... The enemy acknowledged a loss of four thousand five hundred on my front alone; and I lost nearly all my field and line officers.[31]

**General Charles Heckman**

The Massachusetts 23rd historian told of the fighting in the fog: "It is difficult, for one who was not in it, to form a fair idea of the density of that morning's fog.... A column of the enemy ... was only detected by a momentary lift of the fog, showing their massed feet.... [The men] of the 23rd were first made aware of a crushing attack on their ... rear by the splashing of feet ... [in a] pool [of water]."[32] Ben Butler's army retreated to Bermuda Hundred and surveyed its losses.

General Heckman, commander of the Star Brigade, was captured in the fog and imprisoned at nearby Richmond, in Libby Prison.

The Massachusetts 23rd had sent 226 men (all that remained from an original complement of 1,000) into the battle and had lost 89.[33] Company F had 14 men out of its original complement of 100 in the battle of Drury's Bluff and lost half of them. The historian of Company F (one of the few survivors of that battle) wrote: "That night we returned to ... camp [at Bermuda Hundred] from which we had confidently marched forth five days before. It was a sad roll call that evening. Of the fourteen men F had in line, seven were missing."[34]

Five Company F soldiers were taken prisoner in the battle of Drury's Bluff and all died in Confederate prisons:

• William H. Swaney was a seventeen-year-old laborer from Salem who had been with Fred in Company F since it was formed in 1861. Private Swaney was wounded and captured and taken to Libby Prison in Richmond. He died in Libby Prison eight days later.[35]

• David Carlton was a carpenter, who was 34 years old and married when he joined Company F in 1861; he had been wounded in the battle of Kinston in 1862. Captured at Drury's Bluff, he was sent to a prison in Charleston, South Carolina, where he lost his mind amid prison conditions. The Company F historian remembered him: "His indefatigable unselfishness kept him, as long as reason lasted, among the cheeriest and most useful to his fellow prisoners.... After a time, his privations induced the dementia, so commom in the inhuman prison-pens.... He wandered too near the 'dead-line' and was murdered by his guards."[36] The "dead-line," in Confederate prisons, was a line drawn across the prison yard; any prisoner who crossed that line was shot.

• Edward P. Grosvenor was a barrel maker in Salem when he enlisted in Company F in 1862. Captured at Drury's Bluff, he was sent to Andersonville Prison in Georgia, where he died three months later. He was buried, No. 4511, on the prison grounds.[37]

• Alvah Tibbetts was a 21-year-old private who came from a farming town near Salem. He had been in the army only five months when he was captured at Drury's Bluff. He died at Andersonville and was buried, No. 4634, on the prison grounds.[38]

• George O. Hinckley was a Salem junk dealer, who was 21 years old and married when he joined Company F in 1862. Taken prisoner at Drury's Bluff, he died at Andersonville four months later. He was buried, No. 9968, on the prison grounds.[39]

Confederate prisons were inhuman and Andersonville Prison, one hundred miles south of Atlanta was one of the worst. This pine-log stockade in the Georgia countryside, was a place of death where 13,714 Union soldiers died. The prison had just been opened when Fred's captured Company F friends arrived. It soon became severely overcrowded with 32,000 prisoners. No shelter was provided; prisoners "made tents of blankets and ... pieces of cloth, or dug pits in the ground." The "water supply ... became polluted under the congested conditions.... Prisoners suffered greatly from hunger, exposure and disease.... A third of them died."[40]

One prisoner who lived to tell about Andersonville was Charles Hopkins from Boonton, New Jersey. He wrote that he "was convinced ... that the Rebels sought to murder their Yankee prisoners through starvation, disease and mis-treat-ment.... Lice, maggots and flies were everywhere ... . [The] food was vile ... beans crawling with insects.... Water came from a stream [through the prison] which was used for latrines ... [as well as for] drinking water." The prison com-mandant, Capt. Henry Wirz, punished Hopkins by placing him in a stock that stretched him out in the Georgia sun.[41]

Swiss-born Henry Wirz was brought to trial after the war. In August 1865, President Andrew Johnson ordered a military commission to try Major Wirz for abusing prisoners at Andersonville. The Northern public wanted revenge, and Wirz was convicted and sentenced to hang. President Johnson approved the sen-tence, and Wirz was hanged at Washington, D.C., on November 10, 1865.[42] Much has been written about Andersonville, including the best-selling book *Andersonville* by MacKinlay Kantor, which was made into a movie of the same name by Columbia Pictures in 1959. President Clinton signed a bill in Septem-ber 1994 to build a museum at Andersonville to honor prisoners from all Amer-ican wars.[43]

Fred mentioned in his letter that some men in Company K were at Fair Oaks, which was located about seven miles east of Richmond. Fair Oaks was also known as Seven Pines and had been the site of a major battle two years earlier in June 1862.

Fred wrote that some of the men in the 10th Corps had gone to join Grant. Butler's army was made up of the 10th Corps and the 18th Corps. Most of these two corps had been sent to Grant for the battle of Cold Harbor, which was tak-ing place about the time that Fred was writing this June 5 letter. The Massa-chusetts 23rd was in the 18th Corps.

After the battle of Cold Harbor, Grant moved his Army of the Potomac down to City Point, which, combined with Bermuda Hundred, became the base for all Union operations against Richmond.

The "works" Fred mentioned were the five-mile long trench and earthwork fortification across the neck of the Bermuda Hundred triangle.

Dealing with the wounded coming from the battlefields around Richmond was a huge problem. Hospital ships such as the *Matilda* were tied up at the wharves at City Point and Bermuda Hundred to handle some of the wounded.

Fred reported that "The black cavalry do all the duty at this station." Gen-eral Butler was a strong advocate of black soldiers. One of the accomplishments of his career, he states in his memoirs, was his use of black soldiers: "I enlisted ... the first colored troops ever ... mustered into the army of the United States, thus inaugurating the policy of arming the colored race before Congress and the President had adopted it; by so doing, pointing the way to the recruitment ... of colored men to the number of one hundred and fifty thousand, and estab-lishing the negro soldier as a component part of the military resources of the coun-try forever."[44]

**A train of ambulances at City Point bringing the wounded from the battlefield**

The "Mr. Winchester" Fred mentioned was Isaac Winchester, a "stair-builder" from Salem, 44 years old and married. Fred referred to him as "Mr. Winchester" to show respect for an older man. Isaac Winchester survived the war and died in Salem in 1894.[45]

Fred worried about whether Nate had returned to his regiment and hoped he was not participating in Sherman's march through Georgia. According to his military records, Nate had in fact returned to his regiment from sick leave and was with Sherman as he attacked Johnston and pressed toward Atlanta. Sherman got his campaign underway on May 4, in concert with Grant and with Butler on the same date; he was now, in early June, fighting his way toward Atlanta, driving General Joe Johnston's Confederate army before him. Johnston was putting up a tremendous fight; Sherman would not get to the outskirts of Atlanta for another month, well into July 1864.

The answer to Fred's query "Where is Steve?" was that Steve was in the gangrene ward in a hospital at Hampton, according to his military records.[46]

Fred noted, "I have had the chills ... and Vc almost since I came here." The meaning of the term *Vc* is unclear, but it presumably is related to Fred's dysentery.

Fred was still on the hospital ship *Matilda* two weeks hence when he next wrote to his mother. The war was going on all around him, building to a crescendo.

Hospt steamer Matilda
Bermuda Hundred, Va

June 19th

Dear Mother

Yours of the fourteenth was received day before yesterday. The money was all right but I must tell you now what I neglected to in the first place, that State Money is of no more use here than so much brown paper. I should have written to you that greenbacks must be sent. Nothing but specie and greenbacks is current anywhere at the seat of war.

So I shall have to send it back again. Probably the cashier or whoever it was knew just as well as I do that he had no business to give you anything but greenbacks but he couldn't resist the temptation to take advantage of your not knowing the difference. I should just like to be there and have them do so. Now probably he will make a row about giving the greenbacks, but I suppose it is right that I should have the same money as I send home. But I hate to have Jennie or any of you fussing round about it. It isn't the thing for a lady anyway.

So if you cannot get it changed without Jennie or any of you having to do it let it go. It is a shame for her or anybody else to have to. He was very obliging indeed. If he had sent me the order first and then sent me state money he would have known what I thought of him. So if it can't be done without your going about it keep the money and let it slide. I had ought to have sent while Nate was at home. I'll bet he wouldn't have tried it on him. He would [have] known too much.

There hasn't been any news from the front today though the New York papers say Petersburg is taken, but we havn't heard anything about it.

City Point is the station where the business is being done. The Sanitary and Christian commissions have made a rush for there and Point of Rocks.

There have been several ladies here. They were connected with the Christian Commission. There were some from Chelsea, Mass., the Mayor of that city and his adopted daughter. They didn't take much notice of anybody but the 40th Mass.

The Christian and Sanitary commissions are a big institution. The wounded get a great deal that they would otherwise go without.

I have been trying to get over to City Point but havn't had a chance. I suppose some of our boys are there but we have had considerable to do ourselves.

Love to all.

Fred M Osborne

Tell Jennie I am so much obliged for the trouble she took on my account.

Has Nate gone to the West?

Havn't you heard from Steve yet?

Mother, I havn't received the things yet but the express doesn't come so direct as the mail.

F M O

Don't put this back in the bank but get the green backs somehow if you can, but don't worry yourself about it.

Fred was outraged that the bank clerk gave his mother "state money" to send on to him because a soldier could spend only "specie," gold and silver coins, and "greenbacks," paper money issued by the Union government. Before the Civil War, a national currency did not exist. For daily spending, people used gold and silver coins, which had intrinsic value due to their precious metal content, and paper money which was issued by local banks.

Certain banks in a given state were chartered by the state to issue paper bills.

This paper money depended for its usefulness on the confidence of the public in the local bank which issued it; it was thus limited to local use. Fred, a soldier in Virginia, could not spend paper money from a Massachusetts bank.

The first national paper money was issued in 1862 by the Union government to finance the Civil War. These paper bills, which were green on the reverse side, were called greenbacks.[47]

Fred mentioned the battle for Petersburg, a railroad center twenty miles south of Richmond that was attacked by General Butler on June 15th, four days before Fred wrote this letter. The battle was still going on. The capture of Petersburg was a part of General Grant's plan to end the war. After the battle of Cold Harbor, June 1 to 12, 1864, Grant worked out a plan to take Richmond and force the Confederacy to capitulate. Petersburg, the railroad junction feeding supplies to Richmond from the South, was a key element in that plan.

Grant knew that Lee's army, now entrenched in Richmond, would not come out to fight in the open. Grant's plan was simple: starve Lee into surrender. Grant set out to cut Richmond off from the north and west by destroying the Virginia Central Railroad. In his memoirs, Grant states: "The ... [Virginia] Central Road and the regions penetrated by [it are] ... of vast importance to the enemy, furnishing and supplying a large per cent of all the supplies for [Lee's army] and the people of Richmond." Grant ordered Sheridan's cavalry into the Virginia countryside in early June 1864 to destroy that railroad.

To cut off supplies to Richmond from the South required the capture of Petersburg and the destruction of its railroad junction, so Grant ordered Butler to attack Petersburg. Butler sent General Baldy Smith, who had just returned from Cold Harbor with his 18th Corps (including the Massachusetts 23rd), to attack Petersburg. On June 15, 1864, General Smith led an army of 18,000 men toward Petersburg, which was six miles away. General Butler thought it would be a straightforward operation, as he notes in his autobiography: "Smith had with him some eighteen thousand men. There were in Petersburg ... but twenty-two hundred [rebels].... My proposition to him was to go in by an attack and a 'rush.'"[48] General Butler, in a high observation tower, watched out across the flat countryside toward Petersburg for the smoke of artillery and musketry, signs that Smith was attacking, but nothing happened, as Butler explains in his autobiography:

> Hearing nothing from General Smith, early in the afternoon I dispatched Lieutenant Davenport of my staff to General Smith to ascertain ... why he had not attacked ... and with directions for an immediate attack. Davenport reported to me about 7 P.M. that he had found General Smith ... reconnoitring the enemy's position ... [that he] would at once make the attack.... About 9 P.M., I became anxious ... and ... sent ... Davenport back to see General Smith and to say to that officer that I desired to see [an] attack on [the enemy's] works.... Davenport reported to me between eleven and twelve ... that he found nothing being done ... that General Smith [had said] that he had determined to make no ... attack that night.... I sent

Davenport back ... to say to him that I peremptorily ordered an immediate ... attack to be made with all his force.... This order Davenport was
unable to deliver ... owing to the fact that General Smith ... had hidden
himself in a tent pitched among the bushes in the rear of his camp ... and
was there found by Davenport about sunrise.[49]

The attack on Petersburg never took place. General Butler was fuming; "Lee
was caught napping" he later wrote. Petersburg could have been easily taken if
General Baldy Smith had obeyed orders.

Now it was too late. General Lee immediately sent reinforcements to Petersburg, and heavy fighting followed on June 17 and 18. General Grant wrote in his
memoirs: "I believed then, and I still believe, that Petersburg could have been
easily captured at that time."[50] The war would have been shortened by many
months and many thousands of casualties had General Smith been inclined to
attack before Lee sent reinforcements.

General Grant set up fortifications around the city; he says in his memoirs:
"Thus began the siege of Petersburg."[51] The siege of Petersburg would go on for
months, and the Massachusetts 23rd regiment was part of the siege force.

In late June 1864, President Lincoln, who was inquisitive about how things
were going at Petersburg, took a steamer down the Potomac and up the James River,
arriving unannounced at Grant's headquarters at City Point. Colonel Horace Porter,
who served on Grant's staff, wrote to his wife: "We were sitting in front of the General's tent when there appeared very suddenly before us a long, lank-looking per-
sonage, dressed all in black, and looking very much like a boss-undertaker. It was
the President. He said, after shaking hands with us all, 'I just thought I would jump
aboard a boat and come down and see you. I don't expect I can do any good, and
in fact I may do harm, but I'll put myself under your orders and if you find me
doing anything wrong just send me right away'.... [He] remained with us till the
next day, and told stories all the time. He did not ask and said he did not want to
know Grant's plans."[52] General Grant took the occasion to express to the President
his own confidence; he said that his present course was certain to lead to victory.
"You will never hear of me farther from Richmond than now, till I have taken it....
It may take a long summer day, as they say in the rebel papers, but I will do it."[53]

While he was at City Point, Lincoln visited a division of colored soldiers,
who thronged around him "anxious for a chance to touch the Great Emancipa-
tor or his horse in passing.... Tears in his eyes, he took off his hat in salute to
them, and his voice broke when he thanked them for their cheers."[54]

Grant's plan to cut off supplies to Richmond was not working out perfectly.
The railroad junction at Petersburg although under siege was still operational,
still feeding supplies to Richmond. Sheridan's cavalry had been less than successful in cutting the Virginia Central railroad off from supplying Richmond
from the north and west, from the Shenandoah Valley. Railroads had been cut,
but Lee's cavalry had fought back and had driven Sheridan away.

General Lee fortified his position, building miles of fortifications running from east of Richmond down to Petersburg and around to the south of the city. Grant's siege of Richmond and Petersburg began in late June 1864 and would stretch into the months ahead.

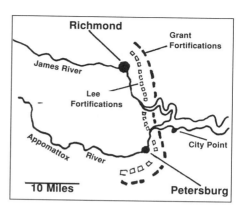

The men of the Massachusetts 23rd regiment, the few men remaining, dug in opposite Lee's earthworks. Fred's Company F, down to seven men — down from the seventy eager youngsters who drilled on Salem Common in the

**Fortifications around City Point**

fall of 1861—"went into the trenches," according to the Company F historian.[55] The historian continued, "Grant's ... lines were now being drawn about the city in python-like folds, whose close embrace was never to be loosened until the end."[56]

Fred referred to City Point as the place "where the business is being done." City Point was indeed the center of things, and General Grant had located his headquarters there. High on the headlands overlooking the junction of the James and the Appomattox rivers, City Point was just across from the Bermuda Hundred triangle. Fred's hospital ship was tied up at a wharf on the shore line of Bermuda Hundred, not far across the water from City Point.

"The Sanitary and Christian commissions have made a rush for [City Point] and Point of Rocks," Fred wrote his mother. Point of Rocks, located on the shoreline of the Bermuda Hundred triangle, had been a large farming estate and was now a Union military installation.[57] General Butler had built a pontoon bridge from Point of Rocks over the Appomattox River to move troops across the river in the maneuvers against Petersburg. General Butler also "built a hospital at Point of Rocks and furnished it with gas and water, and with cows for milk."[58] Time has improved on these war uses of Point of Rocks; it is today a community park where children play.

The Sanitary Commission, which was busy at City Point and Point of Rock, was the precursor of the Red Cross of later wars. It was an important factor in the life of the common soldier. Seldom mentioned by Civil War historians, it was a charity organization which had special concern for wounded soldiers, who have received little attention from historians of the Civil War. Historian Allan Nevins, exceptional in his concern, has called the story of the wounded soldier "almost the darkest side of the Civil War."[59]

The Sanitary Commission, in addition to its concern for the wounded, became interested in the soldier's welfare in camp. This was particularly important because the army showed little interest in the welfare of the individual soldiers, their sanitation, their food, their comfort, or their morale. Except for a few individual officers who had a feeling for their men's welfare, such matters went begging.

The Sanitary Commission needed someone to run the operation. Frederick Law Olmsted, who was at the moment in the middle of creating Central Park in New York City, was their man and charged into the job with enthusiasm. A slender man with a slight limp from a carriage accident, he came to Washington before the first battle of Bull Run, which took place just outside the city. On that June 1861 day, Olmsted had watched soldiers streaming back into the city from the battlefield of Bull Run leaving thousands of wounded men on the ground. Little thought had been given to picking up these wounded soldiers; there were no ambulances, there were no hospitals.

But the Sanitary Commission had to argue to get its help accepted. "General Halleck, commander in chief of the Union army, thought present arrangements quite satisfactory ... that men had to suffer," that was the nature of war.[60] "A general belief continued well after Bull Run that wounded soldiers generally managed to creep back to their lines [without the need for ambulances]."[61] Olmsted and his agents visited army camps and battles in progress, developing an exquisite concern for the soldier's health and well-being both before and after battle.

Not a part of the government and using no government funds, the Sanitary Commission became the funnel through which flowed the huge outpouring of support for the Union cause. Every city and every town, every country crossroads, had enthusiastic groups, especially of women, who wanted to give to the war effort. The Sanitary Commission organized not less than seven thousand such aid societies, setting up warehouses and distribution systems to collect and deliver comfort goods for the soldiers and medical supplies for the wounded. It sent "agents ... to five hundred bloody battles to inspect the conditions under which soldiers lived and fought; it developed relief corps for camp, battlefield and hospital."[62]

Frederick Law Olmsted developed the hospital ship; he modified side-wheel steamboats into hospitals to handle the wounded coming from the battlefields. The mission of the hospital ship was to mitigate the horrors of battlefields "drenched with fraternal blood." Fred Osborne, was on one of the Sanitary Commission hospital ships, the *Matilda*, which took wounded soldiers from the Petersburg battlefields. It was fitting that the first hospital ship was named for Daniel Webster, who had so feared a civil war.

The U.S. Christian Commission that Fred also mentioned was organized early in the war, at about the same time as the Sanitary Commission, by the Young Men's Christian Association, the YMCA. The Christian Commission "worked in conjunction with the U.S. Sanitary Commission for the relief of the soldiers at the front." Free boxlunches and coffee wagons were sent to compete with sutlers selling whiskey.... Special ... kitchens were provided for the ... wounded.... Ladies ... volunteered their nursing skills in hospitals. Its members ... attempted to uplift soldiers's moral and religious spirit.... Reading rooms ... were stocked with Bibles and newpapers from home. The Commission encouraged men to write to their families and provided free writing materials and stamps.[63] The Commission may also have supplied the New York papers mentioned by Fred.

"Has Nate gone to the West?" Fred asked his mother. Nate was with Sherman, approaching Atlanta. It had been a long, hard fight against General Joe Johnston's Confederate army. Sherman would lay siege to Atlanta in a few days, a siege which would last into September 1864.

Fred's inquiry about Steve indicates that he apparently had not heard any news about Steve since they were in the same ward in McClellan Hospital in Hampton, Virginia, back in May. Steve was still in McClellan Hospital and still having trouble with his wounded leg. On June 14, 1864, five days before Fred wrote this letter, Steve was transferred into the gangrene ward in that hospital. Painful gangrene treatment, including the use of caustic fluids to burn the wound, would go on for weeks.[64]

Fred Osborne continued serving on the hospital ship into the summer of 1864, taking the wounded from the fighting around Petersburg.

## CHAPTER SEVENTEEN

# The End of the War

## Summer 1864

It was a slow war during the summer of 1864. The siege of Petersburg went on. Confederate soldiers, dug in behind miles of earthwork fortifications, faced Grant's army lined up behind opposing earthworks. The lines were sometimes only a few hundred feet apart. Fred Osborne's regiment, the Massachusetts 23rd, was in the Union trenches. The Massachusetts 23rd was close to the city of Petersburg, only a mile and a half away. Private Herbert Valentine, historian of Company F, described the situation in the trenches:

> We could hear the [railroad] cars running in and out of Petersburg, and the clang of church bells ... came floating over the lines.... It was hot in the pits on those bright summer days.... There was nothing to screen us from the sun's rays.... In the darkness we were treated to brilliant displays.... The [enemy] mortar firing always attracted attention.... A flash ... was followed by the hollow boom of the mortar, and a little spark of fire could be seen rising slowly in the air, describing a beautiful curve as it reached its height. Beginning to descend, it moved more and more rapidly, the hissing of the fuse sounding louder and louder as it came nearer. Suddenly, coincident with the explosion, came a flash that illumined the whole landscape, and the ensuing darkness could almost be felt....
>
> There was great diversity in the sound of the various missiles [the rebels] hurled at us. The shriek of a Whitworth, seeming to cry, "Which one, which one, which one?" the whirr of a round shot, and the scream of a conical shell.... Some good, honest shells flew over, with a professional directness which insured respect.... Occasionally one appeared, as it were, to stumble along with a sidelong motion and a swaggering noise, which was often interpreted as saying, "Where's that nigger? Where's that nigger?"[1]

Shells were also flying in the opposite direction as Union artillery pounded the city of Petersburg. Private Valentine noted: "A heavy gun ... at intervals of fifteen minutes ... sent a shell into Petersburg.... We could hear the report [of the cannon], then the scream of the missile as it flew overhead on its deadly errand. 'There goes the Express' would pass from lip to lip. In a few seconds came the explosion of the shell, then the reverberations among the buildings."[2]

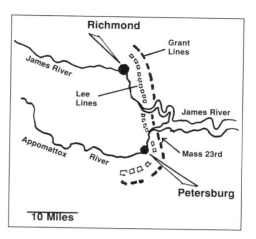

The Massachusetts 23rd took a periodic rest from the trenches at its relief camp three quarters of a mile behind the lines. Another Civil War soldier reported that the tour of duty in the trenches began "at 10 P.M. continuing for forty-eight hours, thus giving one full night in the trenches, the troops always entering and retiring after dark. The period of rest at the rear was the same length of time. We usually entered at about the same place, through what first appeared to us a labyrinth of traverses and covered ways, by which the danger was minimized in approaching the front line."[3]

According to Private Valentine: "Our life in the trenches was ... very monotonous.... We read the papers when we could get them ... principally the New York Herald.... Much of the time was given to sleep.... [There was] some card playing [as] in the old Highlander days."[4] Sometimes there was a temporary truce to exchange newspapers for tobacco: "On one side or the other a paper is raised above the breastworks. Upon return of the signal the men climb over the works and walk out to the middle ground, shake hands, have a few minutes' chat, and separate."[5]

The fortifications built by Grant and by Lee were elaborate. The trenches lay behind raised earthen barriers which were topped by logs to protect riflemen from enemy fire as they shot through openings between the logs. In front of the earthen barrier, poles were installed in the ground at an angle, the tips sharpened to inhibit attackers.

The lines of fortified trenches ran to "redans," or forts, thus forming a system of connected forts. A maze of additional trenches was dug in the rear of the forward line for troops to move in safety to and from the rest camps in the rear. And all the trenches were linked with sunken and covered roads to move guns and supply wagons, protected from enemy fire.

According to historians Johnson and Buel, Grant's men installed forty heavy siege guns and sixty mortars "capable of lofting shells into the enemy trenches. The Confederates soon responded in kind, and the shelling became a daily, deadly factor in the life of the men."[6]

## The Battle of the Crater

As June gave way to July, the stalemate continued. General Robert E. Lee held his line of fortifications. General Grant, who was not able to pierce Lee's defenses, became more receptive to an outlandish idea for breaching the Confederate fortifications. That outlandish idea came from some soldiers in the trenches who came from the coal mining region of western Pennsylvania; they were the 48th Pennsylvania Volunteers commanded by Colonel Henry Pleasants. The coal miners' suggestion for breaking through Lee's line of fortifications was to dig a mine shaft under the Confederate line and blow it up. Grant's soldiers would then charge through the blasted opening and head for Petersburg a short distance away. General Ambrose Burnside, who was now Pleasants's commander, promoted the scheme to General Grant. It would enter history as the "Burnside Mine" or, because of the huge hole in the ground made by the explosion, "the Crater."

This idea was at first rejected, but as the stalemate continued it began to sound good to Grant. He finally gave his approval, and the digging of the mine shaft got underway. The mine shaft, twenty feet under the surface, ran 500 feet from the Union trenches to a point under the line of Confederate fortifications. Because they were not taken seriously by the army staff, the diggers got no help in the way of digging equipment. Colonel Pleasants, who was in charge of the operation, wrote later: "My regiment was only about four hundred strong.... The great difficulty I had was to dispose of the material got out of the mine. I found it was impossible to get any assistance from anybody.... I had to remove all the earth in old cracker-boxes; I got pieces of hickory and nailed them on the boxes [for handles] ... and then iron-clad them with hoops of iron taken from old pork and beef barrels."[7]

Colonel Pleasants had to get blacksmiths to improvise picks for digging since the army would not supply them. He complained: "Whenever I made application I could not get anything.... General Burnside told me that [army headquarters] said the thing could not be done — that it was all clap-trap and nonsense."[8] Army headquarters called the mine shaft "clap-trap and nonsense" because "such a length of mine had never been excavated in military operations, and could not be."[9] Military thinking did not see how fresh air could be supplied to workers in such a long shaft. But the Pennsylvanians worked out a scheme to draw fresh air into the tunnel by using the draft created by a fire in a vertical shaft to the surface above. Warm air from the fire rose up the shaft, drawing fresh air in at the tunnel entrance. The arrangement worked very well.

On July 28, the digging of the mine shaft was completed; 320 kegs of gunpowder were carried into the mine shaft and placed under the Confederate fortifications.[10] By this time General Grant had developed an enthusiasm for the project. "The mine was constructed and ready to be exploded," he says in his memoirs, "and I wanted to take that occasion to carry Petersburg if I could."[11]

He ordered a large force to get ready to penetrate the breakthrough in Lee's line. The Massachusetts 23rd was part of that force. Huge artillery firepower, comparable to the Union artillery used at Gettysburg, was ordered up.[12] Grant was now serious.

Days in advance of the planned explosion, General Burnside had thoroughly organized his men for the breakthrough. He selected two brigades of colored troops to lead the charge through the opening to be created by the explosion; once through the opening they would then establish a Union position, ready to move on toward Petersburg. Historian Shelby Foote explains: "By way of preparation, he had had the two brigades spend the past week

**Colonel Henry Pleasants**

rehearsing the attack until every member knew just what he was to do, and how; that is, rush promptly forward, as soon as the mine was sprung, and expand the gap so that the other ... divisions, coming up behind, could move unopposed ... [to] the rear of the blasted enemy intrenchments, which would give them a clear shot at Petersburg itself."[13]

The mine was scheduled to go off at 3:30 A.M. on July 30, a Saturday. The afternoon before, as Burnside was giving his commanders their final orders, "he was interrupted by a courier from army headquarters bearing a message ... an order ... for the assault to be spearheaded not by ... well-rehearsed Negroes, but one of the white divisions."[14] Ambrose Burnside was stunned. His well-laid plans were destroyed. General George Meade, Burnside's superior officer, at the last moment and only hours before the scheduled explosion, forced Burnside to reorganize his attack plans. Why would the experienced General Meade take such an action, putting the enterprise at risk? Burnside went to Meade and pleaded his case, but Meade was adamant. He thought that it might not look good to the public for Burnside to use Negroes to lead the charge. Burnside was not able to change his mind. The record does not seem to justify Meade's action; but Burnside, not Meade, has taken the historical heat for the debacle that followed. General Grant would testify at a subsequent hearing: "This change ... was provoked by ... racism in reverse. 'If we put the colored troops in front and [the attack] should prove a failure, it would then be said, and very properly, that we were shoving those people ahead to get killed because we did not care anything about them.'"[15] But, Grant testified, "General Burnside wanted to put his colored division in front, and I believe if he had done so it would have been a success."[16]

The division of white soldiers that Burnside was forced to choose to lead the charge had no time for preparation in the few hours remaining before the explosion. They were completely at a loss as to what to do when the blast went off.

In the trenches the night before the blast, the Massachusetts 23rd regiment, got the word to get ready: "On the night before Burnside's mine was blown up we occupied the usual position ... [near] the Appomattox River," reported Private Herbert Valentine of Company F. He was sent out in the darkness to the rifle pits in front of the Union trenches to tell the men of the Massachusetts 23rd to come to the rear and get ready to take part in the assault after the explosion "I crawled [out] and ... as I reached the men I ordered them ... to the rear."[17]

Private Valentine described the scene as the Massachusetts 23rd got ready to go through the rebel line when the mine exploded:

> Moving toward the left [along the Union line, our regiment] took [the] position assigned to us.... We waited until the dawn gave us a view of the scene.... The troops were massed closely and an air of expectation pervaded the whole army. At half past four there was an upheaval of the ground, a mass of rocks and earth ... was thrown up in one tremendous column, the ... roar of an explosion following.... All along the line every cannon opened its ... throat, the air was full of shells, and the roar of musketry was terrific.... It was a magnificent spectacle, and as the mass of earth went up in the air, carrying with it men, guns, carriages, and timbers ... so close were the Union lines that the mass appeared as if it would descend immediately upon the troops waiting to make the charge.[18]

The Confederate fortification was blown into the sky, leaving an enormous crater 200 feet long, 50 feet wide, and 30 feet deep. In the crater, said one eyewitness, were "guns, broken carriages, projecting timbers, and men buried in various ways — some up to their necks, others to their waists, and some with only their feet and legs protruding from the earth."[19]

Both Confederate and Union soldiers were stunned for some minutes. Then Union soldiers began to move forward down into the crater and the Confederate soldiers pulled themselves together and began firing down on the Union men. Union artillery, 160 guns, began to fire to deter the enemy artillery from firing on the advancing Union troops. Confederate artillery, however, caught the Union soldiers who were behind the crater, waiting to advance, in a cross-fire, "sweeping the open field like a tornado," according to a Confederate gunner, who said, "the field looked like an inclined plane of dead men."[20] General Ledlie, who was in charge of the white division leading the assault, was "huddled in a bombproof far to the rear, comforting himself with a bottle of rum. He sat there in safety while his division fell into confusion."[21]

According to a Union major who participated in the battle: "Had General

Burnside's original plan [using the colored troops in the lead] been sanctioned, ... [the Union soldiers] could and would have re-formed and moved on [toward Petersburg] before the enemy realized fully what was intended ... [but] there being no commander present to give orders ... a formation ... was something no troops could accomplish."[22] A Confederate general on the scene commented later: "If the mine — itself a success, making an immense breach in General Lee's works — had been followed up by any vigorous attacking column ... it may not be too much to say that the retreat that [General Lee] ... was

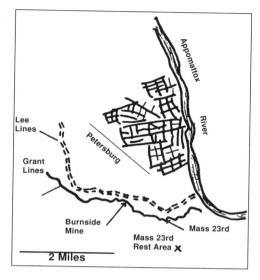

**Location of Burnside's Mine**

compelled to make nine months later would then have been unavoidable. After the explosion there was nothing on the Confederate side to prevent ... opening wide the gates to the rear of [Richmond]."[23]

Bedlam and confusion continued for several hours. "The slaughter was fearful," a Union officer recalled. The dead were, in some places, piled eight deep.[24] The Massachusetts 23rd was never ordered forward. According to Private Valentine, "After the explosion we moved first to the left, then to the right, where we took a position to the right of [Burnside's] 9th Corps. Here we were nearer than ever to our friends of the other side, the opposing lines being so close that hand grenades were thrown from one to the other."[25] But the regiment was not ordered into the fight. By 2 P.M., ten hours after the mine was exploded, the battle of the Crater was over.

The Union lost 4000 men in the battle.[26] Fred probably saw many of the wounded, who were carried to his waiting hospital ship, the *Matilda*, five miles away.

This battle was the end of General Burnside's military career, as historian Shelby Foote notes:

> Resigning from the service, Ambrose Everett Burnside, forty years old, returned to his business pursuits in Rhode Island, where he not only prospered but also recovered the geniality he had lost in the course of a military career that required him to occupy positions he himself testified he was unqualified to fill. In time he went into politics, serving three times as

governor, and would die well into his second term as a U.S. senator, twenty years after the war began.[27]

William Marvel, in a recent book, gives a balanced view of the often-criticized military career of this gentle man who was never eager for great responsibility.[28]

The siege of Petersburg went on with the Massachusetts 23rd back in the trenches that summer of 1864. The stalemate between the Union and Confederate fortifications became something to which both sides adjusted. Private Valentine later recalled: "The boys were very social with the 'Johnnies'.... [We had] an agreement with them not to fire on each other except in case of a general attack."[29]

On August 25, 1864, the Massachusetts 23rd regiment moved a few miles east from the Petersburg trenches to the trenches on Bermuda Hundred, the old "Butler Entrenchment." In a few days, on September 4, 1864, the regiment boarded a ship and went off to New Bern, the scene of its former glory, leaving Fred Osborne at Bermuda Hundred on the hospital ship *Matilda*.

## The March to the Sea

### September 1864

The month of September started off with a bang. Sherman took Atlanta on September 2, to great jubilation in the North. Lincoln's prospects for the upcoming November election, which had been languishing badly that summer, rose dramatically with the news of Sherman's victory.

The war-weary Northern voter, eager to end the conflict with the Southern states, would be able to choose in the November election between Lincoln, who was committed to fighting the war until the South surrendered, and McClellan, Lincoln's former general, who was willing to make a deal with the Southern states leaving slavery in place.[30]

Mary Osborne, at home at 17 Oliver Street in Salem that September, had three boys in the war. Nate was at Atlanta with Sherman. Steve was now in a hospital in Beverly, New Jersey, still undergoing gangrene treatment for his thigh wound. Fred, her youngest

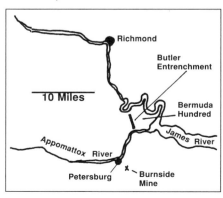

**Location of Butler Entrenchment**

son, with a bad knee and dysentery, was on a hospital ship receiving wounded soldiers from the Petersburg battlefields.

After the capture of Atlanta, Captain Nathan Osborne and the rest of General Sherman's army spent some weeks there recuperating and getting resupplied for the next leg of their campaign through the South. When the siege of Atlanta ended on September 2, 1864, General Sherman set up his headquarters in the court house square and immediately issued an order which caused an uproar throughout the South. Sherman demanded that all civilians leave the city; he didn't want to spend manpower and energy administering a city of captured Southerners. In his memoirs he explained this policy:

> I had seen Memphis, Vicksburg, Natchez, and New Orleans garrisoned by a full division of troops.... Success was actually crippling our armies ... [by using soldiers] to guard and protect ... a hostile population.
>
> I peremptorily ordered that all the citizens ... in Atlanta should go away.... I knew ... that such a measure would be strongly criticized.... I gave notice [to Washington]: "If the people raise a howl against my barbarity and cruelty, I will answer that war is war, and not popularity-seeking."[31]

In September 1864, the Massachusetts 23rd regiment was camped outside of New Bern, North Carolina; the regiment was assigned to picket duty, to alert the city in case of a rebel attack.

An epidemic of yellow fever was raging in New Bern, as the regimental historian noted:

> No one was permitted to enter the city unless driven by urgent necessity.... [New Bern) seemed a dolorous city of the dead.... The pall of smoke filling the streets from fires kept burning at every corner ... utter vacuity and stagnation. One ... saw only those tend[ing] the fires ... [or taking part in] the burial parties. The regiment lost a number of men ... during the epidemic: Austin, Kinsman, Parks, Saunders, Davis, Haskell, Smith, Wonson, Hart, Richardson, Glidden, Goodwin, Reeves and Spear.[32]

On September 26, the three year men in the Massachusetts 23rd regiment, the original members who did not reenlist, started for home. They took a steamer from New Bern to Fort Monroe where they were quarantined for four days, and then traveled by steamer to New York and on to Boston. After receiving the hospitalities of the city at Faneuil Hall, they were dismissed with orders to rendezvous at Lynnfield, near Salem, for muster out.[33]

That was the end of the war for the men who had joined the Massachusetts 23rd with Fred at Lynnfield three years before, but Fred was not with his three-year comrades. Fred was mustered out of the army on September 28, 1864, while on board the *Matilda* tied up at Bermuda Hundred. No particulars are available on Fred's travel back to his home in Salem, Massachusetts, but he was undoubtedly at home when Lincoln was elected to a second term that November.

## November, 1864

"Lincoln was ... nervous on election day, November 8, but the result soon set his mind at rest," recounts historian Peter Parish.[34] McClellan, a strong threat before the election, won only three states, Kentucky, New Jersey and Delaware. The popular vote was:

Lincoln 2,213,645
McClellan 1,802,237

Lincoln's victory ensured that the war against the Confederacy would be pursued with vigor. A major player in this final stage of the war was General Sherman, who was resting his army at Atlanta for a month as he contemplated his next move. Grant wanted Sherman to slice through the eastern half of the Confederacy, the half left after the battle of Vicksburg and the capture of the Mississippi River had cut away the western half. That slicing would shatter the Confederacy; Sherman's idea was to punish the populace so that it would be sick of war. Grant and Sherman's plan called for Sherman to march to Savannah, take over that important Confederate port city and then march toward Richmond through South Carolina and North Carolina.

As it turned out, Sherman would employ a different kind of warfare after he left Atlanta. When he had fought his way down toward Atlanta, his army had been supplied by a railroad running back to his supply depot in Nashville. Leaving Atlanta for the march to Savannah, Sherman decided to cut loose from that railroad and live off the land because it would take too much of his army to patrol and protect that railroad against Confederate attacks. He would do without all those supplies.

On its "march to the sea," Sherman's army would travel light and fast and avoid pitched battles. Pitched battles required lots of supplies and heavy artillery. General Sherman would demonstrate, in his march through the South, that the Civil War need not have been fought primarily with bloody pitched battles such as Gettysburg, Antietam, and Fredericksburg. Although Sherman did not eschew pitched battles because they were brutal — he accepted the brutality of war — he did show that there was a different way of fighting. Different from the bloody set-piece battle, soldiers charging into cannon fire, men falling by the thousands. Killing was the main business of the pitched battle.

According to John Keegan, renowned military historian, the Greeks invented the pitched battle.[35] The Romans copied the Greeks, bringing the pitched battle into Europe along with the Roman Empire; in Europe it came down through time to Frederick the Great. Frederick the Great was the military progenitor of the Civil War generals who were taught his battle tactics at West Point. The pitched battle was the way to make war; high casualties were an accepted feature. There were other kinds of warfare, the hit and run tactics of the Russian Cossacks for example. But the Cossacks were "unmilitary," they galloped away from a superior enemy to fight another day. In the European military tradition that was adopted by our Civil War generals, "the real business was butchery. Men stood ... in rows to be slaughtered," writes John Keegan, who called these battles "slaughter-house scenes."[36]

In the Civil War, the honorable fight was the face-to-face battle, fought by soldiers of do-or-die blind courage. It was honorable to die in battle; it was honorable to walk into cannon fire. The tradition was pervasive; society at home, even mothers, condemned soldiers who took exception to orders sending them to almost certain death.

On November 15, 1864, Sherman's army started for Savannah. Grant writes in his memoirs: "On the 15th the ... march to the sea commenced.... Sherman's orders for this campaign were perfect.... Before starting, he ... sent back all sick, disabled and weak men, retaining nothing but the hardy, well-inured soldiers ... [for] his long march in prospect.... His artillery was reduced.... Small rations were taken in a small wagon train.... The army was expected to live on the country."[37] Captain Nathan Osborne commanded a company in this lightly equipped, fast-moving army.

Sherman destroyed Southern railroads as he went. "The method adopted ... was to tear up the track and bend the rails. Soldiers, to do this rapidly, would form a line along one side of the [tracks] with crowbars and poles, place these under the rails and, hoisting all at once, turn over many [yards] of [rail]road at one time." Fires were built with the wooden ties to heat the iron rails red-hot in the middle; "the soldiers ... one at each end of the rail, [carried it] with force against the nearest tree and twist[ed] it around [the tree] ... thus leaving rails ... to ornament the forest trees of Georgia."[38]

In his usually sober memoirs, General Grant cannot resist including an anecdote of the march:

> The South, prior to the rebellion, kept bloodhounds to pursue runaway slaves.... Orders were issued to kill all these animals.... A soldier picked up a poodle, the favorite of his mistress.... When the lady made a strong appeal to him to spare it ... the soldier replied, "Madam, our orders are to kill every bloodhound." "But this is not a bloodhound," said the lady. "Well, madam, we cannot tell what it will grow into if we leave it behind," said the soldier as he went off with it.[39]

As Sherman's army traveled through Georgia, one officer recalled, "we had ... throngs of escaping slaves, from the baby in arms to the old negro hobbling painfully along the line of march ... negroes of all sizes, in all sorts of costumes, with carts and broken-down horses."[40]

## December 1864

The march to the sea went rather easily, although there was some minor scuffling with Confederate forces outside Savannah. "On December 21, 1864," remembered General Oliver Howard, commander of the 15th Corps, in which Nate was marching, "the campaign culminated as Sherman entered Savannah. He sent a dispatch to President Lincoln [on] ... Christmas eve: 'I beg to present to you, as a Christmas gift, the city of Savannah.'"[41]

In December 1864, Steve rejoined his regiment, after spending eight months in hospitals the surgeons worked on healing the gangrenous bullet wound in his left thigh. His leg finally healed, Steve returned to his regiment on December 5, 1864, joining the Massachusetts 23rd in New Bern, North Carolina.[42] The yellow fever epidemic there had ended.

While Sherman rested at Savannah in January 1865, General Grant was planning Sherman's next move. Grant considered bringing Sherman's army north from Savannah to Richmond in ships because he knew the roads were bad for the movement of the usual kind of massive, heavily laden army. In his memoirs, Grant writes, "I had no idea originally of having Sherman march from Savannah to Richmond or even to North Carolina. The season was bad, the roads impassable."[43] General Grant did not yet appreciate the mobility of Sherman's lightly equipped, fast-moving, living-off-the-land kind of army. Grant had, in fact, already ordered the ships to take Sherman's army by water up to the James River, but according to Grant's memoirs:

> [Sherman] suggested the idea ... of marching north through the Carolinas. I was only too happy to approve this for ... it offered every advantage. His march through Georgia had thoroughly destroyed all lines of communication in that State, and had completely cut the enemy off from all sources of supply to the west of it. If North and South Carolina were rendered helpless so far as capacity for feeding Lee's army was concerned, the Confederate garrison at Richmond would be reduced ... to draw supplies from ... Virginia ... [which was] already exhausted of both forage and food. I approved Sherman's suggestion therefore at once.[44]

Sherman's march through the Carolinas, a killing blow to the Confederacy, might not have happened if Sherman had not had that fast-moving army at the time.

General Sherman wrote to Grant from Savannah: "In about ten days I will be ready to sally forth again.... As to our future plans ... they are as clear as daylight.... I will move by Branchville or Columbia ... ignoring ... Charleston.... Charleston is now a mere desolated wreck, and is hardly worth the time to starve it out.... I would then favor a movement on Raleigh. The game is then up with Lee."[45]

## March 1865

It had been three years since the Burnside expedition had taken New Bern. As part of the endgame of this war, the Union army had decided to strengthen New Bern and other Union holdings in North Carolina, anticipating finally taking over the whole state from the rebels. This strengthening process had started at the end of 1864 when the Massachusetts 23rd returned to New Bern.

As it worked out, North Carolina would be the culmination of Sherman's march through the South. He would stop at Goldsboro to replenish his army. "We are approaching the end of the war," wrote the historian of the Massachusetts 23rd. "The 23rd is to be called upon for its last service in the field. Gen. Sherman's army has been leaving its smoking trail across the Carolinas. He has been subsisting largely upon the country but must soon seek a base for renewed supplies of ammunition and such stores as the conquered country can not furnish. Now comes the opportunity for which we took New Berne nearly three years ago and for which we have held it since."[46]

The Massachusetts 23rd joined in the effort to resupply Sherman's army, an effort which included rebuilding the railroad from New Bern to Goldsboro, Sherman's proposed refueling station. Food and ammunition received at the port of New Bern would go on to Goldsboro via this railroad; reconstructing it and holding it against the enemy were critical elements in the Union strategy. New Bern was still on the rebel frontier, with the enemy always near. To rebuild and hold the railroad to Goldsboro meant operating under the constant threat of rebel attack. Stephen Osborne, in Company G of the Massachusetts 23rd, was in the middle of this railroad rebuilding activity. He was part of "the force improvised to take, rebuild and hold the railroad to and beyond Kinston [on to Goldsboro]."[47] Working on the repair of the railroad near Kinston, Steve, was about to be in a fight, the battle of Kinston, his last battle of the war. One of the participants in that battle has left his account:

> The ball opened on the 7th of March, 1865. There was a general advance [of rebels].... Just before dark the 23rd was ordered into position on the extreme right. Both sides settled down to a quiet night with a very short distance intervening. [The next morning, March 8, 1865] rebel wagon-trains could be seen in motion. Men ... supposed this was a general retreat of the rebels [but] ... the events of the day fairly disabused them of the idea.... The rebels were in sufficient force ... to [break up] our line of battle.... The rebels ... threw a large force ... on our left rear.... Colonel Upham's brigade was ... captured. At the same time there was a sharp attack all along the line. Most of the regimental loss was incurred in the party of skirmishers as they were driven back to the regiment.... The line was withdrawn [but the order to withdraw] failed to reach the 23rd.... When the order to withdraw finally reached Colonel Raymond [commanding the Massachusetts 23rd] ... he sent word to [the brigade commander] that he

could hold his position alone.... [The 23rd] held ... for some time and then fell back to the main line.... The same day the 23rd was moved to the left ... to meet an attack, which was ... repulsed ... then back to its place at the right where it remained until the rebel force, having been repulsed with great loss, had crept away.[48]

It was later reported that "certain rebel officers, in command opposite Colonel Raymond and the Massachusetts 23rd [said that Colonel Raymond's] obstinate holding on to his exposed position made them fear some trick and prevented them from an attack which, they claimed, they had sufficient force to make easily successful."[49] The Massachusetts 23rd performed well in its last battle.

Steve was taken prisoner in that battle of Kinston and was held in the infamous Libby Prison in Richmond.[50]

The South trembled as General Sherman marched north from Savannah. He had left Savannah on December 21, 1864, and marched across South Carolina in January and February of 1865, arriving at Fayetteville, North Carolina, on March 11, 1865, three days after Stephen Osborne was taken prisoner at the battle of Kinston.

Grant had this to say about Sherman's march through the Carolinas:

> Sherman left Fayetteville for Goldsboro.... Frantic appeals were made to the [Carolina] people to come in ... and swell the ranks of our foe [but] the people had grown tired of the war, and desertions from the Confederate army were ... numerous.... Sherman's troops at last reached Goldsboro on the 23rd of the month [March 1865] and went into bivouac; and there his men were destined to have a long rest.... Sherman was no longer in danger. He had Johnston confronting him; but with an army much inferior to his own.... He had Lee to the north of him ... and had [Lee] made his escape [from Richmond] and gotten down to reinforce Johnston ... Sherman would have been able to hold the Confederates at bay for an indefinite period.... He was near the seashore.... Our navy occupied the harbors.... He had a railroad to ... New Bern.[51]

When Nate, arrived at Goldsboro with Sherman's army, he did not meet Steve, who had been captured in the battle of Kinston two weeks earlier and was now in Libby Prison.

The Massachusetts 23rd had helped to hold North Carolina until Sherman's army arrived at Goldsboro. According to regimental historian Emmerton, the soldiers in the regiment watched as a "caravan of six-mule teams file[d] [by] for days ... to haul supplies ... to [Sherman's] troops.... The rail[road] was working to its full capacity.... Long trains of platform cars passed ... with huge piles of boxes."[52]

Grant and Lee, their troops in opposing fortifications which snaked around the two cities of Richmond and Petersburg, carried their stalemate through the winter into March 1865. As March arrived, Grant became uneasy; he later wrote of this time:

> [It was] one of the most anxious periods of my experience during the rebel-
> lion. I felt that ... the Confederate army ... would try to make an escape....
> I was afraid, every morning, that I would awake from my sleep to hear that
> Lee had gone ... running off with his men ... so that we would have the
> same army to fight again farther south — and the war would be prolonged
> another year....
>
> I could not see how it was possible for the Confederates to hold out much
> longer.... Richmond would have been evacuated much sooner than it was,
> if it had not been the capital of the ... Confederacy.... Then, too, deser-
> tions were taking place.... The South was conscripting ... boys from four-
> teen ...and men ... to sixty.... It was my belief that ... the enemy was los-
> ing a regiment a day ... by desertions alone. I was very impatient ... for the
> spring campaign, which I thoroughly believed would close the war ... [but
> after a rainy winter] the roads were impassable for artillery and teams.... It
> was necessary to wait until they had dried [out].[53]

And Grant was thinking about Sherman, who was waiting down in North Carolina to help Grant end the war. He was anxious "lest Lee should get away some night ... and ... push into North Carolina to join with Johnston ... to crush Sherman.... [By the end of March the roads were drying out and] I was enabled to make my plans.... It is now known that ... [Jefferson] Davis and General Lee had ... agreed ... that they must get away [from Richmond] as soon as possible."[54]

While Lee and Grant were maneuvering at Richmond, Steve was released from Libby Prison on March 26, 1865. He was furloughed home but was in such poor condition that he was taken to the army general hospital at Readville, Mass-achusetts, to recuperate.[55]

Lee decided in late March to make a break for it. He arranged an assault on one section of Grant's fortifications around Petersburg to create a diversion for Grant while he, Lee, struck out from Richmond towards the west. The Confederate assault on Grant's line was met, and Lee lost about four thousand men.

Grant, who was determined not to let Lee get away to the west, took some of his forces around the south of Petersburg and to the west to establish a posi-tion at Five Forks from which to attack Lee whom he expected to run that way. Five Forks was a fortified Confederate position, but Grant's men captured it in the small hours of the night of April 2, 1864. Grant, from his field headquarters near the battle scene, sent a notice of the success to the president at City Point. Lincoln, unable to stay in Washington with the war about to be won, had been at Grant's headquarters at City Point for some days.

On April 2, 1865, the same day as the Five Forks battle, Grant's soldiers assaulted Petersburg and found the enemy leaving. According to Grant:

> I entered Petersburg on the morning of April the 3d.... We could see the streets near the bridge [over the Appomattox River] packed with the Confederate army.... I had not the heart to turn artillery upon such a mass of defeated and fleeing men....
>
> Mr. Lincoln was at City Point at the time, and had been for some days. I would have let him know what I contemplated doing [at Petersburg] only while I felt a strong conviction that the move was going to be successful, yet it might not prove so; and then I would have only added another to the many disappointments he had been suffering for the past three years.... The next morning after the capture of Petersburg, I telegraphed Mr. Lincoln asking him to ride out there and see me.... About the first thing that Mr. Lincoln said to me ... was: "Do you know, general ... I have had a sort of sneaking idea for some days that you intended to do something like this."[56]

Grant finally relented and began to tell the President his plans: "He remained for some days near City Point and I communicated with him ... fully by telegraph."[57]

Grant's army followed Lee as he moved in a westerly direction. Grant was ready to finish the war. He ran Lee to ground and accepted Lee's surrender of his army at Appomattox Court House on April 9, 1865.

Three days later, on April 12, 1865, President Lincoln was shot.

Grant was prominent in the funeral service held at the White House on April 19: "At the head of the catafalque, all through the service, stood General Grant, alone ... often moved to tears."[58] Historian Bruce Catton has written: "Grant ... would always be glad to remember that Lincoln had spent most of his final days in Grant's company, and when he tried to sum up the man he could only say: 'He was incontestably the greatest man I have ever known.'"[59]

For Captain Nathan Osborne and General William Tecumseh Sherman, the war was not quite over; they were facing General Joe Johnston's army in North Carolina. If Johnston was not inclined to follow Lee's example and surrender, Grant was prepared to bring his army down from Virginia immediately to help Sherman destroy Johnston's army.[60] General Sherman was apprehensive that Johnston "would ... allow his army to disperse into guerilla bands, to 'die in the last ditch.'... I knew that Johnston's army could not be caught.... The country was too wide open.... The men could escape us, disperse, and assemble again at some place agreed on, and thus the war might be prolonged indefinitely."[61]

But Johnston wrote to Sherman, asking for terms of surrender. Johnston and Sherman worked out the terms of surrender of Johnston's army, but they also included the terms of a general peace treaty between the Union and the Confederacy, giving, many Northerners thought, easy terms to the Confederacy. This action by Sherman caused an uproar in Washington and in Northern newspapers. Many did not want to give such generous terms to the South, especially after the tragedy at Ford's Theater. The point was made that Sherman had no authority to negotiate a general peace agreement. Apparently both Sherman and Johnston were so apprehensive about possible guerrilla warfare that they tried to tie up a peace agreement which would immediately end the war.

President Andrew Johnson disapproved the proposed peace treaty, and Grant hurried down to North Carolina to get Sherman to renegotiate with Johnston, but only for the surrender of Johnston's army. Grant took pains to stay out of sight so that the public would not see Sherman as making a mistake which Grant was trying to correct. Grant kept his Union forces in Virginia on alert in case Johnston did not readily surrender, but Sherman and Johnston came to terms similar to those between Lee and Grant on April 26, 1865.

The war was over.

On April, 30, 1865, the Massachusetts 23rd was ordered to New Bern, where the regiment served as provost guard until June 15, when it was mustered out. The Massachusetts 23rd Volunteer Regiment took a steamer to New Haven and then the train to Boston and on to Readville, "where they remained 'till July 12th, when they received their final discharge and payment and were disbanded as an organization."[62]

# Epilogue

The story of Fred Osborne continues for many years after 1865. Much has been learned of Fred and his relatives in those years, but several mysteries have also developed: the apparent feud between Cornelia, Fred's wife, and Marie, their daughter-in-law; the story behind Mae Crowley; why Fred's daughter was known by two different names; and who saved Fred's letters from the war.

When Frederick Osborne arrived home in the fall of 1864, he was nineteen years old, the youngest in a large family. His father was fifty-nine and his mother was fifty-three. Aunt Jane, his mother's sister, a regular member of the household, was fifty-five. The children living at home included Orville ("Tuvvy"), twenty-four; Lizzie, twenty-seven; Mary Ward, thirty-one; and Jennie, twenty-one.[1]

The family livelihood came from the fur store on Essex Street, No. 191, at the corner of Central Avenue. According to one advertisement, the store was a "Fashionable Hat, Cap, and Fur Establishment."[2] Another advertisement referred to: "OSBORNE'S SABLE ROOMS, the richest furs, the newest styles, and the lowest prices."[3]

Mr. Osborne had owned the store for some years. In 1837, seven years before Fred was born, Stephen Osborne's fur store had been further down Essex Street at No. 183. The Osborne family had lived a few doors away at 311 Essex Street, which was probably an apartment house at the time.[4] The store apparently prospered; by 1842 the family had moved to the house at 17 Oliver Street and the store had moved to 191 Essex Street, a prominent corner location.[5]

Fred and his brothers worked in the fur store. Fred gave his occupation as "clerk," presumably in the fur store, when he joined Company F in 1861.[6] Steve and Nate worked at the store in the years before the war, their jobs given variously as "clerk" and "book keeper."[7] We know from Fred's letters that Orville,

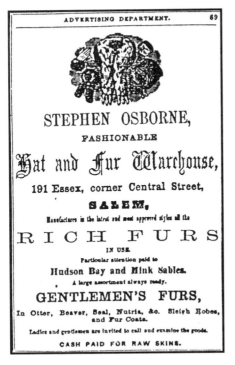

**Advertisement for the Osborne fur store.**

"Tuvvy," worked in the store while Fred was away in the war. When he returned to Salem in October 1864, Fred probably went to work in the store, along with Tuvvy.

Stores were something of a tradition in the Osborne family. In the late 1700s, Captain Stephen Osborne, Fred's great-grandfather, had a grocery store on Essex Street.[8] Captain Osborne was also a shipowner and a shipmaster.

Essex Street was the main shopping and business street in Salem. The iron rails of the Salem Horse Railroad ran down the middle of the street; trolley cars pulled by teams of horses carried people along Essex Street.[9] This prosperous maritime city provided a fine clientele for Mr. Osborne's fur store.

Steve came home in June 1865; he was thirty-one years old, eleven years older than Fred. At five feet five inches tall, he was shorter than Fred's five feet ten, but the two brothers had the same brown hair, blue eyes, and light complexion.[10] Steve joined Fred and Orville to work with their father in the fur store.[11]

In the military as a permanent career, Nate served just after the war as a recruiting officer for the 13th U.S. Infantry at Jefferson Barracks, St. Louis, Missouri. He would in a year be back in action, fighting Indians in the western territories.[12]

Orville Osborne was affectionately referred to as "Tuvvy" in Fred's letters. Tuvvy had artistic ambitions in his youth; at nineteen, his occupation was listed as "artist" in the Salem census.[13] His artistic efforts apparently didn't enable him to earn a living—four years later the record shows him working as a "clerk" in his father's store.[14]

Fred Osborne's life, at this point in our story, is complete to the end of 1865, the year that the Civil War ended. Thousands of Union soldiers came home that year from camps and battlefields to pick up their lives and to make a new beginning. Some were as healthy as when they left, some were impaired by the war. Fred carried the burden of debilitating dysentery and his brother Steve had a damaged thigh. Both would suffer from those handicaps the remainder of their lives.

The events in Fred's life after 1865 are entered under the particular year in which they occurred.

# 1866

Fred continued to work with Steve and Orville in his father's store.

On February 10, 1866, Captain Nathan Osborne (believed to have been at Jefferson Barracks, Missouri, although the record is somewhat obscure) was ordered to organize Company D, 3rd Battalion, 13th Infantry and to take command of that company. On July 1, 1866, he took Company D into the western territories.[15] Nate spent the next months in the Montana Territory and the Dakota Territory protecting white settlers from the Indians.

# 1867

Two years after Fred had returned from the war the Osborne family celebrated Jennie's wedding, the first wedding in the family. On a summer day, July 2, 1867, the Reverend Robert Mills joined Jennie Osborne and David E. Saunders in marriage. She was twenty-three, he was twenty-five.

Jennie's new husband worked as a "paying teller," presumably in a bank.[16] He was the son of David E. Saunders, who lived, when Jennie and Fred were growing up, in a house on Winter Street, one street over from Oliver Street.[17] David's father was a cabinetmaker. He had a shop on Essex Street, at No. 261, a few doors from the Osborne fur store.

Nate was now in the Montana Territory. The regimental history says of this time: "During 1867 the regiment established a post on Sun River, Montana, protected mail stations, established a post in Gallatin Valley, Montana ... [and] built Fort Shaw, Montana.... The marches involved varied from 75 to 207 miles."[18] The regimental history continues: "We started ... with four companies ... and marched to the present site of Fort Shaw.... The officers ... [included] Captains Ide, Osborne, Smith and Parry."[19]

# 1868

Nate was much involved in the settling of the West after the Civil War. The U.S. Army was engaged in protecting the settlers as they moved west into Indian territory. The Indians, of course, took exception to having their land taken away from them. In one battle, Nate was at Camp Cooke, Dakota Territory. The garrison at Camp Cooke, about 200 soldiers, was made up of Company B and Company H. Nate was the commanding officer of Company B. The story of that battle is recounted in the 13th Infantry regimental history:

> At Camp Cooke, May 17th, 1868, hostile Indians [Sioux and Crows] numbering about 2500, surrounded and attacked the post at about one o'clock.... Fearing that the garrison might fall into the hands of the Indians, the wives

of the officers requested that they be placed in the [powder] magazine and
that the magazine be [blown up] in the event of the capture of the post, in
order that they might be saved from falling into the hands of the savages....
The attack [was] continued without intermission until 7 o'clock, when the
Indians were driven off, carrying with them their dead and wounded.[20]

## 1869

Fred was working at the Atlas National Bank in Boston in 1869.[21] He probably commuted to Boston, fifteen miles away, taking the train from the station
on Bridge Street, a five-minute walk from 17 Oliver Street.

Fred lost his father that year. For Mrs. Osborne and the children, it was a
difficult Thanksgiving with Mr. Osborne ill with "lung fever." Stephen Osborne
died just after Thanksgiving Day, on November 29, 1869. He was sixty-five years
old.[22]

Mr. Osborne had purchased a large family plot in the Harmony Grove
Cemetery; he was the first to be buried there.[23] The Harmony Grove Cemetery,
not far from Oliver Street, is an attractive setting today; a visitor finds trees and
steeply rolling grounds, a feeling of history among the walks and gravestones.

Steve Osborne, four years home from the war, now forty, became the head
of the family when his father died, assuming responsibility for the house at 17
Oliver Street as well as for the fur store on Essex Street, which was renamed:
"Stephen H. Osborne and Co."[24]

After Fred's father died, the family continued to live in the house at 17
Oliver Street. Widowed Mary Osborne, now sixty-two, owned the house, which
was valued at $4,000 (it is worth about $400,000 in today's market). Mrs.
Osborne reported a "personal estate" of $12,000 ($120,000 today).[25] Living in
the house on Oliver Street were, in addition to Mrs. Osborne and Steve: Aunt
Jane, now sixty-four; Mary Ward and Lizzie, thirty-six and thirty-two; Orville,
twenty-nine; and Fred, twenty-four. Their servant Mary Barnard, thirty-eight
years old, was still with them. An immigrant from Ireland, she had not had the
opportunity to learn to read and write.[26]

The great hero of the war, Ulysses S. Grant, was elected president in November of that year.

## 1870

Aunt Jane, Jane D. Brace, died on May 11, 1870, five months after Fred lost
his father. She was sixty-five years old; the cause of death was not recorded.[27] Aunt
Jane never married; she was a member of her sister Mary's household for most or
all of her adult life. Fred was close to his Aunt Jane and mentioned her fondly
time and again in his letters, sending his love. In his letter of November 27, 1862,

**The Osborne family plot in Harmony Grove Cemetery. From a photograph by the author.**

he wrote from New Bern: "It is Thanksgiving today.... I suppose Aunt Jane is flying around amongst puddings and pies, putting them on the front of the stove to warm just before dinner, down cellar for a pitcher of cider."

Fred lost two of his anchors that year, his father and his Aunt Jane.

## 1871

Fred, a bachelor of twenty-six, was courting Miss Cornelia Ives, a young lady from a prominent Salem family. Her father, as noted earlier, was an officer in the Bible Society of Salem and handed out Bibles to Fred and the other men of Company F at Lynnfield just before they went off to war in 1861.[28]

Cornelia lived with her family on a spacious property. Her father owned several houses on a large piece of land on Brown Street; his family lived in the house, at 26 Brown Street.[29] Mr. Ives was in the printing and bookbinding business. Cornelia's father and his older brother William published the *Salem Observer* newspaper and they also operated a bookstore.[30] The Ives brothers were members of a trade, the printers, which was developing an increasing influence. The public was hungry for the printed word, for newspapers and books, and the printers were busy feeding that appetite.

Cornelia's older brother Henry also had a bookstore, at 232 Essex Street, a

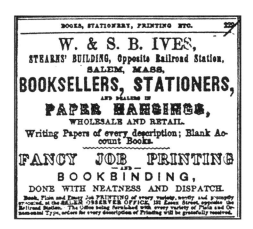

**Advertisement for the Ives Book Store**

few doors from the Osborne fur store.[31]

Cornelia's father was active in local government. According to Salem records, "He ... served in ... the city government for several years, and was president of ... [the city] council.... He was a representative to the State Legislature."[32]

Stephen B. Ives also had strong real estate interests; he owned many properties in Salem, including the John Ward House, a Salem building of such historic importance that it was later moved to the grounds of the Essex Institute, where it can be viewed today.[33]

Cornelia's mother was born Mary Perkins and was a member of the notable Perkins family of Salem. According to local records, "She was always an active worker in the local charities ... for many years ... (a) director of the Seaman's Widow and Orphan Association, and also its president."[34]

David Perkins, Mary Perkins's brother and Cornelia's uncle, was a successful

**The John Ward House**

Salem businessman. As a boy he had apprenticed as a blacksmith, and he eventually became an important manufacturer of carriages, a natural extension of the blacksmith's trade. Another uncle, William Perkins, had a taste for adventure; a Salem historical document states that he "sailed, in 1832, on a trading vessel to the FeJee [Fiji] Islands, where the vessel was wrecked.... He resided for two years among the cannibals of these islands before an opportunity offered to return home."[35]

On June 29, 1871, Frederick M. Osborne and Cornelia A. Ives were married by the Reverend Edward Gusher in a ceremony in Salem.[36] They were both twenty-six years old. Fred's occupation was listed in the marriage records as "clerk";[37] he was still working at the Atlas National Bank in Boston.[38] Cornelia, as was the custom, had "no occupation."

The new couple moved into a house at 30 Brown Street; that house was owned by Cornelia's father, who lived next door at 26 Brown Street.[39] Fred's new home was a five-minute walk from 17 Oliver Street and about the same distance from the railroad station where he continued to take the train to his work in Boston.

Two months after Fred and Cornelia were married Jennie and her husband David, now married four years, had their first child, a little girl born on August 27, 1871.[40] She was named Elizabeth, perhaps for Lizzie, Jennie and Fred's sister. As the first grandchild in the Osborne family, her arrival must have created quite a stir.

# *1872*

In the spring of 1872, Cornelia was pregnant. On August 18, 1872, a son was born. Fred and Cornelia named him Frederick Brace Osborne.[41] Brace was the maiden name of Fred's mother.

Nate was with the 13th Infantry at this time, commanding Company B and contending with Indians in the Montana and Dakota territories. Nate was a bit colorful as a company commander according to a soldier who knew him:

> [In the West] the company commander was far more of a personage than ... in a larger army.... The company and not the regiment was ... the unit of service, and the characterics of the ... companies depended largely upon those of their commanders.... When I joined the regiment it was popularly believed that a B company man could be recognized as far as he could be seen. Captain Osborne, who commanded the company, availed himself of the fact that there was no very direct regulation as to waistcoats ... [and allowed his subalterns] to wear a scarlet waistcoat; but for the enlisted man he insisted that nothing be worn ... except such articles ... as came from the ... quartermaster. Particularly was it a high offence in B company to wear any shoe than the army brogan, for since that was the foot gear in which the soldiers of the rebellion had marched and fought, it must be good enough for the men of his command even at garrison dances.[42]

Nate apparently had a firm view of an officer's prerogatives because in some of his letters, Fred had made comments about Nate and officer privileges. In his letter of June 19, 1863, he had written to his mother: "You needn't write … [Nate] this but as a general thing officers have but little thought for their men.... I am afraid Nate is like most [of] them. His men are things." Later in that letter Fred was contrite: "Tear this up. This letter is letting off some of the mad that I have got pent up."

Nate and Fred clearly had different personalities; Nate liked the military, liked being an officer, and stayed in the military for a career. Fred's personality was gentler; he was not of the military officer type.

## 1873

Cornelia lost her mother this year. Mrs. Ives died on July 4, 1873 and was buried in the large Ives family lot in Harmony Grove Cemetery.[43]

On December 11, 1873, Nathan W. Osborne, a captain since he had entered the army eleven years before, was promoted to major in the 15th Infantry.[44]

## 1876

Fred and Cornelia were still living at 30 Brown Street and Fred was still working in Boston at the Atlas National Bank.[45] Little Fred was four years old.

**The Ives family plot in Harmony Grove Cemetery. From a photograph by the author.**

Early in the new year Jennie gave birth to her second child; on January 12, 1876, a daughter was born.[46] Jennie and David named her Frances. Her sister Elizabeth was now five years old.

Not to be outdone, Fred and Cornelia had their second child three months later, on May 15. She was named Ethel Bradshaw Osborne.[47] Fred was now thirty-one years old.

## 1881

Fred's children were growing. Little Fred was now nine years old and in school. He probably attended the Howard Street Public School, which was just a few steps away from their home at 30 Brown Street. Fred may have found an audience in little Fred for stories of the war, of the battle of Roanoke Island, and what it was like to patrol the streets of the southern city of New Bern.

Ethel was five, expecting to start school the next year.

The fur store at 191 Essex Street was carrying on under Steve's management. Fred's mother was still living at 17 Oliver Street, but big changes and family dislocations were imminent.

## 1882

Major Nathan W. Osborne of the 15th Infantry was promoted to lieutenant colonel of the 6th Infantry on February 6, 1882. The 6th Infantry, then stationed in Utah, had a proud history, which included fighting with General Custer at the battle of the Little Big Horn. According to the regimental history, the 6th Infantry had participated in

> the big Sioux campaign of 1876 ... the drive ... to halt the raiding and pillaging by the Indian nation ... [under] Chief Sitting Bull. The Sioux nation had withdrawn into the Big Country of upper Wyoming and lower Montana.... [The army] was directed to capture Sitting Bull ... to destroy the power of the Sioux.... The Indians [were] steadily pushed into a more localized area.... General Custer led his 7th Cavalry into an ambush and the Battle of Little Big Horn resulted in Custer and 265 of his men being massacred.... A battalion from the 6th Infantry ... in the valley of the Little Big Horn fought several pitched engagements with the Sioux. Sitting Bull escaped the encircling trap and went into Canada.[48]

The Osborne fur store was sold during this year.[49] That sale must have been wrenching because the store had been in the Osborne family for forty-five years. The reason for the sale is not known. The fur store became the "Shawmut Hat Store" with a new proprietor, a Mr. H. D. Rice. Steve continued to work at the store as a salesman for Mr. Rice.[50]

The Osborne family home at 17 Oliver Street was also sold, and the family members who had been living there moved to various locations in Salem. Fred's mother, now seventy-two, moved to a house at 120 Federal Street.[51] Mrs. Osborne's house at 120 Federal Street is still in existence, in the Salem Historic District. Valued at about $400,000 in today's market, it is a substantial structure; one end faces the sidewalk with the entrance and gardens on the side, a charming setting.

Steve, who was now fifty-three years old, relocated his residence to 246½ Essex Street, a block away from his work at the fur store at 191 Essex Street.[52]

Orville, now forty-two, left the fur store and started working as a "shoemaker."[53]

## 1883

Steve applied for a disability pension. In his application for a pension, he wrote:

> Previous to my enlistment in the service of the U.S., in the late war of rebellion, I was a clerk in a hat cap and fur establishment, acting as salesman, book-keeper, and doing such other work as came to hand. Since my discharge ... my occupation has been the same, except the part of book-keeper.... My disability was caused by a ... wound on my left thigh.... It has not entirely disabled me from my duties as clerk at any time, but the wounded limb has always been weak, and has troubled me about stooping and walking. I cannot walk without much fatigue.[54]

The doctor's examination which accompanied Steve's application described Steve's wound as five inches long and three inches wide with a "hard feel"; the doctor wrote, "he says he has suffered much and I don't doubt it."[55] Steve was awarded a pension of $6 per month ($60 in today's money) starting on April 20, 1883; it continued at that rate for the rest of his life.[56]

## 1885

Fred lost his mother in the spring of the year. She died on March 27, 1885, at age seventy-five and was buried beside her husband in the Osborne family lot.[57] She had raised nine children, giving them all a great deal of care, judging from the attention that she gave to her sons in the war, writing to each of them regularly for three years, sending gifts, doing errands by mail, helping them to carry on.

Fred and Cornelia were forty years old. They had changed houses and now lived at 18 Lynde Street.[58] That property, a large house on a large lot, had been owned by Cornelia's father, Stephen B. Ives.[59] Cornelia had probably inherited the house when her father died two years before, in 1883.[60]

Fred was no longer working in Boston.[61] He may well have been having

**18 Lynde Street. From a photograph by the author.**

trouble with the dysentery that he had acquired on St. Helena Island back in 1863, so much so that he could not continue to commute on the train to the Atlas National Bank in Boston. At this time Fred began to work for William A. Clapp at Mr. Clapp's shop, a "bonnet bleachery," at 270½ Essex Street. His job was listed as "clerk."[62] He was able to work only part time because of the dysentery.

## 1887

On March 5, 1887, Frederick Osborne filed papers for a pension stating that he "in the line of duty at St. Helena Island, South Carolina ... contracted dysentery ... was taken with fever and ague ... and have suffered from the same and with the dysentery at intervals ever since my discharge." The petition states that Fred was "partially disabled."[63] In the pension application Fred gave his personal description: "age, 43; height, 5 feet 10 inches; complexion, light; hair, light; eyes, blue."

Fred's application was certified by two old friends from Company F, Ezra Browne and William Chapple. Ezra Browne, a private, an eighteen-year-old leather worker when he enlisted, had been wounded at the battle of New Bern and later at the battle of Cold Harbor.[64] William Chapple was thirty-five and a policeman when he enlisted; he became the Company F commissary, and was the master of Curly, the dog who survived three years of war, had a litter of pups, and came home after the war.[65]

Fred was awarded a pension for the disability caused by his persistent dysentery. The initial amount of the pension is not known but, apparently due to changes in legislation, it increased over the years to an eventual $50 per month ($500 in today's money).[66]

## 1888

Fred and Cornelia moved from 18 Lynde Street to the house next door at 22 Lynde Street.[67] The reason for the move is not known.

Fred and Cornelia were forty-four years old. Their son, Frederick B., was sixteen, their daughter Ethel, twelve.

Nate was promoted to the rank of colonel, commanding the 5th Infantry regiment, on August 5, 1888.[68] Nate took his oath at Salt Lake City, Utah Territory.[69] To command the 5th Infantry regiment was a considerable honor. The 5th Infantry was the third oldest regiment in the United States Army, with a distinguished record in the war with Mexico, the Civil War, and the frontier wars with the Indians.[70] The 5th Infantry regiment was headquartered at Fort Bliss, Texas (near Laredo); Nate would be in Texas for the next few years.

## 1889

Fred's sisters Lizzie and Mary Ward, often mentioned in his letters, moved in with Fred and Cornelia at 22 Lynde Street. Both unmarried, they had been boarding at 3 Barton Square.[71] Lizzie was fifty-two, seven years older than Fred, and Mary Ward was fifty-seven, Fred's oldest sister.

Steve was still working as a salesman at the Shawmut Hat Store; he had rooms at 246½ Essex Street. Such an address on busy Essex Street was probably an apartment above street-level stores

## 1891

Colonel Nathan W. Osborne, commanding officer of the 5th U.S. Infantry, was now in Florida. In May 1891, the headquarters of that regiment left Fort Bliss, Texas, and relocated to St. Francis Barracks, St. Augustine, Florida.[72]

## 1893

Fred had left Mr. Clapp and the bonnet bleachery in 1892 and was now working as a bookkeeper for W. F. Burns and Company in Beverly, a city adjacent to Salem.[73] The business carried on by the Burns company is not known.

## *1895*

In January 1895, Nate was sixty years old and very ill. He was still the commanding officer of the 5th U.S. Infantry, now located at Fort McPherson, Georgia. The post surgeon reported that Nate's health was very poor and that he had suffered from an "extremely severe attack of Influenza ... from which he has never fully recovered." The surgeon itemized problems of poor digestion, nervous dyspepsia, feeble heart action, poor circulation, and gastrointestinal difficulties. He summarized: "In short there seems to be a condition of almost complete collapse." The surgeon recommended a leave, "an entire change of climate ... a sea trip to Bermuda." But before a sea trip to Bermuda could be arranged, Nate became too ill to travel, and he died on January 30, 1895.[74]

Jennie's husband David Saunders traveled to Georgia and brought Nate's body home to Salem.[75] Nate was buried in the Osborne family lot in the Harmony Grove Cemetery.[76]

## *1897*

Fred and Cornelia, now fifty-two, were still living at 22 Lynde Street. Their two children had not left the nest. Frederick B. was twenty-five and working as a "morocco dresser," that is, a leather worker. Ethel was twenty-one; her occupation was given as "student."

**Headstone for Nathan Osborne. From a photograph by the author.**

Fred was still a bookkeeper at the Burns Company in Beverly.

Steve, sixty-eight years old, continued working as a salesman at the Shawmut Hat Store. The Shawmut Hat Store boasted in an advertisement that they had installed an electric sign on the front of the store.[77]

## 1903

Steve was now seventy-four years old. He fell ill in early 1903 and died on February 8. The cause of death was given as "paralysis." Steve was buried with Nate and his father and mother in the family lot in Harmony Grove Cemetery.[78]

## 1908

Lizzie died in 1908 of "cerebral apoplexy" at the age of seventy-one.[79]

Fred was sixty-three and living with Cornelia at the same address, 22 Lynde Street. We do not know what he was doing for work; possibly he had retired because his health was not good.

## 1914

Fred's sister Mary Ward Osborne died in 1914 at the age of eighty-two. The cause of death in her case was also given as "cerebral apoplexy."[80]

## 1915

David Saunders, Jennie's husband, died in 1915 and was buried in the Osborne family plot at Harmony Grove Cemetery.[81] He was survived by Jennie and their daughters Elizabeth and Mary.

## 1918

In 1918, Fred's daughter Ethel, now forty-two years old, had a summer house designed and built in New Hampshire, in the mountain village of Sugar Hill. The gracious and pleasant house is still to be seen at the curve in the road climbing up out of the village. She must have loved the family home at 17 Oliver Street because her Sugar Hill home has a quite similar living room, long with a massive fireplace at one end and lighted on both sides by many windows. The windows look out toward distant hills. In the heart of the White Mountains, Sugar Hill was a summer resort frequented by the well known and the wealthy of the day.

Ethel was known to the villagers as "Aunt Jane" and is still fondly remembered by older residents. The "Aunt Jane" name, rather than Ethel, is a puzzle which has resisted research but was probably connected in some way with Fred's revered Aunt Jane.

Ethel, or Aunt Jane, was much interested in young people and in their education. In the first days of her freshman year at the state university, a Sugar Hill girl received a package from Aunt Jane. That girl still remembers the surprise and the pleasure of being remembered by Aunt Jane with a box of school supplies.[82]

Ethel was a summer resident of Sugar Hill for many years, apparently working in Salem as a secretary for the rest of the year.[83] Eventually she came to live in Sugar Hill as a permanent resident. It seems likely that Fred and Cornelia came to visit Ethel and were familiar with her house and the village of Sugar Hill since train connections to Salem were excellent in those days.

## 1920

Orville, the "Tuvvy" of Fred's letters, died in 1920 of "valvular heart disease" at seventy-nine years of age.[84]

Fred and Cornelia still had their home at 22 Lynde Street. Frederick B., now forty-eight, and Ethel, forty-four, lived at home with Fred and Cornelia. Frederick B. worked for the Post Office as a "letter carrier," and Ethel worked as a secretary at an office on Essex Street.[85]

## 1923

Fred Osborne died on April 25, 1923 at the age of seventy-eight. The cause of death was given as chronic bronchitis and gastrointestinal disease "contracted in [the] Civil War." In his final days, he suffered from the dysentery which he had contracted on St. Helena Island in 1863. He was cremated and buried in the Ives family lot in Harmony Grove Cemetery.[86]

Fred was survived by Cornelia and their children Ethel and Frederick B. Other surviving Osborne family members were Jennie and her two children, Elizabeth and Frances.

Cornelia died a few months later on November 9, 1923. The cause of death was given as myocarditis. She was seventy-nine.[87] Cornelia was cremated and her ashes laid beside Fred's in front of a shared headstone.

A copy of Cornelia's will has survived that indicates that their son Frederick B. was married. Cornelia didn't like his wife, Marie. Her will states:

> To my son Frederick B. Osborne and my daughter Ethel B. Osborne, I give all my furniture and other household goods and effects, to be equally divided between them. To the said Ethel B. Osborne I give one-half of all the residue of my estate, to her sole use forever. If Marie Osborne, wife of

**Headstone for Frederick and Cornelia Osborne. From a photograph by the author.**

said Frederick B. Osborne, shall be living at my death, then I give the other half of said residue to my nephew, Bradshaw Langmaid, of said Salem, in trust, to hold the same and pay the income thereof to the said Frederick B. Osborne. But if the said Marie shall not be living at my death, then I give the said other half to the said Frederick B. Osborne, to his sole use, free of any trust. If the said Marie should die before her said husband but after my death, I direct that my trustee pay over to the said Frederick B. Osborne the whole of said trust estate. If the said Frederick B. Osborne shall die before his said wife, then the estate held in trust for him shall be paid over to the following:

One-half to said Ethel B. Osborne; one fourth to the Salem Animal Rescue League; one fourth to the Salem Young Women's Association. The above bequests of the residue of any estate are read upon the express condition that my children aforesaid shall contribute equally to the support in reasonable comfort of their father the said Frederick M. Osborne; the amount of such contribution to be determined by them; and I direct any said trustee to apply to that purpose as much of the income of the trust fund as may be necessary.

Cornelia wanted to make sure that not only her children but the trustee of her estate would take particular care of Fred. She was also determined that Marie not receive any of her estate directly or by inveigling it out of her son.

## *1929*

Jennie died in 1929 at the age of eighty-six. The cause of death was given as "cerebral embolism hemorrhage." Jennie was buried beside her husband in the Osborne family plot at Harmony Grove Cemetery.[88] She was living in Brookline, Massachusetts, at the time of her death.

## *1944*

Frederick B. Osborne, Fred's son, died in 1944 of "bleeding gastric polyps and pneumonia" at seventy-one years of age. He was living with his sister in the family home at 22 Lynde Street at the time of his death. He was cremated and his ashes were placed beside the headstone marking his parents' grave.[89] His will directed that a "Mae Crowley" receive the bulk of his estate, some $5000 ($50,000 in today's money). Research has not uncovered the mystery of Mae Crowley, who she was and what she was to Fred's son. The cemetery records do not mention Marie, Fred's wife, or Mae Crowley.

## *1951*

Frances, one of Jennie's two daughters, died in a Brattleboro, Vermont, hospital in 1951 at age seventy-five. She was buried in the Osborne family plot in the Harmony Grove Cemetery.[90] Her occupation was given as "music teacher" in the death certificate. She had been married to a man named Morgan, who was not buried with her. Frances had some unhappy years at the end of her life, suffering from "manic-depressive psychosis."[91] Her residence was Brookline, Massachusetts.

## *1956*

In 1956 Elizabeth, Jennie's other daughter, died at eighty-five years of age of heart disease. She was buried in the family cemetery plot, sharing a headstone with her sister Frances.[92]

## *1969*

Ethel B. Osborne had moved to her home in Sugar Hill, New Hampshire, as a year-round resident in her later years. Eventually she moved to the Grafton County home for the aged in nearby Haverhill, New Hampshire, where she died in 1969.

She was cremated and was buried in the Ives family plot in Harmony Grove Cemetery beside her father and mother and her brother Frederick B.[93]

Ethel Osborne was the last of Fred's family.

Fred's story was a piece of the nation's story when it became "drenched in fraternal blood," as Daniel Webster had feared. Fred's privation as a soldier paralleled the stress on the nation as a whole, a nation twisted and strained by this distorted use of men. Fred's personal tragedy, the promise of youth which turned into broken health and lost opportunities for a good life, was paralleled by the tragedy of lost opportunity for the country. Just before the war, in the 1850s, a prosperous future beckoned the country, a future of exciting dimensions, of developing wealth and of promise for the individual. The steam engine had made railroads a miracle of transportation for people and for goods and the telegraph had revolutionized the transmission of news and messages, presaging the modern information era. Steam power was rapidly replacing sails in ocean commerce. Optimism was pervasive among a people eager to learn and to advance. Education was rapidly becoming available to everyone. There was a bright future for all.

The Civil War brought the dreams to a halt. Frederick Osborne and thousands of other young men, from the North and from the South, interrupted their lives and went away to war, Sherman's "dark and cruel war."

# Chapter Notes

## Chapter One

1. Salem Census, 1860.
2. Cemetery records, Harmony Grove Cemetery, Salem, Massachusetts.
3. *The Essex Institute Historical Collections*, vol. 31, index, p. 226.
4. *Ibid.*, vol. 69, p. 171.
5. *Burke's Peerage*, 103d ed., 1963, pp. 1428–29.
6. W. P. Hall and R. G. Albion, *A History of England and the British Empire*, 2d ed. (New York: Ginn, 1946), p. 388.
7. A. Browning, *Thomas Osborne, Earl of Danby and Duke of Leeds*, vol. 1 (Glasgow: Jackson, Son and Co., 1951).
8. Elizabeth K. Reardon, *Salem Historic District Committee Investigation*, vol. 2, p. 128. Not dated. Available in Salem Public Library.
9. Joseph B. Felt, *Annals of Salem,* 2d ed., vol. 2 (Boston: James Monroe, 1849), p. 13.
10. *Salem Directories*, 1836 and following years.
11. *Ibid.*
12. *Ibid.*
13. *Salem Directory*, 1861, p. 241.
14. Caroline King, *When I Lived in Salem, 1822–1866* (Brattleboro, Vt.: Stephen Day Press, 1937); Jane C. Nylander, *Our Own Snug Fireplace, Images of the New England Home, 1760–1860* (New York: Knopf, 1993).
15. Carl Bode, *The American Lyceum,*

*Town Meeting of the Mind* (New York: Oxford University Press, 1956), p. 47.
16. *Salem Directory*, 1850.
17. Bode, *American Lyceum*, p. 75.
18. *Ibid.*, p. 153.
19. *Ibid.*, p. 91.
20. Telephone conversation with Linda Garvert, historian, Lincoln Library, Springfield, Illinois.
21. Phillip S. Paludan, "Lincoln, The Rule of Law and the American Revolution," *Journal of the Illinois State Historical Society* 10, no. 1 (February, 1977):p. 10.
22. Bode, *American Lyceum*, p. 225.
23. *Ibid.*, p. 226.
24. *Ibid.*
25. *Ibid.*, p. 230.
26. *Ibid.*
27. *Encyclopaedia Britannica*, 11 ed., vol. 1, p. 368.
28. Bode, *American Lyceum*, p. 231.
29. *Ibid.*, p. 245.
30. James R. Mellow, *Nathaniel Hawthorne in His Times*, (Boston: Houghton Mifflin, 1980), p. 195.
31. *Ibid.*, p. 202.
32. Terence Martin, *Nathaniel Hawthorne*, (Boston: Twayne, 1983), p. 21.
33. B. A. Hinsdale, *Horace Mann and the Common School Revival in the United States*, (New York: Charles Scribner's Sons, 1898).
34. *Ibid.*, p. 118.
35. *Ibid.*

36. Annual Report of the School Committee of the City of Salem, 1858, p. 27.

37. "Salem School Reports 1848–1860," printed at the *Salem Observer* Office; "Annual Report of the School Committee of the City of Salem, 1857."

38. *The Essex Institute Historical Collections*, vol. 41, p. 251.

39. *Ibid.*

## Chapter Two

1. D. P. Mannix, and Malcolm Cowley, *Black Cargo, A History of the Atlantic Slave Trade* (New York: Viking, 1962), p. 160.

2. *Ibid.*, p. 162.

3. *Ibid.*, p. 190.

4. *Ibid.*, p. 192.

5. *Ibid.*, p. 194.

6. *Ibid.*, p. 107.

7. Thomas Howard, ed., *Black Voyage, Eyewitness Accounts of the Atlantic Slave Trade* (Boston: Little, Brown, 1971), p. 214.

8. Mannix and Crowley, *Black Cargo*, p. 242.

9. *Ibid.*, p. 245.

10. *The Congressional Record*, March 26, 1884, p. 2284.

11. *Salem Directory*, 1842, pp. 3, 46.

12. Henry David Thoreau, *Walden and Other Writings*, edited by William Howarth (New York: Random House, 1981), p. 647.

13. John L. Thomas, *The Liberator, William Lloyd Garrison, A Biography*, (Boston: Little, Brown, 1953), p. 3.

14. Leonard Unger, ed., *American Writers, A Collection of Literary Biographies* (New York: 1979), suppl., part 2, p. 579.

15. Henry Greenleaf Pearson, *The Life of John Andrew*, vol. 1 (Boston: Houghton Mifflin, 1904), p. 131.

16. Walker Lewis, ed., *Speak for Yourself, Daniel*, (Boston: Houghton Mifflin, 1969), pp. 407–8.

17. *Ibid.*

18. *Bartlett's Quotations*, 1992, p. 394.

19. *Dictionary of American Biography*, vol. 18, p. 210.

20. *Ibid.*

21. *Ibid.*, p. 211.

22. Stephen B. Oates, *To Purge This Land with Blood, A Biography of John Brown* (New York: Harper and Row, 1970), p. 181.

23. *Ibid.*, p. 290.

24. *John's Brown's Raid*, U.S. Park Service History Series, Office of Publications, Dept. of the Interior, Washington, D.C., 1974, p. 281.

25. *New York Times*, October 19, 1860.

26. Henry Steele Commager, *The Blue and the Gray* (New York: Fairfax, 1982), p. 40.

27. *Encyclopaedia Britannica*, 11th ed., 1910, vol. 12, p. 826.

28. *Encyclopaedia Britannica*, 15th ed., 1993, vol. 10, p. 874.

29. Stephen B. Oates, *The Fires of Jubilee, Nat Turner's Fierce Rebellion* (New York: Harper and Row, 1975), p. 43.

30. Peter J. Parrish, *The American Civil War* (New York: Holmes and Meier, 1975), p. 227; Steven A. Channing, *Crisis in Fear, Secession in South Carolina* (New York: Simon and Shuster, 1970), pp. 286–93.

31. Oates, *Fires of Jubilee*, p. 61.

32. Channing, *Crisis in Fear*, p. 37.

33. *Ibid.*, p. 41.

34. *Ibid.*, p. 54.

35. Thoreau, *Walden*, p. 354.

36. *Ibid.*, p. 356.

37. Channing, *Crisis in Fear*, p. 84.

## Chapter Three

1. Peter J. Parish, *The American Civil War* (New York: Holmes and Meier, 1975), pp. 69, 86; Steven A. Channing, *Crisis in Fear, Secession in South Carolina* (New York: Simon and Shuster, 1970), pp. 286–93; Mary Newton Stanard, *Richmond, Its People and Customs* (Philadelphia: 1923), p. 160.

2. *New York Times*, Jan. 10. 1861.

3. Parish, *American Civil War*, p. 78.

4. Henry Steele Commager, *The Blue and the Gray* (New York: Fairfax, 1982), p. 40.

5. *Ibid.*, p. 43.

6. *Ibid.*, p. 44.

7. Stanard, *Richmond*, p. 162.

8. *Ibid.*

9. Stanard, *Richmond*, pp. 155–6.

10. Parish, *American Civil War*, p. 132.

11. *Ibid.*

12. Henry Greenleaf Pearson, *The Life of John Andrew*, (Boston: Houghton Mifflin, 1904), vol. 1 p. 173.

13. *Ibid.*, p. 169.
14. *Ibid.*, p. 177.
15. *Ibid.*, p. 185.
16. *Ibid.*
17. John Deegan, *A History of Warfare* (New York: Knopf, 1993), pp. 355–56, 360–61.
18. Shelby Foote, *The Civil War, A Narrative*, vol. 1 (New York: Random House, 1958), pp. 53–54.
19. Pearson, *Life of John Andrew*, p. 191.
20. *Ibid.*, p. 190.
21. Foote, *Civil War*, pp. 53–54.
22. Pearson, *Life of John Andrew*, p. 190.
23. Foote, *Civil War*, pp. 53–54.
24. *Ibid.*, p. 53.
25. Pearson, *Life of John Andrew*, pp. 12–3.
26. James A. Emmerton, *A Record of the Twenty-Third Regiment Mass. Vol. Infantry in the War of the Rebellion, 1861–1865* (Boston: William Ware, 1886); Herbert V. Valentine, *Story of Co. F, 23d Massachusetts Volunteers in the War for the Union 1861–1865* (Boston: W. B. Clarke, 1896).
27. Pearson, *Life of John Andrew*, pp. 202–7.
28. Richard West Jr., *Lincoln's Scapegoat General* (Boston: Houghton Mifflin, 1965), p. 59.
29. *Ibid.*, pp. 60–61.
30. Foote, *Civil War*, p. 54.
31. Pearson, *Life of John Andrew*, p. 214.
32. *Ibid.*, p. 223.
33. *Ibid.*, p. 215.
34. *Ibid.*
35. *Ibid.*, p. 217.
36. *Ibid.*, p. 223.
37. *Ibid.*, p. 225.
38. *Ibid.*, p. 224.
39. *Ibid.*, p. 227.
40. *Ibid.*, p. 224.
41. *Ibid.*, p. 311.
42. Military records of Nathan Osborne, National Archives and Records Administration, Washington, D.C.
43. Foote, *Civil War*, pp. 53–54.
44. *New York Times*, July 26, 1861, p. 2.
45. *Ibid.*
46. Foote, *Civil War*, p. 81.
47. Military records of Nathan Osborne.
48. R. Ernest Dupuy, *The Compact History of the United States Army* (New York: Hawthorne), pp. 88–9.

49. B. H. Liddell Hart, *Sherman, Soldier, Realist, American* (New York: Dodd, Mead, 1929), p. 83.
50. *Ibid.*, pp. 68–69.
51. *Ibid.*, p. 90.
52. U. G. Alexander, *History of the Thirteenth Regiment United States Infantry* (n.p.: Regimental Press, Frank D. Gunn, 1905), pp. 14, 18, 269.
53. Herbert Valentine, *Story of Co. F, 23rd Massachusetts Volunteers in the War for the Union 1861–1865* (Boston: W. B. Clarke, 1896), p. 10.
54. James A. Emmerton, *A Record of the Twenty-Third Regiment Mass. Vol. Infantry in the War of the Rebellion, 1861–1865* (Boston: William Ware, 1886), p. 6.
55. Valentine, *Story of Co. F*, p. 10
56. Emmerton, *Twenty-Third Regiment*, p.6.
57. Valentine, *Story of Co. F*, p. 161.
58. Emmerton, *Twenty-Third Regiment*, p. 4.
59. *Ibid.*, p. 6.
60. Valentine, *Story of Co. F*, p. 15.
61. *Ibid.*, p. 14.
62. *Ibid.*, p. 15.
63. Emmerton, *Twenty-Third Regiment*, p. 6.
64. Valentine, *Story of Co. F*, p. 16.
65. *Ibid.*

## Chapter Four

1. William Marvel, *Burnside* (Chapel Hill: University of North Carolina Press, 1991), p. 31.
2. Shelby Foote, *The Civil War, A Narrative*, vol. 1 (New York: Random House, 1958), p. 227.
3. *Ibid.*, p. 228.
4. Robert W. Daly, "Burnside's Amphibious Division," Marine Corps Gazette 35 (December 1951); pp. 30–37.
5. Herbert Valentine, *Story of Co. F, 23rd Massachusetts Volunteers in the War for the Union 1861–1865* (Boston: W. B. Clarke, 1896), p. 13.
6. Henry Greenleaf Pearson, *The Life of John Andrew*, vol. 2 (Boston: Houghton Mifflin, 1904), p. 249.
7. Henry Greenleaf Pearson, *The Life of*

*John Andrew*, vol. 1 (Boston: Houghton Mifflin, 1904), p. 287.

    8. James A. Emmerton, *A Record of the Twenty-Third Regiment Mass. Vol. Infantry in the War of the Rebellion, 1861–1865* (Boston: William Ware, 1886), p. 12.

    9. *Ibid.*

    10. Valentine, *Story of Co. F*, p. 18.

    11. *Salem Directory*, 1850.

    12. Valentine, *Story of Co. F*, p. 18.

    13. Emmerton, *Twenty-Third Regiment*, p. 15.

    14. *Ibid.*

    15. *Ibid.*, p. 17.

    16. *Ibid.*

    17. Valentine, *Story of Co. F*, p. 22.

    18. Richard Allen Sauers, "General Ambrose E. Burnside's 1862 North Carolina Campaign" (Ph.D. diss., Pennsylvania State University, 1987), p. 53.

    19. *Ibid.*, p. 54.

    20. *Ibid.*, p. 52.

    21. *Ibid.*, p. 53.

    22. William Welch, *The Burnside Expedition and Engagement at Roanoke Island*, 4th series, no. 9 (Providence: The Soldiers and Sailors Historical Society of Rhode Island), pp. 9,10.

    23. Sauers, "Burnside's Campaign," p. 111.

    24. Welch, *Burnside Expedition*, pp. 9–10.

    25. *Ibid.*

    26. *Ibid.*, p. 11.

    27. J. Waldo Denny, *Wearing of the Blue in the Twenty-Fifth Mass. Volunteer Infantry, with Burnside's Coast Division, 18th Army Corps, and Army of the James* (Worcester, Mass.: Putnam and Davis, 1879), p. 50.

    28. *Ibid.*, p. 51.

    29. *Ibid.*

    30. *New York Times*, January 4, 1862, p. 1.

    31. Denny, *Wearing of the Blue*, p. 51.

    32. *New York Times*, January 4, 1862, p. 1.

    33. Welch *Burnside Expedition*, p.11.

    34. Denny, *Wearing of the Blue*, p. 51.

    35. Welch *Burnside Expedition*, pp. 12–15.

    36. R. C. Johnson and C. C. Buel, *Battles and Leaders of the Civil War*, vol. 1 (New York: Century, 1887), p. 663.

    37. *Ibid.*

    38. *Ibid.*

    39. Denny, *Wearing of the Blue*, p. 63.

    40. *Ibid.*

    41. Welch, *Burnside Expedition*, pp. 9,10.

    42. Johnson and Buel, *Battles and Leaders*, p. 665.

    43. Marvel, *Burnside*, p. 48.

    44. Johnson and Buel, *Battles and Leaders*, p. 666.

## *Chapter Five*

    1. Robert W. Daly, "Burnside's Amphibious Division," *Marine Corps Gazette*, 35 (December 1951): 34: Richard A. Ward, "An Amphibious Primer, Battle for New Bern," *Marine Corps Gazette* (August 1952): 36–42.

    2. Thomas F. Edmands, "Operations in North Carolina 1861–1862," Papers of the Military History Society of Massachusetts, Cadet Armory, Ferdinand Street, Boston, 1912, vol. 9, p. 63.

    3. J. Waldo Denny, *Wearing of the Blue in the Twenty-Fifth Mass. Volunteer Infantry, with Burnside's Coast Division, 18th Army Corps, and Army of the James* (Worcester, Mass.: Putnam and Davis, 1879, p. 64.

    4. Daly, "Burnside's Amphibious Division," p. 34.

    5. William Welch, *The Burnside Expedition and Engagement at Roanoke Island* 4th series, no. 9, (Providence: Soldiers and Sailors Historical Society of Rhode Island), pp. 22–23.

    6. James Madison Stone, *Personal Recollections of the Civil War* (Boston: James Madison Stone), p. 31.

    7. Denny, *Wearing of the Blue*, p. XX.

    8. *Encyclopaedia Britannica*, 15th ed., Micropedia vol. 7, p. 608; vol. 18, p. 947.

    9. Shelby Foote, *The Civil War, A Narrative* (New York: Random House, 1958), p. 225; Welch, *Burnside Expedition* , pp. 22–23.

    10. W. P. Derby, *Bearing Arms in the Twenty-Seventh Massachusetts Regiment* (Boston: Wright and Potter, 1883), p. 117.

    11. William Marvel, *Burnside* (Chapel Hill: University of North Carolina Press, 1991), p. 51.

    12. Daly, "Burnside's Amphibious Division," p. 35.

    13. R. C. Johnson, and C. C. Buel, eds., *Battles and Leaders of the Civil War* vol. 1, (New York: Century, 1887), p. 667.

    14. Daly, "Burnside's Amphibious Division," p. 36.

15. Johnson and Buel, *Battles and Leaders,* p. 667.
16. Welch, *Burnside Expedition,* p. 29.
17. Johnson and Buel, *Battles and Leaders,* p. 668.
18. Daly, "Burnside's Amphibious Division," p. 36.
19. Welch, *Burnside Expedition,* p. 31.
20. *Ibid.,* p. 32.
21. *Ibid.,* p. 69.
22. Welch, *Burnside Expedition,* p. 36–37.
23. Edmands, "Operations in North Carolina," pp. 68–70.
24. Johnson and Buel, *Battles and Leaders,* p. 632.
25. Marvel, *Burnside,* pp. 44–45.
26. James A. Emmerton, *A Record of the Twenty-Third Regiment Mass. Vol. Infantry in the War of the Rebellion 1861–1865* (Boston: William Ware, 1888), p. 6.

## Chapter Six

1. James A. Emmerton, *"A Record of the Twenty-Third Regiment Mass. Vol. Infantry in the War of the Rebellion 1861–1865"* (Boston: William Ware, 1888), p. 55.
2. Richard A. Ward, "An Amphibious Primer: Battle for Newbern," *Marine Corps Gazette* (August 1952): 38.
3. R. C. Johnson, and C. C. Buel, eds., *Battles and Leaders of the Civil War,* vol. 1 (New York: Century, 1887), pp. 647, 668.
4. W. P. Derby, *Bearing Arms in the Twenty-Seventh Massachusetts Regiment* (Boston: Wright and Potter, 1883), pp. 77–78.
5. Johnson and Buel, *Battles and Leaders,* p. 647.
6. Ward, "Battle for Newbern," p. 38.
7. Derby, *Bearing Arms,* p. 80.

## Chapter Seven

1. *New York Times,* March 19, 1862, p. 1.
2. W. P. Derby, *Bearing Arms in the Twenty-Seventh Massachusetts Regiment* (Boston: Wright and Potter, 1883), p. 93.
3. *Ibid.,* p. 94.
4. B. E., Wiley, *The Life of Billy Yank* (New York: Bobbs-Merrill, 1952), p. 64.

5. Military records of Nathan W. Osborne, National Archives and Records Administration, Washington, D.C.
6. Salem Census, 1860.
7. *Salem Directories,* 1837 to 1866.
8. J. A. Emmerton, *A Record of the Twenty-Third Regiment, Mass Vol. Infantry in the War of the Rebellion 1861–1865* (Boston: William Ware, 1887), p. 95.
9. Herbert Valentine, *Story of Co. F, 23rd Massachusetts Volunteers in the War for the Union 1861–1865* (Boston: W. B. Clarke, 1896), p. 59.
10. *Ibid.,* p. 64.
11. Emmerton, *Twenty-Third Regiment,* p. 298.
12. *Ibid.,* pp. 57, 327.
13. Beaumont Newhall, *The Daguerreotype in America* (Duell, Sloan, and Pierce, 1961).
14. Emmerton, *Twenty-Third Regiment,* pp. 70, 256.
15. Thomas Edmands, "Operations in North Carolina 1861–1862," Papers of the Military History Society of Massachusetts, Boston, 1912, vol. 9, pp. 80–81.
16. Salem Census, 1860.
17. Wiley, *Billy Yank,* p. 49.
18. *Dictionary of American Biography.*
19. William Marvel, *Burnside,* (Chapel Hill: University of North Carolina Press, 1991), p. 89.
20. Cemetery records, Harmony Grove Cemetery, Salem, Massachusetts.
21. Emmerton, *Twenty-Third Regiment,* p. 280.
22. Luis F. Emilio *A Brave Black Regiment,* (1894; reprint, Salem, N.H.: Ayer, 1990).
23. Emmerton, *Twenty-Third Regiment,* p. 95.
24. *Ibid.,* p. 97.
25. Shelby Foote, *The Civil War, A Narrative,* vol. 1 (New York: Random House, 1958), p. 421.
26. *Ibid.,* p. 422.
27. *Encyclopaedia Britannica,* 11th ed., vol. 19, p. 462.
28. Marvel, *Burnside,* p. 97.
29. *Ibid.,* pp. 90, 91, 97; R. H. Luthin, *The Real Abraham Lincoln* (Englewood Cliffs; N.J.: Prentice-Hall, 1960), pp. 482–85; Peter J. Parish, *The American Civil War* (New York: Holmes and Meier, 1975), p. 522.
30. Marvel, *Burnside,* p. 97.

31. Henry Greenleaf Pearson, *The Life of John Andrew*, vol. 2 (Boston: Houghton Mifflin, 1904), p. 12.

32. *Dictionary of American History*, vol. 2 (New York: Charles Scribners and Sons, 1976), p. 434; *Harper's Encyclopaedia of United States History* (New York: Harper and Brothers, 1905), p. 224.

## Chapter Eight

1. James A. Emmerton, *A Record of the Twenty-Third Regiment Mass. Vol. Infantry in the War of the Rebellion 1861–1865* (Boston: William Ware & Co. 1887), p. 308.

2. *Ibid.*, p. 314.

3. *Ibid.*, p. 273.

4. Garry Wills, "Lincoln at Gettysburg" (New York: Simon and Shuster, 1992), p. 124.

5. From the Webster-Hayne debate in the U.S. Congress, reproduced in Walker Lewis, *Speak for Yourself, Daniel: A Life of Daniel Webster in His Own Words* (Boston: Houghton-Mifflin, 1969), p. 204.

6. Richard S. West, *Mr. Lincoln's Navy* (New York: Longmans, Green and Company, 1957), p. 95.

7. Peter J., Parish, *The American Civil War* (New York: Holmes and Meier, 1975), p. 410.

8. West, *Mr. Lincoln's Navy*, pp. 89–98; *New York Times*, Nov. 17, 19, 25, 26, Dec. 5, 8, 28, 29, 1861.

9. *A Dictionary of American English on Historical Principles,* vol. 2 (Chicago: University of Chicago Press, 1940), p. 870.

10. *A Dictionary of Americanisms on Historical Principles* (Chicago: University of Chicago Press, 1951), p. 548.

11. *What Salem Dames Cooked* (Salem, Massachusetts: The Stetson Press of Boston for the Esther C. Mack Industrial School), p. 14.

12. Emmerton, *Twenty-Third Regiment,* p. 94.

13. William Marvel, *Burnside* (Chapel Hill: University of North Carolina Press, 1991), pp. 92–3.

14. U. G. Alexander, *History of the Thirteenth Regiment United States Infantry, Regimental Press, Thirteenth Regiment* (Frank D. Gunn, 1905), pp. 14, 18, 269.

15. Marvel *Burnside*, p. 94.

16. Adin B. Underwood, *The Three Years*

of Service of the Twenty-Third Massachusetts Infantry Regiment 1862–1865* (Boston: A. Williams & Co. 1881).

17. Thomas Edmands, "Operations in North Carolina 1861-1862," in *Papers of the Military History Society of Massachusetts*, vol. 9, Cadet Armory (Boston: 1912), p. 82.

18. Parish, *The American Civil War*, p. 180.

19. Edmands, "Operations in North Carolina," p. 82.

20. Marvel, *Burnside*, p. 98.

21. "A Dictionary of American English on Historical Principles," vol. 2, p. 870.

22. Marvel, *Burnside*, p. 98.

23. Parish, *The American Civil War*, p. 180.

24. R. C. Johnson and C. C. Buel, eds., *Battles and Leaders of the Civil War* (New York: The Century Company, 1887), p. 652.

25. Emmerton, *Twenty-Third Regiment,* p. 332.

26. *Ibid.*, p. 280.

27. *Salem Directory*, 1861, p. 201.

28. *Ibid.*

29. Marvel, *Burnside*, p. 98.

30. *Ibid.*, p. 99.

31. *Ibid.*, p. 14.

32. Johnson and Buel, *Battles and Leaders,* vol. 2, p. 160.

33. Emmerton, *Twenty-Third Regiment,* p. 105.

34. *Ibid.*, p. 310.

## Chapter Nine

1. William Marvel, *Burnside* (Chapel Hill: University of North Carolina Press, 1991), pp. 99–100.

2. Shelby Foote, *The Civil War, A Narrative,* vol. 2 (New York: Random House, 1963), p. 528.

3. R. C. Johnson and C. C. Buel, *Battles and Leaders of the Civil War,* vol. 2 (New York: Century, 1887), p. 500.

4. Peter J. Parish, *The American Civil War* (New York: Holmes and Meier, 1975), p. 187.

5. Marvel, *Burnside,* p. 111.

6. Parish, *American Civil War,* p. 189.

7. *Ibid.*, p. 239.

8. J. A. Emmerton, *A Record of the Twenty-Third Regiment Mass. Vol. Infantry in the War of the Rebellion 1861–1865* (Boston: William Ware, 1886), p. 108.

9. Foote, *Civil War,* p. 21.
10. Parish, *American Civil War,* p. 194.
11. *Ibid.,* p. 266.
12. Major J. Lewis Stockpile, "The Department of North Carolina under General Foster, 1862 to July, 1863," paper of the Military History Society of Massachusetts, read before the Society, March 2, 1887, vol. 3, p. 87.
13. Marvel, *Burnside,* p. 111.
14. Parish, *American Civil War,* p. 189.
15. Stockpile, "Department of North Carolina," p. 89.
16. *Ibid.,* p. 93.
17. Emmerton, *Twenty-Third Regiment,* p. 125.
18. Military records of Nathan Osborne, National Archives and Records Administration, Washington, D.C.
19. *Ibid.*
20. Stackpole, "Department of North Carolina," p. 95.

## Chapter Ten

1. J. A. Emmerton, *A Record of the Twenty-Third Regiment Mass. Vol. Infantry in the War of the Rebellion 1861–1865* (Boston: William Ware, 1886), p. 106.
2. R. C. Johnson and C. C. Buel, eds., *Battles and Leaders of the Civil War,* vol. 2 (New York: Century, 1887), p. 556.
3. Emmerton, *Twenty-Third Regiment,* p. 106.
4. *Ibid.,* p. 269.
5. Major J. Lewis Stockpile, "The Department of North Carolina under General Foster, 1862 to July, 1863," paper of the Military History Society of Massachusetts, read before the Society, March 2, 1886, vol. 3, p. 90.
6. R. C. Johnson and C. C. Buel, *Battles and Leaders of the Civil War,* vol. 4 (New York: Century, 1887), p. 32.
7. *Ibid.*
8. Emmerton, *Twenty-Third Regiment,* p. 134.
9. W. S. Powell, *The North Carolina Gazetteer* (Chapel Hill: University of North Carolina Press, 1968).
10. Emmerton, *Twenty-Third Regiment,* p. 135.

11. Military records of Nathan W. Osborne, National Archives and Records Administration, Washington, D.C.
12. Emmerton, *Twenty-Third Regiment,* p. 139.
13. *Ibid.,* p. 137.
14. *Webster's Third New International Dictionary.*
15. *American Heritage Dictionary.*
16. James H. Gooding, *On the Altar of Freedom, A Black Soldier's Civil War Letters from the Front,* ed. by Virginia M. Adams (Boston: University of Massachusetts Press, 1991), Introduction.
17. Emmerton, *Twenty-Third Regiment,* p. 139.
18. Luis F. Emilio, *A Brave Black Regiment, A History of the Fifty-Fourth Regiment of Massachusetts Volunteer Infantry 1863–1865* (1894; reprint, Salem, N.H.: Ayer, 1990).
19. *TV Guide,* July, 1994.
20. *New York Times,* December 14, 1989.
21. Peter Burchard, *One Gallant Rush* (New York: St. Martin's, 1965), Foreword.
22. Peter J. Parish, *The American Civil War* (New York: Holmes and Meier, 1975), p. 142.
23. Shelby Foote, *The Civil War, A Narrative,* vol. 2 (New York: Random House, 1963), p. 151.
24. Herbert Valentine, *Story of Co. F, 23rd Massachusetts Volunteers in the War for the Union 1861–1865* (Boston: W. B. Clarke, 1896), p. 84.
25. Emmerton, *Twenty-Third Regiment,* p. 138.
26. A Dictionary of American English on Historical Principles, vol. 1 (Chicago: University of Chicago, 1938), p. 332.
27. *Ibid.*
28. Foote, *Civil War,* pp. 233–34.
29. *Ibid.*
30. *Encyclopaedia Britannica,* 15th ed., vol. 18, p. 809.
31. Military records of Nathan W. Osborne.
32. Parish, *American Civil War,* p. 281.
33. R. C. Johnson and C. C. Buel, *Battles and Leaders of the Civil War,* vol. 1 (New York: Century, 1887), p. 730.
34. *Ibid.,* p. 750.
35. Foote, *Civil War,* p. 225.
36. Johnson and Buel, *Battles and Leaders* vol. 1, p. 731.
37. *Ibid.,* p. 692.

38. *Ibid.*, p. 705.
39. *Ibid.*, p. 719.
40. *Ibid.*, p. 721.
41. *Ibid.*
42. *Ibid.*, pp. 696, 701.
43. *Ibid.*, p. 702.
44. Foote, *Civil War,* vol. 2, p. 225.
45. *Ibid.*
46. *Ibid.*
47. *Ibid.*
48. Fred Osborne, letter of April 19, 1863.
49. Parish, *American Civil War,* p. 429.
50. Foote, *Civil War,* p. 224.
51. *Ibid.*, p. 228.
52. *Ibid.*
53. R. C. Johnson and C. C. Buel, *Battles and Leaders of the Civil War,* vol. 4 (New York: Century, 1887), p. 37.
54. Foote, *Civil War,* p. 229.
55. *Ibid.*
56. Johnson and Buel, *Battles and Leaders* vol. 4, p. 37.
57. *Ibid.*
58. Edwin Tunis, *Oars, Sails and Steam* (New York: World Publishing, 1951), p. 53.
59. *Ibid.*

## Chapter Eleven

1. Pension records for Frederick M. Osborne, National Archives and Records Administration, Washington, D.C.
2. Shelby Foote, *The Civil War, A Narrative,* vol. 2 (New York: Random House, 1963), p. 253.
3. Major J. Lewis Stockpile, "The Department of North Carolina under General Foster, 1862 to July, 1863," paper of the Military History Society of Massachusetts, read before the Society, March 2, 1886, vol. 3, p. 100.
4. *Ibid.*
5. *Ibid.*
6. *Ibid.*
7. James A. Emmerton, *A Record of the Twenty-Third Regiment Mass. Vol. Infantry in the War of the Rebellion 1861–1865* (Boston: William Ware, 1886), p. 140.
8. *Ibid.*
9. R. C. Johnson and C. C. Buel, *Battles and Leaders of the Civil War,* vol. 4 (New York: Century, 1887), p. 40.
10. Stackpole, "Department of North Carolina," p. 97.
11. *Ibid.*, p. 99.
12. Emmerton, *Twenty-Third Regiment,* p. 140.
13. Johnson and Buel, *Battles and Leaders,* vol. 4, p. 13,
14. Stackpole, "Department of North Carolina," p. 102.
15. *Ibid.*, p. 103.
16. Stackpole, "Department of North Carolina," p. 106.
17. *Ibid.*, p. 104.
18. *Ibid.*, p. 103.
19. Salem Public Library, Reference Department
20. Herbert Valentine, *Story of Co. F, 23rd Massachusetts Volunteers in the War for the Union 1861–1865* (Boston: W. B. Clarke, 1896), p. 79.
21. Stackpole, "Department of North Carolina," p. 106; *Encyclopaedia Britannica,* 11th ed., vol. 14, pp. 526–28.
22. S. Casey, *Infantry Tactics,* vol. 1, (New York: D. Van Nostrand, 1862), p. 6 and Foreword.
23. *Ibid.*
24. Valentine, *Story of Co. F,* p. 17.
25. *American Heritage Dictionary of the English Language,* 1969.
26. Emmerton, *Twenty-Third Regiment,* pp. 269, 280.
27. Casey, *Infantry Tactics,* p. 5.
28. Russell F. Weigley, *History of the United States Army* (New York: MacMillan, 1967), p. 229.
29. *Ibid.*, p. 230.
30. *Ibid.*, p. 232.
31. *Ibid.*, p. 231.
32. R. Ernest Dupuy and N. Trevor Dupuy, *A Compact History of the Civil War* (New York: Hawthorn Books, 1960), p. 197.
33. *Ibid.*, 214.

## Chapter Twelve

1. Peter J. Parish, *The American Civil War* (New York: Holmes and Meier, 1975), p. 273.
2. R. Ernest DuPuy and N. Trevor Dupuy, *A Compact History of the Civil War* (New York: Hawthorn Books, 1960), p. 238.

3. Military records of Nathan W. Osborne, National Archives and Records Administration, Washington, D.C.

4. William T. Sherman, *Memoirs of William Tecumseh Sherman, by Himself* (Bloomington: Indiana University Press. 1957), p. 319.

5. R. C. Johnson and C. C. Buel, eds., *Battles and Leaders of the Civil War* (New York: Century, 1887), p. 495.p. 495.

6. DuPuy and Dupuy, *Compact History,* p. 240; Johnson and Buel, *Battles and Leaders,* p. 502; Sherman, *Memoirs,* p. 323, 328.

8. Military Records of Nathan Osborne.

9. Sherman, *Memoirs,* p. 328.

10. Military Records of Nathan Osborne; U.G. Alexander, *History of the Thirteenth Regiment United States Infantry* (n.p.: Regimental Press, Frank D. Gunn, 1905), p. 41.

11. Alexander, *Thirteenth Regiment,* pp. 37, 43.

12. *Ibid.,* Appendix A, pp. 236–37.

13. *Ibid.,* p. 44.

14. Francis B. Heitman, *Historical Register and Dictionary of the United States Army* (Washington, Government Printing Office, 1903), p. 761.

15. *Webster Third International Dictionary,* unabridged.

16. DuPuy and Dupuy, *Compact History,* pp. 38–39.

17. Herbert Valentine, *Story of Co. F, 23rd Massachusetts Volunteers in the War for the Union 1861–1865* (Boston: W. A. Clarke, 1896), p. 91.

18. *Ibid.,* p. 94.

19. James A. Emmerton, *Record of the Twenty-Third Regiment Mass. Vol. Infantry in the War of the Rebellion 1861–1865* (Boston: William Ware, 1886), p. 334: Valentine, *Story of Co. F,* p. 125.

20. Valentine, *Story of Co. F,* p. 91.

21. Cemetery records, Harmony Grove Cemetery, Salem, Massachusetts.

22. Shelby Foote, *The Civil War, A Narrative,* vol. 2 (New York: Random House, 1963), pp. 636–37.

23. Frederick H. Dyer, *Compendium of the War of the Rebellion* (Dayton: Press of Morningside Workshop, 1979), p. 1256.

24. U.S. Grant, *Personal Memoirs of U.S. Grant* (New York: Smithmark, 1994), pp. 327–28.

25. *Ibid.,* p. 332.

26. Sherman, *Memoirs,* p. 334.

27. *Ibid.,* p. 332.

28. *Ibid.,* p. 328.

29. Grant, *Memoirs,* p. 322.

30. Sherman, *Memoirs,* p. 328.

31. Grant, *Memoirs,* p. 322.

32. *Ibid.,* pp. 333, 339.

33. Military records of Nathan Osborne.

34. Sherman, *Memoirs,* p. 331.

35. *Ibid.*

36. Parish, *American Civil War,* p. 283.

37. Foote, *Civil War,* p. 465.

38. *Ibid.,* p. 467.

39. *Ibid.,* p. 531.

40. Garry Wills, *Lincoln at Gettysburg* (New York: Simon and Shuster, 1992), p. 20.

41. *Ibid.*

42. Sherman, *Memoirs,* p. 334.

43. Emmerton, *Twenty-Third Regiment,* pp. 144–6.

44. *Ibid.,* p. 146.

45. *Ibid.,* p. 292.

46. R. C. Johnson and C. C. Buel, *Battles and Leaders of the Civil War,* vol. 4 (New York: Century, 1887), p. 57.

47. *Ibid.,* p. 59.

48. Luis F. Emilio, *A Brave Black Regiment* (1894; reprint, Salem, N.H.: Ayer, 1990), p. 61.

49. *Ibid.,* 1969 edition, Introduction.

50. Emmerton, *Twenty-Third Regiment,* p. 308.

51. *Ibid.,* p. 100.

52. Emilio, *A Brave Black Regiment,* p. 114.

53. *Ibid.,* p. 331.

54. Emmerton, *Twenty-Third Regiment,* p. 314.

55. Valentine, *Story of Co. F,* p. 155.

56. *Ibid.,* p. 94.

57. Emmerton, *Twenty-Third Regiment,* p. 293.

## Chapter Thirteen

1. Herbert Valentine, *Story of Co. F, 23rd Massachusetts Volunteers in the War for the Union 1861–1865* (Boston: W. B. Clarke, 1896), p. 149.

2. *American Heritage Dictionary of the English Language,* 1969.

3. James A. Emmerton, *A Record of the Twenty-Third Regiment Mass. Vol. Infantry in the War of the Rebellion 1861–1865* (Boston: William Ware, 1886), p. 303.

4. *Ibid.*, p. 329.

5. *Ibid.*, p. 303.

6. *Ibid.*, p. 329.

7. Military records of Nathan W. Osborne, National Archives and Records Administration, Washington, D.C.

8. W. T. Sherman, *Memoirs of William Tecumseh Sherman, by Himself*, vol. 1, (Bloomington: Indiana University Press, 1957), p. 346.

9. *Ibid.*, p. 347.

10. U. G. McAlexander, *History of the Thirteenth Regiment United States Infantry* (n.p.: Regimental Press, Frank D. Gunn, 1905), p. 242.

11. Emmerton, *Twenty-Third Regiment*, p. 150.

12. *Ibid.*, pp. 150–51.

13. *Oxford Dictionary of English Etymology*, 1966; *New Webster Encyclopedic Dictionary*, 1970.

14. Shelby Foote, *The Civil War, A Narrative*, vol. 2 (New York: Random House, 1963), p. 782.

15. Sherman, *Memoirs*, p. 348.

16. *Ibid.*, p. 349.

17. R. C. Johnson and C.C. Buel eds., *Battles and Leaders of the Civil War*, vol. 4 (New York: Century, 1887), p. 212.

18. *Ibid.*, p. 207.

19. William Marvel, *Burnside* (Chapel Hill: University of North Carolina Press, 1992), pp. 331, 334.

20. Valentine, *Story of Co. F*, p. 97.

21. *Ibid.*

22. R. C. Johnson and C.C. Buel, *Battles and Leaders of the Civil War*, vol. 1 (New York: Century, 1887), p. 692.

23. Emmerton, *Twenty-Third Regiment*, p. 150; Valentine, *Story of Co. F*, p. 94.

24. Emmerton, *Twenty-Third Regiment*, p. 291.

25. Caroline King, *When I Lived in Salem, 1822–1866* (Brattleboro: Stephen Day Press, 1937), pp. 64–65.

26. Peter J. Parish, *The American Civil War* (New York: Holmes and Meier, 1975), p. 142.

27. *Ibid.*, p. 143.

28. Emmerton, *Twenty-Third Regiment*, p. 239.

29. *Webster's Third International Dictionary*, unabridged.

30. *The Oxford English Dictionary* (Oxford University Press, 1933, vol. 4).

31. King, *When I Lived in Salem*, p. 171.

32. *Salem Evening News*, June 2, 1988, and October 6, 1989, p. 12A.

33. *Yankee Magazine*, February, 1977, p. 19. Mrs. Onassis's secretary, responding to a 1994 letter inquiry by the author, wrote that Mrs. Onassis did not remember the incident.

34. "Ye Olde Pepper Companie" is at 37 Turner Street in Salem.

35. *Salem Evening News*, June 2, 1988.

36. Henry Mayhew, *London Labour and the Poor*, vol. 1 (London: Griffin, Bohn, 1861; reprint, New York: Dover, 1968), p. 203.

37. Emmerton, *Twenty-Third Regiment*, p. 156.

38. U.S. Grant, *Personal Memoirs of U.S. Grant* (New York: Smithmark, 1994), p. 353.

39. *Ibid.*, pp. 381–84.

40. Parish, *American Civil War*, p. 301.

41. Foote, *Civil War*, p. 858.

42. *Ibid.*

43. Military records of Nathan W. Osborne.

# Chapter Fourteen

1. James A. Emmerton, *A Record of the Twenty-Third Regiment Mass. Vol. Infantry in the War of the Rebellion 1861–1865* (Boston: William Ware, 1886), pp. 187–197.

2. *Dictionary of American Biography*.

3. Richard S. West, *Lincoln's Scapegoat General, A Life of Benjamin F. Butler, 1818–1893* (Boston: Houghton Mifflin, 1965), pp. 45–46.

4. *Dictionary of American Biography*.

5. Benjamin F. Butler, *Butler's Book, Autobiography and Reminiscences of Major-General Benj. F. Butler* (Boston: Thayer, 1892), p. 543.

6. *Ibid.*

7. *Ibid.*, pp. 414–418.

8. *Ibid.*

9. *Ibid.*, p. 540.

10. *Ibid.*, p. 543.

11. West, *Scapegoat General*, p. 253.

12. Butler, *Butler's Book*, p. 769.

13. *Ibid.*, p. 930.

14. West, *Scapegoat General*, p. 251.

15. *Ibid.*

16. *Ibid.*

17. Butler, *Butler's Book*, p. 769.

18. *Ibid.*, p. 605.

19. West, *Scapegoat General*, p. 583.

20. Herbert Valentine, *Story of Company F, 23rd Massachusetts Volunteers in the War for the Union 1861–1865* (Boston: W. B. Clarke, 1896), p. 100.

21. *Ibid.*, p. 98.

22. *Ibid.*

23. Emmerton, *Twenty-Third Regiment,* p. 158.

24. Butler, *Butler's Book,* p. 617.

25. Emmerton, *Twenty-Third Regiment,* p. 159.

26. Butler, *Butler's Book,* p. 618; R. C. Johnson and C.C. Buel, eds., *Battles and Leaders of the Civil War,* vol. 4 (New York: Century, 1887), p. 625; Johnson and Buel, *Battles and Leaders,* vol. 1, p. 659.

27. Johnson and Buel, *Battles and Leaders,* vol. 1, p. 659.

28. Butler, *Butler's Book,* pp. 618–19.

29. Johnson and Buel, *Battles and Leaders,* vol. 1, p. 659.

30. Shelby Foote, *The Civil War, A Narrative,* vol. 3 (New York: Random House, 1974), p. 128.

31. *Ibid.*

32. Jay I. Olnek, *The Invisible Hand* (Greenwich, Conn.: North Stonington Press, 1982), p. 175.

33. Foote, *Civil War,* p. 128.

34. Emmerton, *Twenty-Third Regiment,* p. 158.

35. Lloyd Lewis, *Sherman, Fighting Prophet* (New York: Harcourt, Brace, 1932), p. 334.

36. John F. Marzalek, *Sherman, A Soldier's Passion for Order* (New York: Free Press, 1993), p. 249.

37. *Ibid.*, p. 253.

38. W. T. Sherman, *Memoirs of William Tecumseh Sherman, by Himself,* vol. 1 (Bloomington: Indiana University Press, 1957), p. 392.

39. Lewis, *Sherman, Fighting Prophet,* p. 332.

40. *Ibid.*, p. 334.

41. Marzalek, *Sherman, A Soldier's Passion,* p. 254.

42. Lewis, *Sherman, Fighting Prophet,* p. 334.

43. *Ibid.*

## Chapter Fifteen

1. Herbert Valentine, *Story of Co. F, 23rd Massachusetts Volunteers in the War for the Union 1861–1865* (Boston: W. B. Clarke, 1896), p. 102.

2. James A. Emmerton, *A Record of the Twenty-Third Mass. Vol. Infantry in the War of the Rebellion 1861–1865* (Boston: William Ware, 1886), p. 167.

3. Frances A. Lord, *They Fought for the Union* (Harrisburg, Penn.: Stockpile, 1960).

4. Shelby Foote, *The Civil War, A Narrative,* vol. 3 (New York: Random House, 1974), p. 129.

5. *Webster's Collegiate Dictionary,* 5th ed.

6. "Ov" and "Tuvvy" were the same person, Orville Osborne, one of Fred's older brothers. Fred often mentioned Tuvvy and occasionally Ov. He never gave his love to both Tuvvy and Ov, so we deduce that they were the same person.

7. *Salem Directory,* 1866.

8. Emmerton, *Twenty-Third Regiment,* p. 6.

9. Richard S. West, *Lincoln's Scapegoat General, A Life of Benjamin F. Butler, 1818–1893* (Boston: Houghton Mifflin, 1965, pp. 220–22.

10. Valentine, *Story of Co. F,* p. 122.

11. Luis F. Emilio, *A Brave Black Regiment, A History of the Fifty-Fourth Regiment of Massachusetts Volunteer Infantry 1863–1865* (1894; reprint, Salem, N.H.: Ayer 1990).

12. Foote, *Civil War,* p. 104; Emilio, *A Brave Black Regiment,* p. 148 ff.

13. Richard Benson and Lincoln Kirsten, *Lay This Laurel* (New York: Bakins Press, 1973). p. XX.

14. Valentine, *Story of Co. F,* p. 161.

15. U. S. Grant, *Personal Memoirs of U. S. Grant* (New York: Smithmark, 1994), pp. 407–8.

16. Bruce Catton, *Grant Takes Command* (Boston: Little, Brown, 1968), p. 134.

17. Grant, *Memoirs,* p. 409.

18. Grant, *Memoirs,* p. 410–11.

19. *Ibid.*, p. 412.

20. Benjamin F. Butler, *Butler's Book, Autobiography and Reminiscences of Major-General Benj. F. Butler* (Boston: Thayer, 1892), p. 867.

21. Valentine, *Story of Co. F,* p. 102.

22. K. Haeger, *The Illustrated History of Surgery* (New York: Bell, 1988), p. 102.

23. Pension and military records of Stephen H. Osborne, National Archives and Records Administration, Washington, D.C.

24. *Encyclopedia Britannica*, 11th ed., vol. 8, p. 785.

25. Emmerton, *Twenty-Third Regiment,* p. 164.

26. *Ibid.,* p. 165.

27. Butler, *Butler's Book,* p. 638.

28. R. C. Johnson and C.C. Buel, *Battles and Leaders of the Civil War,* vol. 1 (New York: Century, 1887), p. 453.

29. *Ibid.,* p. 456.

30. *Ibid.,* p. 454.

31. V. C. Jones, *The Civil War at Sea,* vol. 3, (New York: Holt, Rinehart, and Winston, 1968), p. 68.

32. *Ibid.,* p. 70.

33. *Ibid.*

34. *Ibid.,* pp. 66–67.

35. *Ibid.,* p. 149.

36. *Civil War Naval Chronology,* p. IV–44.

37. *Ibid.*

38. *Ibid.,* p. II–50.

39. *Ibid.,* p XV–111.

40. Grant, *Memoirs,* p. 408.

## Chapter Sixteen

1. R. C. Johnson and C.C. Buel, eds., *Battles and Leaders of the Civil War,* vol. 4 (New York: Century, 1887), p. 113.

2. Archer Jones, *Civil War Command and Strategy* (New York: Free Press, 1992).

3. U. S. Grant, *Personal Memoirs of U.S. Grant* (New York: Smithmark, 1994), p. 439.

4. Shelby Foote, *The Civil War, A Narrative,* vol. 3 (New York: Random House, 1974), p. 147.

5. Grant, *Memoirs,* p. 451.

6. *Ibid.,* p. 444.

7. Johnson and Buel, *Battles and Leaders,* p. 125.

8. Grant, *Memoirs,* p. 463.

9. Foote, *Civil War,* p. 189.

10. *Ibid.,* p. 191.

11. Grant, *Memoirs,* p. 463.

12. Foote, *Civil War,* p. 241.

13. *Ibid.,* p. 102.

14. Grant, *Memoirs,* p. 483.

15. Benjamin F. Butler, *Butler's Book, Autobiography and Reminiscences of Major-General Benj. F. Butler* (Boston: Thayer, 1892), p. 669.

16. Grant, *Memoirs,* pp. 499–500.

17. Herbert Valentine, *Story of Co. F, 23rd Massachusetts Volunteers in the War for the Union 1861–1865* (Boston: W. B. Clarke, 1896), p. 122.

18. Johnson and Buel, *Battles and Leaders,* p. 220.

19. *Ibid.*

20. Grant, *Memoirs,* pp. 505–6.

21. Butler, *Butler's Book,* p. 638.

22. *Ibid.,* p. 640.

23. *Ibid.,* p. 1061.

24. Richard S. West, *Lincoln's Scapegoat General, A Life of Benjamin F. Butler, 1818–1893* (Boston: Houghton Mifflin, 1965), p. 235.

25. Valentine, *Story of Co. F,* p. 108.

26. West, *Scapegoat General,* p. 235.

27. Valentine, *Story of Co. F,* p. 157.

28. James A. Emmerton, *A Record of the Twenty-Third Mass. Vol. Infantry in the War of the Rebellion 1861–1865* (Boston: William Ware, 1886), p. 308; Valentine, *Story of Co. F,* p. 157.

29. Emmerton, *Twenty-Third Mass* p. 332.

30. *Ibid.,* p. 174.

31. *Ibid.,* pp. 184–85.

32. *Ibid.*

33. *Ibid.,* p. 194.

34. Valentine, *Story of Co. F,* pp. 116, 159.

35. *Ibid.,* p. 116.

36. *Ibid.,* pp. 116, 146.

37. Valentine, *Story of Co. F,* p. 153.

38. *Ibid.,* p. 160.

39. *Ibid.,* p. 154.

40. *Encyclopaedia Britannica,* 11th ed., vol. 1, p. 960.

41. Marc Mappan, *New York Times,* Sunday, February 12, 1995; Charles, Hopkins, *The Andersonville Diaries and Memoirs of Charles Hopkins* (Kearny, N.J.: Belle Grove, 1988).

42. Foote, *Civil War,* p. 1033; Ovid L. Futch, *History of Andersonville Prison* (Gainesville: University of Florida Press, 1968, p. 117; Robert E. Denney, *Civil War Prisons and Escapes* (New York: Sterling, 1993), p. 370.

43. *New York Times,* October 25, 1994.

44. Butler, *Butler's Book,* p. 1035.

45. Valentine, *Story of Co. F,* p. 162.

46. Military and pension records of Stephen Osborne, National Archives and Records Administration, Washington, D.C.

47. P. Studenski and H. E. Kroos, *Financial History of the United States* (New York: McGraw-Hill, 1963), p. 143.

48. Butler, *Butler's Book,* p. 687.
49. *Ibid.,* p. 690.
50. *Ibid.,* p. 515.
51. *Ibid.,* p. 518.
52. Bruce Catton, *Grant Takes Command* (Boston: Little, Brown, 1968), p. 305.
53. Foote, *Civil War,* p. 443.
54. *Ibid.*
55. Valentine, *Story of Co. F,* p. 14.
56. *Ibid.,* p. 128.
57. Butler, *Butler's Book,* p. 847.
58. *Ibid.*
59. William Quentin Maxwell, *Lincoln's Fifth Wheel* (New York: Longmans, Green, 1956), p. v.
60. *Ibid.,* p. 179.
61. *Ibid.,* p. 78.
62. *Ibid.,* p. 9.
63. Patricia L. Faust, ed., *The Historical Times Illustrated Encyclopaedia of the Civil War* (New York: Harper and Row, 1991), p. 140.
64. Military and pension records of Stephen Osborne.

## Chapter Seventeen

1. Herbert Valentine, *Story of Co. F, 23rd Massachusetts Volunteers in the War for the Union 1861–1865* (Boston: W. B. Clarke, 1892), p. 130.
2. *Ibid.,* p. 131.
3. *Death in the Trenches — Grant at Petersburg* (Alexandria: Time-Life Books, 1986), p. 65.
4. Valentine, *Story of Co. F,* p. 131.
5. *Ibid.*
6. R. C. Johnson and C.C. Buel, *Battles and Leaders of the Civil War,* vol. 4 (New York: Century, 1887), p. 545.
7. *Ibid.*
8. *Ibid.*
9. *Ibid.*
10. Shelby Foote, *The Civil War, A Narrative,* vol. 3 (New York: Random House, 1974), p. 532.
11. U.S. Grant, *Personal Memoirs of U. S. Grant* (New York: Smithmark, 1994), p. 524.
12. Foote, *Civil War,* vol. 3, p. 533.
13. *Ibid.*
14. *Ibid.*
15. Johnson and Buel, *Battles and Leaders,* vol. 4, p. 548.
16. *Ibid.*
17. Valentine, *Story of Co. F,* p. 133.
18. *Ibid.,* p. 134.
19. *Death in the Trenches,* p. 78.
20. *Ibid.*
21. *Ibid.*
22. Johnson and Buel, *Battles and Leaders,* vol. 4, p. 533.
23. Foote, *Civil War,* vol. 3 p. 538.
24. Johnson and Buel, *Battles and Leaders,* vol. 4, p. 551.
25. Valentine, *Story of Co. F,* p. 184.
26. Johnson and Buel, *Battles and Leaders,* vol. 4, p. 559.
27. Foote, *Civil War,* vol. 3, p. 538.
28. William Marvel, *Burnside* (Chapel Hill: University of North Carolina Press, 1991).
29. Valentine, *Story of Co. F,* p. 136.
30. Peter J., Parish, *The American Civil War* (New York: Holmes and Meier, 1975), p. 539.
31. W. T. Sherman, *Memoirs of William Tecumseh Sherman, By Himself,* vol. 2 (Bloomington: Indiana University Press, 1957), p. 111.
32. Emmerton, *A Record of the Twenty-Third Regiment Mass. Volunteer Infantry in the War of the Rebellion 1861–1865* (Boston: William Ware, 1886), p. 236
33. *Ibid.,* p. 235.
34. Parish, *American Civil War,* p. 545.
35. John Keegan, *A History of Warfare* (New York: Knopf, 1993), p. 217. See also pp. 232, 244, 249.
36. *Ibid.,* p. 10.
37. Grant, *Memoirs,* pp. 550–54.
38. *Ibid.,* p. 554.
39. *Ibid.,* p. 555.
40. Johnson and Buel, *Battles and Leaders,* p. 666.
41. *Ibid.*
42. Military and pension records for Stephen Osborne, National Archives and Records Administration, Washington, D.C.
43. Grant, *Memoirs,* p.578.
44. *Ibid.*
45. Sherman, *Memoirs,* p. 225.
46. Emmerton, *Twenty-Third Regiment,* p. 242.
47. *Ibid.,* p. 243.
48. *Ibid.,* pp. 244–45.
49. *Ibid.,* p. 245.
50. Military and pension records for Stephen Osborne.
51. Parish, *American Civil War,* p. 589.

52. Emmerton, *Twenty-Third Regiment,* p. 248.

53. Grant, *Memoirs,* pp. 593–94.

54. *Ibid.,* p. 596.

55. Military and pension records for Stephen Osborne.

56. Grant, *Memoirs,* p. 609.

57. *Ibid.,* p. 612.

58. Bruce Catton, *Grant Takes Command* (Boston: Little, Brown, 1968), p. 479.

59. *Ibid.*

60. Grant, *Memoirs,* p. 643.

61. Sherman, *Memoirs,* p. 344.

62. Emmerton, *Twenty-Third Regiment,* p. 249.

## Epilogue

1. Salem Census, 1860.

2. *Salem Directory,* 1850, p. 221.

3. *Salem Directory,* 1864.

4. *Salem Directory,* 1866, map; *Salem Directory,* 1837.

5. *Ibid.*

6. Herbert Valentine, *Story of Co. F, 23rd Massachusetts Volunteers in the War for the Union 1861–1865* (Boston: W. B. Clarke, 1892), p. 157.

7. Salem Census, 1850, 1860.

8. *Essex Institute Historical Collection,* vol. XXXI, p. 125.

9. *Salem Atlas* of 1874; telephone conversation with Essex Institute.

10. Military and pension records for Frederick M. Osborne, National Archives and Records Administration, Washington, D.C; military and pension records for Stephen Osborne, National Archives and Records Administration, Washington, D.C.

11. *Salem Directories,* 1860 and following years.

12. Military and pension records for Nathan W. Osborne, National Archives and Records Admininstration, Washington, D.C.

13. Salem Census, 1860.

14. *Salem Directory,* 1864.

15. Military and pension records for Nathan W. Osborne.

16. Salem City Hall marriage records.

17. *Salem Atlas,* 1874.

18. U. G. McAlexander, *History of the Thirteenth Regiment United States Infantry* (n.p.: Regimental Press, Frank D. Gunn, 1905), pp. 67, 71.

19. *Ibid.*

20. *Ibid.*

21. *Salem Directory,* 1869.

22. Cemetery records, Harmony Grove Cemetery, Salem, Massachusetts.

23. *Ibid.*

24. *Salem Directory,* 1876.

25. Salem Census, 1870.

26. *Ibid.*

27. Cemetery records, Harmony Grove Cemetery.

28. Valentine, *Story of Co. F,* p. 18; Salem Directory, 1850, p. 183.

29. *Salem Atlas,* 1874.

30. *Essex Institute Historical Collection,* vol. 21, p. 57.

31. *Salem Directory,* 1866, p. 93; *Essex Institute Historical Collection,* vol. 21, pp. 57–58.

32. *Essex Institute Historical Collection,* vol. 21, pp. 57.

33. Sidney Perley, *The History of Salem Massachusetts,* vol. 2, (Salem, Mass.: Sidney Perley, 1928), p. 199.

34. *Essex Institute Historical Collection,* vol. 21, pp. 56.

35. *Ibid.*

36. Salem City Hall marriage records.

37. *Ibid.*

38. *Salem Directory,* 1872, p. 141.

39. *Salem Directory,* 1872, p. 141; *Salem Atlas,* 1874.

40. Cemetery records, Harmony Grove Cemetery.

41. Cemetery records, Harmony Grove Cemetery; notice dated January 25, 1944, notarized, to the Probate Court of the County of Essex, accompanying will of Frederick B. Osborne.

42. McAlexander, *Thirteenth Regiment,* pp. 78–9.

43. Cemetery records, Harmony Grove Cemetery.

44. McAlexander, *Thirteenth Regiment,* p. 269.

45. *Salem Directory,* 1876, p. 142.

46. Cemetery records, Harmony Grove Cemetery.

47. Cemetery records, Harmony Grove Cemetery.

48. Ruth Layton, *The Story of Jefferson Barracks and the 6th Infantry* (n.p.: 6th Infantry Association, 1961), p. 53.

49. *Salem Directory*, 1884.
50. *Ibid.*
51. *Ibid.*
52. *Ibid.*
53. *Ibid.*
54. Military and pension records for Stephen Osborne.
55. *Ibid.*
56. *Ibid.*
57. Cemetery records, Harmony Grove Cemetery.
58. *Salem Directory*, 1884.
59. *Salem Atlas*, 1874.
60. Cemetery records, Harmony Grove Cemetery.
61. *Salem Directory*, 1886–87, p. 230.
62. *Salem Directory*, 1888–89, p. 108.
63. Military and pension records for Frederick Osborne.
64. Valentine, *Story of Co. F,* p. 149.
65. *Ibid.*
66. Military and pension records for Nathan Osborne.
67. *Salem Directory*, 1888–89, p. 108.
68. *Ibid.*
69. Military and pension records for Nathan Osborne.
70. Captain Edward Sigerfoos, *Historical Sketch of the 5th United States Infantry* (n.p.: Regimental Press, 1902), p. 18.

71. *Salem Directory*, 1890–1, p. 276.
72. Sigerfoos, *5th Infantry*, pp. 18, 32.
73. *Salem Directory*, 1893–4.
74. Military and pension records for Nathan Osborne.
75. *Ibid.*
76. Cemetery records, Harmony Grove Cemetery.
77. *Salem Directory*, 1897–98.
78. Cemetery records, Harmony Grove Cemetery.
79. *Ibid.*
80. *Ibid.*
81. *Ibid.*
82. The girl was Bertha Grass, the wife of the author.
83 *Salem Directory*, 1920.
84. Cemetery records, Harmony Grove Cemetery.
85. *Salem Directory*, 1920.
86. Cemetery records, Harmony Grove Cemetery.
87. *Ibid.*
88. *Ibid.*
89. *Ibid.*
90. *Ibid.*
91. Death certificate for Frances Morgan.
92. Cemetery records, Harmony Grove Cemetery.
93. *Ibid.*

# Bibliography

## *Books*

*Benet's Reader's Encyclopedia of American Literature*, 3d ed. New York: Harper and Row, 1987.

Benson, Richard and Kirsten, Lincoln. *Lay This Laurel*. New York: Bakins Press, 1973.

Blake, H.G.O., ed. *Early Spring in Massachusetts, from the Journal of Henry David Thoreau*. Boston: Houghton Mifflin Company, 1893.

Bode, Carl. *The American Lyceum: Town Meeting of the Mind*. New York: Oxford University Press, 1956.

_____, and Cowley, Malcolm, eds. *The Portable Emerson*. New York: Penguin, 1957.

Burchard, Peter. *One Gallant Rush*. New York: St. Martin's Press, 1965.

Butler, Benjamin F. *Butler's Book, Autobiography and Reminiscences of Major-General Benj. F. Butler*. Boston: A.M. Thayer and Co., 1892.

Casey, S. *Infantry Tactics*. New York: D. Van Nostrand, 1862 (reprint Dayton, Ohio: Morningside House, 1985).

Catton, Bruce. *Grant Takes Command*. Boston: Little, Brown, 1968.

Channing, Steven A. *Crisis in Fear: Secession in South Carolina*. New York: Simon and Schuster, 1970,.

*Civil War Naval Chronology, 1861–1865*. Washington: Naval History Division, U.S. Government Printing Office, 1971.

Commager, Henry Steele. *The Blue and the Gray*. New York: The Fairfax Press, 1982.

Davis, William C., ed. *Death in the Trenches: Grant at Petersburg*. Alexandria: Time-Life Books, 1986.

Deegan, John. *A History of Warfare*. New York: Knopf, 1993.

Denney, Robert E. *Civil War Prisons and Escapes*. New York: Sterling Publishing Company, 1993.

Denny, J. Waldo. *Wearing of the Blue in the Twenty-Fifth Mass. Volunteer Infantry, with Burnside's Coast Division, 18th Army Corps, and Army of the James*. Worcester: Putnam and Davis Publishers, 1879.

Derby, W.P. *Bearing Arms in the Twenty-Seventh Massachusetts Regiment.* Boston: Wright and Potter Printing Company, 1883.

*Dictionary of American Biography.* 21 vols. New York: C. Scribner's, 1943.

*Dictionary of American History.* New York: Scribner's, 1976.

Dow, George Francis. *Slave Ships and Slaving.* Salem: Marine Research Society, 1927.

Dupuy, R. Ernest, and Dupuy, Trevor N. *A Compact History of the Civil War.* New York: Hawthorn Books, 1960.

Dyer, Frederick H. *Compendium of the War of the Rebellion.* Dayton: The Press of Morningside Workshop, 1979.

Emerson, Ralph Waldo. *Nature, Addresses, and Lectures.* Boston: Houghton Mifflin, 1883.

Emilio, Luis F. *A Brave Black Regiment: A History of the Fifty-Fourth Regiment of Massachusetts Volunteer Infantry 1863–1865.* 2nd ed., Boston: Boston Book Company, 1894; 3rd ed., Salem, N.H.: Ayer Publishing Company, 1990.

Emmerton, James A. *A Record of the Twenty-Third Regiment Mass. Vol. Infantry in the War of the Rebellion.* Boston: William Ware Co., 1886.

Faust, Patricia, ed. *The Historical Times Illustrated Encyclopedia of the Civil War.* New York: Harper and Row, 1991.

Fisher, Sidney George *The True Daniel Webster.* Philadelphia: J.B. Lippincott, 1911.

Foote, Shelby. *The Civil War: A Narrative.* 3 vols. New York: Random House, 1958,.

Futch, Ovid L. *History of Anderson Prison.* Gainesville: University of Florida Press, 1968.

Gooding, James H. *On the Altar of Freedom, A Black Soldier's Civil War Letters from the Front,* ed. by Virginia H. Adams. Boston: University of Massachusetts Press, 1991.

Grant, U.S. *Personal Memoirs of U.S. Grant.* New York: Smithmark Publishers, 1994.

Haeger, K. *The Illustrated History of Surgery.* New York: Bell Publishing Company, 1988.

*Harper's Encyclopedia of United States History.* New York: Harper and Brothers Publishers, 1905.

Hart, B.H. Liddell. *Sherman, Soldier, Realist, American.* New York: Dodd, Mead, 1929.

Hawthorne, Julian. *Hawthorne and His Circle.* New York: Harper and Brothers, 1903.

Heitman, Francis B. *Historical Register and Dictionary of the United States Army.* Washington: U.S. Government Printing Office, 1903.

Hinsdale, B.A. *Horace Mann and the Common School Revival in the United States.* New York: Charles Scribner's Sons, 1898.

*The Historical Times Illustrated Encyclopedia of the Civil War,* Patricia Faust, ed. New York: HarperCollins, 1991.

Hopkins, Charles. *The Andersonville Diaries and Memoirs of Charles Hopkins.* Kearney, N.J.: Belle Grove Publishing Company, 1988.

Howard, Thomas, ed. *Black Voyage: Eyewitness Accounts of the Atlantic Slave Trade.* Boston: Little, Brown, 1971.

Johnson, R.C., and Buel, C.C., eds. *Battles and Leaders of the Civil War.* 4 vols. New York: Yoseloff 1956.

Jones, Archer. *Civil War Command and Strategy.* New York: The Free Press, 1992.

Jones, V.C. *The Civil War at Sea.* New York: Holt Rinehart and Winston, 1968.

King, Caroline. *When I Lived in Salem, 1822–1866.* Brattlesboro, Vt.: Stephen Day Press, 1937.

Krutch, Joseph Wood. *Thoreau: Walden and Other Writings.* New York: Bantam, 1962.

Lewis, Lloyd. *Sherman, Fighting Prophet.* New York: Harcourt, Brace, 1932.

Lewis, Walker, ed. *Speak for Yourself, Daniel.* Boston: Houghton Mifflin, 1969.

Lord, Frances A. *They Fought for the Union.* Harrisburg: The Stackpole Company, 1960.

Luthin, R.H. *The Real Abraham Lincoln.* Englewood Cliffs, N.J.: Prentice-Hall, 1960.

Mannix, D.P., and Cowley, Malcolm. *Black Cargo: A History of the Atlantic Slave Trade.* New York: The Viking Press, 1962.

Martin, Terence. *Nathaniel Hawthorne.* Boston: Twayne Publishers, 1983.

Marvel, William. *Burnside.* Chapel Hill: University of North Carolina Press, 1991.

Marzalek, John F. *Sherman: A Soldier's Passion for Order.* New York: The Free Press, 1993.

Maxwell, William Quentin. *Lincoln's Fifth Wheel.* New York: Longmans, Green, 1956.

Mayhew, Henry. *London Labour and the Poor.* London: Griffin, Bohn, and Company, 1861; reprint, New York: Dover, 1968.

Mellow, James R. *Nathaniel Hawthorne in His Times.* Boston: Houghton Mifflin, 1980.

Miller, Edward H. "Salem Is My Dwelling Place." Iowa City: University of Iowa Press, 1991.

Miller, R.T., ed. *The Photographic History of the Civil War.* 10 vols. New York: The Review of Reviews Company, 1911.

Newhall, Beaumont. *The Daguerreotype in America.* New York: Duell, Sloan and Pierce, 1961.

Nylander, Jane C. *Our Own Snug Fireplace: Images of the New England Home, 1760–1860.* New York: Knopf, 1993.

Oates, Stephen B. *The Fires of Jubilee: Nat Turner's Fierce Rebellion.* New York: Harper and Row, 1975.

———. *To Purge This Land with Blood: A Biography of John Brown.* New York: Harper and Row, 1970.

Olnek, Jay I. *The Invisible Hand.* Greenwich: North Stonington Press, 1982.

Parish, Peter J. *The American Civil War.* New York: Holmes and Meier, 1975.

Pearson, Henry Greenleaf. *The Life of John Andrew.* Boston: Houghton Mifflin, 1904.

Perley, Sidney. *The History of Salem, Massachusetts.* Salem: Sidney Perley, 1928.

Powell, W.S. *The North Carolina Gazetteer.* Chapel Hill: University of North Carolina Press, 1968.

Sherman, William T. *Memoirs of William Tecumseh Sherman.* Bloomington: Indiana University Press, 1957.

Stone, James Madison. *Personal Recollections of the Civil War.* Boston: published by the author, date not available.

Studenski, P., and Krooss, H.E. *Financial History of the United States.* New York: McGraw-Hill, 1963.

Thomas, John L. *The Liberator, William Lloyd Garrison: A Biography.* Boston: Little, Brown, 1953.

Thoreau, Henry David. *Walden and Other Writings,* ed. William Howarth. New York: Random House, 1981.

Tunis, Edwin. *Oars, Sails and Steam.* New York: The World Publishing Company, 1951.

Underwood, Adin H. *The Three Years of Service of the Twenty-Third Massachusetts Infantry Regiment 1862–1865.* Boston: A. Williams and Company, 1881.

Unger, Leonard, ed. *American Writers: A Collection of Literary Biographies.* New York: Scribner's, 1979.

United States Navy, Naval History Division. *Civil War Naval Chronology, 1861–1865.* Washington: U.S. Government Printing Office, 1971.

Valentine, Herbert V. *Story of Co. F, 23rd Massachusetts Volunteers in the War for the Union.* Boston: W.B. Clarke and Co., 1896.

Weigley, Russell F. *History of the United States Army.* New York: Macmillan, 1967.

West, Richard S. *Lincoln's Scapegoat General: A Life of Benjamin F. Butler, 1818–1893.* Boston: Houghton Mifflin, 1965.

Wiley, B.E. *The Life of Billy Yank.* New York: Bobbs-Merrill Company, 1952.

*William Lloyd Garrison: The Story of His Life Told by His Children.* New York: The Century Company, 1885.

## *Articles, Papers and Pamphlets*

McAlexander, U.G. "History of the Thirteenth Regiment United States Infantry." Regimental Press, 1905, Frank D. Gunn.

Daly, Robert W. "Burnside's Amphibious Division." *Marine Corps Gazette*, Vol. 35, December 1951.

Edmands, Thomas F. "Operations in North Carolina 1861–1862." Papers of the Military History Society of Massachusetts, Vol. IX, Cadet Armory, Ferdinand Street, Boston, 1912.

"History of the Fifth United States Infantry," 2d ed. Fort Riley, June 1962.

"John Brown's Raid," U.S. Park Service History Series, Washington: 1974, Office of Publications, Department of the Interior.

Layton, Ruth. "The Story of Jefferson Barracks and the 6th Infantry." Issued by the 6th Infantry Association, date unknown.

"Register of Commissioned Officers of the Sixth Regiment of Infantry, U.S. Army." Fort Thomas, Kentucky: 6th Regiment, 1896.

Sauers, Richard Allen. "General Ambrose E. Burnside's 1862 North Carolina Campaign." Ph.D. diss., Pennsylvania State University, 1987.

Sigerfoos, Captain Edward. "Historical Sketch of the 5th United States Infantry." Regimental Press, 1902.

Stackpole, Major J. Lewis. "The Department of North Carolina Under General Foster, 1862 to July, 1863." Paper of the Military History Society of Massachusetts, read before the society, March 2, 1887.

Ward, Richard A. "An Amphibious Primer: Battle for New Bern." *Marine Corps Gazette*, August 1952.

Welch, William. "The Burnside Expedition and Engagement at Roanoke Island." Providence: The Soldiers and Sailors Historical Society of Rhode Island, Fourth Series, No. 9.

"What Salem Dames Cooked." Boston: The Stetson Press of Boston for the Esther C. Mack Industrial School, Salem, Massachusetts, date unknown.

# Newspapers

*Boston Evening Journal.*
*New York Herald.*
*New York Times.*
*Salem Evening News.*
*Salem Observer.*

# Other Sources

Annual Report of the School Committee of the City of Salem (Massachusetts), 1858.

Death certificate of Frances Morgan (niece of Frederick M. Osborne, daughter of Jennie Osborne).

Interment records, Harmony Grove Cemetery, Salem, Massachusetts.

Letters written by Frederick M. Osborne of Salem, Massachusetts; one letter written by Stephen H. Osborne from North Carolina during the Civil War; a partial letter written by Stephen Osborne, father of Frederick M. Osborne, giving the English heritage of the Osborne family.

Military and pension records of Frederick M. Osborne, Stephen H. Osborne, and Nathan W. Osborne, National Archives and Records Administration, Washington, D.C.

Property records of 22 Lynde Street, Salem, Massachusetts, home of Frederick M. and Caroline A. Osborne after the Civil War.

Records of marriages, births, and deaths, Salem (Massachusetts) City Hall.

*Salem Atlas,* 1874.

Salem, Massachusetts, city directories for the years: 1837, 1842, 1850–1866, 1869, 1872, 1876, 1884, 1886–7, 1888–9, 1890–1, 1893–4, 1897–8.

Salem, Massachusetts, school reports, 1848–1860.

United States Census for Salem, Massachusetts, 1850, 1860, 1870.

Wills of Caroline (Mrs. Frederick M.) Osborne, Frederick B. Osborne (son of Frederick M. Osborne), Nathan W. Osborne (brother of Frederick M. Osborne).

# Libraries

Boston Public Library, Boston, Mass.
Chesterfield County Library, Chesterfield, Va.
Essex Institute Historical Collections, Salem, Mass.
Library of the Chathams, Chatham, N.J.
Lincoln Library, Springfield, Ill.
Lynnfield Public Library, Lynnfield, Mass.
Madison Public Library, Madison, N.J.
Military History Institute, Carlisle, Pa.
Morristown Public Library, Morristown, N.J.

Morris County Library, Whippany, N.J.
Rutgers University Library, New Brunswick, N.J.
Salem Atheneum Library, Salem, Mass.
Salem Public Library, Salem, Mass.
Summit Public Library, Summit, N.J.
Wayne County Library, Goldsboro, N.C.

# Index

*Patapsco* (iron-clad battleship)  126
*Patuxent* (steamship)  54
Pay, soldiers': army procedure for 76;
    colored soldiers 194; Fred Osborne's 87
Peabody, Mass.  36 (map)
Peninsula Campaign: 112, 206; General
    Burnside and 86–88
Pens, writing  13
Pepper Candy Company  172
Perkins, David (Cornelia Osborne's
    uncle)  248
Perkins, Eben (private, Company F)  94,
    95, 115
Perkins, William (Cornelia Osborne's
    uncle)  249
Petersburg, Va.: 220, 221, 222, 239;
    siege of 226; Crater, battle of the
    228–231, 231 (map); Burnside ends
    career at 231, 232; fortifications by
    Grant and Lee 222, 223, 223 (map),
    227 (map); Mass. 23rd regiment in
    trenches at 223, 226, 227; shelling
    described 226, 227
Phillips Grammar School  12
*Phoenix* (steamship)  54
Photography  73, 74, 148
*Picket* (steamship), at Hatteras Inlet  47
Picketing, nature of  67
Pickett, General George  184, 185
*Pilot Boy* (steamship)  54
Pitched battles (slaughterhouse scenes)
    234, 235
Pleasants, Colonel Henry  228, 229
    (portrait)
Plymouth, N.C.: 198; battle of 200–202
Point of Rocks, Va.  223
Pope, General John  98, 99
Porter, Colonel Horace (Grant staff
    member)  222
Porter, Thomas F. (sergeant, Company I)
    198, 199
Portsmouth, Va.  182 (map), 183 (map)
Pratt, Doctor (surgeon of *Matilda*, hos-
    pital ship)  213, 214
Prisoner exchange  176, 180, 181
Prisoners of war  176, 179, 180

*Queen of the West* (ram ship)  200

Raleigh, N.C.  45
Raleigh, Sir Walter  51

Ram ships  198, 200
Raymond, Captain John (commander,
    Stephen Osborne's Company G)  82,
    83, 157, 158, 204
*Recruit* (schooner)  51
Reenlistment  170, 172, 174, 175, 181, 185
Richmond, Va.: 25, 38, 86, 91, 206, 211,
    213, 221, 238; second front against 38,
    76, 77; false rumor of capture 88, 90
Roanoke Island  51, 52, 53 (map), 62
Roanoke Island, battle of  50–61, 53
    (map), 55 (map)
Rodgers, Rear-Admiral C.R.P.  126

Saint-Gaudens, Augustus (sculptor)  194
St. Helena Island, S.C.  114, 116, 118, 121,
    126 (map), 127, 128, 131
Salem, Mass.: 4, 23, 244; antislavery
    movement in 15, 17; colored people in
    7; cultural milieu of 6, 8; literary
    nature of 8; lyceum in 9; maritime
    nature of 4, 5, 8; newspapers in 6;
    occupations of residents 7, 8; popula-
    tion of 7; privateering in 8; schools in
    12–14; slave trade in 15–17; social
    milieu of 6, 8
*Salem Gazette*  37
Salem Horse Railroad  244
Salem Neck  8, 158
*Salem Observer*  17
*Salem Register*  203, 204
Salem School Committee  12, 13
*Sally*  (sailing vessel)  5
Sanitary Commission  220, 223, 224
Saunders, David E. (Jennie Osborne's
    husband)  245, 255, 256
Saunders, Elizabeth (Jennie Osborne's
    daughter)  249, 259
Saunders, Frances (Jennie Osborne's
    daughter)  251, 259
Savannah, Ga.  236, 238
*The Scarlet Letter*  12
Schools: in Massachusetts 13; in Salem
    12–14
*Sea Bird* (schooner)  51
Second front against Richmond  38, 87,
    88
Seven Days, battle of  92
Seven Pines  218; *see also* Fair Oaks
Seven Springs *see* Whitehall, battle of
Shawmut Hat Store  251, 256